CHASING ARCHIPELAGIC DREAMS

CHASING ARCHIPELAGIC DREAMS

THE EXPANSION OF FOREIGN INFLUENCE IN SABAH AMID THE END OF EMPIRE, 1945–1965

David R. Saunders

SOUTHEAST ASIA PROGRAM PUBLICATIONS
AN IMPRINT OF CORNELL UNIVERSITY PRESS
Ithaca and London

Southeast Asia Program Publications Editorial Board
Mahinder Kingra (ex officio)
Thak Chaloemtiarana
Chiara Formichi
Tamara Loos
Andrew Willford

Copyright © 2024 by Cornell University

All rights reserved. Except for brief quotations in a review, this book, or parts thereof, must not be reproduced in any form without permission in writing from the publisher. For information, address Cornell University Press, Sage House, 512 East State Street, Ithaca, New York 14850. Visit our website at cornellpress.cornell.edu.

First published 2024 by Cornell University Press

Library of Congress Cataloging-in-Publication Data

Names: Saunders, David R., 1993– author.
Title: Chasing archipelagic dreams : the expansion of foreign influence in Sabah amid the end of empire, 1945–1965 / David R. Saunders.
Description: Ithaca [New York] : Cornell University Press, 2024. | Includes bibliographical references and index.
Identifiers: LCCN 2024004220 (print) | LCCN 2024004221 (ebook) | ISBN 9781501777738 (hardcover) | ISBN 9781501777745 (paperback) | ISBN 9781501777752 (epub) | ISBN 9781501777769 (pdf)
Subjects: LCSH: Decolonization—Malaysia—Sabah—History—20th century. | Sabah (Malaysia)—Colonial influence—History—20th century. | Sabah (Malaysia)—Politics and government—20th century.
Classification: LCC DS597.336 .S28 2024 (print) | LCC DS597.336 (ebook) | DDC 325.595/3—dc23/eng/20240327
LC record available at https://lccn.loc.gov/2024004220
LC ebook record available at https://lccn.loc.gov/2024004221

For my family

Contents

Acknowledgments ix

Note on Translation xiii

Prologue: Down the Kinabatangan   1

Introduction: The Emergence of a Plan   9

Part One: Resurgent Empire, Fragmented Identities

1. From Company State to Crown Colony   35
2. The (Re-)Emergence of Anticolonial Voices   63

Part Two: Vying Archipelagos

3. The Rise of the Kalimantan Utara Movement   101
4. Maphilindo, the Confederation That Never Was   127
5. Creating Malaysia, "A Shotgun Colonial Wedding"   156

Conclusion: Afterlives   188

Notes 197

Bibliography 237

Index 255

Acknowledgments

The research for this book was made possible by a number of grants awarded during my time at the University of Hong Kong, which enabled me to visit archives and institutions across Asia, the United Kingdom, and the United States. My main source of funding was provided by the Research Grants Council of Hong Kong, which offered annual travel grants for archival research and conference participation. Also of great significance were the Louis Cha Postgraduate Research Fellowship, the Hong Kong University Faculty of Arts' International Experience for Research Postgraduate Students grant, and the National Archives of Australia and Australian Historical Association's Postgraduate Scholarship.

I am deeply grateful for the help provided by the staff at the various archives where I conducted my research. I spent many thrilling months at the National Archives in Kew, between 2015 and 2017, losing myself in obscure North Borneo Chartered Company records and gathering data that would later prove vital for this book. Over the course of many visits, I accumulated some twenty thousand images of government records, colonial memoranda, letters from local political figures, and newspaper articles, among other items. My visits to the Arkib Negara Malaysia in Kuala Lumpur, and the John F. Kennedy Presidential Library in Boston, throughout 2017 and 2018 were equally fruitful and proved to be formative experiences. These archives, in addition to other repositories across Hong Kong, Singapore, the United Kingdom, and the United States, formed the basis of my work, and I am grateful to have had the opportunity to conduct research in so many places.

Although this book was written throughout 2022 and 2023 during my time in work visa limbo in Washington, DC, its essence derives from my research while at the University of Hong Kong. I owe a great deal of gratitude to those who provided me with support and guidance in Hong Kong. First and foremost, I am grateful to my supervisor, Oscar Sanchez-Sibony, who was instrumental in helping me frame my ideas and navigate my research. I am also grateful to David Pomfret, who has supported my work since I first walked into his lecture on the history of the modern world as a wide-eyed undergraduate in 2011. I am also deeply grateful to John Carroll, who offered endless encouragement and great conversation over many lunches at the Senior Common Room. I would also like to extend gratitude to Robert Peckham, who read early versions of my work, and to Peter Cunich, who has served as a mentor for many years, having first encouraged my budding interest in Southeast Asian history during my time as an undergraduate. To my other colleagues and fellow students at the University of Hong Kong, first as an undergraduate, then as a postgraduate, and finally as a lecturer, I also wish to express my sincerest gratitude. I will always fondly remember my undergraduate students in my two courses, HIST2187: Critical Approaches to the End of Empire in Southeast Asia and HIST2192: Introduction to Modern Southeast Asian History. In designing and leading these courses, I was able to pioneer the reintroduction of Southeast Asian history into the history department's curriculum after a twenty-year hiatus, something that I am very proud of. My students displayed incredible enthusiasm and a real hunger to study the lesser-known and rarely discussed aspects of Southeast Asian, global, and imperial history, which was so wonderful to witness.

Beyond Hong Kong, I am grateful to a number of individuals who over the years kindly supported my research, read my work, and offered insights. At Cornell University, I am eternally thankful for the guidance provided by Eric Tagliacozzo, who read early drafts of my work, served as my PhD examiner, and later helped by reading my proposal for this book. I am also appreciative of the advice of Sarah Stockwell, from my time as a visiting doctoral researcher at King's College, London. At Northwestern University, I am indebted to Haydon Cherry, who read early drafts of what would become the first chapter in this book. Finally, I wish to thank all of the individuals who have kindly listened to, and provided feedback on, the work that I shared at various conferences and seminars, the fruits of which can be seen in this book.

For the first-time author, the book publication process will doubtless be daunting, and at times fraught with challenges. My experience working with Cornell University Press, however, has been truly wonderful. I would like to express my deepest thanks to my editor, Sarah Grossman, at Cornell's Southeast Asia Program Publications, who worked tirelessly to help me navigate the publication journey. Since first lodging my interest in publishing my work, through to handling my completed manuscript, Sarah has been invaluable. I would also like to express my thanks to the two anonymous reviewers, who not only produced a pair of fantastic reviews but also understood and appreciated my work and advised me on how to improve my book. Their comments and suggestions provided a final, invaluable boost.

My acknowledgments would not be complete without thanking my family, who unwaveringly encouraged me throughout this journey. My childhood in Hong Kong, spent in the charming west of the island overlooking the South China Sea, was filled with moments that will stick with me forever. Whether roaming the backstreets of Yau Ma Tei and Sham Shui Po with my mother and brother, or taking a sampan across the Lamma Channel with my father and grandparents, these were formative years that instilled in me a love for the region. My wife, Emily Williams, who shares with me a passion for Asia's history and culture, lovingly supported me as I wrote this book. This book is for you.

Note on Translation

Throughout this book various words, phrases, and sources have been translated from Malay Bahasa and various local Sabahan languages. These translations are mostly my own, except for a few instances where I have quoted translated material, such as the tale of Tuwan Nahuda, described in chapter 4. Colonial and other official sources sometimes contain their own translations of words and phrases from local languages, which vary owing to changes across time and place. I have tried to maintain consistency where possible.

CHASING ARCHIPELAGIC DREAMS

Prologue
Down the Kinabatangan

The Kinabatangan River meanders for hundreds of miles through swathes of dense, ancient rain forest, before emptying onto a delta on Borneo's northeastern coast. Shades of vivid green give way to the muddy orange water that carves through the forest.

On March 1, 1883, a young British explorer died while hunting an elephant deep within these jungles. It was less than two years after the establishment of the North Borneo Chartered Company, and the island's uncharted hinterlands—Borneo's so-called terra incognita—had already claimed the life of one of its first employees.[1] Frank Hatton, appointed as a surveyor for the fledgling company, had been journeying up the Kinabatangan to study the region's geology. Starting at Sandakan—the company's newly acquired capital was known previously as Elopura ("Beautiful Town") and colloquially as "Little Hong Kong"—he was venturing into the unknown (see figures 1 and 2). Sabah's interior was perceived by colonials as a wild, dangerous frontier. Coasting down the Kinabatangan on the return leg of his journey, Hatton and his "native" guides spotted an elephant along the riverbank. From the boat, he aimed his rifle and fired at the animal, "wounding it severely," before dashing ashore to give chase. It was here, amid the dense jungle vines, that the young explorer met his end. His father, Joseph Hatton, later described the incident as recounted by his guides, Drahman and Oodeen: "As he stooped to pass under a creeper, he raised his rifle to lift up the obstruction. The weapon became

PROLOGUE

THE JOURNEY BACK.

FIGURE 1. "The Journey Back," illustrating the voyage down the Kinabatangan River to Sandakan prior to Frank Hatton's death on March 1, 1883. Hatton heads the group at the boat's prow. Joseph Hatton, "Frank Hatton in North Borneo," *The Century Magazine* 8 (1885): 444. From the author's collection.

entangled in an unusually strong growth of vines, whereby the muzzle was suddenly twisted towards him, slid down his shoulder, and went off, the trigger being pulled by some twigs of the creeper." Writhing in pain, Hatton called to his guides for help. "Oodeen, Oodeen, *mati sahya! Mati sahya!* (I am dead! I am dead!)" he cried out repeatedly, before succumbing to his wounds.[2]

Only twenty-two years of age at the time of his death, the young man was a promising chemist and geologist in charge of prospecting for oil, coal, gold, and other resources deemed valuable to the new colonial enterprise.[3] His death was a mishap befitting a colonial expedition where scientific and commercial endeavors were sidelined by masculinized pursuits of trophy hunting and conquering the wilderness.[4]

The story of Frank Hatton's death encapsulates the beginnings of a fraught relationship between colonials in Sabah and its indigenous inhabitants, with the natural environment serving as a major point of contest. From the earliest days of company incursion until the end of British rule in September 1963, prospectors, investors, businessmen, and politicians consistently sought to triumph over—and financially benefit from—the land, its resources, and the various communities caught in the fray. Indeed, this heady fixation on extraction and profit persisted even after the creation of the Federation of Malaysia in 1963. Colonial firms continued to operate long after formal decolonization, while today, in the early twenty-first century, the Malaysian state's finances are propped up by the petrochemical, timber, and palm oil products extracted from Sabah and Sarawak.[5] In the colonial period, although Sabah's geography evoked intrigue, it simultaneously bred anxiety. Europeans partook in colonial games such as trophy hunting and explorations into the depths of the jungle as a way of feigning dominance, and yet many of them were terrified by stories of head-hunting, cannibalism, and their apparent inability to extend colonial law across the land. Frequent anticolonial clashes—framed by the colonial state as rebellions and insurrections rather than wars—perpetuated these concerns during the early years, leading to violent crackdowns. Likewise, expeditions revolving around resources, taxation, religious proselytization, policing, and other state functions served as attempts at dominating places ostensibly in need of so-called colonial development.

Colonials at the time did not remark at the irony of Frank Hatton's death. Had he not disembarked to pursue the elephant and instead stuck to his original course charting the mineral wealth of the Kinabatangan basin, he would have survived. For colonials in Sabah, and observers back in Britain, he was a martyr; his death was an inexplicable result of life in the tropics, whose innate hostility and dangerous wildlife were constant sources of peril. In their view, a white man had perished valiantly—and not in vain—in pursuit of domination over Borneo's interior. Reports of his death preached the special respect and adoration displayed by Oodeen, Drahman, and the other accompanying boatmen toward their colonial master. *"Kita lebih baik telah mati!* (Better we had died!)" they cried, worried that the accidental shooting could have been mistaken for murderous mutiny. Satisfied by their accounts, however, officials later lauded their "acts of devotion."[6] As the story goes, the guides rushed Hatton's corpse back to Sandakan, paddling night and day for fifty-three hours continuously down the Kinabatangan. The story of Hatton's death remained a perennial reminder to colonials of the seemingly ever-present dangers of life in the tropics. The colonial enterprise, in turn, used his death to highlight colonial sacrifice and to bolster the notion of the indigenous people's supposed loyalty toward their overlords. Indeed, as Robert Bickers writes, "Death is useful; historians feed off it, and it generates documentation; unexpected death—early, violent, disappointing death—is even more so."[7] Throughout the twentieth century, and even today, numerous geological studies analyzing the region's mineral composition preface their introductions with reverential mentions of Hatton's sacrifice and "tragic death while hunting."[8] A foolish death, but one that has since been eulogized for symbolically granting foreign capital, commerce, and scientific inquiry access to Borneo's rain forests.

Understanding that colonials were fascinated with and yet felt threatened by what was hidden deep within Borneo raises various questions. Simultaneously, Hatton's death serves as a microcosm for understanding colonial dealings throughout the wider region. What were the lingering effects of such incidents on colonial administrative practices? How did this shape relations with indigenous society in later years? How, if ever, were these tensions between the *pesisir* (coast) and the *hutan* (forest) reconciled? And what are its

FIGURE 2. Sandakan Harbor, near the Kinabatangan delta, with Berhala Island in the distance. Lithograph, 1890. *Handbook of British North Borneo* (London: William Cowie & Sons, 1890). From the author's collection.

lasting legacies today, when local and foreign actors alike continue to scramble for territory, influence, and resources in Sabah? Foreign administrators sought to interact with the natural environment as a place where wealth could be extracted, but it was also a place deemed vital to regulate and control. These motivations intensified during the end of empire. Globally, colonial proclivities remained ingrained into the very fabric of foreign domination over marginal, subnational territories, even after the formal end of empire.

The North Borneo Chartered Company's early functionaries left enduring marks on Sabah, but sometimes less through their administrative roles than through their progeny. And as these early administrators worked to incorporate Sabah into the colonial fold, the continuing effects of their descendants would in later years shape the territory's experience of decolonization.

Another surveyor at the time was Ernest Alfred Pavitt. Lured by prospects of adventure and wealth, he emigrated from New Zealand to Sabah in 1881, aged twenty-five. Unlike Frank Hatton, Pavitt did not meet premature death in his explorations. But he was nevertheless immortalized in the colonial archive, not through his death, but through suffering and notoriety all the same. He was employed by the company to survey arable land and indigenous tobacco growing, in order to assess the viability of establishing colonial plantations throughout the Kinabatangan River basin.[9] The two colleagues were stationed in Sandakan in the early 1880s, and they were part of a small but growing community of young colonials tasked with navigating the Kinabatangan and other major arteries into the interior. These early colonial surveyors and explorers were joined by a range of "experts"—agronomists, geologists, chemists, mineralogists, botanists, and hydrologists—who shaped the early company state as it strove to exert influence across the territory.

Colonial interest in Borneo was not limited to imperial strategy and resources. Artifacts, specimens, exotica, and indeed even tales of what lay within its jungles, fanned out across the seas and fueled growing interest in the region.[10] Ashore on Borneo, early European travelers were entranced and perplexed by its flora and fauna. Since the early eighteenth century, fanciful tales of allegedly predatory hominoids (who turned out to be harmless orangutans), giant flesh-eating plants (*Nepenthes rajah*, for example, a pitcher plant species endemic to the foothills of Mount Kinabalu, has leaf traps that exceed forty centimeters in diameter), and birds of paradise were received with great curiosity.[11] These animals and plants, isolated for millennia by Borneo's bounded island geography, resulted in a unique vicariance in biodiversity compared to mainland Southeast Asia.[12] "Borneo has been caricatured in Western literature as the end of the earth," writes Eric Tagliacozzo, "an enormous, impenetrable forest, populated by headhunters and a bevy of strange animals and birds."[13] This popular fixation with the exotic continues to shape perceptions of the island in the contemporary postcolonial era, as it did in the early days of the semi-autonomous chartered company. Despite his ostensible scientific acclaim, Frank Hatton succumbed to the lure of Borneo's wild, while at home in the West many lived vicariously through text and image.

Others, in contrast, adapted to their administrative posts and thrived. Ernest Alfred Pavitt's sojourns into the Bornean hinterland continued throughout the 1880s and 1890s, when he was appointed chief surveyor and acting commissioner of lands, both of which were positions of influence that put him in frequent contact with the territory's indigenous communities and local elite figures. In 1896, Pavitt travelled to a small Kadazandusun *kampong* (village) on the west coast between the colonial settlements of Jesselton and Beaufort. On this trip, he became besotted with a Kadazandusun girl named Kwai. Immediately, Pavitt petitioned her father, Orang Tua (village headman; literally "old man") Limbahau, to be allowed to marry the girl. After considerable persuasion, Pavitt was granted permission to wed the *orang tua's* daughter, with the marriage taking place the following year in 1897.[14]

Although the existence of such interracial marriages was rarely acknowledged by the colonial elite, they became increasingly commonplace.[15] Pavitt's marriage to Kwai, agreed to in a deal with the *orang tua*, serves as a microcosm for understanding the advent of Western colonialism in the region. Like Kwai, who was wed without having a say in the matter, many local leaders and indigenous elites found the land around them suddenly transferred from one overlord to another with neither consultation nor consent. These so-called deals struck between colonials and indigenous potentates—like that which resulted in the formation of the North Borneo Chartered Company itself—served to undermine the traditional patterns of authority relied upon by lesser elites and society at large. Similar forces were at play when Kwai was dispensed by Orang Tua Limbahau in hopes that his *kampong* might receive favorable treatment from the company's fledgling Lands Department. And indeed, these trends were again mirrored in the days leading up to Sabah's eventual merger with Malaysia in 1963. Such were the processes of treaty signing and dealmaking that those whose lives stood to change the most often had the least say.

Ernest Alfred Pavitt's and Kwai's child, Jules Stephen Pavitt, was born later that year and became part of a small but growing number of Eurasians living in the territory. Life for Sabah's Eurasian and mixed-race minorities was characterized by hardship and isolation. Peripatetic company bureaucrats roamed Sabah on administrative tours, leaving behind new families and abandoning relations at the wayside. In 1918, the young Jules Stephen Pavitt became estranged from his father, having accused him of neglecting his family. In an ensuing argument, the elder Pavitt disowned his son and demanded that he stop using the family surname. All of a sudden, Jules Stephen Pavitt found himself with neither a surname nor a reliable link to colonial society, and he was prompted to rename himself Jules Pavitt Stephens.[16] Shortly afterwards, Ernest Alfred Pavitt retired from his post as chief surveyor and emigrated to Australia alone, abandoning his Bornean family and leaving behind a forgotten legacy. The experiences of Eurasians and other minority groups in Sabah were manifestly different to those of the colonial elite. They were often caught between worlds; neither accepted into colonial circles nor considered indigenous. Many were simply left behind or forgotten.

Slavery, though diminishing in prevalence over the years, was still a recurrent issue in Sabah during the late nineteenth and early twentieth centuries. The practice of keeping Chinese or Japanese prostitutes was widespread, particularly among the younger company employees and administrators who were often, but not always, unmarried.[17] In early 1898, Henry William Cope, a wealthy industrialist who made his fortune in Sabah's nascent timber industry, "purchased" a woman from a Japanese merchant vessel docked in Jesselton.[18] The woman—her name forgotten and lost to history—gave birth to a daughter, Edith Cope, later that year. The girl lived in relative prosperity and, unusually for a Eurasian child in Sabah, received a complete Western-style education. In 1920, Edith Cope married Jules Pavitt Stephens. Their child, Donald Aloysius Marmaduke Stephens, was born into a rapidly changing territory shaped by continued colonial attempts at extending influence in a world dominated elsewhere by imperial decline. In his youth, Donald Stephens suffered from leprosy, and as a result he was shunned from colonial society and confined to medical quarantine. The Second World War proved particularly damaging for the Stephens family. Jules Pavitt Stephens was executed by the Japanese in 1944 for his involvement in the Kinabalu Uprising. The site of his killing, at a Japanese concentration camp in Petagas, was just a few miles away from his indigenous family's *kampong*.[19] Donald Stephens, meanwhile, was incarcerated for anti-Japanese activities for much of the war's duration.

Donald Stephens, however, would later be appointed Sabah's first chief minister after its merger with Malaysia in 1963. Having carved himself a niche as the foremost representative of indigenous Kadazandusun society in the 1950s, he became a key mediator between local and colonial groups in the run-up to decolonization.[20] Known affectionately by his Kadazandusun supporters as their *huguan siou* (brave or paramount leader) and pejoratively by colonials as the "King of the Kadazans," and at times as a "black bastard," Stephens followed a remarkable rise from obscurity and ostracization to political prominence.[21] Stephens's role as a newspaper editor and political commentator in the 1950s and 1960s provided him with a platform from which he was able to criticize colonial governance and raise awareness for indigenous causes.[22] But his rise to power was by no means straightforward. Shunned by the colonial elite, subjected to incessant government surveillance, and marked as a destabilizing force, Stephens had to navigate immense precarity. In the late 1950s, Stephens worked alongside local political leaders in Sabah, Sarawak, and Brunei to advance a short-lived plan to form an independent state comprising the three Borneo territories. Although ultimately unsuccessful, the abortive plan for *merdeka* (independence) set Stephens apart as one of Sabah's foremost power brokers. His death in 1976, in an airplane crash, ruptured Sabahan politics during a period of major transition.[23] The legacy of the tragedy continues to shape Sabah today, eliciting public interest as well as allegations of foul play.[24] Situating key individuals alongside broader sociopolitical developments facilitates a more nuanced view of the territory's history, while also enabling a clearer understanding of Sabah's role in late colonial and postcolonial Southeast Asia.

Introduction
The Emergence of a Plan

Travel one hundred miles due southwest from Jesselton, Sabah's colonial capital, and one would reach Kampong Meligan, a sleepy Kadazandusun community with isolated patches of farmland encased within the surrounding dense jungle. Journeying by foot, one would expect to travel for at least five days, likely more. Before the development of major roads and transport links, the trip would have been hard going, with travelers forced to cross numerous rivers and seek refuge at towns along the way. But as with many other indigenous *kampongs* scattered across Sabah in the late colonial period, Meligan was neither isolated from the territory's administrative center nor disconnected from the great sociopolitical and constitutional questions of the day.

In late February 1962, Meligan's residents were grappling with perhaps the greatest question that they would ever face. Should Sabah, together with Sarawak and Brunei, merge with Malaya and Singapore to form a single, greater federation? What pathway toward decolonization should the territory—their country—take? Orang Tua Andulon B. Maga, Meligan's leader, could see the concern in people's eyes as they gathered before him. "It is said by the people in Malaya that they are our brothers," Andulon began. "This is completely untrue," he continued. "We do not know anything about them and we do not wish to know them." The fear and mistrust that diffused throughout Kampong Meligan would soon give way to defiance: "We do not like people from

Malaya and Singapore coming here and taking our land." If pushed, Andulon Maga pledged, "later on we would fight."[1]

Elsewhere in Sabah, however, others welcomed the proposed departure of the British colonial overlords in favor of a new, ostensibly postcolonial Malaysian government. In Jesselton, A. J. Alli Ahmed, a car mechanic, wrote to the Anglo-Malayan Cobbold Commission on Malaysia in February 1962 to express his "full support" for the idea. Ahmed was won over by promises of unity with Malaya, Singapore, and Sarawak. Bound together, he claimed, they would create a defensive archipelagic arc to fend off foreign aggression, be it from the Philippines in the north or Indonesia in the south. Likewise, Ahmed felt that Projek Malaysia (the Malaysia Project) would enable Sabah "to form a bigger voice in the United Nation[s]," which would provide trade opportunities, improved living standards for the "natives," and ultimately, international recognition.[2]

The two decades that followed the brutal Japanese occupation proved immensely difficult for Sabah. Postwar reconstruction was slow and marked by the imposition of a new and intensified form of colonial rule. Society was gripped by many great changes. The new Crown Colony regime that emerged from the ruins of war wielded greater influence over the territory and people's lives than did its autonomous predecessor, the North Borneo Chartered Company. In its efforts to strengthen its authority over the extraction of cash crops, mineral wealth, and timber, Sabah's formal colonial government was paradoxically more pervasive and controlling than ever before. Buoyed by newfound confidence and a belief in the apparent infallibility of British rule in Sabah, colonial bureaucrats on the ground overlooked the rise of local political expression throughout the territory and the prevailing winds of anticolonialism that swept across Asia. In dismissing contrarian views as arising from an insignificant minority of local elites, the colonial state perpetuated unsubstantiated beliefs that Sabah's public was apolitical and detached from constitutional issues. This was a stark irony, considering the dramatic global collapse of imperialism after the Second World War, and the fact that Sabah was plugged into webs of migration and commerce that propelled peoples and ideas across Asia and beyond. And with this came new visions of postcolonial archipelagic unity.

Unsurprisingly, therefore, questions of looming decolonization did indeed trigger strong reactions across Sabah. This was particularly evident among the territory's budding political elites, who in the 1950s began to champion their own unique brand of anticolonialism. Although Sabah was slow to adopt party politics—with ethnic and religious-based parties only emerging in 1961—local political leaders from all corners of the territory had long sought to influence, resist, and at times even paradoxically assist colonial rule. And no time was so pressing as the imminent end of British rule, in which metropolitan officials in London, Malayan nationalist elites in Kuala Lumpur, and colonial bureaucrats in Sabah each worked to advance their own interpretation of, and timeline for, the decolonization process. This moment of constitutional and geopolitical fluidity elicited considerable public interest throughout the Borneo territories and across the Malayan Peninsula. But it also prompted regional uproar and competition among Southeast Asia's recently independent states, with both Indonesia and the Philippines taking keen interest in influencing Sabah's postcolonial transition.

The early 1960s therefore saw Sabah enter unchartered waters, with neighboring Southeast Asian states, and a series of subnational anticolonial movements and state-making concepts, vying for advantage in northern Borneo. The ultimate goal was to extend control over Sabah, a strategic territory perceived as valuable due to its vast tracts of fertile land, untapped resources, and ostensibly pliable indigenous population. This period of political uncertainty, therefore, was marked not just by a fraught pathway toward decolonization but also by fierce competition over the nature of Sabah's postcolonial future. Amid this contestation among the postcolonial states of Malaya, Indonesia, and the Philippines—which each assumed the role of imperial predator, shed begrudgingly by the departure of Western colonial powers—Sabah found itself increasingly unlikely to achieve authentic independence.

This rapidly changing international order thrust Sabah into a deadly mix of competing state making, in which countries with rivaling conceptions of Melayu archipelagic unity jostled for dominance to become the foremost independent power in Southeast Asia. These desires to incorporate or subjugate Sabah were frequently framed under regional security and developmental concerns, be they countering the perceived threat of communism, pushing to secure resource wealth, or expanding proprietary dreams of archipelagic unity.

Plans to merge Sabah within a greater Malaysia, debated across the territory by residents in Kampong Meligan, workers in Jesselton, and countless others from all walks of life, were initially forged in secrecy by British and Malayan policymakers in the late 1950s and early 1960s. Although the British had expressed interest in merging their various Southeast Asian territories as early as the late nineteenth century, it was only in 1961—galvanized by the express support of Malaya's ruling elite—that Projek Malaysia was first revealed to the world. The plan would trigger one of maritime Southeast Asia's greatest periods of geopolitical instability, with the afterlives of unfinished decolonization and continuing territorial strife persisting today.

On May 27, 1961, Malaya's prime minster, the Tunku Abdul Rahman, made an announcement that would forever change the political landscape of maritime

12   INTRODUCTION

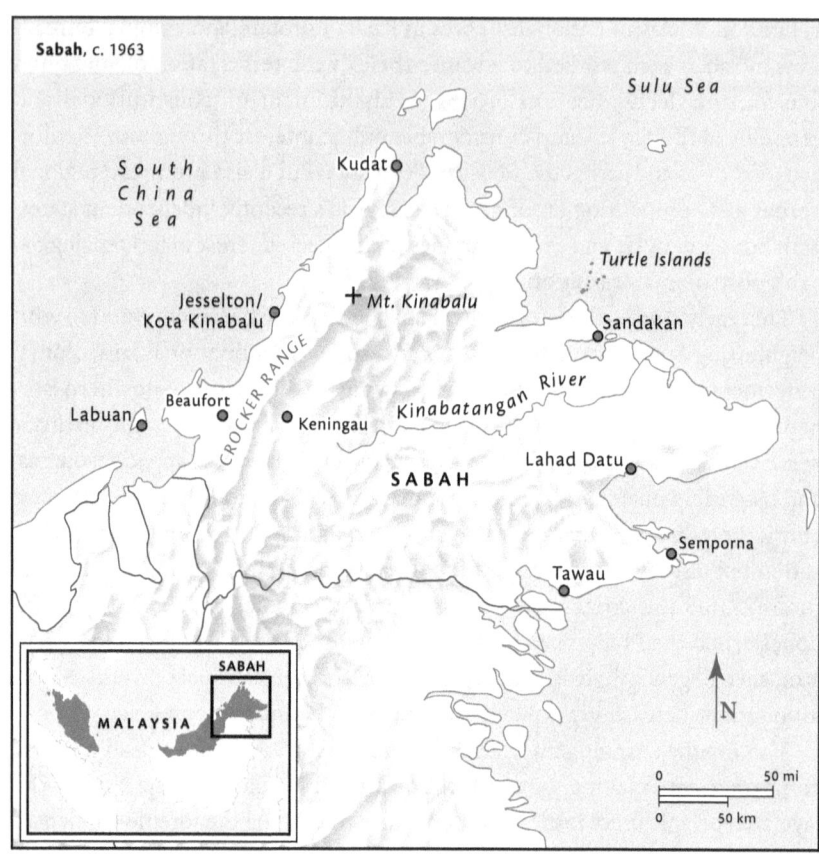

MAP 1. Map of Sabah. Map by Erin Greb Cartography.

Southeast Asia: a proposition to form a greater federation comprising Malaya, Singapore, Sabah, Sarawak, and Brunei. At first glance, the announcement itself appeared nothing out of the ordinary. British colonial bureaucrats and Malayan elites had put forward a range of similar proposals over the years, but to little fanfare and without success. But this day was different, and the Tunku's proclamation of Projek Malaysia thrust Southeast Asia into a hubbub of contentious motion. Speaking before a crowd of reporters and dignitaries during a luncheon at the Foreign Correspondents' Association in Singapore, the Tunku warned of the dangers facing Malaya and of the critical urgency at which it should pursue closer ties with Singapore and the three British Borneo territories. "Malaya today as a nation realizes that she cannot stand alone and in isolation," he proclaimed. Despite the Malayan Emergency drawing to a close the previous year, the perceived threat of communism continued to dominate Kuala Lumpur's political rhetoric. Malaya's and Singapore's Chinese population, the Tunku warned, should "forget China" and instead look toward Malaya, "our one and only home."[3]

As if appealing to Western policymakers, the Tunku invoked the Cold War paranoia of the day: should Malaya be invaded by the Communists, "the result will not be a local war but a global one."[4] Malaya, he argued, needed to merge with the British Borneo territories to offset the perceived ethnic imbalance caused by incorporating Singapore's Chinese-majority population. But beneath this façade of anticommunist urgency lay a desire to expand, enrich, and strengthen the new postcolonial state. Prior to decolonization, Britain had toyed with the idea of merging its Malayan territories with those in Borneo on numerous occasions throughout the 1880s, the 1930s, the late 1940s, and again in the 1950s.[5] Although "this [was] something that which has been thought of, and thought of quite often," plans for merger were repeatedly cast aside by the British over doubts surrounding the ethnic and cultural compatibility of the two distant regions.[6] Similar concerns were conceded by colonial officials who mused on the possibility of union between Sabah and Hong Kong, a distant colonial cousin on the southern coast of China. Such was the malleability of Sabah's postcolonial trajectory in the 1950s and early 1960s that even among colonial elite circles no single decolonization pathway was inherently clear.

These lingering concerns surrounding union between Malaya and Sabah were matched by further unease over the disparity in wealth between the prosperous peninsula and the poorer Borneo territories, and over the sheer distance between them.[7] Yet for Britain, the consolidation of disparate and far-flung colonial dependencies was to become a key strategy for easing decolonization, even if it meant overlooking cultural, economic, and geographic differences.[8] And for Malaya, these incompatibilities were to be swept aside in pursuit of archipelagic expansion and state formation.

The proliferating rivalry between vying postcolonial states of Melayu origin resulted in stiff competition to leverage influence over Sabah. Projek Malaysia, in particular, elicited immediate condemnation across the region. Malaya's continuing affiliation with Britain, especially during the Malayan Emergency, gave rise to allegations that the Tunku Abdul Rahman harbored neocolonial designs and sympathies for British interests. Although the Tunku dismissed such claims as "utterly absurd," the charge of *nekolim* (neocolonialism) would continue to rankle advocates and detractors of Malaysia alike.[9] Indonesia, for instance, viewed the Malaysia proposal as an existential threat, and it set about to block its creation while advancing its own claims. Across the seas in the Philippines, the plan was similarly viewed with suspicion, prompting renewed public interest in staking a claim to Sabah as a long-lost territory of the defunct Sultanate of Sulu. Alongside these burgeoning rivalries between postcolonial states were a sequence of private claims for territory and grassroots anti-Malaysia initiatives. And despite mounting colonial and foreign pressure, emergent local figureheads within Borneo sought to assert autonomy over their own constitutional future. It is small wonder, then, that the Tunku would invoke ostensible security threats and the specter of communism in his push for merger with Britain's colonial territories in Borneo. But these grassroots movements, scrambles for territory, and regional geopolitical disputes seldom figure in the received wisdom concerning the formation of Malaysia and Britain's withdrawal from empire in Southeast Asia, clouding popular awareness.

The story of the creation of Malaysia is often told from the perspective of metropolitan policymakers in London and Malay nationalist elites in Kuala Lumpur who worked to perpetuate colonial systems of governance and resource extraction in the Borneo territories. Official narratives tend to focus on the Westerners' preoccupation with ensuring that they did not leave behind territories vulnerable to communist depredation. Likewise, Malaysia's formation is frequently folded into accounts viewing merger as the final phase in Britain's voluntary and timely departure from the peninsula, an ostensibly enlightened moment following the trajectory laid out by Malayan independence in 1957 and the triumphant end of the Emergency in 1960.

Left out of the equation is the role played by peninsular (West) Malaysia's other half. East Malaysia, as it is known today, comprises the poorer and politically marginalized—and yet vast and immensely resource-rich—states of Sabah and Sarawak on the island of Borneo. In the early 1960s, members of the budding political elite in Sabah conceived themselves as representing their own country. They did not consider Sabah as bound to Malaya by sinews of British administrative tradition or inherent Melayu value, but as bound to its neighboring Bornean states by common precolonial heritage, geographic links, and ethnocultural ties. This incipient push for Bornean statehood was stymied from the outset by British and Malayan officials out of concern that on independence, Sabah would be snapped up by larger states in Southeast Asia eager to expand territorially. Better Malaya than Indonesia, the Philippines, or even communist China, policymakers in London argued. As Singapore's then minister for culture, S. Rajaratnam, warned in 1961, Projek Malaysia "must fill the vacuum left by Britain when she pulls out of Southeast Asia."[10] Yet communism remained the publicized scapegoat. As the official story went, should

Sabah achieve independence alone then it would surely fall to communist subversion. But Sabah bucked the trend as laid out by the Tunku before the crowd of reporters and attendees at the 1961 luncheon. Communism, perceived as the ultimate threat by Western policymakers, was simply not present in Sabah. Even among the territory's large Chinese population—who were often viewed with suspicion and disparaged for their links to China—there was little interest in communism.[11] This presents Sabah as fundamentally incompatible with the prevailing world theory at the time, in which Western policymakers narrowly conceived Asia "as a row of dominos, their fates all interconnected in the Cold War struggle."[12]

Sabah was by no means free from depredation and geopolitical aggression, however. As it coursed toward decolonization in the early 1960s, Sabah emerged as one of the world's most contested territories, with a multitude of state-making attempts, territorial claims, and local political movements each hinging on incorporating it into its postcolonial fold. This harks back to the frenetic period of Western imperial competition over Sabah in the late nineteenth century, which saw myriad attempts at colonization flounder, ranging from private ventures to state-backed bids to establish penal colonies. Nevertheless, the early 1960s was a period of remarkable geopolitical fluidity and contestation. Prior to the crystallization of the Anglo-Malayan plan for Malaysia and Britain's withdrawal from Sabah on September 16, 1963, no single decolonization route appeared certain. The emergence of Kalimantan Utara in early 1963 was but the latest in a string of attempts to form a union of independent Bornean states in the image of the historical Sultanate of Brunei. Nominally independent, the movement later succumbed to Indonesian influence, resembling in its death throes a desperately inauthentic mimicry of popular anticolonial revolution. Although Kalimantan Utara presented as staunchly anticolonial, its roots can be traced to various failed attempts to form a unified Bornean federation comprising Sabah, Sarawak, and Brunei in the late 1950s, an idea propagated at various times by members of Sabah's colonial elite and later by indigenous figureheads. Likewise, the Philippines' territorial claim over Sabah in 1962 sought to capitalize on a groundswell of public interest in reviving the precolonial Sultanate of Sulu and in rejecting the rogue imperial dealmaking that splintered the northern part of Borneo off from the southern Philippine archipelago in 1878. Added to this were the sporadic intimations made by colonial figures within Sabah in the late 1950s and early 1960s that the territory would fare best if its postcolonial future were aligned more closely with Hong Kong, with which it shared deep economic and social ties, by virtue of the sizable population of Cantonese residents in Sandakan, Jesselton, Kudat, and other coastal towns. Local efforts within Sabah to push for a variety of decolonization routes, albeit short lived, and the stark dissonance between colonial and metropolitan agendas in the run-up toward decolonization further cast the region adrift in a sea of contingency and contest.

Such uncertainty serves to denaturalize Sabah's merger with Malaysia. At no point was the process of union guaranteed. Even after the union was formed in September 1963, anti-Malaysia forces continued to proliferate amid the proclamation of President Sukarno's "Ganyang Malaysia" ("Crush Malaysia") campaign that resulted in the Indonesian Konfrontasi (Confrontation). Sabah lay at the tumultuous center of maritime Southeast Asia, contested from all angles by vying postcolonial dreams of archipelagic statehood and territorial consolidation.

Colonization and subordination took many forms, however. Colonial and official administrative records, preserved in archives across Britain and Malaysia, tell only one side of the story. Family histories, memoirs, and local oral traditions can aid in supplementing the official view. Accordingly, in addition to examining the vying scrambles for territory and influence in Sabah, it is vital to trace the experiences of individuals and their descendants who lived through and shaped these periods of major sociopolitical change. The shifting fortunes of those whose lives were intertwined with the rise and fall of foreign administrative ventures in Sabah illuminate the rarely seen shades of late colonial governance and local civic development during periods of fluidity and upheaval. Such human stories, seldom considered within the context of political history, are intertwined with the story of Sabah's transition from a site of semi-autonomous colonial extraction into a contested cornerstone of postcolonial statehood.

Scrambles for Territory

Sabah's history was fraught with geopolitical challenges. Few places in Asia were so contested. Throughout the nineteenth and twentieth centuries, a stream of states, colonization projects, corporate ventures, and local grassroots movements met with failure in Borneo. All of this, Maya Jasanoff writes, turned the island into "a morass of rebellions, wars of succession, and border squabbles."[13]

These competing attempts at staking a claim to Borneo were heightened by the perceived wealth of the island. Control over Borneo's shores enabled access to the resource-rich interior, a place brimming with precious minerals, timber, and other valuable primary products. Geopolitically, too, the island was strategically located at the center of maritime Southeast Asia during a time of colonial expansion and indigenous resistance. Its coasts served as a nexus connecting local and foreign maritime traffic from the Philippine archipelago to Java, Sulawesi, Sumatra, the Malayan Peninsula, and to China, Japan, India, and beyond. Similarly, its strategic natural harbors offered ships shelter from perilous waters, convenient enclaves that would be eyed by Western imperial powers in the late nineteenth century as potential refueling stations for onward voyages. Although Borneo soaked up regional cultural and economic influences, foreign incursions were typically transient and short lived. Permanent settlement and authority proved incredibly difficult to implement on the island. Indeed, Borneo's foremost local polities—whether the Sultanates of Brunei, Sulu, or Bulungan—also struggled throughout history. Their influence waned considerably in the eighteenth and nineteenth centuries, when they were reduced to ruling strips of often-overlapping coastal territory and seldom able to exert direct control inland, where a multitude of semi-autonomous *pangerans* (princes), warlords, and local chiefs reigned supreme. The consequent lack of any singular local polity or dominant state in Borneo during this period shaped the island as a site vulnerable to foreign incursion, rather than a source for projecting power regionally.[14]

Early foreign involvement in Borneo has been traced to at least the fifth century CE, when the Chinese monk Fa Hsien was recorded to have first made landfall on the island. Fragmentary evidence of Chinese interactions across the wider region stretches further still into the past, with archaeological discoveries revealing that Chinese porcelain, coins, and other artifacts had long been transported to the island in exchange for an array of jungle produce. Although Chinese connections with Borneo were primarily mercantile, they were remarkably pervasive. As Eric Tagliacozzo describes, "Few Bornean societies, from the Kelabit deep in the interior of the island to the Bajau communities scattered along the coasts, can be said to have escaped these fluctuations altogether."[15]

Western colonial involvement in the region was initially spasmodic. Despite brief periods of European activity dating to the early sixteenth century, it was only in the nineteenth century that Western interest intensified. The proliferation of European trade with China in this period resulted in increased shipping and navigation throughout the South China Sea, especially after the colonization of Singapore and Hong Kong. With this swelling maritime traffic, Borneo's importance as a strategic location—as well as a site "abounding in vegetable and mineral resources"—became rooted in the imperial psyche. Lord Thomas Brassey, speaking in the House of Lords in 1892, described how "Borneo lies on the high road of our great trade to China and Japan. Its northwest coast . . . is hundreds of miles in extent, and it possesses several secure and capacious harbours."[16] These strategic harbors were made further available to imperial powers by the declining influence of the Brunei Sultanate, which also "presented opportunities for independent adventurers and traders."[17]

For centuries, Brunei had been the foremost polity along Borneo's northwestern coastline. Together with lesser local states, the sultanate oversaw expanses of coastal territory and utilized rivers to project maritime authority into Borneo's interior. By the early nineteenth century, however, these systems had all but faltered. The effects of increased competition with Western adventurers and traders, as well as the collapse of once-lucrative tribute systems with interior communities, severely weakened the sultanate. Brunei was "on the brink of disillusion, riven by civil wars, increasingly unable to defend against raiders based to the east . . . and struggling to adapt to European penetration of trade."[18] Western entrepreneurs and colonial agents alike "used piracy as a lever against the sultans, forcing them to sign treaties banning the practice, and then intervening when they didn't."[19] It was amid this chaos that James Brooke secured a cession for territory in Sarawak along Borneo's west coast in 1841, which he later established as an autonomous kingdom and ruled as its "Rajah."[20] In this period, formal British imperial interests were confined to the small island of Labuan off the coast of Brunei, which Britain later annexed in 1846 with the intention of establishing it as a trading port akin to Hong Kong or Singapore.[21]

Although Rajah James Brooke's private annexation of Sarawak persisted, virtually all other Western colonization attempts in Borneo failed. In 1861, Duke Leopold—the heir to the Belgian throne who would later gain notoriety for his brutal, dehumanizing rule over the Congo Free State—sought territory in Borneo.[22] Having witnessed Brooke's successes in Sarawak and the Netherlands' nominal control over the southern half of the island, Leopold wanted in, now convinced that "the idea of buying control of a country" as personal property "was not necessarily outrageous."[23] Although Leopold's efforts in Borneo were ultimately futile, these ideas proved remarkably portable. Indeed, these Southeast Asian experiences served as a trial run that later informed Europe's relentless colonization of Africa in the 1880s and 1890s. Borneo was a proving ground for unconventional state making at empire's peak in the nineteenth century, as it was for postcolonial territorial expansion decades later in the mid-twentieth century.

Another notable, if ultimately unsuccessful, colonization attempt by a venture from the United States in 1865 characterizes this period of frenzied territorial expansion. Having secured a ten-year land title from Pangeran Tumonggon, heir to Brunei's throne, a contingent of American speculators, led by Joseph William Torrey, arrived at Kimanis Bay, a prized stretch of coastline near Sabah's present-day capital of Kota Kinabalu. Torrey and his followers selected Kimanis Bay with the intention of establishing a trading and farming settlement, called Ellena, to cultivate tobacco and sugarcane. At Ellena, Torrey was crowned "Rajah of Ambong and Murudu," a move doubtless inspired by Brooke's successful adoption of royal titles in Sarawak.[24] Prospects of American colonization of Borneo's northwest coast alarmed the British officials stationed nearby at Labuan, who declared that any American incursion would be "attended by serious prejudice to British interests in Borneo." The colony at Kimanis Bay, however, soon met with disaster. Within months, Ellena's small population of Chinese laborers, lured from Hong Kong by promises of secure employment, faced famine, illness, and abandonment. A series of riots followed, and by 1866, most settlers had either died or fled the encampment.[25] Few would make it home. Ellena was no more: the trading colony had vanished almost as suddenly as it had emerged, Torrey fled to Hong Kong, and Kimanis Bay seemingly reverted to its natural state.

But no sooner had one colonial undertaking failed than a new scramble for Bornean territory arose in its place. Bankrupted and dejected, Joseph William Torrey sold off his land titles at a loss to Baron Gustavus von Overbeck, a German diplomat based in Hong Kong who subsequently traveled to Borneo to seek extensions to the initial territorial grant. Subsequently, and with new titles purporting to cover larger portions of the Bornean interior, Overbeck attempted to sell his rights to the German government for a profit.[26] He was met with a cold reception, however. Not swayed by the lure of potential land and wealth, Chancellor Bismarck chose not to pursue the opportunity during a period of antiexpansionist policy in the 1870s.[27] Deutsch Nordborneo was not to be.

Having failed to lure German interest, Overbeck returned to Hong Kong to take his deeds elsewhere. In 1878, he managed to sell some of his titles to Arthur Dent, who headed Dent & Co., an important *hong* (colonial business or trading firm), which, together with rivals Jardine Mathieson & Co., Russel & Co., and Swire, financed much of Hong Kong's early economic activity. Overbeck and Dent collaborated to acquire further territorial cessions from Sulu Sultan Jamal ul-Azam and lobbied in London for a royal charter, leading to the establishment of the North Borneo Chartered Company in 1881. Even after its formation, agents working for the early colonial enterprise continued to secure further grants from local Bornean leaders over the subsequent two decades, such as those illustrated in figures 3 and 4.

Despite the proliferation of British commercial activity in Sarawak and Labuan in the 1840s, colonial interest in Borneo from other countries did not diminish. Following the collapse of the ill-fated American venture in 1866, yet

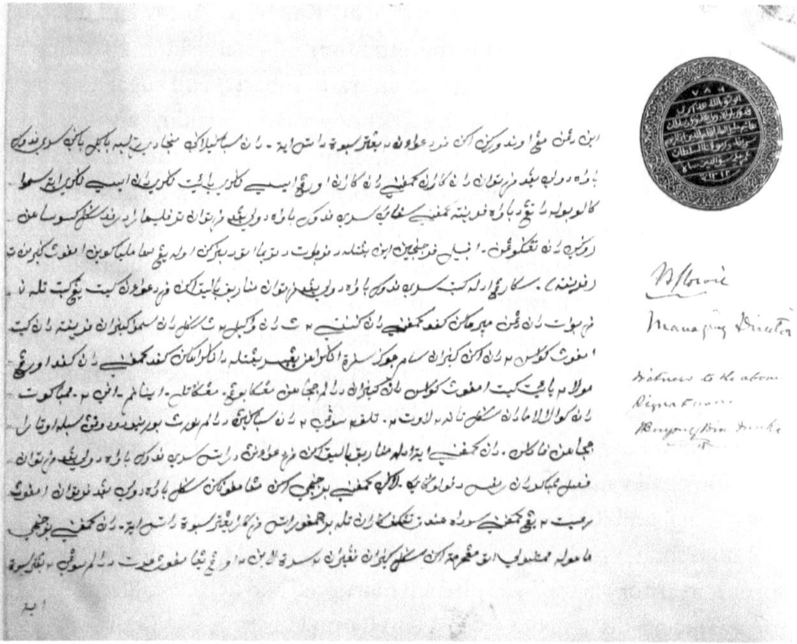

FIGURE 3. "Grant of sovereign rights over Inanam, Menggatal, Api-Api, Membakut, Mengkabong and Kuala Lama," March 30, 1898. Signed by Sultan Hashim Jalilul Alam Aqamaddin of Brunei and William Clark Cowie, North Borneo Company Managing Director. Cession Deeds, CO 874/54, the National Archives (TNA), Kew, England.

FIGURE 4. "Grant of Mengkabong," March 30, 1898. Signed by Sultan Hashim Jalilul Alam Aqamaddin, *Pangeran* Omar Ali, *Pangeran* Anak Siti Khatijah and William Clark Cowie. Cession Deeds, CO 874/54, TNA.

another emergent Western imperial power wanted in on Borneo. In early 1870, an Italian naval vessel laid anchor in Gaya Bay on the west coast seeking to establish a penal colony. This followed previous failed attempts by the Italian government to establish overseas penal settlements—modeled on Australia—in Abyssinia, Socotra, and the Nicobar Islands. The Italian officers saw in Gaya Bay the "finest anchorage" in the region, and beyond it, a vast interior suited for colonization. The British authorities stationed nearby at Labuan again declared in outrage that such a penal colony "would corrupt the people of Brunei" and obstruct British interests.[28] But by 1873, the Italian government would abandon its Borneo dreams. What the Italians lacked, in contrast to the contemporaneous United States, British, and Hong Kong–based ventures, were the paper deeds and cession documents signed with local leaders that supposedly enabled the purchase of sovereignty through treaty. These treaties were inherently dubious, often coerced and seldom translated into local languages. Such processes of semi-autonomous colonization, described by Steven Press as a legal "loophole," enabled state actors and private adventurers alike to "claim eminent domain over all land and mineral wealth within a given territory," in addition to the "traditional state prerogatives" of overseeing taxation, diplomacy, trade, lawmaking, and the lives of the inhabitants within.[29]

Perhaps the sternest challenge to British influence in Borneo, however, came from the Spanish colonial authorities across the Sulu Sea in the Philippines. Spain—a weakened power that had long sought to conquer the Sulu Sultanate's territories in Borneo—was alarmed by the establishment of the North Borneo Chartered Company in 1881.[30] Since the 1840s, British traders had ferried cargo via Labuan toward Manila and onward to southern China, eating into Spain's commercial dominance. The new chartered company venture appeared a major threat. Through varying claims of suzerainty over Sulu, Spain extended an assertion of authority over the northeastern parts of Borneo and sought to crack down on foreign trading in the area.[31] This was followed by Spanish attempts to blockade Sandakan, Kudat, and other centers of colonial-indigenous trade along Borneo's coast. Although these punitive expeditions failed to oust the British, they caused considerable distress among European merchants active in the region. With German help, Britain eventually forced Spain to relinquish its claims over Borneo in 1885.[32]

Even after Spain withdrew its territorial claims, security patterns within Sabah revealed major administrative vulnerabilities. The early days of chartered company rule were marked by frequent indigenous uprisings. This period of instability, termed by James Francis Warren as Sabah's "unsettled years," saw tenuous company control largely confined to the coastal extremities and select lowlands along the west coast.[33] But age-old scrambles for territory persisted, and in January 1942 the North Borneo Chartered Company was decisively expunged from Sabah by the invading Japanese during the Second World War. A calamitous period of stagnation followed; virtually all foreign trading ceased, while local agriculture and commercial activity diminished significantly. Sabah's liberation from Japan in 1945 prompted Britain to formally annex and colonize the region, unwilling to countenance any return to semi-autonomous corporate rule. The subsequent period of Crown Colony governance under formal British rule prompted a paradoxical increase in colonial influence amid the contemporaneous decline of imperialism elsewhere across the world.

Chasing Archipelagic Dreams accordingly examines this sharp increase in colonial interest in Sabah after the Second World War, alongside the proliferation of scrambles for territory across the region in the 1950s and 1960s. Sabah attained heightened commercial significance for Britain at a time when colonies across the world were ceasing to be operable under traditional forms of imperial rule. The transition from natural rubber cultivation to commercial logging, and later palm oil production, strengthened Sabah's economic position by enriching enterprises run by colonial and local elites. Central to this book, however, is a close examination of the competing Indonesian, Malayan, Philippine, and local attempts in the late 1950s and early 1960s to incorporate the British Borneo territories into proprietary visions for postcolonial statehood. Although these vying attempts to secure Bornean territory proliferated amid the demise of Western imperialism, they were each predicated on a heady combination of colonial-style rule and ostensible precolonial legacies. Cultural, ethnic, and historical ties were recalled, invoked, and at times even fabricated in attempts to lure Sabah's public toward one of numerous postcolonial state-making projects. The lack of any popular nationalism in Sabah at the time—incorrectly cited as an indicator of political naïveté—led numerous states to attempt to (often forcedly) include Sabah within their respective postcolonial spheres as a subordinate colony. In many cases, the same treaties and cessions that had facilitated initial nineteenth-century colonial incursions were once again contested, reimagined, and brought to the fore. In so doing, each of these competing projects sought to impose its own vision of geopolitical, cultural, and economic control over Sabah.

Situating Sabah in History

Chasing Archipelagic Dreams is the first book on the end of empire in Sabah and its critically understudied role in the formation of the Federation of Malaysia. The book covers the tightening of British imperial control over Sabah after the Second World War; the emergence of influential local power brokers; the competing attempts by the Philippines, Indonesia, and Malaya to incorporate the territory into their respective archipelagic spheres; and finally, its merger with Malaysia in 1963. Each of these vying attempts at extending influence resulted in a sharp increase in foreign, colonial-style control over Sabah. Alongside this main thrust, the book also casts light on geopolitical disturbances and rivalries across the South China Sea, the fates of minority and subaltern communities bisected by (post)colonial borders, and the shifting social, economic, political, and environmental landscapes of Southeast Asia. Together with these key regional concerns, the book also traces the lives of local figureheads and elites, such as Donald Stephens and Mustapha bin Harun, contending that their ability to draw widespread public support rendered them key power brokers in the formation of Malaysia. Importantly, however, these figures were not akin to the revolutionary, intellectually charged anticolonial leaders that emerged elsewhere in the decolonizing world. They espoused a unique brand of politics, prioritizing personal advancement, communal—not national—affinity, and a willingness to collaborate with foreign and colonial powers to meet their ends. These figureheads present an important case study for analyzing civic-political change in a territory often dismissed as naïve or underdeveloped. In so doing, this book further demonstrates how they leveraged Malayan archipelagic ambition, Western Cold War paranoia, and local political potentiality to shape Sabah's postcolonial transition.

This exploration of Sabah's role in late colonial and postcolonial Asia brings into sharp focus the tensions in historiography between the popularity of mainstream studies analyzing clearly defined nation-states and the pressing need for fresh scrutiny on subnational, marginal, or otherwise understudied places. Sabah in particular, by virtue of its experience of unfulfilled decolonization, loses out vis-à-vis other territories that emerged from the clutches of Western imperialism as fully independent states. Its continuing status as a subnational territory, as with numerous other cognate examples of colonies-turned-provinces across the world, has clouded academic attention and thus popular access to its history. Nevertheless, as this book shows, analyzing Sabah's role as a central component in a series of contemporaneous state-making projects offers valuable nuance for scholarship on the end of empire, geopolitical contests, the fates of grassroots and minority voices, and the continuation of colonial-style governance in the postcolonial era.

Decolonization therefore serves as one of the core threads in this book. Conventional historiographical explanations for decolonization are rooted in analyses of waning imperial power relative to the rising influence of local or international anticolonial movements.³⁴ Declining metropolitan strength is often considered alongside the rise of national liberation struggles in the colonies. These widespread views, as Wm. Roger Louis explains, are predicated on the idea that the end of empire occurred in a scenario akin to the fall of Rome, "with infirmity in the metropole and insurgency in the provinces" dictating imperial collapse.³⁵ The issue with such "suspiciously whiggish" approaches is that they risk being teleological or reductive, or at the very least, too simplistic.³⁶ In the case of the British Empire, it is often said that once entering its phase of decline—"felt instinctively" by many historians to be the aftermath of the First World War, when "much of the crude self-confidence had drained out of British imperialism"—an interminable process of decolonization was sure to follow.³⁷ Yet, as Louis notes, events that are generally accepted as watershed end-of-empire moments, such as the Suez crisis in 1956, can also be interpreted as sparking periods of revival, in which British influence across the Middle East paradoxically increased based on its controlling of centers of oil production between 1957 and 1971.³⁸ Likewise, imperial apologists of the day were known to claim success amid catastrophe.³⁹ Linear approaches to conceptualizing decolonization fall short when considering broader shifts in imperial history: "Colonial emancipation is not necessarily a sign of metropolitan weakness. Virtual independence was conceded to Canadian, Australasian, and South African nationalists before 1914, when Britain was at her strongest. Conversely, when she was much weaker, during the inter-war years, the Empire reached its greatest extent, with the addition of much of the Middle East and more of Africa."⁴⁰

Indeed, Sabah was formally colonized in July 1946 at a time when Britain's empire lay in ruin and when it could barely manage to feed its domestic population back home. With this, Wm. Roger Louis raises important issues in understanding the paradoxes of the end of empire. In viewing decolonization as the inevitable conclusion to a rise-apex-decline trajectory in imperial history, particularity and detail are often overlooked.⁴¹ Despite these risks, historians have long worked to compartmentalize the end of the British Empire (and indeed Western imperialism itself) into a neat periodization, or into specific themes or geographic zones. This has served well in outlining general trends, but in seeking patterns and predictability, key nuance has been lost. Naturally, territories such as Sabah have lost out in these historians' attempts at identifying uniformity. In many such linear or chronological delimitations, Sabah's decolonization fits in better with the African timetable—in which most of Britain's African dependencies were decolonized in the early 1960s—than it does with that of its neighboring Southeast Asian colonies. Martin Shipway's comparative study of decolonization discusses the role of emergent postwar "nationalist realities" across Southeast Asia in sparking Western imperial decline.[42] While this is true in the cases of Myanmar, Indonesia, and Vietnam, among other places, it does not paint a comprehensive picture of Southeast Asian decolonization. Important case studies are left out of the equation. As with many other territories, Sabah's decolonization experience does not fit into this concept of emergent nationalism and radical anticolonialism, and for that matter, neither does Malaya's.[43] As discussed in chapters 1 and 2, the postwar years were characterized not by an upsurge of nationalism, but rather by an increase in colonial authority and the emergence of influential local power brokers. Indeed, against virtually all the odds the new Crown Colony administration implemented a form of colonial rule that was more extractive, pervasive, and profit oriented than that of its embattled chartered company predecessor, all the while collaborating with local mediators and foreign (mainly Malayan) elites to facilitate continuity beyond the decolonization moment.

Piero Gleijeses has adopted a similar approach to Martin Shipway in his describing of patterns in Western decolonization. It "would come in waves, at times bloody, at times peaceful," he writes. Gleijeses identifies decolonization's "first wave" in Asia, in which the Philippines, India, Indonesia, and Vietnam achieved constitutional independence by the late 1940s and early 1950s, followed by a subsequent "wave" in Sub-Saharan Africa and the Caribbean in the 1960s.[44] That British Borneo's end-of-empire experience was thematically and chronologically distinct from Asia's decolonization archetypes means that it seldom features in such texts. Added to this, that neither Sabah nor Sarawak became an independent state has resulted in hasty explanations for decolonization that gloss over the merger process. Was Sabah, like Hong Kong, the exception that proved the rule?[45] Sabah's story has been irrevocably tied to Malaya, where it remains today a constituent—and thus subordinate or peripheral—state in the Federation of Malaysia. In so doing, Sabah's role is often cast as passive, relegated to footnotes and addenda. Few studies adequately differentiate between archetypal moments of independence (as attained by India or Indonesia, for instance) and coordinated handovers (as experienced by Hong Kong or Macao). Where does Sabah fit on this scale? Many scholars perpetuate official explanations, while others fail to weigh in on this at all. This is a product of the British Borneo territories being dismissed as an inconsequential sideshow in scholarly debates in favor of the Malayan-Singaporean center stage. And where Sabah and Sarawak are mentioned, their roles are explained in such a way that normalizes the artificial links struck between Borneo and the Malayan Peninsula. These links were devised and imposed by metropolitan policymakers in the late colonial era and actively consolidated by Malayan and local Sabahan elites in the postcolonial period.

Indeed, as described in chapter 5, Sabah had long maintained major demographic, economic, and political links with other regions in Asia, most notably with Hong Kong, where close-knit patterns of migration and trade brought the two territories into a close embrace. The events of history have all but eradicated these links, while cementing others.

Although Sabah was prioritized in Philippine, Indonesian, US, British, Malayan, and even Australian postwar foreign policy, much of this has been forgotten or lost to history.[46] By using Sabah as a touchstone for better understanding nonmetropolitan perspectives, it is possible to cast light on asymmetric end-of-empire transitions in places that did not attain independence and in places that have since been subjected to new or continuing colonial-style domination. Through this, the book presents important contextual and thematic corollaries with other localities across the world that similarly do not figure in conventional, linear explanations of decolonization. In so doing, this book rejects teleological arcs that paint the enfeebled, declining imperial power and the triumphant independent state as the natural order of the late colonial and postcolonial world. The reality on the ground was vastly more complex.

By utilizing Sabah as a case study in reinterpreting decolonization, this book makes it clear that normative explanations of imperial withdrawal do not always hold up. Accordingly, this book provides a portable and adaptable methodology for examining an array of cognate territories that either were unable to transition to full independent statehood or have faced continuing threats to their autonomy—or very existence—after official decolonization. The Bornean case, and by extension of this, that of wider Southeast Asia, serve as salient reminders that uneven processes of postcolonial state formation and their legacies still dominate our world today. Separatist and insurgency movements operating across wider Southeast Asia—spanning from Aceh and West Papua to Myanmar, among other places—demonstrate the problematic legacies of colonial-era boundaries and their contemporary effects on stateless nations and subnational minorities.

A quick look at the Indonesian case can help elucidate these issues. While official Western narratives in the 1950s and 1960s depicted postcolonial Indonesia as an all-powerful, and often malignant, force in Southeast Asian geopolitics, recent interventions have demonstrated the extent that it was a crisis-ridden state ruptured by separatist movements, economic disarray, and the ever-lingering threat of foreign depredation. As Vincent Bevins argues, the complicity of the United States in the 1965–1966 mass killings and the eradication of the Indonesian Communist Party prompted Indonesia to cease "rocking the boat," as it had done previously in the 1950s and early 1960s, and thus "fall off the proverbial map."[47] Likewise, while Malaya was traditionally considered a conformist actor in Southeast Asia—with its leaders supposedly embodying the image of rational, liberal statesmen—recent scholarship suggests that the Tunku Abdul Rahman was bent on expansionism.[48] Indeed, Wen-Qing Ngoei further describes Malaysian and British activities in Sabah during the Konfrontasi as tantamount to the waging of a "clandestine war against Indonesian troops in Borneo," as opposed to merely a reactionary counterinsurgency conflict.[49]

Elsewhere across Asia, issues deriving from (post)colonial state-making and unfulfilled decolonization continue to dominate contemporary grassroots resistance movements. The 2019 prodemocracy protests in Hong Kong, for instance, galvanized by the public's frustration at the state's suppression of suffrage and the encroachment of Beijing's influence into local autonomy, reveal how dissatisfaction with contemporary governance frequently leads to debates over the colonial legacy and even fresh calls for independence.[50] In Sabah, too, movements such as Sabah Sarawak Keluar Malaysia (Sabah and Sarawak Leave Malaysia), and talk of "BorneoExit," have gained momentum in the twenty-first century, casting further scrutiny on the legacies of postcolonial state formation.[51]

Similar dynamics are at play beyond Asia, where in Eastern Europe the legacy of the Soviet collapse and the formation of the modern state of Ukraine in 1991 remain contested amid the war between Ukraine and Russia from 2022.[52] In Palestine, too, contemporary rivalries and geopolitical struggles derive from the uneven effects of colonial-era state making and subsequent decolonization. That Palestinian nationalism took shape with, and in many ways after, colonial rule has sparked fierce debate over territorial borderlines and state legitimacy. As Muhammad Muslih writes, orthodox analyses of the development of Palestinian nationalism tend to "underrate" local forces and internal actors, while overemphasizing the role played by Zionism and the state of Israel.[53] Scholars have since explored the extent that nationalism was fomented by the late colonial state to promote imperial strategy, offering valuable explanations for cases that do not track with the normative progression of nation building as portrayed in the received wisdom.[54] Likewise, as Yair Wallach argues, issues deriving from colonial-era border delimitations persist in the contemporary Arab-Israeli context, where maps of Israel and Palestine—despite being "almost identical in shape"—are used by both Palestinians and Israelis, "from their unequal power positions," as celebrated national symbols.[55] Returning to Sabah, similar issues persist to this day, in which postcolonial states (such as the Philippines) and subnational actors (the representatives of the Sultanate of Sulu) continue to stake territorial claims, sometimes with dramatically violent consequences.[56] The armed standoff between Sulu insurgents and Malaysian security forces at Lahad Datu in Sabah in 2013 comes to mind here.[57]

This book draws on a wide range of sources. Administrative records, treatises, government publications, surveys, reports, and diplomatic correspondence provide insight into the numerous dimensions of colonial rule and postcolonial transition. This documentation, extracted from archives across the United Kingdom, Malaysia, the United States, Singapore, and Australia, is complemented with local stories, traditions, and oral records, as well as a range of biographies, reminiscences, and memoirs. Although the local, grassroots voice is all too often silent in the official record, a careful reading of transcribed interviews, memoranda, and correspondence aids in working toward a more representative set of evidence. As Michael Dove writes, "We cannot really understand the wider, global systems if we do not understand these local actors."[58]

Likewise, newspaper articles and other reportage provide crucial nongovernmental, and in some cases local, viewpoints. Read together, these sources present a cohesive body of material. While the use of colonial sources is not without its problems, when read with a keen eye to official bias it is possible to obtain a clearer understanding of the administrative priorities and concerns that shaped the state as it navigated opposition and crisis. "All writing is an act of translation. It turns something you see or sense into something you say," writes Maya Jasanoff.[59] In this sense, it is also possible to glean from what is silent, forgotten, or intentionally withheld from view in official records. The work of Ann Laura Stoler is particularly useful here, showing how colonial documents "serve less as stories for a colonial history than as active, generative substances with histories . . . of their own." Writing about the Dutch colonial administration in the East Indies, Stoler describes how "grids of intelligibility were fashioned from uncertain knowledge" and notes that such uncertainty "repeatedly unsettled the imperial conceit that all was in order."[60] In a similar vein, Mary Margaret Steedly's ethnographic history of the Karo highlands in Sumatra—"one of the many stories of Indonesian independence that could be told from the outskirts of the nation"—serves as a reminder that a multitude of perspectives exist beyond the conventional, tidy explanations emitted from the national capital or colonial bureaucracy.[61] These experiences can disrupt colonial narratives and contemporary nationalist realities, while also providing a crucial touchstone for marginalized voices.

Not all marginalized or underrepresented voices can be uncovered through a close reading of available archival sources, however. The role of women in the history of Sabah's decolonization and merger with Malaysia remains among the most underserved and difficult-to-elucidate topics. Colonial and local sources, a reflection of the social norms and biases of the day, fail to provide adequate insights into the ways that the female voice shaped society and politics in Sabah. The unavailability of credible sources in the colonial archive, popular material, and other records makes it difficult to parse gender in the complex web of Sabah's late colonial and postcolonial history. And in cases where women do crop up in official and public records, they are often relegated to a sideshow or used as leverage to undermine local elites or advance colonial agendas. Take, for instance, the colonial state's efforts to disparage Mustapha bin Harun in the early 1960s, in which it tracked and derided his apparent proclivity to associate with numerous women. That these women were portrayed as a vice, alongside alcohol and the "bright lights" of city nightclubs, is revealing of how women were viewed within the entrenched colonial system.[62] Similar character faults were identified in Sheikh Azahari bin Sheikh Mahmud, the radical anticolonial activist behind the Kalimantan Utara movement, who had two wives and was designated in the press as a "woman-chaser."[63] Newspapers at the time focused on his wives, Raja Shamsiati binte Raja Putra and Saibah Azahari, and both of their struggles to secure a divorce.[64] Despite the media scrutiny, neither was accorded any agency and they remained as voiceless bystanders. Although this book does not focus on gender, an effort has been made to analyze the entrenched colonial system, and its postcolonial successor, with a critical lens. Nevertheless, much work needs to be done in the fields of Southeast Asian and imperial history to further elucidate the role played by women and other underrepresented voices.

Despite recent interventions in imperial history, much of Sabah's history remains propped up by colonial-era literature. Yet there is little to be gained through engaging these orthodox histories head on, especially those written many decades ago. Although contributing at the time toward a greater understanding of Borneo's role in Asia, they ultimately offered a colonial-sponsored take on events.[65] Indeed, due to a lack of contemporary publications—with the exception of important contributions by Danny Wong Tze Ken, Amarjit Kaur, and Ooi Keat Gin—these early texts have remained popular well into the twenty-first century.[66] Official narratives must be read with a discerning eye for colonial interference, however. Kennedy Tregonning's publications on Sabah remain popular, but some of his work was sponsored directly by the Colonial Office.[67] Declassified records reveal how, when submitting his manuscript to the Colonial Office for inspection, Tregonning was ordered to "tone down" some of the "sting" in his frank portrayal of the colonial government in Sabah.[68] Yet in their attempts to censor critique, these same sources also go some way toward vindicating Tregonning, who expressed concern that his manuscript might become a "stiff covered Annual Report."[69] R. N. Turner, Sabah's chief secretary at the time, stated in 1958 that Tregonning "suffers, in a comparatively mild form, from the well-known disease of anti-colonialism."[70] Understanding these historiographical nuances enables a greater awareness of how the official view permeated early scholarship and continues to shape academic and popular understandings of the region's history. It was in the colonial (and postcolonial Malaysian) interest that Sabah's history be folded into that of the wider Malaysian Federation as a constituent part. As explored in this book, the important and at times sui generis nature of Sabah's history disrupts official narratives of postcolonial state building and their contrived foundational myths. Uncovering this history offers a valuable template for assisting the study of other contested regions across the world.

Structure of the Book

Underpinning these broader historiographical contentions, *Chasing Archipelagic Dreams* advances three main arguments relating to the history of Southeast Asia, imperialism, and postcolonial state formation. Firstly, growing international anticolonialism and regional geopolitical competition over Sabah from the late 1940s to the 1960s elicited a considerable increase in colonial power and influence on the ground. Secondly, ethnic, social, and political heterogeneity in Sabah contributed to local fragmentation and disunity, which undermined the development of a cohesive anticolonial movement but nevertheless gave rise to a class of influential local power brokers and elites. And finally, this book demonstrates that Sabah never fully decolonized. Its merger with Malaysia prompted an extension of colonial-style rule, resource extraction, the suppression of local autonomy, and the imposition of an externally configured national identity.

To develop these arguments, the book is divided into five chapters. Chapter 1 examines the devastating aftermath of the Second World War. It discusses how Australian officials, in charge of the postwar Allied military administration, sought to bring Sabah under permanent Australian rule as a defense against future Japanese aggression. It then addresses Sabah's formal colonization by Britain in 1946, exploring how this simultaneously paved the way for a more penetrative form of foreign rule and elicited regional anticolonial ire in the Philippines and Indonesia. Finally, it examines the purported changes to colonial economic policy, driven by resurgent desires to extract mineral wealth and cash crops. The chapter concludes by reflecting on the effects of an abortive economic recovery, in which food cultivation and humanitarian aid were cast aside in favor of marketable cash crops.

Chapter 2 extends the analysis of the colonial state's heightened economic penetration into Sabah, adopting a granular approach by exploring how this impacted local lives and marginalized communities across the territory. It shows how asymmetric economic recovery contributed to the emergence of a nascent form of anticolonial opposition. Although not yet in direct pursuit of independence, this budding cohort of anticolonial skeptics—hailing from a diverse range of ethnic and social groups—sought greater economic equality and political representation. As this opposition was compounded with the advent of new forms of print media, marked changes to systems of political association, and the emergence of new political identities, the late 1950s saw Sabah enter unchartered waters.

Chapter 3 examines the effects of the proliferating anticolonial movement in neighboring Brunei in the early 1960s. It explores how changes to forms of public communication and media—notably the rapid popularization of radio in the late 1950s—contributed to major sociopolitical shifts across Southeast Asia. The chapter then covers the rise of the Indonesian-funded Negara Kesatuan Kalimantan Utara (the Unitary State of Northern Borneo) in early 1963, which threatened colonial interests and heightened public and administrative anxieties throughout Sabah, arguing that it ultimately gave rise to new forms of technologically proficient anticolonialism.

Chapter 4 disentangles Anglo-Philippine geopolitical disputes over a series of island territories off Sabah's northern coast, exploring how this set the stage for decades of geopolitical volatility and resurgent territorial claims over Sabah. It then focuses on the escalation of private claims over Bornean territory in the early 1960s, which spurred the Philippine government to launch its own official assertion of authority in December 1962. With these claims failing to materialize, the chapter explores how, having secured tentative support from both Indonesian and Malayan policymakers, the Philippine government proclaimed the emergence of Maphilindo, a transnational confederation between the three postcolonial states and a theoretical route for ousting Britain from Borneo.

Finally, chapter 5 examines how, with a growing number of private and official territorial claims lodged over Sabah, and with increasingly frequent armed clashes occurring off the territory's coast, Projek Malaysia gained increased urgency and importance for Britain and Malaya. It discusses how British and Malayan policymakers worked in concert with local power brokers and indigenous elites across Sabah to convince the public to support the Malaysia proposal. Despite their best efforts, the proposal remained highly divisive, and it was extremely unpopular among sections of Sabah's indigenous and Chinese communities. It presents a stark departure from the received wisdom, which suggests that Sabah's assimilation into Malaysia was orchestrated solely by peninsular strategists, and that it was all but certain by 1963. This chapter concludes by demonstrating how Sabah's diverse public served as the engine of the territory's history and how, without Sabah, Malaysia would never have come into being.

Part One

Resurgent Empire, Fragmented Identities

CHAPTER 1

From Company State to Crown Colony

Sabah emerged from the tumult of the Second World War a battered territory on the cusp of major change. Historically insulated from the rising tide of anticolonial thought that was sweeping the world, the territory was irrevocably altered by the experience of wartime occupation—not least the swift colonial defeat in January 1942. The North Borneo Chartered Company that had ruled circumscribed stretches of Sabah's coastline and small interior outposts since the 1880s had all but vanished, and British policymakers in London were unwilling to countenance supporting its return to semi-autonomous corporate control. As the wider empire was coming under increased global scrutiny, prospects of reverting to atypical, outdated modes of colonial governance were out of the question for Britain.

Initially, there was little talk of independence among Sabah's local communities in the immediate postwar period. Despite the common desire to oust the Japanese during the war, there was no real sense of territory-wide unity or popular support for statehood in Sabah in the late 1940s. Indeed, at this time the sternest opposition to Britain extending greater controls over the territory was voiced by Australian bureaucrats serving within the interim Allied Military Administration that oversaw the war-torn territory in late 1945 and 1946. Their concerns, however, arose less from anticolonial leaning or opposition to British influence in Asia than from fear of potential Japanese aggression in the future. But talk of transferring a series of poorly developed, semi-autonomous territories to Australian control failed to gain any traction beyond Sabah's temporary Allied custodians and dissipated as the dust of war settled and the costs of colonial economic rehabilitation were fully realized.

Postwar recovery in Sabah was painfully slow. The temporary Allied administration provided little in the way of aid or support. On "liberation," the scenes of destruction were exacerbated by the unchecked spread of hunger and disease. As one British member of Parliament who toured the region after the war later described the situation, "To this undeveloped country the war brought many untold disasters only revealed after its liberation." At the port of Jesselton, only three permanent structures remained standing: the clocktower, the general post office, and the survey hall. Everything else had been obliterated: shelled during the initial Japanese invasion, ravaged by fires, or subsequently bombed by American and Australian airplanes in the war's closing months. Across Sabah, "Of the 890 government buildings . . . 614 were completely destroyed and 266 badly damaged."[1] There was a near-total absence of supplies, and the makeshift attempts to rehabilitate civil and medical infrastructure offered little reprieve for the struggling residents.[2] Virtually the entirety of Sabah's west and north coasts experienced similar patterns of destruction. Coastal towns were visibly scarred by occupation and violent "liberation," and by some estimates, 10 percent of the population had perished.[3] Orang Tua Oman, of Kampong Benoni in the west coast's Papar district, claimed that "everything was *habis* [finished, devastated, or ruined]." Freshly liberated prisoner of war and former North Borneo Chartered Company employee Ronald J. Brooks remarked that "all enquiries lead to one conclusion: everything had been flattened; not a town, not a building was left standing!"[4] Japanese soldier Ueno Itsuyoshi recalled how incessant shelling from Allied warships in the bay had flattened Jesselton, an exposed city pressed close to the shore by the hills and forests behind it.[5]

Beyond the ports and *kampongs* that dotted Sabah's coastline, the interior also bore evidence of the struggles of war. Trade in essential foodstuffs, medicines, and other commodities had ground to a halt. The networks of colonial administration that had tenuously facilitated prewar chartered company rule had been dislodged. The dirt roads and "rentices" that once connected port to market, colonial settlement to interior *kampong*, and indigenous headman to district officer, had all but become overgrown and lost to the jungle.[6] Little was known among administrative circles of the war's impact on Borneo's hinterland. To many colonial observers, Sabah's interior had appeared to revert to its untamed and impenetrable precolonial status.

Yet across the entire island, remote indigenous communities had played an active role in the war. Despite prevailing colonial perceptions that Sabah's indigenous groups were dislocated from coastal centers of administration (and thus the bulk of wartime hardship), anti-Japanese resistance had hinged on the participation of people from all over Borneo. Allied soldiers, who parachuted into distant hills in Sabah and Sarawak from American and Australian air bases in the Pacific, joined forces with indigenous fighters who were eager to resist the Japanese. In missions and operations seldom acknowledged in the immediate postwar period, bands of Muruts, Kadazandusuns, and other indigenous groups, armed initially with traditional weaponry such as *parangs* (knives) and later increasingly rifles, joined Allied fighters in driving out pockets of Japanese soldiers.[7] The effects of the war on Sabah's interior were considerable, if less immediately palpable than the devastation across the coastal lowlands. Most importantly, however, the war showed "that white man was no sort of unshakeable divinity."[8] It revealed that foreign control over Sabah could be excised, as it had been in 1942 and again in 1945 with Japan's defeat.

The Crown Colony government, established on July 15, 1946, following Britain's annexation of the territory from the defunct North Borneo Chartered Company, ushered a new period of formal colonial domination.[9] The new colonial government was chiefly concerned with the implementation of territory-wide authority. It sought to replace the previous company and Japanese administrations with a more centralized system. Greater influence over the territory's interior, it was hoped, would yield infrastructural and civil development and, as in company days, profit.

Although there were concerns about the impact of wartime defeat on colonial-local relations, the new administration in Sabah swiftly came to prioritize commercial development and economic self-sufficiency over stable food cultivation. Efforts to sponsor material repair and aid were slow, and widespread poverty and hunger persisted into the early 1950s. Agricultural policies revealed true colonial intentions: while the cultivation of locally produced foodstuffs was initially prioritized, administrators impatiently sought to reinvigorate the age-old reliance on nonedible cash crops. Colonial bureaucrats hoped that the attempted revitalization of rubber plantations would jumpstart Sabah's war-weary economy. Yet enduring fears of labor shortage—and the adverse effects of indigenous depopulation in the interior—threatened to undermine the territory's potential for economic growth. Alongside perceptions of Borneo's demographic emptiness, this contributed to radical colonial plans to import labor from elsewhere in the British Empire.

This chapter is divided into five sections, beginning with a discussion of the unsteady implementation of colonial rule during the postwar period, in which regional attempts to radically rethink Sabah's strategic purpose undermined British colonial designs. The chapter then examines how Britain annexed

Sabah, with the contention that while politicians sought to imitate due process in Sarawak, the accession of Sabah into the empire was covertly undertaken in metropolitan boardrooms to best serve shareholder interests. The third section considers how the territory's finances persisted in a ruinous state even after colonization. Lacking formal rehabilitation programs or metropolitan aid, postwar revitalization was unsteady and dependent on a narrow set of private initiatives. With revitalization efforts proving ineffective, the territory's future seemed increasingly uncertain. The final two sections of the chapter explore how the government was caught between promoting food cultivation and the growing of nonedible cash crops. Drought and widespread food shortages persisted well into the late 1940s, with the government seeking to remedy these issues with radical plans for labor importation. Together, this analysis of Sabah's postwar experience casts crucial light on how the territory was reformulated as a crucial asset for subsequent state-making designs amid the end of empire.

Untidy Liberation and the Imposition of Colonial Rule After the Second World War

The end of the Second World War in August 1945 brought neither peace nor stability to Sabah. Although the temporary Allied Military Administration had extended its control over the territory's main towns and ports, widespread pockets of Japanese resistance continued to cause disruptions. Amid the Allied coastal landings in mid-1945, many isolated Japanese soldiers fled inland to continue the fight, having failed to receive word of the official surrender.[10] Even after the formal end of the war, the Allied administration recruited parties of armed men from local *kampongs* to scour out the remnants of the Japanese occupying force.[11]

Along the coast, the severity of war damage wrought on the colony was grimly apparent. In addition to physical ruin, the absence of functioning commercial networks and the inability to procure essential goods, including foodstuffs, continued to wreak havoc on port towns and lowland *kampongs*. Many of these communities—comprising large populations of Malays, Chinese, Kadazandusuns, Muruts, and others who had relocated to Sabah's coast in search of prosperity—were not self-sufficient in food; the threat of famine loomed large. While some refugees opened stalls to sell fish, sago, tapioca, turtle eggs, wild game, fruits, and other items gathered from the sea and nearby forests, these were not enough to meet demand. Smugglers and black-market operators took advantage. In some cases, entire *kampongs* faced starvation and were forced to migrate to makeshift colonial ration centers at Papar, Tuaran, Jesselton, and other coastal towns.[12]

The territory's returning colonial communities, though a comparatively smaller contingent of Sabah's population, also experienced hardship in the aftermath of the war. Little comfort was found in the fact that Sabah was still, for the time being, nominally under the aegis of the North Borneo Chartered Company. The firm was in financial disarray and controlled the territory only in name. Although many local residents and rank-and-file colonial officers initially believed that it would resume its administration of the territory, the company's executives in London had different plans. In August 1945, they quietly entered talks with the British government to discuss alternatives for the future administration of Sabah.[13] Functionally, the chartered company was unable to wind back the clock to its prewar status as a profitable enterprise, while politically, its position as an anachronistic relic had become untenable.

The creation of the British Borneo Civil Affairs Unit in mid-September 1945—a more formalized transitionary body that replaced the temporary Allied Military Administration—signaled a major change.[14] For the first time, the entirety of the northern and western parts of Borneo was combined into a single administrative unit. Prior to colonial rule, the sultanates of Brunei, Sulu, and Bulungan, as well as numerous smaller polities, had for centuries fought for control over Borneo, claiming stretches of territory that overlapped in tangled webs of sovereignty.[15] These same regions were subsequently split between the "White Rajahs" in the south and the chartered company in the north, with the two colonial regimes seldom interacting. That the Civil Affairs Unit was (albeit nominally) in charge of the entire region suggested that the days of autonomous private statehood in Borneo were numbered.

Not only was the Civil Affairs Unit unable to deliver meaningful aid and economic relief; its botched creation also heralded a period of uncertainty for Sabah's future. Although the British government had begun preparing for a resumption of civilian (i.e., chartered company) control over occupied Borneo as early as 1943, with the establishment of the Borneo Planning Unit (alongside the Malayan Planning Unit), the Allied Pacific advance took a different course during the final months of the war.[16] As the Allied war effort progressed in 1945, the civil affairs staff tasked with administering postwar Malaya were placed under the Southeast Asian Command under Lord Mountbatten. The Borneo planners, in marked contrast, were consigned to the South West Pacific Area Command under US general Douglas MacArthur, firmly beyond the British remit.[17] This functional division between colonial planning units frustrated British attempts at coordinating postwar administration in its colonies, even portending a loss of imperial control. According to Graeme

Sligo, British officials received "sporadic US enquiries as to their post-war intentions in relation to Sarawak and North Borneo," prompting widespread suspicion within the Colonial Office of American anti-imperialist rhetoric and "possible post-war ambitions" in the region. British officials fought desperately to avoid a situation in which American troops recaptured Borneo from the Japanese to enable an American takeover.[18] But by mid-1945, it was primarily Australian soldiers who were spearheading the liberation offensive, due to MacArthur's reluctance to "commit . . . American land forces in the Borneo campaign."[19] With Australian soldiers on the ground in Borneo, officials under the South West Pacific Area Command envisioned Australian, rather than British or American, officers taking up the role of postwar administration. Despite the Allies' military successes against the Japanese, the transition to civil administration in Borneo was beset with confusion caused by logistical issues and last-minute operational changes. Indeed, although some British civil officers had been dispatched to Australia in December 1944 to prepare for postwar reoccupation, the bulk of Britain's Borneo Planning Unit did not reach Australia until mid-1945. These delays prompted Australian general Thomas Blamey to argue for postwar rehabilitation in Borneo to be built on Australian, rather than British, administrative foundations.[20]

While British politicians strove to preserve colonial interests in the region, sections of the new Borneo administration had different aims. Although nominally headed by Charles F. C. Macaskie, a senior North Borneo Chartered Company official, the British Borneo Civil Affairs Unit's rank-and-file staff primarily comprised Australian civil servants, military officers, and academics.[21] Owing to a lack of available British personnel, the Australians filled a crucial manpower gap, but they did not have any prior experience in Borneo. While many of the Australian administrators on the ground had briefly served under the postwar Australian New Guinea Administrative Unit, they had not dealt with a territory that had "suffered . . . [such] terrible devastation" as Sabah.[22] With the chartered company appearing increasingly unlikely to resume its governance of the territory, Australian administrators sought to extend their influence over the various "liberated" colonies in what was effectively an unprecedented power vacuum. Senior Australian members of the Civil Affairs Unit, such as Colonel Alfred Austin Conlon, worked to ensure that Australia be well placed to take over Sabah, Sarawak, and Brunei as "trust territories under the auspices of the yet to be established United Nations."[23] Conlon was a divisive figure. A medical student before the war, he lacked any military or administrative experience, and he rose to power through his participation in the Directorate of Research and Civil Affairs, a controversial think tank reputedly linked to intelligence organizations.[24]

Alfred Conlon argued that following a transitionary period under Australian rule, the British Borneo territories could bolster the region's strategic interests as a buffer state against future Japanese aggression.[25] Indeed, as Gavin Merrick Long has written, Conlon requested that initial Civil Affairs Unit detachments to Sabah be "predominantly Australian" in order to limit British influence on the ground. To achieve this, Conlon "instructed that [the British officers] . . . concentrate at Ingleburn [Australia]," where they would serve "as a rear headquarters" until it was "prudent to send them in." The attempts by Australian officers to block British involvement in Borneo—facilitated in part by the tangled chains of command among British, American, and Australian forces—caused "confusion and distress among the British Borneo officers who had arrived [in Australia] to perform a task for which they had long been preparing."[26] Ultimately, such active attempts to stymie British efforts to reassert influence in Borneo reveal the contested nature of the Allied liberation of Southeast Asia. The war had left indelible marks and irreparably damaged Britain's imperial standing.

The surrender of colonial armies to Japan in late 1941 and early 1942 served a fatal blow to Western empires across much of Asia. Even in regions that had not witnessed the rise of significant anticolonial movements before the war, the experience of Japanese occupation precipitated major shifts in attitudes to colonial rule. For many in Sabah, the botched defense and swift defeat of British forces evaporated myths of colonial invincibility. As David Phillips writes, colonial officials "were painfully conscious of a corrosive 'loss of face' and decline in respect for European rule."[27] Alfred Austin Conlon lamented the swiftness of the Japanese conquest and argued that it was reflective of the "scant loyalty [of the indigenous communities] towards their colonial masters" and a reciprocal lack of effort on the part of the imperial power. He complained that by the time the Japanese reached Jesselton in January 1942, the small colonial defense force had already surrendered and laid down its weapons. Conlon argued that there was an urgent need to rethink the purpose of colonial territories such as Sabah.[28] Politicians in Britain conceded that unsatisfactory defense capabilities during the war had allowed the Japanese to use Borneo as a "stepping stone to Australia and the South Pacific."[29] While there was agreement across the commonwealth that this could not be repeated, Britain was reluctant to sanction the transfer of Sabah from chartered company to Australian control for this purpose.

But such attitudes continued to pose a major problem for Britain. Although markedly different to the tide of anticolonialist thought that was contemporaneously sweeping much of Asia, they demonstrated to British authorities that asserting control over Sabah would be no easy task. Indeed, these changes came at a major juncture in public and official thinking toward the empire in Britain. While there was growing acknowledgment that colonialism was increasingly untenable, imperialist thought still pervaded virtually all echelons of the metropolitan government. While there was talk in the new ruling Labour government of commencing the "real socialisation of the Colonial Empire," when pushed to defend colonial interests in Southeast Asia, policymakers were quick to fall back on tried-and-tested imperialist measures. Significantly, among these measures were renewed efforts of outright colonization in an attempt to strengthen the empire's grip on strategic regions. The difficulties involved in adhering to the belief that the "Empire could not endure, and was not worthy to endure, except on the basis of full consultation with the Colonial peoples," while creating new crown colonies in Borneo, proved a complex balancing act.[30]

The Road to Cession and Formal Colonization

Alongside Sabah, Britain faced similar difficulties in nearby Sarawak, where the resumption of civilian administration in 1945 was overshadowed by uncertainty about the future of the "White Rajahs" who had ruled the territory as a private kingdom since 1841. Much like its company-administered neighbor to the north, Sarawak had been controlled by an autonomous regime only nominally connected to the British Empire as a protectorate. Rather than reporting to a board of directors or company shareholders based in London, however, Sarawak had for the past century been the personal fiefdom of the Brooke dynasty, who in the eyes of many observers had "plundered the island all the time they had been there."[31] After the war, prospects of returning to despotic rule were widely accepted as untenable, especially considering the finances required to rehabilitate the territory. Rajah Vyner Brooke conceded this and entered talks to facilitate Britain's formal colonization of Sarawak. During a House of Commons debate in February 1946, while there was cross-party consensus among members of Parliament in favor of Britain annexing Sarawak, concerns were raised that such a move might provoke anticolonial uproar. MP John Langford-Holt, for instance, stated that in view of the "undesirability of the extension of any form of imperialism at this time . . . [it would be necessary to] bear in mind that justice should not only be done but should seem to be done."[32] Politicians were therefore cognizant of the unpopularity of colonial expansion: any such activity would need to be finessed carefully. To the south of Borneo, the Indonesian anticolonial struggle against the Dutch raged on, while elsewhere in Asia the attempted return of colonial governments stimulated great fury.[33]

The situation in Sarawak, as in Sabah, was complicated by a failure to gauge the population's stance on issues of annexation and formal colonization. "It is very difficult to get a real expression of public opinion of the people of Sarawak," stated MP George Hall. "There has been no system of electoral voting and the Rajah has always been regarded as the mouthpiece of all the people." Although many British officials believed Rajah Vyner Brooke's assurances that the population would accept annexation, others remained wary. Unable to propose any arrangements to assess the public's purported "desire to join the Empire," the British government decided that the question of annexation should proceed to a vote in the territory's Council Negri (State Council).[34] With all executive members handpicked by the rajah, however, the council would be hard pressed to reflect actual public opinion in Sarawak.

The Council Negri vote on May 17, 1946, nevertheless exposed stark divisions. Although the rubber-stamp council passed the cession bill, with nineteen voting in favor and sixteen against, the close vote laid bare the differences between colonial and local elite interests.[35] The majority of the British councilmembers toed the rajah's line, eager to cash in and move on from private statehood toward formal colonization. Among the British elites, many of whom maintained commercial interests in Sarawak's rubber and oil industries, which were increasingly dependent on metropolitan investment, it was widely believed that formal colonization would offer the best chances of reinvigorating productivity.[36] It was a different story for the indigenous and non-European council members, most of whom opposed the bill and annexation by Britain. But these anticession views were downplayed by the British government, which asserted that the decision "reached among the non-Europeans of the Council Negri against the Cession Bill . . . did not afford grounds for rejecting the cession of the territory." Members of Parliament in Britain were assured by colleagues such as George Hall, secretary of state for the colonies, that cession would be, "broadly speaking, acceptable to the inhabitants of Sarawak." Added to this thinking was the fact that the local and indigenous council members did not proportionately represent Sarawak's population; the views of these members were summarily dismissed as not reflecting the true will of the people. Malay elites appointed by the rajah comprised 65 percent of the non-European seats in the Council Negri, but ethnic Malays numbered only 25 percent of Sarawak's population. In contrast, the Dayaks (Sarawak's largest indigenous ethnic group, comprising 50 percent of the population) and the Chinese (25 percent of the population) were granted a mere 15 and 12 percent of the council's seats respectively.³⁷ It was no surprise, therefore, that when Sarawak was annexed by Britain on July 1, 1946, the territory was gripped by intense opposition, particularly among its Chinese and indigenous communities. The anticession movement continued to escalate, reaching a head in late 1949 when Duncan Stewart, Sarawak's new colonial governor, was assassinated only two weeks after taking office.³⁸ Throughout much of this period, Sarawak's colonial police forcefully suppressed anticession voices. In one such incident in late 1946, the Sarawak Constabulary reportedly "toured the native quarters of Kuching . . . intimidating members of the native population and tearing down posters expressing opposition to the cession."³⁹

Britain's plans to annex Sabah advanced in tandem with the developments in Sarawak but followed a different approach. Where in Sarawak Britain attempted to present a vague narrative of legitimacy through the Council Negri vote, no such efforts were made in Sabah during the takeover of the defunct North Borneo Chartered Company. In an ending befitting only the most commercial-oriented and resource extraction-focused colonial enterprises, the primary concerns discussed by British officials and company executives centered on cash settlements to placate anxious shareholders in London. Charles F. C. Macaskie, representing the company, assured British officials that "there [was] no question but that all communities in North Borneo would welcome the proposed transfer." He further claimed that among many of Sabah's Kadazandusun, Murut, Malay, and Chinese communities there was "general recognition of the fairness and justice of Chartered Company rule" and widespread belief that colonization "would accelerate the development of the country and bring with it a consequent increase in prosperity."⁴⁰ But given Sabah's long tradition of indigenous antigovernment dissent in the early colonial period, culminating in a sequence of violent uprisings between 1888 and 1915, outright public support for annexation was by no means guaranteed.⁴¹ The postwar period was "a time of confusion, rumour, and suspicion in which the imposition of colonial rule was never uncontested."⁴² Administrators on the ground would later come to realize this, with concerns over the potential for the public's rejection of colonial rule increasingly voiced in 1947.⁴³ But in mid-1946, those opposing cession had little, if any, opportunity to express their discontent publicly: society was gripped by continuing food scarcity, and once-thriving towns along the coastal lowlands remained in a ruinous state. British officials ultimately anticipated less resistance to cession in Sabah than in Sarawak.

This attitude shaped the colonization process. In a show of brazen disregard for public opinion in Sabah, cession terms were debated in secrecy at the

North Borneo Chartered Company's London headquarters, some seven thousand miles away and out of sight from the war-damaged streets of Jesselton and Sandakan.⁴⁴ Not only was Sabah's public considered incapable of voicing opinions on matters of annexation, but amid claims of political immaturity they were deemed unlikely to react either way. As early as August 1945, however, rumors were leaked to shareholders in London about Britain's intentions to buy out the company's territorial rights, stoking excitement on the stock exchange and concern in Sabah. Speculation of a large payout caused company shares to almost double in value compared to May 1945, rising from 9s. 3d. ($1.86) to 18s. 3d. ($3.68). This surge in share price complicated cession negotiations, prompting some British politicians to raise suspicions about the legitimacy of the trades in chartered company shares. MP John Barlow, for instance, complained that the shares, for a company that had done absolutely nothing since being ousted by the Japanese in 1942, "suddenly rose without any apparent reason."⁴⁵ Barlow further alleged that surging share prices unfairly boosted the company's negotiating position in its attempts to secure higher compensation. Nothing was formalized until June 1946, when the company's president, Neill Malcolm, reached an agreement with British representatives to cede its territorial rights to the Crown in exchange for a partial cash settlement of £860,000 ($3.46 million) to tide investors over. This was a considerable sum, 45 percent greater than Sabah's total revenue for 1946.⁴⁶ But on June 19, Malcolm rejected the government's subsequent offer to buy out the company's remaining shareholders for £2.2 million ($8.87 million), determined instead to hold out until a more lucrative deal could be struck.⁴⁷ According to some reports, shareholders were pushing for a liquidation distribution in excess of £3 million ($12.1 million).⁴⁸

Although the North Borneo Chartered Company was effectively defunct, its shares continued to hold value and were traded excitedly on the London stock exchange even after it had ceded its territorial rights to Britain.⁴⁹ In late June 1946, the company was a mere shell, with neither functioning operations nor any future outlook. But rumors of a payout greater than the total share value stoked enthusiasm. Interest continued to grow, and "city gamblers" wanted in on the act.⁵⁰ But Neill Malcolm's wager would eventually backfire when negotiations with the government collapsed in late 1947.⁵¹ Following the conclusion of an independent inquiry in early 1949, company shareholders were awarded a final liquidation payout of £1.4 million ($5.64 million), 40 percent less than the initial 1946 offer of £2.2 million, a considerable reduction from the anticipated £3 million.⁵² That the cession question was characterized by debates over metropolitan financing and shareholder payouts rather than broader issues of postwar reconstruction in Sabah speaks volumes about

Britain's colonial priorities in the late 1940s. Years later, in October 1962, following the completion of the liquidation payouts, a final balance of only £35 (320 Malayan dollars; $141) remained in the company's coffers. This was an amount that the liquidator deemed "too small to justify [the company's] reconstitution," but that would instead be appropriate if it were passed to Sabah's Social Welfare Committee "for charitable use" in the colony. It is likely that Sabah's public never saw a penny, with the £35 "small gift" instead symbolizing "the last occasion on which an official letter from the old Chartered Company [was] written."[53] And thus a chapter in Sabah's history closed in much the same way as it had begun: with a letter from the company symbolizing deep rifts, an exchange of territory for cash, financial gain in the metropole, and local economic disenfranchisement.

Whereas sizable sections of Sarawak's public came out in opposition to the territory's cession to Britain on July 1, 1946, there was little visible opposition in the streets of Sabah's main towns when it too was formally colonized two weeks later, on July 15. That Sabah's population appeared to quietly accept colonization with neither overt fanfare nor dismay reveals stark differences between the two cases. The reasons for this were twofold: first, the continuing effects of wartime devastation across Sabah's coastal towns meant that already-marginalized anticolonial sentiments were fragmented and distracted.[54] Sarawak, in contrast, having endured considerably fewer Japanese and Allied bombardments during the war, saw everyday life and commerce spring back more quickly and, with it, anticolonial murmurs. Second, local elites in Sabah's towns and ports grudgingly accepted colonial promises that assimilation into the British Empire as a Crown Colony would facilitate speedier economic, social, and infrastructural development. Their own commercial interests might well be boosted by injections of colonial aid; self-governance could wait.

These differences, alongside the pronounced discrepancies in public reactions to cession, have contributed to divergences in historiographical interpretation concerning the two territories. While there is a strong consensus among scholars that Sarawak was ceded to (and formally colonized by) Britain in July 1946, few extend the same logic to Sabah.[55] The received wisdom instead contends that Sabah returned to civilian control "quietly and without fuss" after a brief interregnum period under the Japanese, with little to no mention of any cession controversy.[56] The lack of any widespread public opposition to Britain's annexation of Sabah in 1946 is taken as evidence that it was merely a resumption of the prewar status quo, rather than an act of formal annexation or colonization. But in so doing, scholars fail to acknowledge the weight attached to the region by imperialists in Britain and the fact that continued British control over Sabah in the aftermath of the war was by no means assured. It was in once-autonomous territories such as Sabah—where anticolonialist and nationalist thought was relegated to fringe politics—that policymakers saw the future of Britain's empire and the preservation of its international relevance.

International reactions to Britain's colonization of Sabah, however, reveal that there was little ambiguity about the inherent coloniality of the act of cession at the time. There was immense public outcry across the Philippines, which itself had transitioned to independence only two weeks earlier, on July 4, 1946. If the timing of Britain's colonization of Sabah stung, then so too did the symbolism of an imperial power formally taking over its closest neighbor. The persistence of colonialism was a major issue for many politicians and public figures in the Philippines, for whom independence was a stymied affair.[57] Orchestrated by the United States, the declaration of Philippine independence left people wanting more. Despite official decolonization, American military bases remained active; American corporations and businesspeople retained unhindered access to resources and land; and American politicians continued to frame independence as something "granted," reflecting an ostensibly unique brand of enlightened liberalism.[58] All of this could not have been more different from the contemporaneous independence struggles waged in Indonesia, India, Burma, and elsewhere across the colonized world.

Although Britain's colonization of Sabah and Sarawak sparked anger in the Philippines, support was won over from advocates of imperial expansion across the globe. The American vice-consul in Singapore, Max Seitelman, for instance, lauded Sarawak's cession as a moment in which the British Empire was "increased by an area almost as large as England." Seitelman contended that although this appeared on the surface "a retrograde step," the empire "appears the more suitable candidate to perform the task . . . [of] social, political, and economic development" compared to despotic rule by the Brookes or the chartered company.[59] Many supporters, therefore, advocated formal colonial rule as the best route toward postwar rehabilitation and development.

Others similarly saw in the colonization of Sabah and Sarawak an opportunity for Britain to pivot toward a more active strategic role in Southeast Asia. With India appearing all but lost, prospects of a new Southeast Asian-oriented empire gained popularity in the late 1940s. The procolonial editorial board of the *Straits Times*, for instance, ran a series of articles in 1946 exalting Britain's annexation of the Borneo territories as the final step in the process of creating "an empire within an empire," with Malaya at its "heart." One such article produced by the *Straits Times*' editorial staff a few weeks prior to cession boasted of how the incorporation of Sabah and Sarawak into the British Empire, along with the formation of a new Political Committee for Southeast

Asia, would lead to the creation of a "Little Empire" that "offers great possibilities for building up a powerful defence position, and for the economical advancement of the group as a whole."[60] Ardent colonialists across Southeast Asia saw in this so-called "Little Empire" the opportunity to strengthen and consolidate British colonial interests in a world increasingly hostile toward imperialism. Borneo and Malaya, rather than India, might just offer the key to preserving Britain's empire, they reasoned. "If they were united . . . either as a self-governing Commonwealth country or as a unit in a British Southeast Asian Federation," claimed Lord William Hare, "they would surely stand a much better chance."[61] Indeed, amid the ruins of war, the temporary Civil Affairs Unit had demonstrated that once fragmentary, autonomous states could be pooled together to create new opportunities for strategic consolidation and streamlined economic advancement. Dreams of archipelagic unity—forging new links between Sabah, Singapore, Sarawak, and Malaya—voiced as early as the 1880s, were again mooted in the late 1940s amid the onset of imperial decline. In each of these archipelagic imaginings, the northern coast of Borneo was key.

"Bullet Spattered and Beflagged:" Colonial Regeneration and Decay

Sabah's new Crown Colony government, established on July 15, 1946, ushered in a period of expanded colonial control. The new administration set out to broaden its reach beyond the coastal and lowland regions that had previously circumscribed company rule. Colonial officials sought to replace the outgoing company and wartime Japanese administrations with a more standardized system of governance akin to colonial regimes elsewhere across the empire. The government hoped that greater influence over Borneo's interior and its resources would yield dividends in colonial development, security, and, as in company days, profit.

But colonization proved a complex task. The proclamation of the new colonial state elicited neither public excitement nor protest in Sabah. The bombed-out streets of Jesselton appeared quiet, as if its residents were morose or fatigued. With only three permanent structures left standing—the Atkinson Clocktower, the general post office, and the survey hall—the new administration would have a difficult time shaking off the dust of war.[62] Of these buildings, only the last was remotely suitable for holding official events. As one observer described, "The ceremony of cession took place in the bullet spattered and beflagged survey hall."[63] Weary officials were to take over the mantle of administration in a territory described as one of the most devastated in the British Empire.[64] The image of the new Crown Colony flag draped over bullet-ridden walls appeared intensely bleak. If anything, it was a reflection of the continuing hardship that was to come.

Sabah received little formal aid and support. Britain itself was in a state of war ruin, preoccupied with its own diminishing presence on the international stage. As David Phillips writes, "The shackles of closer metropolitan control . . . were not accompanied by the substantial flow of development funding promised as a substitute for the loose personal loyalties of pre-war Borneo."[65] In terms of rehabilitation, therefore, Sabah was on its own. Meanwhile, while few sources of fiscal aid were made available for reconstruction and recovery in Sabah, metropolitan investors poured large sums of money into prospecting for minerals and resources across the territory. Between 1946 and 1956, amid continuing dilapidation and food insecurity, over £4 million ($16.1 million) was spent in Sabah on "research and prospecting" for oil, though ultimately without "any satisfactory result." In neighboring Sarawak, already a stable exporter of petrochemicals, new prospecting licenses for bauxite and other minerals were similarly awarded to colonial speculators.[66] But none of this helped ameliorate the dire conditions afflicting everyday communities on the ground.

During this period, various private charitable funds were established by local Sabahans to kickstart recovery. Some of these funds were framed as anti-Japanese organizations, indicating that many communities continued to operate as if on a war footing, despite the proclamation of peace in August 1945. The Chinese War Victims Relief Association, for instance, was founded after the war in October 1945 but later became known as the Anti-Japanese Chinese Martyrs' Affairs Office.[67] While these charitable endeavors injected much-needed relief into Sabah's coastal and lowland populations (typically channeled toward Chinese families and businesses), indigenous groups across the remote hinterland received little support. Elsewhere in Sabah, other sources of aid were tinged with colonialist undertones and were devised to secure the loyalty of indigenous communities. In October 1947, for example, a troupe of British and Australian soldiers, led by Major H. Jackson and Major R. K. Dyce, visited Sabah to retrace the route previously taken by thousands of European prisoners of war during the forced "death marches" from Berhala Island, near Sandakan, to the town of Ranau deep in the interior. Peter Lovegrove, a journalist who accompanied the expedition, reported that two hundred Kadazandusuns were given money, clothing, and medicine "as a tribute from the two countries who [had] not forgotten what they did out of loyalty and regard for white men."[68] Perceptions of colonial racial superiority were rife, and efforts to deliver aid were conducted with the express purpose of cementing indigenous-colonial hierarchies.

It was only in late 1947 that the new colonial government began to finally address the dire conditions and poor living standards affecting Sabah's remote Kadazandusun and Murut communities. Food shortages and illnesses were rampant. The North Borneo War Victims Fund Ordinance, established in December 1947, was conceived to distribute money to dependents of the war dead and to those who had been incapacitated or maimed, ostensibly "without distinction of class or nationality."[69] But with little money reaching the dependents, the initiative proved inadequate. It took an appeal by Governor Edward Francis Twining to the British public for charitable donations to avoid failure.[70] Prior to this, government relief was largely limited to the distribution of imported foodstuffs and emergency supplies. That private funds had predated official schemes by almost two years came as a major embarrassment to the new Crown Colony government.

Sabah's finances were in a particularly ruinous state. In mid-1947, the Colonial Office declared that it "does not intend to carry on the banking system as formerly was done" by the North Borneo Chartered Company. In London, the metropolitan government invited major banks to submit proposals to take over the colony's banking, but without success. Back in Sabah, meanwhile, numerous British-owned plantation companies and trading firms faced complete fiscal deadlock, having had their assets frozen since the start of the war. Although the "freezing of those bank balances caused very serious embarrassment" to the firms, the Colonial Office was unable to expedite the release of their assets.[71] Efforts to free the funds were further complicated since "practically all pre-war accounting records . . . were destroyed during the war." Arthur G. Tubb, Sabah's postwar accountant general, noted that the records that had survived the war were of limited use, having been drafted "in accordance with the principles of the Chartered Company" and its outdated "commercial practice." This placed the colonial government and metropolitan advisors in an onerous position. Despite intentions to modernize and standardize the "nondescript system" of company-era fiscal management, officials soon came to believe that any changes made in the short term "would only lead to further confusion." The implementation of standardized "colonial procedure," Tubb declared, would have to wait until at least the end of the decade.[72]

The colony's dire state of financial affairs, and its inability to provide monetary relief, provide only a partial image of the problems facing the new administration. As the months wore on, the realities of crop failure, food shortage, and commercial dislocation revealed the extent of the hardships facing the newly colonized territory.

Agriculture for Food or for Profit? The Duality of Colonial Recovery

Among the most pressing challenges facing foreign colonial regimes in Borneo was the perennial issue of food shortage. The uneven availability of staple foods among rural communities rendered large sections of Sabah's hinterland susceptible to famine. Labeled by the government as the "barometer of native prosperity," the cultivation of *padi* (rice) and sago seldom increased beyond subsistence levels (see figures 5, 6, and 7).[73] Disruptions to farming, such as in times of drought or conflict, amplified these vulnerabilities. Alongside famine came cognate issues of ill health, depopulation, and wider socioeconomic deterioration in marginalized communities. The new Crown Colony government faced a revival of these age-old pressures amid the continuing postwar disruption.

Before the war, recurring threats of famine shaped interactions between the chartered company government and Sabah's indigenous Murut and Kadazandusun communities. The proliferation of tobacco estates in the 1890s, followed by rubber cultivation in the 1910s, upended traditional socioeconomic patterns. Colonial plantations depended on steady sources of labor for survival: cash crops needed to be tended year round, and rubber tapping was particularly

FIGURE 5. A *padi* farmer leads a water buffalo across a flooded field in Inanam, a Bajau community north of Jesselton. According to George Cathcart Woolley, these fields were unirrigated and therefore subject to natural variations in water levels. In times of drought or low rainfall, *padi* cultivation ceased. Photograph by George Cathcart Woolley, 1937, in CO 874/463, TNA.

FIGURE 6. Bajau women sow *padi* in the newly plowed fields. Photograph by George Cathcart Woolley, 1937, in CO 874/463, TNA.

FIGURE 7. Months later, the *padi* has started to grow. Photograph by George Cathcart Woolley, 1937, in CO 874/463, TNA.

labor intensive. Despite horrific conditions—reports of brutality, illness, and indentured bondage bordering on slavery were widely recorded—many Kadazandusuns and Muruts were lured from interior *kampongs* to take up work at estates across the coastal lowlands.[74] This undermined traditional political hierarchies by reducing the authority of indigenous elites and *orang tuas* over their subjects. Perhaps most importantly, however, it contributed to a loss of labor for the cultivation of traditional foodstuffs among subsistence communities.[75] In addition to steady coastal-bound migration, a growing number of indigenous *kampongs* and private smallholders turned to the cultivation of rubber and other nonedible cash crops, further reducing rice and sago production.

Borneo was a vast island with "one of the lowest densities of population in the Far East."[76] Sabah, in particular, had long suffered from depopulation among indigenous groups, and commercial ventures in the territory were frequently hindered by labor shortages.[77] While census data collected since 1891 indicated that the colony's overall population was gradually increasing due to immigration, many Murut *kampongs* were declining sharply.[78] In the early twentieth century, the chartered company believed that population decline among Sabah's Murut ethnic minority was a product of ill health, ostensible behavioral defects, and widespread alcohol addiction.[79] Little was done to investigate further or ameliorate conditions, however. The severity of Murut depopulation was not fully realized until 1931, when updated census data revealed the scale of mortality and *kampong* abandonment.[80] There were enormous gaps in the official understanding of Borneo's population: not only were censuses difficult to conduct owing to environmental and logistical pressures, but they were also "taken exceptionally cheaply by any standards," at times costing as little as 1,500 Malayan dollars (£164; $660).[81]

Despite receiving generous land grants and tax waivers, Sabah's corporate plantations struggled to compete with rival estates in Malaya due to frequent labor shortages and the high costs associated with exporting goods from Borneo.[82] Throughout the 1920s and 1930s, rubber bosses continually lobbied for increased importation of foreign labor, resulting in a steady rise in migrant workers from China, Hong Kong, and Java.[83] This contributed to major demographic shifts and heightened the territory's dependence on imported food, which also prompted concerns to be raised in the Colonial Office and in Parliament, where bureaucrats and politicians noted that "one of the dangerous aspects of affairs in North Borneo is . . . that a country situated in a wonderful climate in the Inner Antipodes should be importing food" rather than being self-sufficient.[84]

But Borneo's climate was not always so "wonderful." Although its equatorial location offered seasonal stability and shielded it from typhoons (giving rise to the moniker "the land below the wind"), droughts were "a significant component of tropical rainforest dynamics" on the island.[85] Periods of drought were particularly damaging to communities that depended on water for agriculture, such as wet *padi* growing.[86] In 1915, for instance, a protracted drought led to widespread crop failure and political instability across Sabah. Murut leaders claimed that the drought was caused by spirits angered by colonial rule and the implementation of taxation.[87] Within months, critical levels of food shortage, combined with long-standing anger toward the chartered company, triggered an armed uprising in the Rundum District in the distant south. Led by Ontoros Antanum, a Murut chief, the Rundum rebellion brought to a head decades of seething anticolonial feeling. Although the rebellion was decisively crushed by company police, its legacy persisted for many years in the colonial government's institutional memory and in wider public consciousness.

When "exceptionally dry" conditions developed in 1946, Sabah faced a similar juncture to 1915. Agricultural conditions were dire, and discontent simmered. The Department of Agriculture recorded that "unseasonable weather conditions which prevailed during the normal *padi* planting season seriously affected the total area planted."[88] By the end of 1946, the reduced rice yields could only meet a quarter of the colony's requirements.[89] Food shortages were also exceptionally costly, with government expenditure on agriculture outweighing revenue by a ratio of fifteen to one.[90] Although colonial officials believed that drought-induced crop failure and consequent food shortages risked stoking anticolonial resistance, resources were stretched thin and the government resolved to do little to improve conditions in the short term. But even when regular precipitation returned in 1947, food production continued to be insufficient for the needs of the colony, indicating systemic issues.[91]

Rice and rubber had long served as the twin pillars of agricultural output in Sabah, but colonial administrators remained divided over which was more important. Rice was a critical local food source, while rubber was the primary colonial export. Unsurprisingly, as soon as the drought subsided, the territory's leading bureaucrats pushed to prioritize the revitalization of rubber and other nonedible cash crops. As a newly formally colonized territory, Sabah's viability within the British Empire hinged on it becoming a money-making venture. Indeed, as Wm. Roger Louis writes, the empire was "a self-generating and self-financing system," in which there was little room for deadweight territories.[92] In this sense, many in Sabah's new colonial government, under Governor Edward Francis Twining, favored a return to cash crop cultivation to promote economic self-sufficiency. Where the temporary postwar Civil Affairs Unit had prioritized food cultivation between 1945 and 1946, the Crown Colony government increasingly urged a renewed focus on commercial and nonedible products. Officially, food cultivation was still encouraged, but this was considered the domain of indigenous subsistence communities and received little government support. The Department of Agriculture declared in its policy recommendation for 1947 that while "self-sufficiency in the production of staple foodstuffs still takes priority . . . it is essential in the interests of general welfare and improvement of living conditions amongst the peasant agriculturalist, that due consideration should be afforded to the rehabilitation of cash crops."[93]

Proclamations such as these revealed the colonial government's stance toward colonial development and socioeconomic advancement. Many in government argued that rejuvenated exports of nonedible cash crops would enable greater prosperity to trickle through the entire population. But smallholders and local rubber producers were seldom as competitive as the large plantation estates operated by metropolitan and colonial elites. Added to this, colonial plantation estates were exempted from paying export duties "to help British companies to pioneer in the growing of rubber."[94] With major shareholders and plantation owners based in Britain (including numerous members of Parliament), profits were rarely redistributed within Sabah. In contrast, "native" growers were often dismissed as producing "wild rubber" of variable quality and were liable to pay the very export duties from which their colonial competitors were exempt.[95] The system was rigged against ordinary growers and everyday agriculturalists. Colonial criticisms of indigenous smallholders, who could never match the scale of output of big colonial firms, were also rooted in the belief that they should instead focus on food cultivation.

Some in Parliament, however, believed that even commercial-scale cash crop cultivation was misguided. In early 1949, Labour MP Ernest Kinghorn argued that "countries like Borneo which fed themselves before the war, are being so pressed into producing commercial products, groundnuts and that kind of thing, that many of them are rapidly leaving their villages and are not producing the food that they should produce to keep themselves and their families [fed]." According to Kinghorn, Sabah would be better suited if its "basic industry [was] that of producing food, not only for itself but for export."[96] At play was the opportunity to fundamentally rethink the purpose of Sabah as a new colony. As with the lofty discussions about the Borneo territories kick-starting a "Little Empire" in Southeast Asia in 1946, colonialists in 1949 sought to derive utility from Sabah's new status as a Crown Colony. It was no secret that Sabah was failing to compete economically vis-à-vis its neighbors and competitors. Long-standing issues of population shortage and administrative malpractice under chartered company rule had rendered Sabah's rubber exports less competitive than neighboring Malaya's. Likewise, Sarawak had long boasted capable petrochemical exports that Sabah could not match.[97] Similarly, Jesselton and Sandakan, Sabah's premier port towns, had failed to imitate the commercial successes of Hong Kong, Singapore, and other colonial entrepôts. And finally, total wartime devastation had left Sabah particularly ravaged and weary. But such destruction also presented a clean slate on which the colony could be shaped anew. Could Sabah, as touted by Kinghorn, serve as the bread bowl for Britain's postwar Southeast Asian empire? This level of colonial ambition was indicative of the sense of opportunity (and the desire for imperial preservation) that British bureaucrats and politicians saw in Sabah, and wider Southeast Asia, following the loss of India in 1947.

Ernest Kinghorn's opinions did not reflect the dominant views held by colonial and metropolitan elites, however, with the majority instead advocating a revival of Sabah's rubber industry through massive importation of labor. Although in the late 1940s the market for natural rubber was severely weakened due to the proliferation of cheaper American-produced synthetic alternatives, demand remained high across Asia and Europe.[98] As a result, the government resolved to prioritize the recovery of commercial rubber, though not among indigenous smallholders, who were expected to boost food output instead. "Wild rubber" growing, which had been popularized among Kadazandusun and Murut smallholders, continued to be disparaged. In its annual report for 1948, the territory's Department of Immigration and Labour declared that greater food cultivation among indigenous agriculturalists was key for the territory's survival. The report claimed that the rice harvest was the "tie which binds natives most firmly to their villages" and that efforts to "preserve village organisation" could only be reinforced by bolstering traditional agriculture and political systems.[99] As Kinghorn's lofty ambitions for redesigning Sabah as a food-generating hub for Britain's other Southeast Asian colonies fell largely on deaf ears, colonial policymakers doubled down on their attempts to encourage indigenous subsistence food production, while boosting immigration and commercial agriculture. This was key in the colonial state's thinking: "natives" who were tied to their *kampongs* by traditional power structures and agriculture were considered less likely to engage in the radical anticolonialism and "narrow nationalism" that were increasingly circulating through Southeast Asia's ports and cosmopolitan hubs.[100]

Labor Policy and the Reinvigoration of Cash Crops

The late 1940s was a time of immense social and demographic upheaval across much of Asia. In Hong Kong, turbulence across the border in China precipitated a major refugee crisis and unprecedented population growth in the city. Although long considered the "Great Emporium of the East," Hong Kong was to enter a period of great socioeconomic transformation.[101] Reeling from the Second World War and crises up north, Hong Kong saw its population expand in the late 1940s by an estimated ninety thousand a month, an extraordinary pace of growth that placed enormous pressure on the city and its administration.[102] But this also served as an opportunity: Hong Kong was powered by "cheap human labor . . . the Colony's greatest economic asset." As described in a tourism booklet detailing everyday life in Hong Kong in this period, "Hundreds of thousands of destitute refugees, mostly ill-educated and untrained, compete[d] for jobs paying as little as a few cents per day."[103] Indeed, by the 1950s and 1960s, Hong Kong had cemented its "transformation from an entrepôt to an industrial city." Crucially, this functional shift toward manufacturing and export industrialism was triggered by external forces and not by colonial design. As Ho Yin-Ping writes, "drained of its traditional source of income," namely entrepôt trade with China, "Hong Kong was forced to choose a different livelihood."[104]

Sabah faced a similar loss of livelihood, but it lacked the steady influx of labor needed to reorient itself economically on such a scale. Added to this, old sources of labor had dried up. In 1948, during the Indonesian war of independence, the embattled Dutch colonial administration banned the export of workers from Java. Migrants from India, too, were prevented from reaching Sabah owing to strict labor laws in Singapore, through which they would typically transit on their voyage east. And while steady numbers of working-class immigrants arrived from Hong Kong, "sponsored individually" by established Chinese landowners in Sabah, the colonial government considered this "fraught with problems of a political order."[105] These apparent political risks were felt more keenly by metropolitan politicians in London, who expressed annoyance that their colonial colleagues in Sabah continued to allow Chinese migrants to enter from Hong Kong. In April 1950, for instance, speakers in the House of Lords called for all Chinese "to be ruled out as settlers" in Sabah amid fears of communist contagion.[106]

Despite a critical labor shortage, the colonial government continued to pin its hopes of recovery on commercial rubber growing. Across the coastal lowlands, new *Hevea brasiliensis* trees were planted at great cost, and tappers were pressed into service to revive latex extraction from derelict prewar plantations. But due to high labor overheads and a lack of viable cultivars (fresh rubber saplings took between five and seven years to mature before tapping could begin), production could satisfy neither market demand nor government targets.[107] Similar patterns were observed across Malaya and other rubber-producing regions, causing natural rubber prices to soar on the world market. Although natural rubber had been "extremely plentiful and cheap" in the 1930s, its demand was later undercut by the introduction of cheaper petroleum-based alternatives developed by the United States during the Second World War.[108] And although the US's demand for rubber remained at an all-time high—accounting for 70 percent of the world's consumption in 1946—its requirements were increasingly met by domestically produced synthetics.[109] Natural rubber was to remain uncompetitive until the 1973 oil crisis, which prompted a short-lived revival of interest in *Hevea brasiliensis* tapping.[110]

Agricultural revitalization depended on labor, and the government sought to expedite recovery through importing workers from across the world.[111] These concerns were shared by politicians in Britain, too, who were quick to lament that Sabah, which had "soil and rainfall such as [were] not generally found except in the Belgian Congo," should suffer such "a labour problem."[112] At the behest of the metropolitan government, a range of schemes were devised to alleviate the labor shortage. One such scheme, for instance, explored the feasibility of importing workers from Italy to cultivate unused land across Sabah.[113] The plan faltered, however, due to concerns about Italians effectively integrating with indigenous society and adapting to the tropical climate, as well as the logistical difficulties of bringing in labor from so far away.[114]

The plan to import Italian labor, however, was but one of many schemes devised to populate Borneo with foreign migrants. In late 1947, Sabah's Department of Immigration and Labour formulated an ambitious plan to import 20,000 workers from Mauritius, which, in contrast to Sabah, was considered critically overpopulated.[115] The scale of this proposal was remarkable, especially considering Sabah's postwar demography. Census data revealed that in 1948 Sabah's total population was 336,000, with only 20 percent (approximately 67,000) estimated to be engaged in some form of wage-earning work. Of the remaining 80 percent of the population, those of working age were typically subsistence farmers or traders. The scale of the Mauritian plan was large: in 1948, the total number of laborers employed on commercial estates in Sabah amounted to 13,600 individuals, compared to 20,500 before the war in 1940.[116] In this regard, the proposed influx of 20,000 new immigrants would have radically altered the territory.

Initially, the Mauritian immigration scheme was envisaged to bring in labor "to develop rice cultivation."[117] But the plan was swiftly revised to bolster cash crop cultivation as the drive for profit once again dominated administrative policy. In November 1948, concerns were raised in the Colonial Office that the proposal might strain the territory's finances.[118] Who would bear the costs of importing 20,000 individuals? How might such a scheme boost the territory's economic outputs? What was initially envisioned as a mutually beneficial scheme to ameliorate both Sabah's food production woes and Mauritian overpopulation had by 1948 transformed into a mechanism to reinvigorate the territory's floundering cash crop industry. Yet most of the plantations that supposedly stood to benefit from such immigration were derelict and overgrown following years of wartime abandonment. In many areas, the surrounding jungles had encroached into the once-orderly rubber estates, transforming them into unruly entanglements of vines and shrubbery. Moreover, the territory's surviving plantations lacked the capital required to support the costs of passage to bring the Mauritian laborers to Borneo, having had their assets frozen or seized during the Japanese occupation. Fierce debate thus arose concerning the logistics of the proposal, with some officials objecting to the colonial state "assuming financial responsibility for a scheme . . . [that was] primarily in the interests of private enterprise." Others, in contrast, argued that government sponsorship would be "in the interests of North Borneo as a whole."[119] Indeed, direct governmental involvement in jump-starting the colonial economy was not a new feature in Sabah. In what was long perceived to be "a commercial and geographic backwater," the government considered it vital "to offer additional incentives" to lure foreign businesses and investors to Sabah who might otherwise seek opportunities in Malaya or Hong Kong.[120]

Despite initial reservations, Sabah's labor commissioner, R. C. Wilkinson, concluded in 1949 that a small-scale trial should be implemented. The compromise stipulated that "fifty families"—rather than twenty thousand individuals—should be sent to work at the Darvel Tobacco Estate to grow vegetables. While the scheme was judged "well worth trying," potential complications remained. Plantation bosses were now skeptical because the plan no longer purported to offer free labor for cash crop cultivation. Alongside this, concerns were raised that Sabah was "by no means so well fitted for human habitation as is Mauritius." Nevertheless, Wilkinson concluded that if the Mauritians were willing to "put up with the bare necessities without ornament or luxury" then they may well prosper at the "frontier of civilisation."[121]

Although the Mauritius plan elicited controversy, support was won among those who opposed indigenous employment at plantation estates. As in the chartered company era, the lure of wage-earning employment contributed to the steady migration of Kadazandusuns and Muruts away from the interior, a pattern that undermined indigenous agriculture and diminished the hold of *kampong* leaders over their traditional subjects. The Immigration and Labour Department noted with concern how, of the 13,600 people employed at plantation estates in 1948, 56.4 percent were "natives," an increase from the 46.3 percent recorded in 1940. The Department argued that this was due to the government's premature emphasis on commercial regeneration, in which "the indigenous native is being drawn from his traditional ways of life into wage-earning employment." This signaled a revival of age-old colonial concerns about maintaining the accord of indigenous elites, some of whom in past decades had stoked rebellions over taxation, food shortages, and perceived threats to their political authority. As one official noted, "That there is a potential danger in the trend, in a country dependent for a large part of its national income on the variations of the unpredictable world markets for rubber, timber and coconut products, is obvious . . . [but] the native village agronomy must remain undisturbed and the employment figures watched for anything resembling an exodus from the *kampongs*."[122] The colonial government found itself in a difficult position. Leading bureaucrats such as Governor Twining believed that Sabah's postwar recovery and economic self-sufficiency depended on rejuvenated cash crop exports. But the overall health of the territory was also contingent on steady food production. The government's chosen solution was to promote labor importation to develop the former, while encouraging (and in many cases compelling) indigenous agriculturalists to facilitate the latter. This meant that indigenous communities were increasingly pushed out of the production of cash crops and the wider colonial economy. Jungle rubber, unsurprisingly, continued to be denigrated. Such policies reveal deep-rooted colonial perspectives on race, employment, and civil participation in the colonial economy.

Although the Mauritian plan failed to boost Sabah's commercial outputs, a range of similar proposals were developed in the late 1940s and 1950s to reallocate labor from within the British Empire toward Sabah. Between 1948 and 1955, some 75 percent of the population of the Cocos Islands was relocated to Sabah and Singapore after the Cocos were ceded to Australia.[123] Similar efforts to relocate indentured laborers from Christmas Island to Sabah were discussed when it too was transferred from British to Australian control in 1958.[124] Likewise, in April 1950, Lord William Hare proposed alleviating high population density and rampant unemployment in the West Indies through mass emigration to Borneo: "It would be a long distance, but, in many respects, West Indians would be extremely suitable. I think they would find conditions of life in Borneo congenial to them. After all, they are agriculturists, they live in a somewhat similar climate and there is not a big difference between the average man's standard of living in the West Indies and the standard of living in Borneo." While few places were considered as sparsely populated as Sabah, Lord Hare argued that nowhere else in the empire "suffer[ed] more cruelly from over-population than the Islands of the West Indies." Another advantage of Caribbeans' labor, according to Hare, was that they would not "introduce Communism into Borneo."[125] Also considered ideologically inert and free from communist influences were the scores of people enticed into Sabah from Portuguese Timor-Leste in the 1950s, though these alone could not alleviate Sabah's "paucity of population."[126] These proposals were but the latest in a long-standing tradition of labor reallocation toward Sabah throughout the early twentieth century. Colonial bureaucrats delved into metropolitan records, scoured historical policy documents, and drew from methods honed in previous decades in their attempts to cure the age-old dearth of labor. Among these sources of inspiration were, for instance, the British foreign secretary's calls in 1920 to forcedly migrate the *entire* Assyrian population to Sabah amid the collapse of the Ottoman Empire.[127] Although these calls went unheeded, they demonstrate the extent to which Sabah remained in the imperial psyche a dumping ground for the dispossessed, the disenfranchised, and the overcrowded.

By the end of the decade, Sabah was on the path to recovery. But postwar revitalization, as conceived by the new Crown Colony regime, was markedly uneven and predicated on the widespread marginalization of indigenous agriculturalists and workers. Attempts to reorder Sabah's demographic makeup through a series of radical labor reallocation programs had fallen short. These schemes to transplant people from places as disparate and unlikely as Italy, Mauritius, the Caribbean, Timor-Leste, and the Cocos and Christmas Islands revealed the extent to which colonial and metropolitan bureaucrats viewed labor as data on a balance sheet. Labor—extracted from disenfranchised populations across the empire—was a resource to be pumped through imperial hydraulics from high-density territory to low-density territory in order to facilitate colonial development and demographic equilibrium. Simultaneously, despite these labor woes, the government retained company-era prejudices over indigenous participation in the colonial extraction economy. By the early 1950s, however, it became increasingly evident that despite colonial beliefs, new industries and new economic ventures would become necessary. As in Hong Kong, Sabah faced having to "choose a different livelihood."

Sabah emerged from the trauma of the Second World War as the most devastated territory in the British Empire. Although the occupation served to erase the North Borneo Chartered Company's hold over the territory, its legacy of autonomous corporate governance left indelible marks and continued to shape the patterns of colonial administration. Britain's creation of a new colonial state in Sabah after the war, although intended to promote self-sufficiency and commercial viability, remained bogged down by institutional memory of and a proclivity to perpetuate old company-era administrative practices.

Although this is seldom acknowledged in conventional scholarship, this chapter has demonstrated that Sabah was formally assimilated into the British Empire in July 1946 by a process of direct annexation and colonization. This act of imperial expansion, amid the ruins of war and the contemporaneous rise of anticolonialism, elicited criticism at the time. But it also won support among ardent colonialists who sought to reimagine Britain's imperial purpose in an Asia after India's independence and the loss of face induced by wartime humiliation. In these dreams of imperial revival, Sabah was to play a key role. But the nature of this role remained fluid and divisive. As a strategic stepping-stone, perhaps, between Hong Kong to the north, Australia to the south, and the Malayan peninsula to the west, or as a revitalized imperial bread bowl, Sabah's complicity in a reinvigorated "Little Empire" garnered interest and support. As this chapter has demonstrated, however, the transition from despotic company rule to Crown Colony administration was fraught with difficulties. Might Sabah have been better suited to defend Australian strategic interests, as suggested by Australian colonel Alfred Conlon? Or might the colony have benefited Britain's Southeast Asian dependencies if it had been reimagined as a *padi*-growing territory? Sabah would later transition from the postwar period into a state undermined by institutional and public confusion over its role and function. The colonial government brandished promises of socioeconomic development and continued to barter for loyalty among its ethnically diverse and politically divided population. Sabah's renewed purpose for Britain as a newly formalized colony lay instead in its capacity to become a stable exporter of primary products, such as timber, whose ostensibly undeveloped status would feasibly insulate it from the rising tides of anticolonialism and emergent nationalism. But as chapter 2 will discuss, increasingly exclusionary and exploitative policies of resource extraction, and the emergence of politically vocal local leaders, would transform local politics and society.

CHAPTER 2

The (Re-)Emergence of Anticolonial Voices

The implementation of formal colonial rule in 1946 precipitated an intensification of resource extraction and a sharp growth of administrative influence in Sabah. Postwar recovery initially prioritized the regeneration of the rubber industry while failing to combat widespread poverty and food insecurity among the territory's poor and disenfranchised. All of this contributed to lingering discontent in both elite and grassroots circles. Simultaneously, despite the rise of anticolonialism across Southeast Asia, colonial bureaucrats failed to accord Sabah's public a sense of agency, reducing it to merely a population to be governed. Furthermore, that the Crown Colony government perceived the lack of any proindependence or anticolonial movement in Sabah as an indication of the population's ostensible lack of political maturity led to a heady confidence in the longevity of colonial rule.

The Crown Colony government met with its fair share of good fortune, too, further boosting commercial activities in Sabah as neighboring colonial territories succumbed to rising anticolonialism. As if immune to prevailing socioeconomic pressures, Sabah's colonial economy also defied disaster amid the precipitous decline of the global rubber market in the late 1940s and 1950s through a timely transition toward viable alternatives. This enabled even greater foreign penetration into Sabah's resource-rich interior while strengthening the colonial grasp over the territory. As in neighboring Sarawak, where the nascent petrochemical industry expanded sharply, which portended immense economic growth, colonial prospectors and business elites in Sabah turned to commercial logging during a period of increased demand across Asia.[1]

This swift transition to logging, however, precipitated major social and political changes. Fundamental to the fabric of the territory was the tenuous balance among interior and coastal commerce, society, and politics. For generations, the indigenous economy had been predicated on small-scale swidden cultivation and the steady outflow of traditional jungle products, both of which were dependent on unhindered access to the rain forest. Unable to compete with the big colonial firms situated along the coastal lowlands, locals in Sabah had long turned to the forests in order to supplement their food supply and provide produce to sell. This jungle economy, although dismissed by colonials as marginal, served as a fundamental component of the indigenous way of life. Traditional elites also depended on these commercial networks for their own wealth and influence. But after the war, heightened colonial logging served to upend this tenuous balance.

These economic shifts contributed to the emergence of anticolonial voices in Sabah, signaling a return to the instability of the late nineteenth and early twentieth centuries. This chapter argues, however, that renewed public and elite opposition in Sabah was vested not in ideological anticolonialism, but rather in desires to improve access to wealth and influence. Social transformations, too, such as the rise of locally produced print media, contributed to a growing interest in ideas of communal affinity, indigenous identity, and advocacy for local resource rights among everyday communities. In focusing on the (re-)emergence of anticolonial voices, this chapter examines traditional elites who wrought major effects on late colonial society and politics, and later on Sabah's proactive role in Projek Malaysia (the Malaysia project) in 1963. Donald Stephens, who by 1960 had become the Kadazandusun *huguan siou*, emerged as a vociferous critic of colonial rule and a unifying voice for Sabah's largest indigenous community. Similarly, Orang Kaya Kaya ("rich rich man") Mustapha bin Harun, the foremost representative of the territory's Muslim indigenous groups, became an active political power broker and a staunch opponent of British colonialism.[2] Alongside these elites, this chapter discusses the various forms of emergent grassroots anticolonialism and communal identity that took hold in Sabah in the 1950s.

This chapter is structured into eight sections. The first section explores the development of commercial logging in Sabah. Although logging was highly controversial for many local Sabahans, the timber industry enabled the colonial government to tighten its grasp over the interior, regulate economic productivity, and engender a new class of compliant local collaborators. Section two examines the process of local elite formation, showing how company-era policies of inducement and collaboration contributed to the rise of a compliant class of indigenous functionaries. Section three considers the development of anticolonial discontent among elite circles and corresponding colonial attempts at surveilling opposition and soliciting continued support. The rise of Donald Stephens, discussed in sections four and five, provides an important context that lays the groundwork for the emergence of local print media, examined in section six. The final two sections discuss emergent locals' attempts to stake a claim to their *tanah ayer* (homeland) and the corresponding clashes between colonial systems of patronage and Sabah's newly empowered elites.

The Expansion of Logging in Sabah

Borneo has been tapped for its natural resources since the earliest days of human habitation on the island. As Michael Dove argues, "The involvement of the land and people . . . in commodity production is not a modern phenomenon."[3] Local consumption of, and foreign competition over, the island's primary products have long shaped sociopolitical and economic interactions across the wider region. Indeed, records of early explorers and traders from China and the Middle East, who reportedly reached the island as early as the fifth century CE, underscore the extent that Borneo had been a focal point of regional economic interest long before the advent of Western colonialism.[4]

Although subsequent colonial economic ventures primarily involved experimental cultivars, such as coffee, hemp, tobacco, and, most successfully, rubber, Sabah's colonial government also placed considerable emphasis on noncultivated primary products.[5] Mineral resources and timber existed in such abundance that the limiting factors in overall output instead were local labor shortages, logistical impediments, and international market fluctuations.[6] In the late 1940s, for instance, Sabah's timber mills "produced to the limit of their abilities" but struggled to find buyers in postwar Hong Kong owing to "political troubles in China," where the bulk of the timber had been previously reexported. Similarly, shipments to Allied-occupied Japan were tightly regulated and only permitted to resume freely in 1947, following negotiations with the supreme commander of the Allied Powers.[7] The 1950s, however, saw Sabah's logging industry grow on an unprecedented scale, eventually outpacing rubber—once the darling of the defunct North Borneo Chartered Company—as the colony's primary export. In the aftermath of the Second World War, in 1946, logging firms in Sabah felled 1,176,000 cubic feet of timber, of which less than 40 percent was exported. Yet by 1958, over 85 percent of Sabah's timber output (a staggering 34,683,000 cubic feet out of a total of 40,773,000 cubic feet) was exported to markets across Asia. Within twelve years, the volume of timber produced in the colony had increased by over 3,500 percent. Exports grew even more dramatically: in 1947, the volume of timber exports increased by 500 percent compared to the previous year, and by 1958, shipments had ballooned by over 7,400 percent compared to 1946.[8] And this trend only accelerated in the early 1960s, boosted by the insatiable demand for raw materials in postwar Asia and the ostensibly limitless bounty contained within Sabah's forests.

Indeed, after the Communist victory in China in 1949, the Chinese market for Bornean hardwoods slowly began to return, underscoring Hong Kong's historic role as a commercial entrepôt. But Hong Kong's rapid industrialization in the 1950s soon saw the city's demand for raw materials from Borneo outstrip even that of its larger neighbor to the north, as it became one of Sabah's primary export partners in its own right. In fact, by 1957, buyers in Hong Kong were acquiring over 21 percent of Sabah's hardwood timber exports, 10 percent of its rubber exports, and 100 percent of its firewood exports for local use.[9] This shift in Sabah from selling goods primarily to Britain and other Western countries toward new markets in Japan, Hong Kong, Singapore, and elsewhere in Asia was critical. Whereas in the late 1940s Britain served as Sabah's largest trading partner, accounting for over 20 percent of its total exports, by 1960 the colonial metropole had slipped to only consuming 8.3 percent of its products (mainly hemp and trace amounts of rubber). Demand in Japan, by contrast, had by 1960 increased to account for 43 percent of Sabah's total exports, with Japanese buyers purchasing almost two-thirds of the territory's timber (65 percent) and copra (62 percent), among other goods.[10]

Bornean hardwoods were a prized resource. Although comparatively little old-growth jungle remains today in the early twenty-first century, the "forests of Borneo and Sumatra [continue to] represent a fortune of many billions of dollars in timber value," as they did in the 1960s and 1970s [11] Sabah's forests comprise particularly vast trees, beaten in height only by the towering *Sequoia sempervirens* redwoods of the North American West Coast. The largest of Sabah's trees, dipterocarps such as *Shorea faguetiana* (the world's tallest documented angiosperm), have been recorded to reach up to 330 feet (100 meters) in height.[12] Other dipterocarps, such *Parashorea malaanonan* and *Parashorea tomentella*, can reach similar heights. In addition to the sheer size of these trees, Sabah's jungles were renowned for their high resource density and yield. As William Bevis writes, whereas in Sarawak in the 1960s the typical yield was eight tons per acre, loggers could expect to extract twice as much in the forests of Sabah.[13] The sheer size and volume of timber produced is illustrated in figures 8, 9, and 10.

FIGURE 8. Officials inspect a felled log of *Parashorea tomantella*, known colloquially in Borneo as *urat mata*, a species of hardwood tree native to the island, in March 1959. This log measured 30 meters (98 feet), while other specimens have been known to grow up to 65 meters (213 feet) tall. CO 1069/548, TNA.

FIGURE 9. A section of a *Parashorea malaanonan* log is slowly loaded onto a cart on a narrow-gauge railway, 1932. CO 1069/537, TNA.

FIGURE 10. A snaking raft of logs is floated out toward a barge off Sabah's east coast, 1932. CO 1069/537, TNA.

The increased demand for Bornean timber was fueled by massive postwar industrialization in places that lacked sufficient forest reserves, such as in Japan and Hong Kong.[14] During this period, Sabah was to become one of the world's primary sources of timber, fueling manufacturing and economic growth across Asia on an unprecedented scale. As described in chapter 1, whereas in the late 1940s metropolitan policymakers sought to reimagine Sabah as a potential producer of edible cash crops for Britain's reinvigorated "Little Empire" in Southeast Asia, by the 1950s circumstances had changed and the once economically marginalized territory attained new value and purpose.[15] Indeed it was precisely this proven record of resource wealth—and its capacity for future productivity—that made Sabah so attractive to regional state-making and territorial expansion projects in the early 1960s.[16] This newfound market for prized Bornean hardwoods was not limited to Britain and its commonwealth partners as imperial policymakers would have intended, instead serving the interests of a range of economies beyond the so-called "Little Empire," from Japan and Taiwan to the United States and Italy, among other places.

Importantly, the shift from cash crop cultivation toward timber extraction wrought major changes to how Sabah was governed, in which the colonial state sought to exert greater influence over interior jungle regions.[17] Sabah's dense rain forests, which colonials had previously considered impenetrable, existed in stark contrast to the settled coastal lowlands that were dominated by regimented plantation estates and burgeoning ports and townships. This state of difference, typified in colonial ontological frames as an irreconcilable tension between the *pesisir* (coast) and the *hutan* (forest), had long shaped administrative practices and colonial-indigenous relations. During the chartered company era, practically all economic activity was centered on coastal plantation estates and lowland timber mills, with only a steady trickle of jungle produce traded from interior *kampongs*. There was little motivation to push inland, where colonial control had been secured nominally through local collaborators and functionaries. Colonial administrators such as Owen Rutter claimed that "within twenty miles of the coast alone there are more than two million acres of commercial forest," and although he declared that "the areas beyond this coast belt are almost unlimited," Sabah's lowlands offered ample resources.[18] In addition to this, for much of the early twentieth century, colonials saw Sabah's interior as synonymous with rebellion and disorder.[19] Violence, drunkenness, ill health, and, in earlier times, rumors of head-hunting colored racist perceptions of the *hutan* and informed colonial policy.[20] The postwar Crown Colony administration, however, driven by a need to reassert its relevance and purpose in a world increasingly hostile to colonial rule, and faced with economic uncertainty amid the collapse of the natural rubber market, sought to control Sabah's jungles and the interior communities within through expanded forest regulation and a renewed focus on local collaboration.[21]

The voracious appetite for Bornean hardwoods in postwar Asia provided the colonial government with a convenient pretext for greater forest regulation. By supporting the expansion of the logging industry, the government was in theory able to appease both colonial and local elite interests while shoring up the colony's productivity and fiscal security. Colonial firms, and select indigenous elites, were granted exclusive concessions to conduct logging operations in prime forest reserves. This facilitated the economic reaping of the land while appeasing traditional elites who were simultaneously gaining influence as local leaders. The state's new emphasis on logging and commercial forestry led to a substantial increase in the size of the colony's administrative workforce. Under earlier company rule, the forestry division was small and underfunded, but by 1955 government hiring had expanded to include an array of conservators, rangers, botanists, ecologists, and cartographers, together with cohorts of "forest guards," mahouts, and bearers, largely funded through colonial development and welfare schemes.[22] Alongside this expanded bureaucracy were the growing number of private sector industrialists and the timber firm employees who were sent into the interior to oversee logging operations.

Harry G. Keith, the territory's long-term conservator of forests, was appointed in 1931 during the height of the rubber boom to oversee jungle administration. Although he was an advocate of scientific surveys to "mark out forests for conservation," Keith's "designated tasks" also included the "promotion of agriculture" and commercial cultivation in ostensibly ecologically dead zones ravaged by "native" deforestation.[23] Although colonial deforestation was vastly more industrial in scale, the territory's forestry bureaucracy had long been concerned with what was dubbed the "native waste of virgin jungle," in which indigenous farmers were alleged to burn stretches of jungle to make way for low-value subsistence crops.[24] The colonial regime simultaneously presided over expanded deforestation while bemoaning indigenous land use as inefficient, careless, and ecologically damaging. This echoed condemnations of locally cultivated jungle rubber as inferior to colonial estate products.[25] Although the colonial tendency to disparage indigenous agriculture was not a new phenomenon, disputes over land use became increasingly commonplace and inflammatory during the postwar period.

But raw timber outputs, being harder to differentiate than those of traditional cultivars such as rubber, threatened to level the playing field between colonial and local enterprises. In 1960, for instance, 98 percent of Sabah's timber exports were sold as unprocessed logs, with only the remaining 2 percent comprising sawn and refined wood. This rendered it virtually impossible to distinguish between the material produced by colonial-owned mills and that of local competitors. Only through seeking to control access to the land itself was a degree of regulation possible. By presiding over who could obtain timber licenses, the colonial government sought to act as the arbitrator of wealth in a territory gripped by a logging frenzy. The extents of these attempts to regulate resource access were considerable. While politically misaligned or less influential individuals were denied licenses, those who were considered useful or crucial to appease were granted access to Sabah's forests in the form of single-year concessions. Annual renewal depended on continued allegiance and promises of productivity. Alongside controlling licenses, the colonial government also manipulated the availability of commercial forest through changing reserve boundaries, as was the case for the Kawang, Mount Cochrane, and Lema'as reserves in 1960, which were resized to control timber output.[26]

Colonial attempts to regulate commercial logging and stymie local participation proved remarkably effective, in part because timber exports were not so easily smuggled out of Sabah. Large-scale operations left conspicuous scars on the environment; logging was simply more visible than other industries. The most sought-after trees were enormous: felling them required expensive machinery, such as bulldozers, tractors, cranes, and on-site narrow-gauge railways (the import of which was tightly controlled by colonial authorities), in addition to access to roads, rivers, and other logistical networks. The largest operations were managed by foreign-owned firms, such as the British Borneo Timber Company, North Borneo Timbers, the Bombay Burmah Trading Corporation, and the Kennedy Bay Timber Company, which could leverage foreign capital and preferential colonial treatment to outhire and outcompete local rivals.[27]

Although the burgeoning logging industry enabled the colonial government to tighten its grip on Sabah's forested interior, oversee economic output, and promote the rise compliant local collaborators, it simultaneously contributed to the growth of anticolonial opposition and ethnic rivalries. Newly galvanized voices reacted with anger at the government's flagrant attempts at monopolizing the territory's resources and granting preferential treatment to select elites. Where in the past, indigenous anticolonial opposition had traditionally arisen over local-level grievances with the state, by the mid-1950s there was growing antagonism toward economic disenfranchisement on a territory-wide scale. Indigenous claims to ancestral lands were sidelined by colonial contracts with foreign-owned firms, while traditional *kampong* leaders struggled to make their voices heard over competing elites from rival ethnic groups who were able to leverage their positions as state-certified chiefs and government functionaries.

In addition to this, increased logging also wrought unprecedented ecological devastation. The felled trees and desolate muddy clearings left behind served as poignant reminders to Sabahans of the realities of colonial rule. Their land was being irreparably scarred in ways that would take decades, perhaps centuries, to recover from. Politically, too, these transformations in Sabah occurred during a period of declining colonial rule elsewhere in the world, in which new anticolonial aspirations abounded. In Sabah's rapidly urbanizing port towns, whispers of alternatives to colonial rule diffused among the urban residents and new migrant communities from Hong Kong, Java, Sulawesi, and Malaya, while new newspapers and pamphlets raised awareness among the literate. Emergent indigenous leaders, and growing numbers of "politically alert" individuals, began to question the validity of colonial rule in Sabah.[28] Yet as the territory coursed toward an uncertain future, the government doubled down on exclusionary resource extraction. This was done under the guise of economic development in an attempt to justify continued colonial rule.

Local Elite Formation

The population of Sabah was characterized by major ethnic rivalries. Pronounced differences in language, custom, religion, and political leaning had long existed among lowland, upland, and coastal communities. This fragmentation, exacerbated by Borneo's densely forested and mountainous environment, historically precluded the rise of any singular, territory-wide identity. Even the foremost indigenous groups experienced considerable divides based on locality, dialect, profession, and custom. Over time, these distinctions intensified through contact with the steadily growing populations of Malay, Chinese, and other Southeast Asian traders along the Borneo coast. While some communities were enriched by these connections, others were marginalized and pushed out of regional circuits of goods, capital, and opportunity.[29] Sabah's demographic and socioeconomic heterogeneity meant that no single ethnic group became dominant, even prior to the colonial period. While the interior was populated by the Muruts, and the lowlands settled by the Kadazandusuns, the territory's coastal entrepôts were spaces in which colonials, Malays, Chinese, and various émigrés increasingly jostled for commercial preeminence. Indeed, where colonial territories elsewhere underwent massive sociopolitical transformations amid the rise of popular anticolonial nationalism after the Second World War, no such unified movement or identity emerged in Sabah.

Economic and social issues, rather than ideological or political motivations, instead served to galvanize grassroots and marginalized communities across the territory. And it was in this arena, in which day-to-day concerns prioritized food supply, taxation, health care, and access to land and resources, that government-approved local elites assumed considerable sway in the early colonial period. Beginning in the 1910s and 1920s, local collaborators, rather than independent chiefs or colonial district officers, increasingly served as the primary points of contact between distant *kampongs* and the government. These functionaries, however, were initially manufactured by the colonial state as a way of extending its influence into the interior and mediating with dissident groups. Elites willing to advance the colonial agenda were granted official titles, salaries, and pensions, while those who were noncompliant were deprived of these privileges.[30] Over time, many elites put aside grievances with the state in order to further their ambitions and attempt to help their communities overcome hardships. First kickstarted by the North Borneo Chartered Company in the early 1910s, the codification of local leaders expanded in the years leading up to the Japanese occupation. By the time Sabah formally became a Crown Colony after the war, a considerable proportion of the territory's local elites were categorized as either Grade III, Grade II, or Grade I chiefs, the first being the most junior, and the last holding considerable clout over large districts beyond the remit of the government.[31] The most senior classifications were typically synonymous with the traditional epithet *orang kaya kaya*, which denoted wealth and supremacy over lesser elites. Those who failed to serve the state's interests lost out amid the growing symbiosis between local elites and the colonial government. But with the territory lacking a credible anticolonial movement, and with ethnic rivalries abounding, administrative neglect and stagnation set in, prompting little social development in the years leading up to the Second World War.

As in virtually all imperial contexts across the world, the colonial regime in Sabah was dependent on indirect rule. The promotion of cooperative local elites—in part to streamline efficiency in understaffed and underfunded bureaucracies, and in part to combat dissidence in remote regions—was systematically undertaken in late colonial states across Asia, the Middle East, and Africa.[32] Existing scholarship on political elites in colonial Southeast Asia builds on the formative work of Harry Benda. These studies typically focus on ruling elites hailing from the territory's primary ethnic group, rather than religious or minority leaders from "secondary groups" or traditional elites from vying autochthonous communities. Although granting too much significance to the concept of the "national elite" in the colonial (and thereby largely prenational) context, Benda categorized local leaders as either "intelligentsia elites" or "modernizing traditional elites," which is an important distinction. Where intelligentsia elites derived political authority "from their Western-style education" and bureaucratic experience, traditional indigenous elites were typically "recruited on an ascriptive basis" dependent on ethnic group or preexisting political authority.[33] Although in Sabah there were few, if any, intelligentsia elites that might adhere to Benda's definition, the territory was replete with traditional elites from competing ethnic communities and minority groups who were by the 1950s eager to "modernize" by experimenting with new forms of political expression.

Recent contributions in the 2010s have cast important light on the role played by traditional elites in governing Southeast Asia's remote fringes. As Rini Kusumawati and Leontine Visser describe in the case of the Indonesian province of East Kalimantan, indigenous elite collaboration (and correspondingly friction) with the state today forms the backbone of decentralized governance.[34] But such systems of patronage and indirect rule, described as "elite capture," were not inherent in the initial colonial period in places like Sabah, instead developing later through active, coercive attempts by the state to extend its influence.[35]

Indirect rule was also central to the theories underpinning late colonial governance at the time, considered synonymous with the concepts of "trusteeships" and "dual mandates." Although indirect rule arose to suit administrative and economic convenience—local elites knew the land better and were cheaper to hire than colonial counterparts—colonials argued that trusteeships were indicative of progressive governance. Evidence of local collaboration was utilized by metropolitan policymakers to advertise Britain's unswerving commitment to fostering development in the colonies. Indeed, as MP Harold Nicolson claimed in 1938, local trustees were "taught to believe in their own rights . . . [and were] educated to aspire to their own future."[36] Although hinting at eventual self-governance, this colonial framing of indirect rule as enlightened and for the benefit of the colonized peoples underscores the continuing popularity at the time of ideas of the civilizing mission. Popular in the early twentieth century, this faith in colonial stewardship and progress remained prominent during Sabah's eventual decolonization in the 1960s, and its legacies were even perceptible during the empire's final throes in Hong Kong in the 1990s. But beneath the surface, these elite-colonial relationships remained transactional, rather than ideological.

As Ma Ngok writes in the case of Hong Kong, while the British "needed to democratize or prepare local elites" for self-governance, they did not want "upstarts to rise so fast as to challenge the last days of colonial rule."[37] In Hong Kong, as in Sabah, these efforts were complemented by the expansion of civil-administrative bodies to include select elites as a way of boosting local political participation while preserving colonial authority. Indeed, Hong Kong presents a particularly salient corollary because, like Sabah, full independence and suffrage was never truly on the table in the run-up toward decolonization.[38] Only on the "eve of their departure," writes Ming K. Chan, was there an "eleventh-hour change of heart" to push for democracy in Hong Kong, but even this was beset with "missed opportunities, deliberate non-actions, and even antidemocratic manoeuvres."[39] In such cases, collaboration with elites was fundamental in suppressing anticolonial and proindependence thought, and in preserving business interests.

The relationship between local elites and the colonial state in Sabah evoked similar dynamics to that of Hong Kong, despite fundamental demographic differences, in which Sabah's elites were shaped by considerable ethnic heterogeneity and rivalries. Under the anachronistic chartered company regime, little, if any, consideration was given to the idea that Sabah would someday attain self-governance or independence; indirect rule was merely a matter of convenience. Following formal colonization in 1946, however, Crown Colony bureaucrats had to respond to the concomitant threats of rising international anti-imperialism and growing local criticism in Sabah toward economic disenfranchisement and poor administration. But unlike in other colonial territories, local opposition never presented as an ideologically charged anticolonial movement. Administrators believed it possible to keep a lid on simmering discontent and thus prolong colonial rule indefinitely. Elite capture and collaboration, combined with the faintest semblance of constitutional modernization, therefore, became key tools of late colonial governance in Sabah during the 1950s and 1960s.

Seeking to Remain Their "Own Masters" over the Forests

Local elites across Sabah struggled to make their voices heard. Prior to the late 1950s, there were no official forums through which public concerns could be articulated.[40] The Legislative Council was staffed by colonial bureaucrats and business elites. News and information from the *hutan* reached the government in Jesselton only through sporadic communication between salaried chiefs and their district officers. Official visits by colonials to interior communities were infrequent, resembling more a formality than any attempt to gain an understanding of local issues.[41] If specific grievances did reach the government, it was through the interpersonal channels of communication between elites and their colonial minders. Most local issues fell on deaf ears.[42] The lack of any popular access to print media, radio, or other forms of news and information prior to the mid-1950s further stymied organized dissent and the pooling of oppositional thought.

Sabah's foremost indigenous elites in the early twentieth century—such as Orang Kaya Kaya Gusanad Kina, chief of the Kadazandusuns and Muruts, labeled the "King of the Interior"—exercised considerable autonomy in the remote uplands. Beyond the interior, however, their influence remained circumscribed and parochial. Indigenous power structures seldom translated into high office, status, or privilege in colonial-urban contexts. In political, as well as economic and environmental terms, therefore, the divisions between Sabah's *pesisir* and *hutan* remained pronounced. While the colonial government considered elites like Gusanad Kina useful, others were acknowledged only for doing "what little was required of them," whether this was showing fealty to district officers, quashing dissent, presiding over "native courts," or encouraging annual poll tax payments.[43]

The story of Arusap bin Sokongan, a house servant under the employ of Sabah's conservator of forests, Harry G. Keith, and his wife, famed author Agnes Newton Keith, casts important light on these indigenous-colonial dynamics. In her writing, Agnes Keith explored themes relating to the perennial struggle of extending colonial influence into Borneo's deep hinterland and the tensions with its indigenous groups. Keith described Sabah's Kadazandusun and Murut communities as consisting of independent-minded people who strove to remain their "own masters" over their lands.[44] Although she painted colonial administrative efforts as valiant, Keith believed that Sabah would always remain fiercely autonomous. The expansion of commercial forestry and logging after the Second World War, she suggested, upset existing balances and reignited frictions between locals and colonials. Keith condemned the territory's indigenous groups as untamable and lazy, racist stereotypes that remain in common usage across postcolonial Malaysia, especially toward the Muruts in Sabah and the Orang Asli across the Malay Peninsula.[45] Keith described how Arusap bin Sokongan, her house servant, would frequently abandon his duties to return to Kampong Pau, his hometown in the interior, only to resume his work months later. She decried this as symptomatic of a poor work ethic and complained that "when a native feels like a holiday he takes it!"[46] But Arusap's activities were indicative of his attempts to advance his career and socioeconomic positioning beyond a life of servitude, rather than acts of laziness. During one such sabbatical, in 1935, Arusap was involved in helping American documentarists Martin and Osa Johnson hire local Murut workers to accompany them on their travels across Borneo and to care for captured exotic animals that were to be brought back to New York's Central Park Zoo.[47]

More significant, however, was the fact that Arusap's visits to the interior enabled him to later become *orang tua* of Kampong Pau. The rise of minor elites such as Arusap, who rejected servitude in favor of village leadership, reveals the difficulties facing those who sought to participate in the colonial economy while advancing their sociopolitical standing as indigenous leaders. The memoirs of other Muruts, such as Saudin bin Labutau, who traveled extensively across the United States in the 1930s, similarly bring into sharp focus the systemic prejudices and obstacles undermining indigenous attempts to access the world beyond Sabah's interior. In his recollections, Saudin described his fear of being dismissed as "just a jungle man" while traveling from Singapore to Ceylon and from South Africa to the United

States.⁴⁸ Such discrimination also pervaded Sabah's port towns and administrative enclaves, where indigenous and minority groups struggled to compete with wealthier, better educated, and politically connected rivals. While the colonial state did not perceive the emergence of new petty elites such as Orang Tua Arusap bin Sokongan as a direct threat, the rise of other prominent figures precipitated major concern.

Indeed, the postwar period witnessed the re-emergence of anticolonial voices in Sabah. Although the territory had a long history of anticolonial dissent, with early wars and conflicts violently suppressed by the colonial state, the latter period of chartered company rule met with no major opposition until the Japanese invasion in 1942. But so violent and chaotic was the initial chartered company period, with the 1880s to 1910s dubbed the "unsettled years," that indigenous freedom fighters such as Ontoros Antanum and Mat Salleh continue to evoke popular and scholarly interest in Sabah today.⁴⁹ In the 1950s, however, the colonial government grew concerned about renewed public discontent. Whereas previously grievances were confined to interior *kampongs*, new and outspoken elites were increasingly expressing their dissatisfaction. Given the contemporaneous decline of Western empires and the surge in popular anticolonial movements across the world, British officials were keenly aware of these vulnerabilities. Although cognizant of external pressures, the government continued to believe Sabah's public to be politically immature and thus immune to the kind of organized anticolonialism that had developed across India, Indonesia, and Vietnam, among other places. In such cases, anticolonial revolutions were led by ideologically charged intelligentsia elites. But Sabah's emergent local leaders, by comparison, were considered ideologically inert and motivated by ethnic rivalries, and it was thus deemed possible to pacify them with inducements and kickbacks. Added to this was the fact that Sabah had suffered disproportionately during the Second World War. As ex-governor Edward Francis Twining noted in 1963, the Japanese occupiers "administered a devasting blow by the mass execution of all the intelligentsia on whom they could lay their hands . . . several thousands perished."⁵⁰ The mass killing of local Chinese elites, Eurasians, and other locals following the 1943 Jesselton Revolt left enduring marks on Sabah's nascent urban society. Nevertheless, despite the continuation of colonial beliefs that Sabah's public had yet to "advance [to] political maturity," administrators on the ground voiced concern about the potential emergence of new anticolonial opponents.⁵¹

These colonial concerns were amplified in the mid-1950s when new forms of indigenous political authority and communal leadership began to gain traction and assail traditional elites and their colonial overlords. The emergence of new local elites aimed to collectivize the public under communal goals, whether rallying against poor living standards or promising to end civil disenfranchisement. Many of these new elites converged in clubhouses, societies, and tearooms across Jesselton and other port towns, breaking with tradition and increasingly inserting themselves into the territory's budding political and urban scenes. Whereas in the past, colonials had fetishized local hierarchies as naïve jungle polities controlled by "native" chiefs, by the 1950s the territory's foremost ethnic groups were producing leaders and spokespersons who were increasingly plugged into radical politics and abounding with fresh ideas of Sabahan identity.

Donald Stephens (later known as Tun Fuad Stephens), who by 1960 had become the territory-wide *huguan siou* of the Kadazandusuns, precipitated major shifts in how Sabah's largest indigenous group interacted with the colonial government. Similarly, Orang Kaya Kaya Mustapha bin Harun, the foremost representative of Sabah's Muslim community by the late 1950s, signaled for the first time in Sabah the crystallizing of local identity based on religious affinity rather than ethnic background. Other emergent elites, such as the sons of Orang Kaya Kaya Gusanad Kina, the once-dependable "King of the Interior" who collaborated with the chartered company in the early twentieth century, wielded considerable influence over Kadazandusun and Murut groups in the territory's uplands. Crucially, these new elites could count on support beyond the circumscribed scale of traditional *kampongs* that were historically isolated and disparate. This shift threatened to upend the tenuous colonial hold over compliant petty elites that had been the status quo since the 1910s.

In response, the colonial state doubled down on its attempts to control the creation of new elites. Indeed, the management and overseeing of elite formation were elevated to the forefront of Sabah's colonial bureaucracy, alongside forestry and commercial expansion. Officials, tasked with nurturing compliant "natives" to political maturity, compiled dossiers of candidates and biographical surveys complete with records of communications, infractions, and character traits. Colonial rule could be prolonged, it was believed, through the "fostering of potential leaders" who would take up the reins of administration in the future through serving as dependable disciples rather than anticolonial antagonists.[52] The government also considered colonial-sponsored elite formation a viable shortcut toward improving the public's quality of life, particularly in marginalized communities that lacked humanitarian and development programs. By shifting the burden of the community's welfare onto local elites, the government reasoned that it could also dodge any attendant blame that came with socioeconomic hardship.

While colonial officials proclaimed that those selected by the state were fortunate to have been identified and elevated as future leaders, these local elites remained second-class citizens. Importantly, many of those who were designated by the government were already-prosperous individuals who hailed from families that had long ruled over *kampongs* or who had maintained successful business interests. But even they struggled to assert themselves within colonial elite circles as serious candidates, among whom they were considered useful only in tending to tedious interior affairs. There were some notable exceptions, however, in which teachers, small-business owners, and school graduates were noted in colonial surveys as promising individuals fit for future administrative roles. But these opportunities were limited and transactional, and they ultimately came too late to make a difference. At Semporna, a remote coastal town in the distant east, once known as Hujung Hutan (edge of the forest), officials identified Sanin bin Pandin in early 1963 as an "intelligent young man" who, with "a little further experience, should go far" in administrative service.[53] Others "noticed" by the government included Tho Yeo Ping, who owned a radio shop in Lahad Datu; Orang Tua Alam bin Datu Jinurain, head of Kampong Kunak; and Chan Wing Cheong, an English-language teacher at Semporna.[54] But on the eve of decolonization in 1963, it was too little, too late. Although many such individuals emerged as promising future civil servants, few with humble origins secured administrative roles. It was the territory's foremost traditional elites—particularly those who had already secured key positions of indigenous leadership, and those with entrenched business interests—who emerged as the primary contenders to take on growing political duties.

The Rise of Donald Stephens

Analyzing the experiences of Donald Stephens, who would later serve as Sabah's first chief minister following the territory's merger with Malaysia in September 1963, offers valuable insights into colonial-indigenous relations during the late colonial period. Born in 1920, Stephens was part of a cohort of young and increasingly politically active Sabahans, who were often referred to as "Anak Sabah" (Son of Sabah).[55] During the mid-1930s, he became a member of a youth group known as the "West Coast Boys," who identified more with local indigenous ideals than with entrenched colonial society. In their discussions, the West Coast Boys broached political topics and stated that their loyalties lay with the idea of an indigenous Sabah.[56] Despite existing under the aegis of the chartered company, the Sabah that they experienced in the 1930s would have been an exciting environment for educated local youths who were interested in pushing back against colonial society (see figures 11 and 12).

The eldest son of Jules Pavitt Stephens and Edith Cope, the young Donald Stephens experienced a tumultuous childhood, moving around Sabah due to his father's itinerant employment at the Public Works Department.[57] As a child, his family spent time in Sandakan before moving to Jesselton in the west, then to the remote interior town of Keningau, and finally to Kudat in the far north. In each of these childhood locales, Stephens was exposed to a range of different indigenous communities, where he learned to converse in the Kadazandusun, Murut, and Bajau languages. But Stephens was caught between worlds, neither a colonial, nor fully "native." Although his father was the son of an indigenous Kadazandusun woman named Kwai, Stephens's paternal grandfather, Ernest Alfred Pavitt, was one of the first employees of the North Borneo Chartered Company and a central figure in early colonial efforts to chart Sabah's interior regions. Donald Stephens's mother was also of mixed heritage, as the daughter of Henry William Cope, a colonial industrialist, and a Japanese slave whom he had purchased at the Jesselton dockyards in 1898.[58] A popular figure, whose life ended in tragedy on June 6, 1976, in a fatal airplane crash, Donald Stephens has drawn popular and scholarly attention as one of the foremost political figures in Sabah.[59]

The status of Eurasians and mixed-race individuals in Sabah, as in much of colonial Asia, was perennially insecure.[60] Donald Stephens was routinely subjected to racism and prejudice by members of the colonial elite, and his

FIGURE 11. A street scene depicting shop houses in Sandakan, circa 1930s. CO 1069/527, TNA.

FIGURE 12. View of Sandakan and ships in the harbor, circa 1930s. CO 1069/527, TNA.

attempts to assimilate with colonial society were met with suspicion and disapproval. Some opportunistic officials, however, saw value in his multiracial identity, with his Western-style education and command of numerous local languages allowing Stephens to bridge the gaps between indigenous and colonial societies in a way that few European officers could match.[61] Sabah's colonial administrators sought local leaders who could appeal to indigenous groups without inciting nationalistic beliefs, while maintaining perceived colonial sensibilities and an affinity to the government. A tall order, perhaps, but the continued reaping of Borneo's resources depended on controlling the population and steering public opinion away from anticolonialism. Stephens' mixed-race identity purportedly presented such an opportunity. In a government file on local timber applications in 1960, Stephens was described as being simultaneously European enough to be dependable and "native" enough to appeal to the public as an authentic leader.[62] These were qualities that marked him out as a candidate fit to receive a lucrative timber concession. Indeed, in official correspondence, Stephens was noted for the "European blood in his veins," though at times also dismissed as untrustworthy.[63] Such prejudice had its roots in the chartered company era, when according to Danny Wong Tze Ken, "Eurasians were considered inferior in status to the Europeans" but were nevertheless "placed higher than Asians."[64]

Although Donald Stephens received a full education and straddled colonial and indigenous societies in his youth, his early years were marred by hardship.

In 1937, he applied to work at the Sandakan Public Works Department, which required candidates to pass both an entrance examination and a medical inspection.[65] It was here that Stephens was diagnosed with leprosy, which precluded him from employment. Following his diagnosis, Stephens was forcedly confined at a government quarantine camp at Berhala off the coast of Sandakan, an island noted for its sheer cliffs and fortress-like silhouette.[66] The Japanese had previously utilized Berhala during the war as the site of a notorious prisoner of war camp, where much of Sabah's colonial population was interned prior to the infamous Sandakan "death march."[67]

In contrast to tropical diseases that evoked colonial anxieties, such as "Borneo fever," leprosy was a known illness.[68] But without readily available treatment at the time, leprosy was managed through containment, and suffers were stigmatized and ostracized from their societies.[69] Victims in Sabah were sent to "leper colonies," neglected outposts that lacked even basic medical care. As P. J. Granville-Edge writes in her biography of Donald Stephens, unlike the colony's tightly regulated "lunatic asylums," "the leper colony on Berhala Island was not kept in strict isolation," meaning that "lepers in the early stages of the disease . . . often managed to escape the island and mix with Sandakan Society." Stephens resolved not to be confined at the leprosarium, and later in 1937 he managed to escape. He spent the next three years in hiding from the colony's medical authorities at a friend's agricultural estate to the south of Jesselton.[70] Colonial officers, however, eventually caught on to Stephens's illegal abscondment, alleging that his father, Jules Pavitt Stephens, had aided his escape. Soon afterwards, in 1941, Stephens's father arranged for his son to travel to Singapore to seek treatment, resulting in the family again running afoul of colonial law, since sufferers of leprosy were banned from foreign travel. As a result, Stephens's father was dismissed from his job as a Sanitary Board health inspector, with official records noting that he was forced into "early retirement."[71] Granville-Edge, however, argued that the official reason given for his dismissal by colonial authorities was the diagnosis of "encroaching senility," despite his relatively young age of forty-one.[72] The dismissal was widely alleged to be a politically motivated punishment in response to helping his son's escape to Singapore.

The Second World War was particularly difficult for the Stephens family. In Singapore, Donald Stephens had to navigate living under its new Japanese occupiers. Together with a few other West Coast Boys who had also emigrated to Singapore, Stephens "eked out a gruesome living by burying the dead." Stephens avoided internment at Japanese camps through claiming to be a Kadazandusun laborer before later returning to occupied Sabah aboard a Japanese vessel in 1943.⁷³ Back in Sabah, tragedy befell the Stephens family. In October 1943, Jules Pavitt Stephens joined a major uprising against the Japanese. Under the leadership of Albert Kwok, the elder Stephens joined a multiethnic band of rebels, comprising local Chinese, Suluks, Bajau, Kadazandusuns, and Muruts from across Sabah. Together, their efforts represented a significant, if brief, moment of interethnic unity in the territory. Alongside Kwok, various *orang tuas* and elites urged their followers to take up arms against the Japanese, in what later became known as the "Kinabalu Uprising."⁷⁴ The rebellion was short lived, however, and was crushed decisively by the Japanese Kenpetai, who later oversaw the mass execution of all the rebels at the town of Petegas on the west coast.⁷⁵

Despite these hardships, Donald Stephens's fortunes improved after the war. Over the next decade, he rose to prominence as a businessman with extensive timber holdings and served as a successful newspaper editor, which facilitated his newfound role as a popular spokesperson for indigenous groups.⁷⁶ With financial backing from his wealthy father-in-law, Henry William Cope, Stephens founded the *North Borneo News & Sabah Times*, a newspaper that ran weekly editions containing editorials, news, and a popular "letters to the editor" series.⁷⁷ For the first time in Sabah, locals were able to write to a newspaper to voice their concerns and thoughts about current affairs and social issues in Chinese, Kadazandusun, and other non-English languages. This was a privilege previously available only to English-speaking elites and colonials through official forums and the government-sponsored *North Borneo Herald*. Following the publication of its first issue on January 21, 1953, the *North Borneo News & Sabah Times* swiftly gained popularity among the small but growing numbers of literate Kadazandusuns in Jesselton, Sandakan, and Kudat, for its hard-line stance championing indigenous causes and its criticisms of colonial policy.

The 1950s was a decade of considerable change in Sabah. With the advent of new forms of print media, the small but increasingly vocal public had gained an outlet for news and politics that were crucially distinct from, and often at odds with, official colonial discourse. Simultaneously, emergent elites such as Donald Stephens sought to leverage their newfound role as media proprietors by interacting with entrenched colonial and business leaders. In the late 1950s, Stephens even built up a rapport with then governor Roland Evelyn Turnbull. This budding relationship raised Stephens's profile and reputation, ending only with Turnbull's death in December 1960. Ultimately, where traditional *kampong* elites struggled to elevate themselves as territory-wide figures, Stephens and other modernizing elites were able to boost their popularity and standing during a period of intensifying public interest in the territory's political future.

From a "West Coast Boy" to "King of the Kadazans"

In times of crisis or conflict, indigenous elites in Sabah had long turned to hierarchical structures with a view toward promoting unity and mediating against external threats. This was at variance to colonial perceptions of "jungle" politics as disaggregated and dysfunctional. Indeed, the role of the Kadazandusun *huguan siou* was akin to serving as the "chief diplomat of the community." During the precolonial period, the *huguan siou* had historically played a decisive role in resisting incursions from the coastal sultanates of Sulu and Brunei and in facilitating negotiations with foreign envoys and travelers.[78] But by the time Orang Kaya Kaya Gusanad Kina ascended to the role in the early twentieth century, indigenous leadership had been gutted of much of its power, instead serving a largely symbolic, ceremonial function in spaces permitted by the state.

Following the death of Gusanad Kina in January 1930, the role of the "King of the Interior" became vacant. With no clear successor, with chartered company bureaucrats dismissive of local political affairs, and with wartime occupation, devastation, and protracted recovery in the 1940s, the role remained unfilled for much of the next three decades. It was only following the rise of Donald Stephens in the 1950s that a new candidate arrived who was deemed suitable for territory-wide preeminence. Stephens, however, embodied a new cohort of Sabahan who did not adhere to traditional precedents, with his Eurasian background, Western-style education, and itinerant childhood setting him apart from traditional *kampong* elites. In contrast to previous Kadazandusun leaders, Stephens and his associates were mixed race, they unashamedly and publicly coveted access to the territory's resource wealth, and, crucially, they were willing to play the political game by appealing to both colonial and traditional corners for support. Referred to by colonial officials as part of a new cohort of young indigenous "intelligentsia" and increasingly active as a businessman and newspaper proprietor, Stephens had by the late 1950s become the de facto leader of the increasingly politically active Kadazandusuns along the coastal lowlands. And by 1960, the Kadazandusuns would declare him their new *huguan siou*.[79] According to government sources, Stephens's role as the territory's foremost Kadazandusun representative had long been apparent, with some officials even branding him—replete with pejorative colonialist connotations—the "King of the Kadazans" as early as 1957.[80] As Herman Luping noted, however, the Kadazandusuns "had no kingship system," and Donald Stephens "was not a king."' As *huguan siou*, while Stephens was "superior to the village headmen in all important questions of justice, ceremony and war," his most important function was to be the spokesperson of the community.⁸¹ This was a role for which his bureaucratic links and control over the *North Borneo News & Sabah Times* particularly suited him.

The process of elite formation in Sabah was a contested space in which the colonial government often held the upper hand. As with the rise of Orang Kaya Kaya Gusanad Kina in the chartered company period, elites with widespread clout were only permitted to remain in power as long as they suited the colonial agenda, or at the very least did not threaten official interests. And yet colonial claims to directly control the rise of indigenous elites appeared spurious, and at best overconfident or exaggeratory. To regulate elite formation—or stake a claim to the role of kingmaker—was to keep a lid on anticolonial murmurs. This was a difficult undertaking, perhaps, but one that embodied an assertion of colonial authority over "native" affairs that few local leaders could oppose if they wished to remain in power. The state therefore went to great lengths to not only encourage compliant functionaries where possible but to profess its control over the entire process. For much of the chartered company and subsequent Crown Colony periods, this resulted in a denial of local agency over the very process of traditional elite formation, a precedent broken only by the arrival of Donald Stephens, Mustapha bin Harun, and other new elites in the 1950s. Although the government initially sought to oversee and manage these new leaders, they soon outgrew any need to acquiesce to their colonial minders. By leveraging business interests and access to news and information, and by staking claims to represent newly defined socioethnic groups, these emergent power brokers shattered the government's monopoly on elite formation.

Indeed, much to the concern of leading colonial officials, Donald Stephens was not a compliant functionary. In one surveillance report compiled in 1957 detailing Stephens's activities, administrators wrote with express concern that he "nursed a feeling of resentment" toward the government.⁸² Further alarm was raised in October 1960 when Stephens was embroiled in a highly publicized spectacle at the Sandakan Recreation Club, in which he traded insults with a "drunken European."⁸³ Stephens was so prioritized in colonial surveillance activities that the territory's assistant commissioner and the Sandakan resident were called up to brief the chief secretary, R. N. Turner, about the incident.⁸⁴ Sabah's commissioner of customs, G. R. Johnson, recalled the incident to Turner:

> A man whose name I believe is Douglas Hunter . . . provoked an argument with Mr. Donald Stephens. He had obviously had a lot to drink. I don't know how it started as it was under way before I became properly aware of it. Certainly Mr. Stephens did not start it, but I recalled that

Hunter was most insulting to him. . . . I was later told Hunter had used the expression "black bastard."

Soon after this Mr. Stephens went over to Hunter at the bar. . . . I heard him say "white trash" and he said that he had challenged Hunter to settle it outside but Hunter had backed down.

He had been badly insulted and there was little else that any man could have done in retaliation.[85]

While G. R. Johnson appeared sympathetic toward Donald Stephens, he did not comment further on the use of racially charged terms such as "black bastard" or "white trash." Stephens's sociopolitical standing as a Eurasian in Sabah remained blurred and tenuous: although he was a participant in the colonial social arena, this was by no means a safe space. The nature of the incident, and the government's responses, however, reveal that little sympathy was felt toward the victims of such racial abuse, particularly when it occurred within colonial circles. Indeed, colonials were quick to paint Stephens as an agitator and a destabilizing presence. Since 1957, he had been outlined in a "character profile" as a problematic figure. Officials noted with concern that he was becoming "increasingly anti-European in outlook." To explain this, officials cited a series of possible "grievances," which included "his discharge from Government when suffering from leprosy," his belief that he should be accorded the honorary title "Tuan," and his treatment by colonials. The biographical profile further outlined that "his sense of humour does not allow him to be made fun of by anybody, particularly Europeans. He is addicted to violent verbal attacks on Europeans, brought on by their lack of respect for him."[86]

As early as 1954, Donald Stephens had already featured prominently in official discussions as an individual with the capacity to emerge as a future leader, should he not turn to radical anticolonialism. He was also aided by powerful colonial connections. In particular, his wealthy father-in-law's friendship with the then governor, Roland Evelyn Turnbull, enabled Stephens to tap into important administrative circles and even gain access to inducements in the form of lucrative logging concessions. Ronald J. Brooks, head of Sabah's Information Office, reported that one of Turnbull's first steps as governor in 1954 was to nominate Stephens to the Legislative Council.[87] Turnbull sought to usher in a new generation of local leaders who were sympathetic toward colonial rule and capable of taking up greater responsibility for running the territory. Stephens was quick to utilize his new official position to call for improved living conditions for the Kadazandusuns. While some colonials branded these discussions as "radicalism," others saw value in his calls for greater literacy and improved education among indigenous groups.[88] As Brooks claimed, "Stephens had become, quite rightly, a vociferous critic of Government measures, or lack of them, in cases where he thought action was necessary. By bringing him into the inner circle [the Legislative Council], he would then appreciate the more fundamental problems [facing] . . . the Government."[89]

Writing in the 1990s, some three decades after Sabah's decolonization, Ronald Brooks would have witnessed just how important Stephens would later become in postcolonial Malaysia. But as always, colonial administrators were quick to stake their claim to the process of elite formation, even if the elites in question were already noteworthy public figures in their own right. Brooks further wrote that "Sir Roland also had the foresight and wisdom to identify in Donald a potential political leader who had the ability to stir political thinking and create the atmosphere and background against which political parties could be formed. Political development was essential if ever the country were able to shake off the yoke of imperialism and become a country capable of standing on its own feet."[90] Despite the ostensible role played by colonial bureaucrats in "identifying" new elites, Donald Stephens remained very much an outsider in official circles. Although he benefited financially, he was also condemned as a rabble-rousing newspaper owner, slighted for his covetous attempts to secure timber concessions, and caricatured as the "King of the Kadazans."

The Emergence of Local Print Media

Indigenous affairs in Sabah attained a vital platform with the emergence of the *North Borneo News & Sabah Times*. Having received generous funding in 1948 from his father-in-law, Donald Stephens worked to prepare the newspaper for its first issue on January 21, 1953. Although the publication started strong, securing over one thousand subscribers by the year's end, its early popularity among indigenous groups has been debated.[91] While Fausto Barlocco emphasizes the newspaper's importance in disseminating news and information in the colony's main languages, with the intention of "reach[ing] as many people as possible," the bulk of its content was in English.[92] Anthony Reid, in contrast, downplays the paper's early successes, claiming that most subscribers were curious (and often concerned) European and Chinese residents.[93] With the territory still facing critically low literacy rates well into the 1950s, only a small proportion of the indigenous population would have been able to read the newspaper. As Margaret Roff described, prior to 1953 only a select minority of "mission schools were providing anything more than the merest rudiments of literacy, and it was mainly the Chinese who took advantage of this." By the mid-1950s, although a number of new "Native Voluntary Schools" had been set up in remote *kampongs*, they remained little more than "rough huts or mere roofs on stilts."⁹⁴ But they demonstrated the popular desire for increased educational facilities and improved literacy among Sabah's Kadazandusuns.

Eager to build greater communal kinship among disparate Kadazandusun groups, Donald Stephens published articles dealing with local issues and indigenous affairs. Soon after the launch of the *North Borneo News & Sabah Times*, Stephens debuted the "Kadazan Corner," a column written in a Romanized form of Kadazandusun dialect native to the populous Penampang and Papar regions along the west coast.⁹⁵ While the reach of the indigenous-focused column was limited to those who could read the Penampang and Papar dialect, the "Kadazan Corner" was nevertheless an important development. On one level, it positioned the Kadazandusun language on a symbolically comparable footing to the Chinese, English, and Malay languages. On another level, it represented an important step in the development of Kadazandusun identity and new opportunities to voice political opinions.

Due to the early successes of the *North Borneo News & Sabah Times*, Donald Stephens received a British Council grant to study journalism in the United Kingdom. Within weeks, however, he abandoned his studies in order to return to Sabah to deal with the paper's struggling finances.⁹⁶ Despite his efforts, the paper failed to expand its sales, and throughout much of the 1950s it suffered from critical staff shortages and budget constraints. The paper persisted, however, and increasingly served as an outlet for Stephens' personal political ambitions. At times, Stephens served as its only writer, managing its day-to-day operations, budget, and content, which was a source of contention for many observers who criticized the paper for its lack of impartiality, diversity, and professionalism.

The government kept close tabs on Stephens's newspaper. In their monthly compilations of the local press, officials expressed their alarm at the paper's increasingly critical anticolonial tone. The *North Borneo News & Sabah Times* spearheaded a sharp rise in the number of locally produced publications in the colony and in neighboring Sarawak. Between 1949 and decolonization in September 1963, some fourteen newspapers were established. But these were primarily English- or Chinese-language publications that failed to attract significant indigenous readership. Since the establishment of *North Borneo News & Sabah Times*, there have only been two other publications utilizing the Kadazandusun language: the *Daily Express*, founded in 1963 shortly after Sabah's merger with Malaysia, and the *Borneo Mail*, founded in 1988.⁹⁷

Facing allegations that the newspaper was becoming little more than a personal mouthpiece for his political ambitions, Donald Stephens began to write some articles using a nom de plume in the late 1950s in an attempt to convey varied authorship to his readers. But under the guise of "Roderick," Stephens intensified his anticolonial tone, authoring criticisms of government policy that highlighted administrative failures and colonial prejudices. The government's monthly press reviews soon came to reflect a condensed assemblage of "Roderick's" comments. Everything Stephens wrote was meticulously recorded and logged, no matter how trivial: "Roderick deplores Jesselton airport building," one summary noted. "Roderick praises service at new hospital," another one recorded. Sometimes, these comments touched on deeper issues: "Roderick discusses situation in Indonesia; fears Jakarta may covet further territory in Borneo," "Roderick urges introduction of elections," and so on.[98] But colonial officials appeared less concerned about content detailing administrative failures than they were about the calls for Kadazandusun unity and political advancement. While issues of underdevelopment and administrative neglect were palpable and thus hard to deny, the attempts to boost Kadazandusun political awareness, particularly with a view toward promoting communal affinity, elicited harsh condemnation and even claims of "radicalism." Even faint whispers of a nascent Kadazandusun "nationalism" evoked stiff concern among Sabah's colonial circles. Colonial rule benefited from the petty divisions within indigenous groups and the complicity of local functionaries, with disputes among rival *kampongs* on the micro level mirroring broader antagonisms among larger communities. Growing talk of a functioning unity among the once disparate and disunited Kadazandusuns—previously only attained symbolically through the *huguan siou*—was perceived as a threat to the colonial status quo. These historic divisions among Kadazandusun communities were both cultural and political in nature. As Margaret Roff described, in the past the "Penampang and Papar group [of Kadazandusuns] were thought in Tuaran to be dangerously outspoken and unattractively assertive," while "the Rungus tribes in the north were denied kinship because of their backwardness." In an attempt to overcome these divisions, Stephens sought to extend the use of the Kadazandusun language, "to standardize it," and to improve its standing relative to other languages.[99]

In February 1955, for instance, Stephens ran a series of articles intending to "show the Kadazandusun community in a better light."[100] By displaying the "cultural strengths" of the Kadazandusuns, Stephens aimed to counter the condemnations of so-called primitive behavior at annual harvest festivals, and the allegations of widespread drinking that accompanied ceremonies, that had long afflicted indigenous groups.[101] Writing as "Roderick," he called for funding to be allocated for the publication of English-Kadazandusun and Kadazandusun-English dictionaries.[102] But even seemingly innocuous requests such as this fell on deaf ears.

More broadly, the 1950s marked a growing public disillusionment toward the colonial government. Many *orang tuas* and local chiefs had firsthand experience of the profit-minded, exclusionary approach to governance employed by the previous company administration. The postwar years had demonstrated that little had changed under the new Crown Colony government. The urgency with which colonial bureaucrats pushed for the reinvigoration of rubber cultivation, and later commercial logging, exposed the government's priorities and its failings. And by the mid-1950s, it was evident to many local leaders that the promised benefits of Crown Colony status had fallen short, with its administration differing little from the despotic, profiteering approach of the North Borneo Chartered Company. Alongside these sweeping changes, the *North Borneo News & Sabah Times* confirmed to people across the territory that their experiences were not unique; that indigenous Kadazandusuns, alongside Muruts, Bajaus, and Suluks—and even many Chinese, Malays, Eurasians, and other minorities—were being functionally excluded from gaining a proper education, partaking in the economy, and voicing their political opinions.

Indigenous Attempts to Stake a Claim to the *Tanah Ayer*

By the end of the 1950s, while public discontentment across Sabah continued to grow, few individuals actively pushed for independent self-governance. Economic and social issues, be they the high costs of living, the inaccessibility of food and land, or the lack of educational and medical infrastructure, remained the primary talking points among Sabah's grassroots communities. Although he was a vocal proponent of greater prosperity and improved living standards, Donald Stephens struggled to stoke public interest in the concept of political independence. As early as June 1955, again writing as "Roderick," Stephens disseminated increasingly ideologically charged proindependence content. Although Stephens spoke of his "praise" for "the particular brand of *merdeka* [independence] found in North Borneo," his attempts to galvanize the public failed.[103] In this period, talk of *merdeka* was confined to the margins of Sabah's educated society, and even then, intelligentsia elites viewed it as a goal fit only for the distant future. Ethnic rivalries and socioeconomic hardships hindered the development of any singular proindependence movement. Although many Sabahans opposed colonial rule, the persistence of deep ethnocultural divisions contributed to widespread fears that, following independence, rival communities might gain the upper hand.[104] There were concerns among Kadazandusun groups, for instance, that ethnic Malays would oversee the spread of Islamic values, while others warned of the rising economic and political dominance of Sabah's Chinese population. For many Sabahans, colonial rule was a known entity that served a mediating role, preventing local rivalries from spiraling out of hand.

Despite failing to elicit popular interest, Sabah's emergent local elites continued to publicize their own visions of *merdeka*. The government kept a close watch. In July 1957, just a few weeks prior to Malaya's own transition to independence on August 31, Donald Stephens, together with Mustapha bin Harun and Orang Kaya Kaya Mohammed Yassin bin Haji Hashim (a Kadazandusun leader from Sipitang on the west coast), publicly announced their intention to push for *merdeka* in what was a rare demonstration of communal solidarity between rivalling indigenous groups. Days later, Stephens gave a speech in the Legislative Council in which he called for "self-government" in Sabah and broached the possibility of forming an independent Bornean federation with Brunei and Sarawak. Referred to as "Stephens' plan for *Merdeka*," his 1957 Legislative Council speech also called for the rapid "Borneanization" of the civil service to prepare for independence.[105]

The reasons why these calls for independence failed to galvanize local support are critical in explaining Sabah's decolonization story. While Donald Stephens' calls for improved education, health care, economic integration, and prosperity elicited public interest, talk of *merdeka* proved less popular, particularly among minority communities beyond his direct purview. In response, colonials suggested that Sabahans were neither "politically alert" nor mature enough to turn their discontent into support for independence.[106] For decades, scholars have perpetuated this assumption, labeling the territory as "politically dormant."[107] But independence was not a clear-cut scenario: *kampong* leaders voiced their concern over who would replace the British, fearful that rival ethnic groups would gain undue influence at their expense. These entrenched socioethnic divisions, combined with the long distances separating Sabah's coastal settlements from its interior *kampongs*, stymied the popularization of *merdeka* from the outset. But rather than political naïveté or dormancy, it was widespread concern among the Kadazandusuns that wealthier Malays or Chinese might come to power after independence (and these sentiments were felt reciprocally, too, of course) that undermined support for *merdeka*. Indeed, by the late 1950s, "fear of domination" by Malays who were alleged to maintain ties to Malaya (and by Chinese with ties to China) had become widespread across Sabah's interior *kampongs*.[108]

Cognizant that discussions of independence were unlikely to induce popular backing, Stephens, together with other emergent local elites across Sabah, later worked to galvanize supporters over pressing economic and civil issues. In December 1957, Stephens disseminated material condemning the colony's poll tax, claiming that it was devised with the express purpose of "prov[ing] . . . that they [the indigenous communities] are the most backward people in the world."[109] Stephens further stated that

> The natives have been pushed out of everything which can bring in the dollars. . . . The natives of Sabah who should have first right to the good earth of their *tanah ayer* have in fact been robbed in broad daylight.
>
> Unless the natives get the New Deal for which the time has come, it will not be long before they find that discontent is the only meat left in their dish; discontent that can and will breed communalism and hatred more dangerous than anything we have known in the country in the past.[110]

Stephens's assertions, disseminated across Sabah in English, Chinese, Malay, and the Penampang and Papar Kadazandusun dialect, were met with forceful indignation by colonial authorities. The district officer for Labuan, for instance, wrote to the colony's chief secretary to inquire whether what Stephens had written was illegal, in the hope that some action could be taken against him. Colonial bureaucrats condemned what they saw as a "dangerous piece of rabble-rousing" and sprang into action to suppress the material.[111] Elsewhere, the district officer for Papar, P. M. Hewitt, bemoaned that virtually every issue of the *North Borneo News & Sabah Times* carried articles that were either highly critical of the government, or "boosted . . . [Stephens's] abilities, integrity and purpose."[112] Despite the strong colonial blowback, Stephens continued to make further incendiary claims, arguing that the government sought to actively disenfranchise Sabah's indigenous peoples. He alleged that administrative neglect was designed to "keep them in their *kampongs* and their hill tops."[113] These comments pushed Stephens further out of favor with the colonial elite but turned him into a hero in the eyes of ordinary Kadazandusuns. Although few could access these publications, word swiftly spread, and Stephens's claims proved to be a popular rallying cry among the colony's poor. The idea of *merdeka* may have failed to garner support—few believed Sabah was ready to fend for itself as an independent, unified country—but calls for lower taxes, improved access to resources, and fairer distribution of land galvanized many Kadazandusuns, alongside Muruts, Chinese, and other minority groups. In so doing, Stephens placed unprecedented scrutiny on the entrenched colonial economic system.

Anticolonial Opposition and Systems of Colonial Patronage

As Sabah's timber industry reached new heights in the 1950s, public interest in issues of economic disenfranchisement increased. This was despite colonial claims that the population was politically immature. The emergence of new and expanded logging ventures transformed how big businesses conducted wealth extraction in Sabah. Whereas previously, colonial firms were confined to lowland rubber plantations, postwar industrial logging drastically increased the demand for indigenous ancestral lands in old-growth forests that formed the basis of Sabah's traditional jungle economy. Similarly, attempts by emergent elites to gain access to forest resources increased tensions between vying ethnic groups and the government. But above all else, logging proved a particularly incendiary issue, and there was growing talk among local communities that their *tanah ayer* was being "robbed." Yet the colonial administration contended that the territory's very existence hinged on the profitable extraction of wealth from the forests, and it believed that large colonial firms were best suited to achieve this. At the same time, however, strict forestry regulation threatened to alienate key local elites, on whom the tenuous balance of indirect rule was dependent.

Government control over resources was closely tied to policies overseeing elite management. In previous decades, colonial bureaucrats had acted as kingmakers, investing compliant indigenous elites with power over far-flung districts and granting them exclusive access to jungle produce within their spheres while sidelining opponents. But by the mid-1950s, this system had all but collapsed, with once-compliant local leaders, such as Mustapha bin Harun and Donald Stephens, now resembling protonationalists and borderline independence activists. Likewise, active colonial attempts at pacifying these elites no longer produced desired outcomes. Rather than hushing discontent, the awarding of economic concessions provoked jealousy, ethnic tensions, and allegations of impartiality.

This did not stop the colonial government from seeking to influence local power structures, status, and wealth through issuing logging licenses. Official sources claim that the awarding of these licenses was an equitable process.[114] Sabah's chief secretary, for instance, stated that prospective license holders were assessed on a case-by-case basis to determine their capability and commitment to the job. But in reality, it was their record of service or loyalty to the state that would have mattered more. Licensing was thus mired in corruption and discrimination. In this sense, when elites were denied timber licenses (ostensibly due to a lack of requisite capital, manpower, equipment, or even experience), many felt that they were being rejected due to political affiliation or a lack of patronage, indicating preferential treatment of rivals. Irrespective of merit and intent, it was the already-established elites who were typically rewarded by the government with concessions.

But even those with demonstrable clout over large communities struggled to gain access to Sabah's timber wealth. Mustapha bin Harun, who was by the late 1950s firmly positioned as the foremost representative of the territory's indigenous Muslims, was repeatedly prevented from establishing a permanent logging enterprise on Jambongan Island, off Sabah's northeastern coast. As Mustapha's influence among local Muslim followers continued to grow throughout 1959 and 1960, he petitioned to colonial officers to reconsider its refusal. Observing growing local agitation among Mustapha's followers, the government was compelled to compromise, and it eventually granted Mustapha an annual license to operate a limited venture on the outskirts of the town of Kudat.[115] Not only was this a temporary license, but stringent controls were placed over where the timber could be sold, which was allowed only within the local Kudat area. This proved problematic for Mustapha; there would be little local demand for his product across Sabah's north coast. Local communities were virtually self-sufficient in the provision of timber, and the town of Kudat itself represented an oversaturated market. The prime buyers were located overseas in emerging industrial cities like Hong Kong, Tokyo, and Singapore.

Not only did Mustapha bin Harun's new license offer little in the way of profit, but it also triggered allegations among Kudat locals that the government was reviewing applications unfairly. John Dingle, a retired colonial officer and Kudat resident, reported to the conservator of forests in late 1960 that growing accusations of government favoritism were circulating throughout the town. Kudat's local Chinese community, in particular, were publicly opposed to Mustapha's new license. As Dingle noted, "Pak Min Chu [a Chinese leader in Kudat] . . . keeps moaning to me about the unfair treatment he has received over his timber application and his surprise at hearing D. M. [Datu Mustapha] is getting a licence, which he has already flogged to the Chinese."[116]

On hearing these complaints, R. N. Turner, the chief secretary, urged Kudat's district officer to investigate "the allegation" that Mustapha had had showed off his license to his rivals.[117] By granting Mustapha a license, the government had prompted communal rivalries to flare up. But had they continued to deny him a license, they risked alienating one of the territory's most powerful elites. Indeed, within weeks, scores of other *orang tuas* and local elites submitted new applications for timber licenses. Having witnessed Mustapha's successful application, Orang Tua Haji Abdul bin Rahim, a Jambongan Island resident, petitioned for a license to extract timber. Haji Abdul explained that he and his subjects wished to "jump on the timber band-wagon and grab a share of the profits" before it was too late, as "there soon may be no timber left on the island."[118] Many applicants, like Haji Abdul, hailed from families that had resided on Jambongan for generations, and they felt betrayed by the state's selective awarding of licenses to wealthier, more powerful local elites from Borneo's mainland.

Nevertheless, colonial attempts to pacify and appease Mustapha bin Harun ultimately failed, and his involvement in politics in the early 1960s became increasingly radicalized. Initially echoing the antigovernment sentiments of other prominent figures, such as Donald Stephens, Mustapha's speeches later adopted a volatile and at times even militant tone. On numerous occasions, debates came to a head in the territory's Legislative Council, which by 1962 had devolved into shouting matches divided along ethnic lines.[119] Initially envisioned to boost local representation and accountability in the governing of the territory, colonial efforts to expand local participation in the Legislative Council exposed the extent to which factionalism and ethnic discord now dominated Sabahan politics. Once a bastion of colonial orthodoxy and an echo chamber for metropolitan views, the council was increasingly beset by disputes between representatives of Sabah's main ethnic groups.

On the one hand, the rising ethnic discord proved fortuitous for the government because it largely drowned out the criticisms against colonial policy that had previously rattled administrators who were wary of "radicalism." On the other hand, these rivalries threatened to spill out onto the streets, which had hitherto been spared from ethnic discord and violence. These issues later proved problematic in Britain's and Malaya's push for strategic union between the Borneo territories and the Malayan Peninsula. During a Legislative Council meeting on July 13, 1963, ethnic tensions appeared to reach a boiling point. Mustapha bin Harun was renowned for being a particularly incendiary figure. In the council meeting he debated with the leaders of Sabah's Chinese community, Khoo Siak Chiew and Kwan Yui Ming, over issues of public support, and he later accused them of attempting to "buy over" and bribe his followers in Kudat. Since the 1940s, Kudat had witnessed major demographic change, with its already-sizable Chinese population boosted by steady immigration from Hong Kong and southern China. For years, Mustapha had vied with

Kudat's wealthy Chinese elites for supremacy. During one particularly aggressive exchange, Mustapha declared that if he lost influence to the Chinese—and if the Chinese "came into power" after decolonization—his supporters would take matters into their own hands. "My people will set fire to the houses of Chinese and kill them," he proclaimed. "Just think, my people are all over the place, on the hills and on the sea."[120] Mustapha, as a key Muslim leader, boasted of having supporters beyond Sabah's shores, among Suluk and other Muslim-minority communities scattered across the southern Philippines.[121] He sought to demonstrate to his rival council members and to colonial bureaucrats that his supporters were irrefutably loyal and existed in great numbers. Tensions were emerging too between Mustapha's Muslim followers and Donald Stephens's animist or Christian Kadazandusuns, both of which sought to present themselves as Sabah's original indigenous inhabitants.

Mustapha bin Harun was a complex figure. Although he purportedly sought to improve the lives of his supporters, he openly boasted of his desire for wealth, status, and personal gain. Colonial officials, ever wary of ambitious local elites and critical of those who deviated from stereotypical behavior, made detailed lists of his apparent vices. Government records on Mustapha noted his infractions, while memorandums sent between bureaucrats in Jesselton and Kudat derided him as a "womanizer" who sought the "bright lights" of London's clubs rather than uplifting his followers from poverty and hardship.[122] His threats of violence, while initially taken seriously, were later discounted as mere bluster. In an earlier biographical profile written in May 1960, for instance, officials condemned his habits as extravagant, as "reports continued to filter through . . . [of his] purchase of top hats, 40 suits," among other luxuries, during a trip to London to participate in English classes.[123] R. N. Turner described him as having "a very high idea of his own importance as a future leader of North Borneo" while also suffering from "an inferiority complex vis-à-vis his present colleagues (and possible future rivals)" such as Donald Stephens, Khoo Siak Chiew, and Kwan Yui Ming.[124]

Although the government largely dismissed Mustapha's rhetoric, he continued to espouse strong condemnations of the colonial system, declaring in 1962, for instance, that

> My words were mild—they were just like a hand grenade. At the next LegCo [Legislative Council] meeting in October, my speech will be like the explosion of an atomic bomb set to attack the government. These white people are still not contented. They have been exploiting the natives for a long time. At this juncture, when they are about to leave this place, they have instigated the Chinese into setting up political parties

to make an enemy of me. If I come to power one day, I will first deal with the big white men's firms.[125]

But little came of these threats, and gradually, they became part of Sabah's volatile and complex political landscape. Colonial bureaucrats, critical of Mustapha's vices—his ostensible covetousness, flamboyance, and apparent ill temper—believed that they had called his bluff. Although he condemned colonial rule, officials believed that he could still be pacified through promises of political power, status, and wealth. Ultimately, however, they did not have to pacify him, as local elite ambitions increasingly aligned with colonial interests in the run-up toward decolonization in the early 1960s.

Parallel to Sabah's transition from a rubber-producing territory under anachronistic company rule toward a reliance on timber exportation under formalized colonial control, were the major sociopolitical changes that took hold in local society. These changes—the emergence of local power brokers, the proliferation of indigenous-focused print media, and the deepening of ethnocultural identities and rivalries—radically altered life in the colony. While contributing to Sabah's constitutional development, these transformations also underscored its tenuous geopolitical positioning in an increasingly volatile Southeast Asia. Perhaps most significant, however, was the fact that much of this change was prompted not by colonial tutelage, but by local activism and community-driven desires for prosperity. And alongside these changes were the personal ambitions of—and interpersonal rivalries between—local elites, who cast scrutiny on colonial governance, resource extraction, and the territory's constitutional path.

As this chapter has demonstrated, Sabah emerged from a period of intense postwar suffering with its own brand of anticolonialism. Driven neither by the ideological propulsion of intelligentsia elites, nor by the emergence of any singular national identity, these local aspirations for change in Sabah were instead stirred by calls to end socioeconomic hardship and disenfranchisement and by the crystallization of elite ambition. Nevertheless, these local trends have been sidelined in traditional scholarship, which instead cites the absence of any conventional anticolonial movement, and the public's wider lack of interest in the concept of independence, as evidence of political inertia in Sabah. These were views initiated by colonial bureaucrats at the time who were confounded—if ultimately relieved—by the stark absence in Sabah of the type of anticolonialism that had emerged elsewhere in the colonized world. Indeed, this early historiographical precedent has been propped up by a continuing scholarly focus on metropolitan strategy in London and state-making designs in Malaya, at the expense of local agency in Sabah. This in turn underemphasizes the role played by the Borneo territories in configuring late colonial strategy and postcolonial state formation. Although Britain and Malaya were the primary architects of the Malaysia proposal, whose constitutional and ideological lineage can be traced to earlier attempts to consolidate and federalize the empire, its successful creation was predicated on the complicity of Sabah's local elites and the willingness of its wider population to embrace merger.

The public's early lack of interest in calls for political independence in Sabah—posited experimentally by local elites in the mid-1950s—and the commensurate intensification of ethnocultural divisions based on race, religion, and political opinions, laid the foundations that later enabled the Malaysian Federation. As demonstrated in this chapter, the deepening factional rifts among Stephens's Kadazandusuns, Mustapha bin Harun's Muslims, Khoo Siak Chiew's Chinese, and scores of minor elites led to a paradoxical acceptance of continued colonial mediation. Fearful of rival communities gaining power and influence, Sabah's emergent local elites begrudgingly lent the ineffectual colonial regime support. As will be discussed in chapter 5, this set a precedent later followed by elites as they navigated Anglo-Malayan policymaking amid the end of empire.

This chapter's focus on the legacies of chartered company–era indirect rule has also cast crucial light on the prevailing sociopolitical change and upheaval in Sabah. Whereas in the early twentieth century the company state professed its control over elite formation through certifying *orang tuas* and discrediting their noncompliant rivals, by the 1950s this system had all but collapsed. Newly energized elites, who assumed traditional as well as colonial roles, voiced their opposition to exclusionary resource extraction policies yet demonstrated a willingness to work within the colonial system. In the Legislative Council, as in remote *kampongs*, and increasingly through newspapers and public speeches, elites such as Donald Stephens and Mustapha bin Harun sought to advance their personal influence and standing, as well as the prosperity of their followers. Ultimately, the (re-)emergence of anticolonial voices in Sabah ushered major sociopolitical changes that set the territory on an uncertain path amid rising regional geopolitical interest and foreign desires for territorial expansion.

Part Two

Vying Archipelagos

CHAPTER 3

The Rise of the Kalimantan Utara Movement

The early 1960s was a period of immense change and uncertainty in Sabah. The emergence of outspoken local elites and a rising sense of political consciousness among marginalized indigenous groups over the previous decade contributed to major societal shifts. Since formal colonization in 1946, the new colonial state had demonstrated its reluctance to embrace change, instead relying on resource extraction and the compliance of local functionaries lured by kickbacks and inducements. But across Sabah, new aspirations abounded. The proliferation of print media, and the popularization of radio among urbanizing societies, rendered many in Sabah increasingly receptive to new politics, information, and ideas. Initially, this was beyond the colonial state's capacity to control.

Alongside this growing political engagement, however, came heightened fears of external domination. Contrary to the received wisdom, in which metropolitan bureaucrats (and successive generations of scholars) assumed that communism was the primary threat facing Sabah, public concerns centered on fears of subjugation by and assimilation into already-independent neighboring countries.[1] These public fears were not unfounded: by the early 1960s, Sabah lay at the epicenter of competing visions for postcolonial state formation and territorial expansion. This resulted in a sense of insecurity among rival elites and power brokers, in which desires for independence from Britain appeared increasingly contingent on acquiescing to foreign control from elsewhere in Southeast Asia. Regional powers expressing interest in acquiring Sabah was no new phenomenon. In Indonesia, following independence in 1949, politicians voiced their ambitions to incorporate British Borneo into an expanded Nusantara (Indonesian Archipelago).[2] Likewise, in the Philippines, the government drew on claims maintained by descendants of the Sulu Sultanate to lodge its own territorial assertions over Sabah.[3] Malaya, too, was viewed critically by indigenous Kadazandusuns and Muruts in Sabah who denounced the dictatorial and expansionist policies espoused by politicians in Kuala Lumpur.[4] And in Sabah, unimpeded by any credible nationalist or unified anticolonial movement, the colonial government operated with the bold assumption that it would remain in power until at least the 1970s.[5] For many observers and policymakers, the territory appeared too politically divided and too ethnically diverse to push for independence alone. Nevertheless, the road toward impending decolonization triggered regional instability. But rather than a local push for independence, it was the Anglo-Malayan plan to form Malaysia that thrust Sabah into geopolitical strife. Formally announced in mid-1961, Projek Malaysia was deeply controversial and spurred regional anticolonialists and expansionists alike to act on long-standing concerns about rising Anglo-Malayan influence. In neighboring Brunei, where anticolonial Bornean nationalists found refuge in the emergence of new political parties, Projek Malaysia incited public ire and led to a major uprising in December 1962. Led by Sheikh Azahari bin Sheikh Mahmud, the rebellion in Brunei failed to oust the British, but it led to the founding of Negara Kesatuan Kalimantan Utara (the Unitary State of Northern Borneo) in January 1963.

As this chapter demonstrates, the Kalimantan Utara movement materialized amid the failures of the Brunei Rebellion and swiftly capitalized on regional desires to undermine British colonialism in Borneo. Scattered across Southeast Asia, and eventually settling in Indonesia, Kalimantan Utara operated as a state-in-exile, assuming the form and function of an independent government without actually controlling any territory directly. Indonesia provided the lifeblood for Azahari's movement, and it was through the development of "The Voice of the Freedom Fighters of Kalimantan Utara," or Radio Kalimantan Utara, in early 1963 that the movement broadened its reach and sought to counteract Projek Malaysia with an alternative vision for a federation of Bornean states. Crucially, however, Radio Kalimantan Utara's broadcasts, with its proclamations tinged with foreign-sounding Malay Bahasa, failed to capture the hearts and minds of Sabah's public. The ensuing months saw people shy away from imaginings of independent Bornean statehood in favor of the Anglo-Malay plan to form Malaysia. It was in Projek Malaysia that many people found a more stable and peaceful decolonization alternative. Although observers considered Sabah's public receptive to foreign ideology and information, Kalimantan Utara's violence-tinged broadcasts and overt support for Indonesia's *revolusi* (revolution) paradoxically alienated the very grassroots communities in Sabah that it sought to impress.

Section one of this chapter explores the impact of the Malaysia plan on Southeast Asia, suggesting that it was part of a broader British attempt to expedite decolonization and an eagerness in Malaya to expand territorially by incorporating the British Borneo territories. This section further contends that contrary to conventional scholarship, Malaya's designs in Borneo reflected a wider pattern of geopolitical jostling between postcolonial states and revealed the expansionist ideals and archipelagic dreams harbored by its nationalist leaders. The second section examines Sheikh Azahari's ambitions of attaining independent Bornean statehood through looking at the failures of the Brunei Rebellion and the subsequent founding of the Kalimantan Utara movement. The emergence of provocative, often caustic, anticolonial and anti-Malaya radio broadcasts, covered in section three, played a crucial role in intensifying public and official anxieties over threats of foreign subversion. Section four argues that Sabah was gripped by rapid technological changes in early 1963, in which Radio Kalimantan Utara jostled for airtime and popularity with its rival colonial station, Radio Sabah. Finally, this chapter concludes by examining how despite its access to cutting-edge radio equipment and calls for violent anticolonial revolution, Kalimantan Utara withered away into obscurity and obsolescence. Calls for independent Bornean statehood had by mid-1963 become tinged by Indonesian influences, which paradoxically boosted the popularity of the rival Malaysia plan among Sabah's diverse public.

Aggression Archipelago

The Anglo-Malayan plan to create the Federation of Malaysia was first revealed publicly during a speech delivered by Malaya's prime minister, the Tunku Abdul Rahman, at a Foreign Correspondents' Association luncheon on May 27, 1961.[6] Devised to combine peninsular Malaya with Singapore, Brunei, Sabah, and Sarawak, the plan purported to transform what was once a loose colonial bloc into a Malay-majority postcolonial state.[7] Almost immediately, it thrust Southeast Asia into a contentious tumult.[8] Prior to decolonization, Britain had considered the idea of merging its Malayan territories with those in Borneo on numerous occasions throughout the 1880s, the 1930s, the late 1940s, and again in the 1950s.[9] Despite this pattern of continual interest, plans for merger were repeatedly dropped by the British, who cast doubt on the ethnic and cultural compatibility of the two disparate regions. Added to this was the fact that in the early 1960s, British colonial administrators, and indeed even many Malayan politicians and local Sabahan power brokers, believed that Sabah was not yet capable of transitioning to independent self-governance alone.[10] Postwar educational, social, and infrastructural development remained critically slow and ineffectual. Furthermore, Sabah had yet to fully recover from the effects of crippling wartime atrocities, in which, for instance, the Japanese had in 1944 engaged in the "mass execution of all the intelligentsia on whom they could lay their hands."[11] Many also considered Sabah strategically vulnerable to Philippine and Indonesian aggression.[12] Projek Malaysia was spun as a solution to these issues.[13] It was a pragmatic option for Britain, which wanted to streamline its imperial withdrawal, as it was for postcolonial Malaya, which actively sought territory, resources, and an ethnically malleable indigenous population whom it could reclassify as Malay *bumiputera* (sons of the soil).[14] Publicly across wider British Borneo, it was portrayed as a way of decolonizing from Britain while retaining strategic backing from another metropole, only this time Kuala Lumpur rather than London.[15] And for those fearful of foreign influence, Projek Malaysia was advertised as a defense against subversion and depredation. British and Malayan policymakers argued that without such safeguards, Sabah would surely fall to advances from either Indonesia or the Philippines, or as feared by those in the West with Cold War mind-sets, perhaps even the Soviet Union or China.[16]

The proclamation of the Malaysia plan nevertheless elicited widespread condemnation across Southeast Asia. Although initially popular among the political elite in Malaya, Singapore, and even in Brunei, it swiftly drew international criticism over its ostensibly expansionist undertones. Malaya's continuing affiliation with Britain, especially during the Malayan Emergency, fueled further allegations that the Tunku Abdul Rahman harbored neocolonial designs and sympathies for British interests. As discussed in chapter 1, Britain's ambitions of colonial consolidation, revived amid the ruins of the Second World War, saw imperial policymakers turn increasingly to Southeast Asia in an attempt to salvage international influence and relevance. Indeed, it was in Southeast Asia that Britain managed to paradoxically enlarge its colonial empire in 1946 through the annexation of Sabah and Sarawak at a time of imperial decline elsewhere. This was a particularly significant, if rather ironic, process, considering the protracted wars of colonial suppression waged contemporaneously in Southeast Asia by the Dutch and the French that ended in catastrophic failure. Likewise, Malaya's peaceful independence transition in 1957, and its partnership with British and commonwealth forces during the Emergency, presented a very different image of postcolonial statehood to that which arose from the outcomes of the bloody independence wars nearby. In fact, the notion of the "Little Empire" that was popularized in the late 1940s, with Malaya at its heart as a miniature metropole, appeared alarmingly close to fruition.[17] This was especially the case with regard to the unfolding Cold War drama of the late 1950s and the early 1960s, in which the Tunku Abdul Rahman's vocal anticommunism and Malaya's victory over the communists during the Emergency came as a boost to British (and indeed American) foreign policy interests.[18]

In conventional historiography, Malaya is seldom considered an expansionist power.[19] For decades, scholars have perpetuated orthodox colonial assurances that Malaya was a rational and conformist actor in postcolonial Southeast Asia. Traditional Cold War narratives draw from descriptions of the Tunku Abdul Rahman an image of a "relaxed, tolerant, and affable" statesman who "carried the imprimatur of English politicians."[20] This was a leader who could not be more different from President Sukarno, who was contrastingly described as a "demagogue" set on territorial expansion.[21] Such perceptions of the Tunku conveniently supported wider characterizations of Southeast Asia as a place divided by Cold War ideologies. This was a bipolarity in which liberal, Western-oriented states ostensibly served as a defense against communism and territorial aggression.[22] But the reality was vastly more complex and Southeast Asia was beset with fears of expansionism from all corners. Whether the spread of communism on the one hand, or the extension of (neo)colonialism on the other, every state saw itself as vulnerable to some form of foreign subversion or another. For Indonesia, the perceived continuation of colonial influences in neighboring countries presented an existential threat. Indeed, few places were more threatening to Indonesia than Malaya and the British Borneo territories, the former a Melayu archrival, and the latter a colonial thorn in its side. But for British and American policymakers who lauded the Tunku's anticommunist convictions and willingness to work with Western security bodies such as the Southeast Asian Treaty Organization (SEATO), it was epistemologically impossible to consider Malaya neocolonialist or expansionist. Furthermore, it was politically advantageous for Britain that Malaya was presented as both nonthreatening and as a decolonization success story. On the eve of the formation of Malaysia in 1963, for instance, George Petty-Fitzmaurice, Marquess of Lansdowne and minister of state for commonwealth and colonial affairs, declared that there was no reason to judge Malaya's actions "in any way antagonistic to Indonesia."[23] Inundated with glaring inaccuracies, such statements set the tone in the West, and these attitudes have remained largely steadfast ever since. Indonesian condemnations of Malaya as expansionist, and descriptions of the Malaysia plan as the embodiment of *nekolim* (neocolonialism) are frequently dismissed as Konfrontasi-era bluster and opprobrium.[24]

This has clouded scholarly and wider public perceptions of Malaya's role in Southeast Asia in the 1950s and early 1960s, especially concerning the experience of the British Borneo territories. By the early twenty-first century, however, recent historiographical interventions have cast new light on the role of Malaya in aggravating regional tensions in the years preceding the formation of Malaysia in 1963.[25] This builds on two broader strands in Southeast Asian history that mark an important departure from colonial-sponsored orthodoxy and Cold War bipolarity. First, the focus on American and British subversive activities and covert operations in the 1950s and 1960s has led to renewed scrutiny of policies advocating communist containment and regime change in Indonesia, in which Malaya was actively complicit.[26] Second, a reconceptualization of Indonesia that indicates the extent that it was a crisis-ridden and vulnerable state that had to respond to the concurrent threats of internal fragmentation, socioeconomic disarray, regional political instability, and external pressures.[27] This has enabled scholars to step beyond the conventional analyses of Indonesian foreign policy that are so frequently riven by colonial-era panic and ideological bias.

It is with this in mind that the renewed attention paid to Southeast Asian rivalries attains added importance. Indeed, as Wen-Qing Ngoei points out, postcolonial Malaya was a state "bent on regional expansionism."[28] And although the Tunku Abdul Rahman was widely perceived as a conciliatory and decorous public figure, Joseph Chinyong Liow contends that he was "equally capable of *realpolitik* readings of the geopolitical circumstances confronting his country and of the 'Machiavellian' politics . . . necessary to secure" its interests.[29] Likewise, while Projek Malaysia "served the Tunku's expansionist ambitions," it was not the first time that Malayan policymakers had expressed their interest in absorbing the Borneo territories into an enlarged federation, with intimations made as early as 1957.[30]

But Borneo was not the sole target of Malaya's interest. Across the Straits of Malacca, in Sumatra, where locals shared with their counterparts on the Malayan Peninsula a long-standing "aversion to Javanese dominance," the Malayan government found a strategic outlook in rising secessionist ambitions along the Indonesian periphery.[31] With the outbreak of full-scale rebellion in Sumatra in early 1958 and the subsequent founding of the breakaway Peremintah Revolusioner Republik Indonesia (Revolutionary Government of the Republic of Indonesia) (PRRI), Malaya was quick to support the secessionist cause.[32] Malaya actively facilitated American and British support for the Sumatran rebels: arms and strategic materiel were airdropped into Sumatra "from airfields in the Philippines, Taiwan, Thailand, and Malaya," with numerous airplanes flying directly from Singapore's Changi Airport.[33] Although the Malayan government publicly denied its involvement in the affair, little effort was made to hide its support for the Sumatran rebels. Much to Indonesia's resentment, Malaya granted Sumatran revolutionary exiles a safe haven in Kuala Lumpur, from where they continued to spin their calls for secession, conduct fund-raising exercises, disseminate propaganda, and even "utilise Malaya's military facilities for their operations."[34] The Sumatran exiles found an eager audience in political circles across Kuala Lumpur, amplifying their rhetoric considerably.[35] Perhaps more important, however, were the Malayan government's calls for Sumatra to secede from Indonesia and merge with the Federation of Malaya.[36] Many of Malaya's ruling elite considered Sumatra "an integral part of the Semananjung Melayu [the Malay Peninsula]," and most were "outright pro-Sumatran."[37] These sentiments were heightened by the long-standing sense of rivalry between Malaya and Indonesia: each vied for primacy in maritime Southeast Asia and touted competing visions of archipelagic unity.[38] In addition to this, there was a wider ontological tension in Malay thought between perceptions of revolutionary *semangat* (spirit) and *permuda* (youth), as advocated in postcolonial Indonesia, and the "bureaucratic finesse and elitism that characterised the relationship of traditional Malay leadership with their colonial counterparts" in Malaya.[39] This tension further manifested in distinctions between Indonesia's experience of independence through violent struggle and Malaya's peaceful decolonization, which skeptics dismissed as "counterfeit independence" and "a gift from the colonial power."[40]

By the late 1950s, Southeast Asia was embittered by heady rivalries and attempts to reorder the region's geopolitical composition by means of subversion and territorial aggression. With the announcement of Projek Malaysia in May 1961, these tensions only continued to intensify.

Dreams of Bornean Statehood: A Failed Uprising

Although lauded by Anglo-Malayan policymakers as a grand solution, the newly proclaimed Malaysia plan was not welcomed across all quarters. Official enquiries indicated that public opinion in Sabah and Sarawak was split evenly among strong support, firm opposition, and indecision toward the proposal.[41] But anticolonial and nationalist sentiments had been stirring across wider Borneo since the mid-1950s, most prominently in neighboring Brunei.[42] The founding of Parti Rakyat Brunei (the Brunei People's Party) in August 1956 by Sheikh Azahari bin Sheikh Mahmud signaled the rise of local political consciousness in a territory historically dominated by its absolute monarchy. A leftist organization that strove to bring about greater political representation and eventually independence, Parti Rakyat Brunei threatened the status quo, in which the Brunei Sultanate enjoyed considerable autonomy and colonial interests were safeguarded.[43] As one editorial stated in 1957, "Prodded by the People's party, the young men of Brunei are gradually getting angrier."[44]

These anticolonial sentiments were later amplified by the announcement of Projek Malaysia in 1961. Parti Rakyat Brunei's followers were typically young, working-class individuals employed on rubber plantations, on logging estates, and in grassroots businesses.[45] Many of them grew increasingly outraged because they did not want their country to be subsumed by a dominant peninsular Malaya. Colonial advisors in Brunei were quick to disregard this opposition, however, with Dennis White, the British high commissioner, dismissing Parti Rakyat Brunei as a mere "boyscout camp."[46] These sentiments were shared by many in the British government, with one official remarking in early 1959 that "the party today is in its doldrums."[47] This failure to take the movement seriously allowed it to develop right under the colonial watch. When this rumbling unrest reached a violent head in Brunei on December 8, 1962, the uprising was described by the British as coming as a "complete surprise."[48] In an attempt to explain their mishandling of the situation, metropolitan policymakers lamented that it was "extremely difficult to be in the possession of first-class intelligence" in such a territory with "vast tracts of jungle."[49]

Despite failing to take the movement seriously and lacking credible intelligence, colonial forces crushed the uprising decisively. But widespread public skepticism toward Britain and the Malaysia plan lingered across Brunei.[50] The revolt was led by Sheikh Azahari, leader of Parti Rakyat Brunei and its paramilitary arm, Tentara Nasional Kalimantan Utara (the National Army of Northern Borneo).[51] Under Azahari's leadership, the movement sought to bring about independence and to establish a Bornean state comprising Brunei, Sabah, and Sarawak, referred to as "Kalimantan Utara." Although faced with military defeat, Azahari claimed in December 1962 that "the struggle will continue and we will not lay down arms until the last British colonizer is expelled and until an independent Kalimantan Utara state is born."[52] Azahari argued that independence for, and unity among, the three Borneo territories was key to resisting foreign territorial overtures. He further appealed to public concerns over political subversion across the region, arguing that "if we merge with Malaysia we will be controlled by the communists."[53] Although Azahari found a continuing audience among radicals in Borneo who opposed foreign influence, he expressed bitter disappointment at the public's failure to participate in the anticolonial uprising. "The rebellion aimed to liberate their country from occupation," he complained, and the "action of the British army is a cruelty to the people of Brunei."[54] The uprising failed to achieve any of its objectives, and in its wake, Parti Rakyat Brunei was dissolved and its members cast adrift.[55]

But the movement was far from over. After the failures of December 1962, the group scattered transnationally across Asia. Sheikh Azahari and his close followers fled to Manila, and others dispersed across the seas to Singapore and Hong Kong, while many of the movement's rank-and-file members melted into Borneo's interior, seeking refuge in distant *kampongs*.[56] In Brunei, close contacts who remained were arrested, including Azahari's wife, Shamsiati.[57] In Singapore, defiant supporters circulated pamphlets that foretold the impending "Revolusi Nasional Kalimantan Utara" ("National Revolution in Northern Borneo").[58] Adrift in Hong Kong, one former Parti Rakyat Brunei member defected and handed themselves in to the British, fearing assassination.[59] Azahari, meanwhile, having received a warm welcome in Manila, formally proclaimed the founding of Negara Kesatuan Kalimantan Utara (the Unitary State of Northern Borneo), his proposed state that was devised to counteract the Malaysia plan.[60] Its territorial extents, as proposed by Azahari, are detailed below in map 2. He declared himself Kalimantan Utara's prime minister, appointed his closest aides to key ministerial positions, and drafted a manifesto for excising British colonialism from Borneo.[61] At thirty-five years of age, Azahari was young and charismatic. Alex Josey, writing for the *Straits Times* in January 1963, gained exclusive access to interview Azahari, who was guarded night and day by Philippine secret police at an undisclosed hotel in Manila. Josey described Azahari as "well dressed, confident and relaxed" and as a "remarkable orator" who spoke about his anticolonial movement's plans with "enormous vitality." Azahari's arrival drew considerable excitement. One Indonesian resident living in Manila even described him as a "good junior Sukarno" who would soon become the "Sukarno of Borneo," a comparison intended to bestow great flattery.[62]

Kalimantan Utara's nascent cabinet-in-exile was remarkably young, and the movement drew on a stream of followers from the defunct Parti Rakyat Brunei.[63] Azahari appointed Zaini Haji Ahmed, who was twenty-eight years old, as his minister for economics, while Awang Abdul Hapidz bin Laksamana and Abang Ahmend Zulkipli, both in their mid-twenties, were selected as minister for labor and lieutenant general of the Tentara Nasional Kalimantan Utara, respectively.[64] Alex Josey described how these ministers appeared to unwaveringly back Azahari when he proclaimed that while his "army is in the jungle . . .

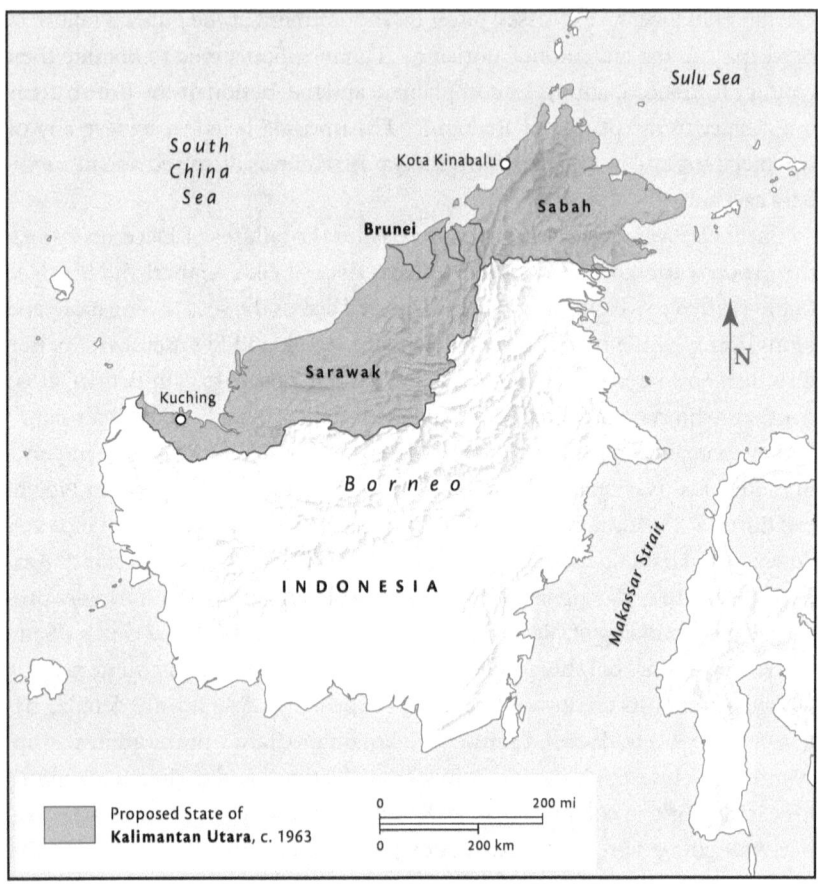

MAP 2. Map detailing the proposed state of Kalimantan Utara, comprising Sabah, Brunei, and Sarawak, circa 1963. Map by Erin Greb Cartography.

if tomorrow I ordered them into the streets to fight, they will obey."[65] But many colonial administrators and Western analysts continued to disregard the movement as an empty threat, with L. C. Hoffman, editor in chief of the *Straits Times*, dismissing Azahari as having "a complete lack of knowledge of what went on in Brunei."[66]

Although disregarded by observers, Kalimantan Utara soon established itself on the international stage. And no platform was better for cementing anticolonial intentions than that of the Non-Aligned Movement. Indeed, Sheikh Azahari sent a delegation to the February 1963 Afro-Asian Conference in Moshi, Tanganyika, led by a Bruneian youth named Abdullah Salim Mohamed, who served concurrently as Kalimantan Utara's minister of state and ambassador to Indonesia.[67] Mohamed's attendance at the conference in Tanganyika sparked widespread controversy over his staunchly anti-Malaysia agenda and alleged Indonesian ties.[68] Decrying Projek Malaysia as a "disease," Mohamed called on the participants to instead recognize Kalimantan Utara's anticolonial struggle and its plan for a unified Bornean federation.[69] It was here that the rivalry between Malaysia and Kalimantan Utara attained increased international attention. Kalimantan Utara's participation, coupled with the emerging geopolitical rifts over the formation of Malaysia, dominated the event and split the Non-Aligned Movement into two camps. Having witnessed an emergent rupture in the movement between support for either Indonesian or Malayan interests, pundits declared the Moshi summit a "fiasco."[70] But the Tanganyika Conference was a boon for Kalimantan Utara. Having stood shoulder to shoulder with representatives from independent postcolonial states at the conference, the movement could now claim a veneer of legitimacy. This proved particularly valuable for Azahari as such conferences were "arena[s] to reify new Asian post-colonial states."[71]

And it was reification that Kalimantan Utara needed most urgently. With its ministerial positions filled, with the promise of regional support from Indonesia secured, and with the hope of drawing support from across Borneo and wider Southeast Asia still alive, Kalimantan Utara had assumed the architecture of an anticolonial state-in-exile. All the movement needed was physical territory, funds, materiel, and concrete evidence of public support in Borneo. Indeed, by early February 1963, it had appeared to rise from the ashes of the failed uprising in Brunei; it had attended a Non-Aligned Movement conference; it had poured additional scrutiny on allegations of Malayan territorial expansionism; and it had attracted considerable international media coverage throughout. Drawing from the wealth of past nationalist and independence movements that lingered in recent memory in Southeast Asia, Kalimantan Utara under Sheikh Azahari feigned functionality, legitimacy, and even statehood, mimicking past anticolonial victories with heady confidence.[72]

But not everyone was convinced. British colonial officials continued to downplay the movement, while members of the public, too, voiced their skepticism. During a period of particularly devastating flooding in Borneo during the monsoon season in January 1963, one commentator in Singapore attempted to call Azahari's bluff, questioning what the "self-styled Prime Minister . . . has done for his people. Did he order his 'army' to help the refugees? Did he order his 'government' to send funds . . . ?" Then the commentator asserted that "the answer must be in the negative for he [Azahari] has neither army nor money."[73]

Although many disregarded the movement as little more than a publicity stunt, regional anticolonialists sought to take advantage of the opportunity presented by Kalimantan Utara to aid their own struggle against British colonialism, Malayan influence, and Projek Malaysia. The exiled movement desperately needed political and financial support, and though it had failed to oust the British, its fervently anticolonial cause continued to resonate among some elements of society in Brunei, Sabah, and Sarawak, and across wider Southeast Asia. Although shrouded in controversy, the Anglo-Malayan Cobbold Commission of Enquiry conducted earlier in 1962 had indicated that roughly one-third of Sabah's and Sarawak's publics remained staunchly opposed to the idea of Malaysia.[74] For Kalimantan Utara, there was hope that this contingent of Malaysia-skeptics would latch onto ideas of attaining authentic *merdeka*. In addition to independence, Azahari pledged to introduce a "guided national economy" in which "workers would be especially safeguarded."[75] Regionally, the movement proved popular among political elites in the Philippines and Indonesia who saw it as an opportunity to undermine British and Malayan influence in Borneo. Across Southeast Asia, many flocked to court the young revolutionaries with offers of assistance. But all of this threatened to turn Kalimantan Utara, like Sumatra's secessionist rebels in 1958, into a pawn in Southeast Asia's spiraling geopolitical divisions.

Soon after arriving in Manila, Sheikh Azahari entered talks with Cipriano Cid and Ignacio Lacsina, leaders of the Philippine Trade Union Council and Katipunan ng Manggagawang Pilipino (the Union of Filipino Workers), who offered to send "volunteers to fight in Borneo."[76] Aided by Filipino supporters, Azahari even held "secret meetings" with descendants of the Sulu Sultanate, such as Princess Tarhata Kiram, to divide Bornean territory between them. Others in the Philippines, such as Congressman Godofredo Ramos, were also supportive of Kalimantan Utara in principle but stopped short of advocating armed intervention. Although Ramos urged the Philippine government to extend "sympathy and support" to Azahari's cause, he stressed that it must "oppose the recognition of Kalimantan Utara so long as it included North Borneo [Sabah]," for this was, he claimed, a Philippine domain.[77]

Contemporaneously in the Philippines, a succession of private claims and lawsuits had been lodged against Britain over contested territory in Sabah.[78] Since 1961, the Sabah question had dominated Filipino politics, culminating in President Diosdado Macapagal's announcement in 1962 of a formal territorial claim over Sabah.[79] In this period, numerous Filipino descendants of the defunct Sultanate of Sulu petitioned Britain asserting their "equal and legitimate rights" over Sabah.[80] Nicasio Osmeña, a prominent Filipino lawyer, supported many of these claims pro bono, having publicly opposed British colonialism in the region for decades.[81] His frequent lawsuits and public declarations attracted significant media attention across the Philippines, Sabah, and Malaya, and made him a well-known, if divisive, figure.[82] On hearing of Azahari's arrival in the Philippines, Osmeña approached him with offers to serve as his lawyer, seeking to capitalize on the movement's notoriety following the Brunei revolt.[83] Azahari would take all the help he could get; Kalimantan Utara now had a legal team.

But due to conflicting aims, their relationship was short lived. The mood swiftly soured in late January 1963 after it transpired that Azahari would not allow his movement to be used to further Osmeña's goals of bringing Sabah under Philippine rule. And like Godofredo Ramos, Osmeña was unwilling to support Kalimantan Utara if it conflicted with the Philippines' claims over Sabah. Eventually, Osmeña ceased to support the movement, but not before publicly disavowing it and castigating Azahari as a liar. "That man Azahari has told me so many lies," declared Osmeña, "he is so irresponsible. He's a bum, he's a liar. He's nuts." Media outlets across Southeast Asia eagerly picked up on this public humiliation, with some ridiculing Azahari as an unhinged "rebel," a "woman-chaser," and a "self-styled Prime Minister . . . whose own lawyer describes him as 'a bum.'"[84] In Sabah, colonial officials increasingly disregarded him as a spent force.

But rumor and hearsay continued to spread. Newspapers in Malaya ran frequent publications questioning what had happened to Kalimantan Utara, weighing up the various possibilities and serializing the story as if it were a work of fiction or a soap opera.[85] The cast was young, enigmatic, and, for opponents and supporters alike, deeply fascinating. The setting—the jungles of Borneo—evoked intrigue for urbanites in Singapore, Kuala Lumpur, Ipoh, and Johor Bahru, as it did for those in Jesselton, Kuching, and Sandakan. Some reporters suggested that having outstayed its welcome in Manila, Kalimantan Utara had fled to Jakarta, while another wrote fancifully that Azahari had "parachuted into the Brunei jungle from a Garuda Airways airliner" to serve his people, with a *parang* (knife) in hand.[86] One column in the Malayan newspaper *Berita Harian*, titled "Kesenyapan Azahari" ("Azahari's Silence"), offered updates regarding his purported whereabouts. "The world must have wondered what had happened to the Brunei rebels," it wrote to an eager readership, blending rumor with conjecture.[87] It explored various scenarios before concluding that Azahari was most likely in Indonesia, because "it is hard to believe that Azahari would have returned to Brunei," where he would face immediate arrest.[88] Despite this voracious public appetite for information, few details could be verified at the time, and for a brief period in February 1963, all went quiet in Borneo.

The Sound of Terror

One evening in early March 1963, an unsettling sound was projected across the airwaves over Borneo. Between 7:50 p.m. and 8:30 p.m. on March 5, those who were tuned in to the 25-meter band of shortwave radio would have heard the first chilling broadcasts of a new radio station.[89] It proclaimed itself anti-British, anticolonial, and vehemently anti-Malaysia. Its declared purpose was to stand for the oppressed peoples of British Borneo and deliver them *merdeka*. Later that month, on March 25, the same radio station ran a series of threatening proclamations, speeches, and even "poems."[90] Amid bursts of static and radio noise, one such "poem" declared:

> We shall destroy the Malaysia Federation by every method possible
> Those who obstruct us
> Will be killed by us, we shall drink their blood,
> Slice their flesh and break their bones.[91]

And so, "The Voice of the Freedom Fighters of Kalimantan Utara" had come on air. With its radio waves broadcast over hundreds of miles of dense jungle, the projection of foreign ideologies across Borneo had suddenly become markedly more penetrative. Anyone with access to a radio receiver would have been able to listen to its daily multilingual broadcasts.[92] Colonial officials scurried to discern how Kalimantan Utara's threats of revolution, murder, and impending attack were being broadcast so far and wide. That the programs were broadcast using advanced radio transmission technology caused great alarm within the colonial administration. Little could be done to assuage public fears.[93]

What characterized this new form of radio-based anticolonialism as unusual in Borneo—especially in comparison to historical instances of localized rebellion—was the fact that it was a technologically advanced and foreign-aided project. The radio transmissions sought to not only counter Western colonialism and Malayan expansionism but also shift public opinion toward supporting Kalimantan Utara as a viable alternative to Projek Malaysia. Through this, Kalimantan Utara could advance the revolutionary traditions of *semangat* (spirit) and *permuda* (youth) that had been popularized by Indonesia since its war of independence. In so doing, however, Azahari's movement also purported to align with Indonesia's goals of incorporating the entirety of Borneo under its sphere of influence, as part of an enlarged Nusantara.[94] Although this risked undermining promises of independent Bornean statehood, it was a symbolic way of resisting Malayan influences and the perceived threat of assimilation into an expanded Semananjung Melayu. Although Azahari had resisted overtures from anticolonial leaders in the Philippines, his movement's survival later depended on securing assistance from Indonesia, even if this meant acquiescing to its national goals.[95] Initially, alignment with Indonesia proved fruitful for Azahari and his movement: his state-in-exile had gained an audience at the Afro-Asian Conference; it had secured vital funds; it had obtained advanced radio apparatus; and it had ostensible backing from a leading postcolonial state. But this positivity did not last long, and its Indonesian links were swiftly viewed with deep suspicion across Sabah and Sarawak, where people were more tolerant toward British colonialism and the idea of Malaysia and where an aversion toward Indonesian influences was widespread.[96]

The advent of subversive radio in early 1963 came as a shock to Sabah's public. Those who owned radios, and those who gathered at shops, teahouses, and public venues with wireless receivers listened with anxious curiosity to the daily broadcasts of "The Voice of the Freedom Fighters of Kalimantan Utara" (also referred to as Radio Kalimantan Utara). Across Borneo, some listeners "expressed annoyance that such hostile propaganda should be directed at their country."[97] Others simply turned their receivers off. But importantly, the serialized rumors that had played out in the pages of *Berita Harian* and the *Straits Times* suddenly sprang to life over the airwaves, interrupting people as they went about their daily lives with threats of death and destruction. Some now wondered if Azahari had actually parachuted into the jungles of Borneo; perhaps the stories were true after all. Indeed, since late 1962, rumors had circulated of the existence of a guerrilla army hiding in the borderlands separating Sabah and Sarawak from Brunei.[98] The broadcasts breathed life into fanciful tales and rumors that had permeated communities across Sabah. In January 1963, it was claimed in the *Straits Times* that as many as twenty-one battalions comprising "between 800 and 1,200" soldiers were roaming the jungles of Sabah and Sarawak, stoking public alarm. Colonial authorities later concluded that the number of "rebel remnants" in Borneo numbered as few as 300, but concerns persisted.[99] The "rebel" fighters were believed to be everywhere, and yet nowhere. The public was on tenterhooks.

Initially, no one knew where the radio broadcasts were coming from. Colonial officials, concerned about their destabilizing effects, brought in specialists from Britain to conduct radio triangulation exercises. They soon concluded that the radio station was operating from a distance of at least five hundred miles, and for the signals to cover the entirety of Borneo, the broadcasts must have originated from somewhere with "good studio and transmission facilities." Fingers were pointed toward Indonesia after "radio direction finding tests . . . made it abundantly clear" that the station was operating from

Jakarta.¹⁰⁰ Other capable transmission facilities were later known to exist in the neighboring Indonesian city of Bogor.¹⁰¹

Radio Kalimantan Utara heralded a new era of energized and technologically advanced anticolonialism in Borneo. While the politicization of the airwaves was neither a new nor a unique phenomenon globally, it signaled the rapidly shifting pace of opposition toward British colonialism and Malayan influence in Southeast Asia, which was increasingly spearheaded by Indonesia.¹⁰² Crucially, however, these new anticolonial radio transmissions sought to not only unravel Western imperialism but also supplant it with a new form of territorial expansion that was itself markedly colonial in nature. Although Kalimantan Utara initially professed to push for independent Bornean statehood, it swiftly became a vehicle for advancing Indonesia's dreams of an expanded Nusantara. These disputes echo the events in Sumatra in 1958, in which the local uprising received foreign assistance, at the risk of being subsumed into Malaya's own visions of archipelagic unity via an enlarged Semananjung Melayu. But in Borneo, many of Sabah's indigenous communities had long been skeptical of foreign rule under any form, whether British, Japanese, or indeed even Malayan. And locally, there was rising antagonism toward prospects of Indonesian domination.¹⁰³

The Battle for the Airwaves

Throughout the summer of 1963, Radio Kalimantan Utara's broadcasts continued to reach communities across Sabah and Sarawak. Transmissions such as the strident anti-Malaysia "poem" aired on March 25 marked an intensification of Kalimantan Utara's subversive efforts. The radio broadcasts elicited disquiet among Sabah's ruling colonial elite too. For many colonials in Borneo, the radio transmissions and the threats of bloodshed emanated from distant regions in ways that recalled age-old fears of "native" insurrection. While historically, colonial anxieties in Borneo had derived from orientalized and often exaggerated or fictionalized physical threats—whether "headhunters," man-eating tigers, jungle uprisings, or mysterious tropical diseases—they were now fueled by clandestine radio broadcasts that gripped the territory with little sign of reprieve.

This was the first time that radio had been used in such a way in Sabah, although radio was not a new phenomenon in late colonial Southeast Asia.¹⁰⁴ Indonesia's rapid transformation from a Dutch colony to a bastion of anticolonialism after the Second World War significantly altered regional geopolitics in Southeast Asia. Amid these major changes—shaped by strife and uncertainty—radio transformed from a primarily colonial cultural phenomenon into a political tool for promoting postcolonial national unity. Radio first emerged in the Dutch East Indies in 1925 when a group of enthusiasts founded Bataaviasche Radio Vereening (the Batavia Radio Association), an amateur station that aired Western music from a hotel room in Jakarta. The popularity of radio grew rapidly over the subsequent decade. By 1934, Bataaviasche Radio Vereening was designated an official government station, but it remained "primarily a medium for entertainment and culture rather than news and information." After the Second World War, although radio's popularity continued to grow, the prewar colonial stations did not reappear in Indonesia.[105] They were swiftly replaced by a series of postcolonial, state-controlled initiatives such as Radio Republik Indonesia, which took over the old Dutch broadcasting facilities to deliver political messages and proclamations across the entire archipelago.[106]

Compared to Indonesia, where incipient broadcasting emerged initially for entertainment before transitioning into a tool for nationalist propaganda, radio in Sabah had different origins. With a smaller population, and with its port towns considered less developed than other Southeast Asian settlements, there was initially a reduced demand for bespoke radio-based entertainment. Despite this, radio infrastructure did progress in Sabah at a rapid pace, although it was primarily curated for colonial ears and administrative functions. As early as 1908, the North Borneo Chartered Company pursued the construction of an ambitious network for radio telegraphy to replace its aging and vulnerable overland communications system. Contact between colonial outposts, separated by stretches of intractable jungle, remained a priority for administrators. The government quickly understood that radio communication could better penetrate the interior compared to traditional overland, river, or air-travel routes. Wireless systems also afforded greater reliability than the older systems of wired telegraphy, which were frequently disrupted by floods, landslides, and even herds of wild elephants that were known to stampede through the jungle. After the Second World War, however, much of Sabah's early radio infrastructure lay in ruin, having either been bombed or neglected after years of disuse. Reestablishing facilities for communication was one of the postwar administration's primary objectives, but as with much of Southeast Asia, repair projects were undercut by crippling resource and manpower deficits.[107]

Public demand for entertainment and news services grew rapidly in the postwar years.[108] But it was only in the late 1950s that radio in Sabah fully emerged as a viable competitor to print media, fueled by the arrival of cheaper plastic radio receivers from Japan and Hong Kong. The popularization of these receivers rendered the British Borneo territories increasingly receptive to radio-based propaganda. Ronald Brooks, director of Sabah's newly founded Information Office, warned of the potential dangers posed by "subversive" radio as early as 1952.[109] But these concerns were not initially shared by the Colonial Office in London. Metropolitan officials instead prioritized the perceived threat posed by communism in Southeast Asia through clandestine associations and the infiltration of migrants from China, for whom Sabah's ports were popular destinations.[110] Brooks contrastingly argued that the "greatest threat to the security of Sabah might well be the voices coming over the airwaves." While Sabah had made considerable gains in the 1950s relative to the immediate postwar years, much of its population remained in poverty. These "less well off" people who had "suffered badly during occupation," Brooks warned, were most vulnerable to foreign subversion over the airwaves. Under Brooks's direction, Sabah's Information Office sought to preemptively "combat hostile thought coming out of the air" by "swamping the air channels with [their] own story of events."[111]

This led to the establishment of Radio Sabah in early 1952 to deliver "experimental" midday news and cultural programs in English, Malay, Mandarin, Cantonese, and Hakka. Ronald Brooks claimed that these daily broadcasts rapidly became popular. Indeed, by late 1952 it was reported that "there was hardly a Chinese shop in the main streets of Jesselton which did not have its set tuned loudly listening to [the] broadcasts."[112] Gradually, the government took notice and Radio Sabah's operators later received specialist training at the Canadian Broadcasting Corporation (CBC) and the British Broadcasting Corporation (BBC), funded by Colombo Plan grants.[113] By the late 1950s, Radio Sabah's transmissions had joined the ranks of the English, Malay, Cantonese, and Mandarin channels of the BBC's Overseas Service in disseminating empire-curated news and information. Listeners of Radio Sabah from Sandakan and Kudat, and even as far away as Hong Kong, "expressed appreciation of the radio coverage" that contained a "programme of music" and even "quiz programmes" that were particularly popular among schoolchildren.[114] Requests were repeatedly made for the addition of a regular Kadazandusun-language series to Radio Sabah.[115] Across Sabah, the public's appetite for radio consumption was voracious, painting a picture of a society that was plugged into the very latest in cultural, informational, and political content.

As Indonesian hostility intensified in the late 1950s, the colonial government sought to strengthen the coverage and quality of Radio Sabah's transmissions, which were still reliant on hastily built postwar infrastructure.[116] The existing facilities in Jesselton and other coastal towns were small and could only broadcast within certain areas. The forested interior, where most of Sabah's poorer communities lived, suffered from patchy radio quality. Individuals in Ranau,

THE RISE OF THE KALIMANTAN UTARA MOVEMENT   119

in the interior, and Kalabakan, in the far southeast, wrote to the *North Borneo News & Sabah Times* to express their disappointment at Radio Sabah's "poor reception."[117] These issues were confirmed in 1958 when efforts to chart signal range revealed critical transmission gaps.[118] Improvements would be necessary for the radio to pervade and feasibly inculcate the entire colony. Yet in the absence of any powerful transmission facilities, and with limited funds, the Information Office had to improvise. In seeking a novel solution, it planned to boost signal quality by relocating a radio transmitter 3,000 meters up the slopes of Mount Kinabalu, a considerable way toward its 4,095-meter summit.[119] As Kinabalu is one of Southeast Asia's highest mountains—with considerable topographic prominence relative to the surrounding jungles—the colony's engineers hoped that elevating the transmitter to such a high altitude would be a cost-effective way of enhancing Radio Sabah's coverage. On its completion, however, the relocated transmitter proved woefully insufficient, and the government was left with radio equipment stranded on a steep and inaccessible mountain.

After the first attempt to improve Radio Sabah's capabilities had failed, a major upgrade project was undertaken in early 1961 to construct a new recording studio with state-of-the-art transmission equipment in Jesselton. By this stage, Radio Sabah had received greater backing from the colonial and metropolitan governments. British policymakers had come to believe in the value of spreading colonial-sponsored radio propaganda among the public. Lessons were learned from the Malayan Emergency, and officials promoted the winning of hearts and minds in Borneo with heightened vigor. To aid in the studio's installation, advisors were brought in from neighboring Sarawak, which had undertaken similar upgrades. When interviewed about the project, Sarawak's chief broadcasting engineer, J. R. Sandison, declared that the upgrade would make Radio Sabah the "best built and equipped radio station in Southeast Asia."[120] Yet unbeknownst to Sandison and Brooks at the time, Indonesia was also enhancing its own radio facilities, which would soon enable Radio Kalimantan Utara to broadcast across Borneo. By the early 1960s, therefore, there was a growing fixation on shaping public opinion by means of radio transmission.[121]

Radio served a practical purpose. Considering Borneo's densely forested, rivered, and mountainous topography, it was widely accepted that curated news and propaganda were best dispersed over the air. Additionally, low literacy rates, particularly among Sabah's poorer indigenous communities, meant that radio was more accessible for those who could not read newspapers, which were overwhelmingly published in English or Chinese rather than in the local Kadazandusun or Murut languages.[122] Throughout 1963, Sabah emerged as the focal point in a spiraling technological arms race for supremacy over the airwaves, in which Radio Sabah jostled for airtime, coverage, and popularity with its Indonesian-funded adversary. Indeed, Radio Kalimantan Utara was quick to take aim at its rival station, decrying Radio Sabah as a Malayan puppet, the "voices of the devils and the satans [sic]," and "the voice of the ill-mannered Tunku Abdul Rahman."[123] Radio Sabah and its counterpart station in Sarawak responded in turn by airing a mass of pro-Malaysia material, including a song that chanted the refrain "Merger and Malaysia are sure as the sun rises! Merger and Malaysia are sure as time goes by!"[124] Over the weeks, infectious tunes such as these pervaded shop houses and schoolyards across Borneo, shrouding the colony in a cacophony of politicized shortwave radio. As Indonesia's opposition to Malaysia further intensified, countersongs and counterslogans were aired with increased regularity on channels across Borneo and the Indonesian Archipelago to sway public opinion. As described by Steven Farram, Indonesian popular songs played over the radio contained verses explicitly condemning the Tunku Abdul Rahman and Projek Malaysia, such as "Ganjang," which went as follows: "Be prepared Tengku, I am coming to obstruct your plans. Face up Tengku, I will block your intentions."[125]

Despite the prevalence of radio in late colonial Southeast Asia, it seldom features in existing scholarship on decolonization and state formation in Borneo, which remains fixated on the counterinsurgency, strategic, and pedagogical dimensions of the Konfrontasi and the wider Cold War.[126] The competing colonial and anticolonial attempts to weaponize radio underscore the extent that Sabah's decolonization experience was shaped by technology and transnational rivalries and was in turn contingent on local responses to foreign political influence.

Kalimantan Utara Falls Apart

By mid-1963, Radio Kalimantan Utara had become a feature of daily life in Borneo. As Malaysia's proposed formation date drew closer—initially scheduled for August 31, 1963, although later delayed to September 16—matters became particularly desperate for Sheikh Azahari's movement.[127] Between March and June, Radio Kalimantan Utara's transmissions developed an increasingly anti-Malaysian tone. During its evening broadcasts it issued direct threats to Malaya's prime minister, declaring on June 6, for instance, that the "Tunku Abdul Rahman, by his defiance to our independence movement, will end in disaster. He will be defeated politically . . . he might even be liquidated physically by our secret agents, if he continues this piratical exploitation."[128]

The threats of "secret agents," combined with rumors of militants in the jungle, stoked further public anxiety. Some colonial officials and pro-Malaysia elites in Sabah feared assassination, while others worried about the potential for social unrest. According to David Easter, even the Tunku himself was a "regular listener to Radio Kalimantan Utara," while other bureaucrats also kept abreast of the latest broadcasts.[129] Locals across Sabah were regular listeners, too, and reacted negatively to the barrage of propaganda that interrupted their normal programs. Some expressed fears of violence and voiced their opposition to what they saw as a combination of Malayan and Indonesian interference. An anonymous Kudat resident, for instance, writing to the government, expressed their "pleasure of hearing . . . Radio Sabah" but felt "strongly against to join Malaysia [sic]," owing to fears of reprisals and political chaos. Their greatest concerns centered on the perceived risk of foreign domination and violence, citing the social disarray that developed in Indonesia amid its anticolonial struggle: "I can guarantee . . . that some assassinations will going on [sic]. Indonesia is an example."[130] Elsewhere along the Malayan Peninsula, Indonesian-backed radio broadcasts fomented racial tensions, and they later contributed to the outbreak of race riots in Singapore.[131]

By mid-1963, a new voice had risen to prominence on Radio Kalimantan Utara. Lieutenant General Abang Ahmend Zulkipli, one of Azahari's close associates, assumed control over the group's propaganda arm.[132] Zulkipli was particularly critical of the Tunku, vowing to personally "crush his bones to powder."[133] Alarmed by the intensification of these threats, Sabah's colonial government labeled these transmissions as sources of "lies and violence" and "open incitement[s] to murder."[134] While some of these broadcasts were particularly bellicose, Radio Kalimantan Utara's mainstay was propaganda that encouraged the people of Sabah and Sarawak to take up arms and replicate Indonesia's anticolonial *revolusi*.

Many Western policymakers failed to recognize the voracity of this desire for total independence among everyday anticolonialists in Southeast Asia. Prospects of a colonial-sanctioned decolonization through merging Sabah and Sarawak with Malaya and Singapore (labeled by detractors as "counterfeit independence") simply did not weigh the same as the idea of *merdeka*. The same anonymous contributor from Kudat explained in their letter that "most of us prefer to become independent than joining the Malaysia [plan]."[135] Authentic independence was an attractive concept, and Projek Malaysia faced backlash because many interpreted it as a thinly veiled attempt at imposing foreign rule, along with the radically controversial Kalimantan Utara plan that made little effort to hide its Indonesian links. Previously, in December 1962, during a meeting between US consul general Bob Donhauser and the British commissioner general for Southeast Asia, George Douglas-Hamilton, in Singapore, it was suggested that Indonesian aggression would likely dissipate if Brunei was granted "immediate" independence while retaining British civil servants and a "security treaty" with Malaya. Interpretations of independence clearly varied, and in this case a starkly anachronistic view had prevailed. Donhauser and Douglas-Hamilton both believed that "independence from colonial rule was [Indonesia's] major objective and if that [was] satisfactorily undertaken [in Brunei] they would 'overlook' British involvement."[136] But this could not have been further from reality: Indonesia opposed the Malaysia plan and sought to extend its influence over the British Borneo territories to counteract what it saw as Malaya's attempts to expand territorially and to preserve colonial interests. And even if Kalimantan Utara was designed in part to prevent the Borneo territories from joining Malaysia, for the movement to have any chance of survival, it would have to acquiesce to Indonesian control.[137]

This helps explain the marked disjunction between Kalimantan Utara's stated objectives and its actions, which both appeared to be out of step with local political sentiments across British Borneo. Nevertheless, Sabah's and Sarawak's highly diverse publics continued to envision a variety of routes toward decolonization. This was a particularly fluid moment in Borneo's history, in which no particular decolonization trajectory was certain. Interpretations of *merdeka* varied from *kampong* to *kampong*, and goals differed between rival ethnic groups. Unlike British and American officials, Sabah's colonial government expressed concern that decolonization via the Malaysia route would appear underwhelming for those with strong anticolonial or anti-Malayan convictions. Indeed, in late 1957 Sabah's governor, Roland Turnbull, even advanced his own proposal to form a union of Sabah, Sarawak, and Brunei. Crucially, Turnbull's proposal was functionally akin to Sheikh Azahari's original Kalimantan Utara concept, prior to his alignment with Indonesian goals.[138] Colonial bureaucrats in Sabah feared that desires for an authentic independence might still evoke major interest among Sabah's public, even after the proposed merger with Malaysia.[139] But like the Malaysia plan, Azahari's attempt to incorporate Sabah into Kalimantan Utara was not a pathway toward genuine independent statehood. Instead, it resembled an alignment shift from one archipelagic power to another. Concerns about this possibility were keenly felt throughout Sabah, not least among its Chinese communities.[140]

Many of Southeast Asia's past independence movements were "contested and often violent" struggles for freedom that resulted in a total severance from the colonial power.[141] Initially, this was the version of *merdeka* that Azahari promised through Kalimantan Utara: a laborious, violent if necessary, struggle for independence. But gradually, like Projek Malaysia (and indeed like Malaya's support for the 1958 Sumatran rebellion), it too could only promise decolonization through merger with, or rather absorption into, a larger, wealthier, and already-independent state.[142] Sabah's public appeared to be growing weary of the Kalimantan Utara option.

Simultaneously, by mid-1963, Radio Sabah was winning the battle for the airwaves, and public opinion was gradually warming to prospects of merger with Malaysia. In contrast, Azahari's movement struggled because it alienated the very demographic it sought to impress. Within months, Radio Kalimantan Utara's revolutionary camaraderie had devolved into threats of brutal death, dismemberment, and even cannibalism for those who dared resist. These threats were interspersed with blind reverence to Indonesia, underscoring the extent to which Kalimantan Utara had fallen out of touch with local political aspirations. No sooner had a more veritable independence cause been advertised than it was supplanted by voices of intimidation tinged with foreign coercion over the airwaves. Azahari's state-in-exile, which had been so close to conjuring itself into existence through mimicking other anticolonial movements, had by mid-1963 withered into a series of desperate radio broadcasts and virtue signaling toward Indonesia. Crucially, while Sabah's public continued to hear these broadcasts, they no longer listened to them.

Investigating Indonesia's simultaneous role as Kalimantan Utara's lifeblood and death knell is critical in understanding the movement's rapid demise in mid-1963. Although Radio Kalimantan Utara's violent discourse drove many potential supporters away, it was its frequent praising of President Sukarno and Indonesia's revolutionary tradition that became its final undoing. In what was described by colonial officials as "fulsome flattery," Azahari, Zulkipli, and the other voices on the radio called on Borneo's people to imitate Indonesia's revolutionary example.[143] This failed to resonate with local leaders and their followers in Sabah, who had long been wary of Indonesian political aggression and the influence of Javanese migrants in the territory.[144] Although concerns over Malayan domination were rife, and suspicions about the Tunku's colonial-style designs widespread, such sentiments were soon outweighed by more pressing fears of Indonesian subversion. Suspicions over Indonesian influence trickled down to local hierarchies in even the most remote of Sabah's jungle *kampongs*. Ironically, on the eve of decolonization, it was Indonesian aggression, and not British imperial rule or allegations of Malayan neocolonialism, that elicited the most public ire in Sabah. Although prospects of a completely independent Bornean state remained compelling for many in Sabah—particularly among the Chinese population and sections of the

Kadazandusun and Murut communities—Kalimantan Utara's threatening tone and pro-Indonesia outlook precluded it from achieving its goals. Above all else, the public sought peace and prosperity.

Few scholars accord Sabah's public a sense of agency in their decolonization struggle. But these perceptions of "foreignness" and threats of neocolonial expansion that tinged Radio Kalimantan Utara were patently obvious to locals in Sabah, who were quick to reject it on their own terms without direction from Britain, Malaya, or the colonial government. Almost immediately, listeners in Sabah complained that Kalimantan Utara's speeches were "generally given in a form of Malay quite different to that spoken [in Sabah] and sometimes in very poor English."[145] Signs of Indonesian involvement were unmistakable by the time Sukarno publicly declared his support for the movement in May 1963: "The enemies of the Indonesian revolution . . . are even now trying to encircle the Indonesian Republic with their practices of neo-colonialism as is evident in the concept of Malaysia . . . it is on the basis of this principle that we sympathise with the Kalimantan Utara people's heroic struggle."[146]

But Indonesian policymakers had cause for concern, too. In his speech, Sukarno voiced fears that the Malaysia plan would be "yet another ploy to expand Malaya's influence." According to Wen-Qing Ngoei, Projek Malaysia was "a move that brought the Tunku's proven record of aggression against Sukarno right to the Indonesian border in Borneo." Indonesian officials later confided in American diplomats their fears that Malaysia would enable Malaya and Britain to "recreate" the destabilizing conditions of the 1958 Sumatran rebellion in Borneo "and tear Indonesia asunder."[147] These concerns actively shaped Indonesia's policy toward the Malaysia plan and influenced its support for Kalimantan Utara. Public figures across Malaya and Singapore eagerly fanned these Indonesian anxieties. Later in 1963, for instance, the spokesperson of the Singapore-based Malayan People's Action Party Front claimed to launch a "counter confrontation" against Indonesia by threatening to "support any rebellion in Sumatra." Stoking insurrection would be easy, the spokesperson claimed, due to the large numbers of Indonesian nationals and "former rebels in exile" in Malaya who were eager to "restore democracy in Indonesia."[148] Threats of rebellion and foreign-funded subversion were disseminated across Southeast Asia from virtually all directions, emanating not just from Indonesian broadcast facilities.

Kalimantan Utara struggled amid this regional instability. It remained trapped as a phantom state, ubiquitous on the airwaves, but barely noticeable on the ground. It would go down in popular memory as a performative country-in-waiting that was confined to the jungles, to radio broadcasts, and, ultimately, to the public's imaginations and fears. Although the injection of Indonesian financing, training, and radio infrastructure provided much-needed sustenance to the weakened movement, Sabah's merger with Malaysia appeared increasingly likely by mid-1963. This was the case even prior to the outcome of the United Nations inquiry into the formation of Malaysia, which later concluded that Sabah and Sarawak "emerge[d] . . . to the status of self-government," albeit as an "autonomous component of [a] larger unit" rather than an independent sovereign state.[149]

Nevertheless, Sabah and Sarawak remained contested cornerstones in Malayan, Indonesian, and Philippine efforts to extend influence into Borneo. Matters became even more fraught as the Malaysia plan progressed, giving rise to Sukarno's "Ganyang Malaysia" campaign, which led to Konfrontasi in 1963.[150] While Kalimantan Utara remains in public consciousness as a very real disturbance, its story has been largely forgotten by contemporary scholars. Few historians specializing in the formation of Malaysia, the Konfrontasi, decolonization, or even regional geopolitics in Southeast Asia have focused on the technological edges of anticolonialism, the active participation of local communities in Borneo, and the role played by foreign states in stoking, funding, and outfitting rebellions. That the two competing pathways toward decolonization in British Borneo were based on rival paradigms—continued Anglo-Malayan cooperation versus Indonesian-led nonalignment—underscores the extent to which Sabah was a lynchpin in Southeast Asian state formation and geopolitical restructuring. Likewise, that both decolonization routes amounted to assimilation into a larger unit, rather than true independent statehood, is indeed telling. Crucially, however, these geopolitical struggles were neither a one-sided defense against Indonesian neocolonial aggression nor a manifestation of Cold War ideological contestation. In marked contrast, they were reflective of acute, multidimensional rivalries over competing dreams of archipelagic unity. These rivalries manifested on the one hand as a struggle between Malaya's Semananjung Melayu and Indonesia's Nusantara, and on the other hand as the locals' attempts in Sabah to cling onto a sense of agency as their territory hurtled toward decolonization.

Negara Kesatuan Kalimantan Utara was unable to conjure itself physically beyond the airwaves, where it remained as a phantasmic, static presence. The movement's violence-tinged propaganda and its links to Indonesia were its ultimate undoing. This chapter has examined the rise and eventual collapse of Sheikh Azahari's anticolonial movement. It has charted its emergence following the failed Brunei Rebellion in December 1962; its formative days confined to a hotel in Manila and strewn across Southeast Asia in January 1963; its sudden entrance onto the international stage in Tanganyika in February; and, eventually, its technological expansion and demise in Jakarta's radio rooms between March and August. By the time Sabah, Sarawak, Singapore, and Malaya entered union to form Malaysia on September 16, 1963, Kalimantan Utara had vanished from the airwaves almost as abruptly as it had appeared just nine months earlier.

Despite its brief history, Kalimantan Utara wrought significant changes to Southeast Asia by intensifying regional anticolonial sentiments and stoking international opposition toward Malaysia. The movement's activities furthermore reveal how Sabah's public lay at the forefront of rejecting subversion and embracing the Anglo-Malayan status quo. But local Bornean experiences are seldom discussed in conventional scholarship, which remains largely peninsular Malayan and Konfrontasi-centric in its outlook. As this chapter has demonstrated, the received wisdom has broadly overlooked the foundational effects of Malayan-Indonesian rivalries in shaping the conditions on the ground in Borneo that gave rise to grassroots anti-Malaysia sentiments. Although the Brunei Rebellion and the subsequent Kalimantan Utara movement failed to capitalize on public support, unite British Borneo, and block the eventual formation of Malaysia, they shaped the merger process. In a broader sense, this serves to denaturalize prevailing explanations of decolonization by showing that if not for local support and contingency, Malaysia might not have come about. Conventional scholarship frequently assumes that the formation of Malaysia was largely uncontested until the proclamation of Sukarno's "Ganyang Malaysia" policy in 1963.

Finally, the discussion of the methods employed by Sheikh Azahari and his Kalimantan Utara functionaries to mimic statehood reveals the importance of technology, ideology, culture, language, information, and broader issues of peace and stability in appealing to Sabah's increasingly informed and politically conscious public. This resembled a significant shift in Sabah, in which the unwieldy colonial bureaucracy treated governance as a top-down process whereby social conditions were balanced alongside economic issues without due consideration for public opinion. The threat posed by Kalimantan Utara, and later Indonesia, forced Britain and Malaya to pay deeper attention to issues of local public opinion. Ultimately, the increased prevalence of radio and propaganda exchanges reveals that while Sabah's public was increasingly receptive to information over the airwaves, it was the promises of peace and prosperity, and not threats of destruction and conquest, that elicited the greatest responses.

CHAPTER 4

Maphilindo, the Confederation That Never Was

For generations, the flow of peoples, goods, and ideas brought the northern coast of Borneo into a close embrace with the southern Philippines. The scattered isles that dotted the Sulu Sea in between served as essential waypoints for traders, travelers, and fortune seekers navigating the archipelago. Throughout history, the natural harbors along Borneo's northern coast had attracted nascent commerce and contributed to the emergence of local maritime polities. Precolonial states, and their colonial and postcolonial successors, drew from the legacies of these transnational circulations. In addition to being separated by the Sulu Sea—a body of water noted for its perilous currents, jutting sea rocks, and rogue waves—Borneo and the Philippines were also bisected by divergent colonial systems.[1] Although it was initially arbitrary, in later years the colonial-imposed maritime boundary segmenting Sabah from the Philippines pulled the two regions further apart.[2] Politics as well as geography, therefore, threatened to hinder established links. As this chapter argues, however, long-term social and cultural connections endured. Although territorial claims and geopolitical rivalries continue to shape relations between Sabah and the Philippines today, contemporary traders, migrants, and even raiders echo the journeys of their forebears.[3]

For centuries, the northern coast of Borneo has been under near-perpetual contest, pulled in virtually every direction. Local and foreign polities alike wanted in on slices of coastal territory and river access to tap the island's interior resources. Foreign prospectors from across Asia, the Middle East, and later Europe were all drawn to Borneo by promises of "jungle produce" and mineral resources.[4] These early merchants were followed by speculators and colonists in the nineteenth century, leading to the formation of semi-autonomous colonial states. And as Western colonization took hold, Borneo's land—a resource deemed virtually limitless in abundance—became an essential commodity in the proliferation of plantation estates and logging ventures, as well as the consolidation of empire.[5]

In addition to these economic stimuli, emergent Southeast Asian postcolonial states in the 1950s and 1960s increasingly configured Borneo as an essential component in plans for nation-building and state formation. The island had long existed as a nexus between the Muslim-dominated worlds of Indonesia and Malaya to the south and to the west and the Christian-majority Philippine Archipelago to the north. Each of these regions of Melayu heritage converged on Borneo, which lay at the center of maritime Southeast Asia, a place cast simultaneously as an ancient land embodying precolonial tradition and as a resource-rich bounty for future postcolonial development. The island was so vast—almost continental in scale—that unlike much of maritime Southeast Asia, which is characterized by archipelagos and chains of small islands, Borneo's lengthy land borders pushed vying states toward uneasy contact. Sabah, in particular, was perceived as an essential building block for postcolonial state projects emphasizing precolonial heritage.[6] By the late 1950s, it had become a keystone for new ideas of national and archipelagic unity, notions vested in perceptions of a common Melayu heritage, ethnicity, and culture. As this chapter shows, Sabah also became a focal point of considerable interest among Southeast Asia's publics, with its vast expanses of land and resources enrapturing people across the Philippines, Malaya, Brunei, and beyond. Critically, this led to numerous private claims for territory. As discussed in chapter 3, Indonesia supported the Kalimantan Utara movement in its pushback against Western colonialism and Malayan expansionism and, in so doing, sought to exert greater influence over the island to preserve its national interests and extend its tradition of anticolonial independence. As will be explored in chapter 5, Malaya viewed the incorporation of Sabah (along with Sarawak and Brunei) into the proposed Federation of Malaysia as critical in offsetting perceived ethnic imbalances, in safeguarding regional security, and in acquiring territory and resources. In a similar vein, this chapter focuses on the Philippines' attempts to propagate historical claims over Sabah while at the same time positing ideas for transnational cooperation and Melayu unity through the proposed Maphilindo confederation.[7] In each of these three vying plans for postcolonial state formation and archipelagic unity, Borneo's northern coast became a hinge for strengthening new national goals while denying rivals the commercial, territorial, ideological, and even demographic gains that it purportedly offered.

This chapter accordingly turns to Sabah's maritime zone. The first section examines the making of overlapping maritime boundaries in the Sulu Sea, which interrupted established patterns of commerce and migration. It argues that semi-autonomous colonial statehood developed through a combination of rogue dealmaking and indigenous attempts at pitching vying colonial states against each other. Section two disentangles this territorial overlap by analyzing the Philippines' successful bid to administer British-controlled Sulu Sea islands off the Sabah coast in the late 1940s. This territorial transfer set important legal and personal precedents that paved the way for the Philippines' claim over the entirety of Sabah, with Filipino politicians and public figures citing it as a formative moment. The third section looks at the escalation of private claims for territory in Sabah lodged in the Philippines in the early 1960s, which spurred governmental action. Section four examines the Philippines' official claim over Sabah, which was lodged by President Diosdado Macapagal in June 1962. The final two sections of the chapter focus on the Maphilindo confederation, an idea posited in July 1963 that purported to offer a solution to maritime Southeast Asia's deadlock over Projek Malaysia. Although it ultimately failed to come to fruition, Maphilindo was a formative idea developed during a period of geopolitical fluidity and contingency amid the end of empire in Sabah.

The Making of Maritime Boundaries in the Sulu Sea

In the traditional Suluk folktale "Tuwan Nahuda," the death of Tuwan Nahuda Kalayakan is described by his wife while at sea on their voyage back to Borneo.[8] A Suluk navigator and "great warrior" from Sandakan, Tuwan Nahuda Kalayakan features prominently in local tradition and folklore across the region. As their boat sails back to Sandakan from Jolo, Tuwan Nahuda's wife depicts the voyage across the Sulu Sea frequented by generations of Suluk and Bajau sailors from across Borneo and the Philippines. These coasts appear as one and the same, with the archipelagic sprawl of Sulu Sea islands serving as waypoints and navigational landmarks in a world of maritime exploration.[9] And while Tuwan Nahuda's milieu was an interconnected and uninterrupted expanse, it is today segmented by Malaysian and Philippine territorial boundaries. The folktale describes a world in motion, dotted with countless islands great and small, situated within wild, often perilous, waters. On this final voyage, Tuwan Nahuda's wife calls to her dying husband to observe the passing islands in the Sulu Sea as they sail southward. They drift past Tulayan, the island "where people pass by"; then Sulari, "where boats dock, coming and going"; then Tapul, "a traveler's stopover"; then Siasi, "with its odd mountain top"; then the distant island of Tahau; then Taganak, which "looks so tiny"; before finally sailing past Berhala Island at the mouth of Sandakan's vast natural harbor. They arrive at Sandakan, gateway to Borneo, but it is too late.[10]

In other versions, Tuwan Nahuda Kalayakan is depicted as an itinerant sultan, wise and powerful. He is fabled to have journeyed as far as Java and Malacca and to have conquered swathes of Borneo, the Sulu Archipelago, and even Luzon.[11] Such folktales, passed down the generations through oral tradition, underscore the prominence of cultural and political links spanning Borneo, the Sulu Sea, and wider maritime Southeast Asia. These tales also serve as local reminiscences of precolonial thalassocratic empires, such as the sultanates of Sulu, Bulungan, and Brunei. At varying points in history, these sultanates occupied stretches of coastal territory, extending webs of archipelagic influence across Southeast Asia's seas and landmasses.

Initially based out of the island of Jolo in the south of the Philippine Archipelago, the Sulu Sultanate grew to operate within a vast maritime realm, claiming slices of coastline across Mindanao and northern Borneo.[12] Sulu resisted Spain's attempts at colonization, and it continued to oversee trade and collect taxes as an autonomous polity. Although it was historically dismissed for its alleged piratical tendencies, scholars have since shown that the Sulu Sultanate was an adaptive polity capable of a variety of diplomatic and military responses to the pressures it faced.[13] In the late seventeenth and early eighteenth centuries, Sulu played a decisive role in a major Bruneian civil war, subsequently enlarging its territorial holdings along the northern coast of Borneo. This new overseas territory served as the lifeblood for Sulu, enabling it to prosper as other indigenous polities in the Philippines fell to Spanish colonial advances.[14] Its authority over stretches of Bornean coastline also enabled control over the outflow of valuable goods and commodities destined for the southern Philippines.[15] These products, ranging from edible birds' nests and dried fish to slaves and spices, were in high demand and excited interest from merchants hailing from as far as China, Sulawesi, and India on their annual visits to the Sulu Archipelago.[16]

Throughout the eighteenth and nineteenth centuries, the links between coastal communities across Borneo and the southern Philippines gradually formalized under Sulu control. Raiders-turned-merchants, fishermen, and settlers put down roots in new lands.[17] These economic and political ties built on centuries of trade, migration, and the transfer of Islamic culture. Alongside Brunei and the myriad sultanates that dominated the region, Sulu was a product of Islam's eastward expansion into Southeast Asia since the thirteenth century.[18] Although culturally and religiously enmeshed with one another, these sultanates developed distinctive characteristics. Unlike Brunei's absolute monarchical system, for instance, Sulu exercised indirect control over its disparate maritime holdings, in a system in which local *datus* (chiefs) and *panglimas* (governors) held the sultan's authority in check.[19] These elites also sat on the sultan's Ruma Bechara (governing council), a body devised to limit despotic rule and decide on crucial matters of state.[20]

As a central polity in early modern Southeast Asia, Sulu's presence acted as a buffer defying Spain's southward advance into Borneo. Simultaneously, Sulu merchants plied the trade routes between Borneo and the Philippine Archipelago with intricate knowledge of the "ill-defined" coasts "strewn with rocks and shoals."[21] With the intensification of Western colonial interest in the region in the nineteenth century, Sulu's importance grew as one of the last independent holdouts in the region. Like Aceh in northern Sumatra, which had long defied Dutch colonial expansion, Sulu was considered a rebellious, piracy-ridden state disparaged for its refusal to accommodate Western interests.[22] Nicholas Tarling has suggested that "though Sulu's contacts with Spain lasted for three centuries, British policy in the later nineteenth century was decisive in determining its fate."[23] Indeed, it was the sultanate's dealings with private adventurers and autonomous imperial agents based in Hong Kong that brought about its eventual demise. When Baron Gustavus von Overbeck and Arthur Dent secured a cession for territory in northern Borneo in 1878 from Sultan Jamal ul-Azam, the Sulu Sultanate was relegated to a few small islands.[24] This followed Overbeck and Dent's similar purchase of land from Brunei a few months prior, which further eroded local Bornean sovereignty.

Private colonization attempts—which gave rise to the "White Rajahs" in Sarawak and the North Borneo Chartered Company in Sabah—were decisive in subduing maritime Southeast Asia's last independent states. As Steven Press argues, "rogue" agents of Western imperialism traveled across Borneo to colonize territory for commercial gain, challenging conventional laws "while only briefly winning approval from Western legal institutions." These rogue dealings, imposed on unwitting indigenous leaders by European adventurers, were characterized by a "sense of fraudulence" through their use of Western legal procedures and spurious assurances of patronage and alliance. Borneo was a proving ground for rogue, semi-autonomous imperial expansion, in which a mere explorer-speculator could be ordained as a maharaja. James Brooke's similar purchase of Sarawak from the Brunei Sultanate in 1841, for instance, set in motion a sequence of successive private colonization ventures in Borneo, a template later applied elsewhere by imperial agents during the "Scramble for Africa."[25] Sultan Jamal ul-Azam's sale of land in Borneo to Dent and Overbeck (who was subsequently styled Maharaja of Sabah and Rajah of Gaya and Sandakan) arose out of a similar process of deceptive colonization through transaction. In pursuit of titles and cession deeds, Overbeck and Dent deployed Western legal practices and compliant intermediaries to coerce local elites. Under growing pressure, vulnerable and embattled indigenous polities were compelled to liquidate their holdings in exchange for sums of money and, in the case of Sulu, vague promises of security and diplomatic support.

Sultan Jamal ul-Azam had long been wary of Spanish pressure from the north.[26] "Fearing imminent Spanish conquest," wrote Ian Black, the sultan "wished to involve" the British as a way of pitting competing imperial powers against each other. The sultan believed that ceding land to the Hong Kong–based consortium would protect his interests from Spain while enabling him to retain "a morsel of his sovereignty" in Borneo.[27] But Jamal ul-Azam's decision making revealed a grave lack of understanding of what the 1878 cession entailed to Overbeck and Dent. Accordingly, although the sultan sold off his territorial rights in Sabah "until the end of time," he remained convinced that lasting cultural affinity—and the presumed fealty of local *panglimas*, *datus*, and other Ruma Bechara elites—would enable him to retain a foothold in the region.[28] Indeed, Jamal ul-Azam may have relinquished his legal title over the land, but he believed that his people remained in Sabah and that he remained their sultan.[29] But colonial law was unforgiving and operated without concern for the local hierarchies it dismantled. When Overbeck and Dent later sold off their Borneo titles to the nascent North Borneo Chartered Company in 1881, verbal promises made at the time were lost, and Borneo's coastline was incorporated into a new colonial enterprise. The sultan's chances appeared slim.

The 1878 cession has elicited considerable controversy ever since, particularly following the Philippines' transition to independence and Britain's formal colonization of Sabah in 1946.[30] Writing in 1946, Henry Otley Beyer argued that the legality of the 1878 cession was doubtful because the sultan acted without consulting the Ruma Bechara. Beyer further claimed that "there can be no doubt but that the North Borneo territories were state property of the Sulu Sultanate and not personal property of the sultan and his heirs."[31] British officials, in contrast, maintained that their sovereignty over Sabah was "undoubted."[32] These lasting questions over sovereignty continue to elicit debate today, with varying interpretations of translations and the legal fine print.[33]

The 1878 cession remains important, however, because it involved the transfer of territory that was so vague and ill defined at the time that even those who stood to receive it did not realize its full extent. How many Sulu Sea islands were there? Who owned them? Precisely how far did Sulu's lands extend into the Bornean jungle? For colonials in the late nineteenth century, Borneo's northern coast and the Sulu Sea were poorly understood regions. And they were considered dangerous, inundated with piracy, dangerous currents, and jutting sea rocks that would splinter any ship that strayed too close. Hence, colonial state-making endeavors relied on imprecise cartography and only a vague grasp of the region's geography and bathymetry.[34] Of the many islands in the Sulu Sea, few were accurately mapped, and even fewer were formally brought under a form of centralized authority. Many island territories existed in a state of abeyance, neither formally colonized nor permitted to remain as independent territories.

These issues continued to shape relations between the nascent North Borneo Chartered Company and the Sulu Sultanate after Jamal ul-Azam's reign. Following the United States' colonization of the Philippines in 1898, the Sulu Sultanate faced increased pressure from the north. A year later, in 1899, Sultan Jamalul Kiram II petitioned to William Cowie, the chartered company's chairman, for permission to seek refuge in Sabah and "look after those islands which were not included [in the 1878] agreement."[35] Cowie refused Kiram's desperate request, unwilling to shield the sultan from the American advance. These maritime territories, known locally as the Turtle Islands, were a group of seven islands off the northeastern coast of Borneo loosely administered by the company but not specified in any cession deeds. They were to remain in a state of geopolitical flux. Sultan Jamal ul-Azam's gamble with European speculators in 1878 had ultimately failed: in Sulu's time of need it was unable to seek refuge in Borneo and pit vying colonial states against each other. By the early twentieth century, Sulu was irreparably weakened and by 1915 it would be suppressed by the American colonial administration.[36]

Disentangling Territorial Overlap

The subjugation of indigenous polities through rogue colonial dealings left lasting marks on Sabah and its surrounding maritime region. The seas around Borneo were particularly contested during the late colonial period. The same chain of islands that is depicted in the traditional folk tale "Tuwan Nahuda," and which Sultan Jamalul Kiram II requested to administer in 1899, was by the late 1940s enveloped in renewed controversy following the Philippines' transition to independence.

Taganak Island, part of the Turtle Island shoal and situated close to Sabah's port of Sandakan, symbolized the lasting effects of muddied and intertwined maritime boundaries in the Sulu Sea. The islands were caught in flux, trapped between rival colonial states and obscured on poorly drawn imperial maps.[37] Although administered in practice by the North Borneo Chartered Company, the islands were neither demarcated within British or American colonial boundaries nor formally described in any territorial deeds. It was only in 1930 that they were finally defined as falling within American-controlled waters, despite their proximity to the Sabah coast. While they were considered part of the American-controlled Philippine Archipelago, British and American officials agreed in 1930 to maintain the status quo and allow the chartered company to continue administering the islands "in perpetuity."[38] The Turtle Islands had attained considerable navigational value to the company following the construction of a lighthouse at Taganak Island in 1923. The Taganak lighthouse, along with similar navigational beacons at Batu Tinagat, Tanjung Trang, and Kalampunian Island elsewhere along the Sabah coast, served imperial shipping interests in the seas around Borneo.[39]

After the Philippines transitioned to independence in July 1946, however, these islands came under heightened scrutiny.[40] Within months, on September 19, the Philippines announced its intention to formally administer the Turtle Islands, marking the newly independent state's first major foreign policy engagement.[41] The Philippines won support from some in the departing American administration. In February 1947, Francis B. Harrison, former colonial governor of the Philippines, wrote to Philippine vice president Elpidio Quirino to question whether the Philippines was also willing to extend a territorial claim over the entirety of Sabah. Accompanying Harrison's letter was a "portfolio of papers" concerning Sabah, over which, he claimed, "the Sultanate of Sulu has held sovereignty" since 1714. Harrison, who later became a naturalized citizen of the Philippines, was a vocal critic of Britain's resurgent colonial activities after the Second World War. He argued that Britain's annexation of Sabah from the chartered company in July 1946—mere days after Philippine independence—was "done in derogation of the rights of the Sultanate of Sulu."[42] Harrison's support for Sulu was highly ironic, however, because it was during his governorship of the Philippines from 1913 to 1921 that the sultanate was finally subjugated under the colonial yoke. Under Harrison's authority the US colonial administration compelled Sultan Jamalul Kiram II in 1915 to recognize the United States' sovereignty over the entire Philippine Archipelago, thereby reducing the sultan to merely the "titular spiritual head of the Mohammedan Church in the Sulu Archipelago."[43] When the Philippines transitioned to independence in 1946, the new postcolonial government replaced the United States as Sulu's overlord and successor-in-interest. The sultanate's legacies subsequently attained newfound importance in the Philippines, which led to heightened public interest in staking a claim to the territory.[44] The Turtle Islands were the first port of call.

Although small, isolated, and sparsely populated, the Turtle Islands attained powerful symbolism as a reflection of nascent Philippine statehood and its dreams of archipelagic unity. Likewise, the islands' embodiment of precolonial Sulu statehood and indigenous defiance ostensibly positioned the Philippines among the ranks of Asia's foremost postcolonial nation-states. Perhaps most importantly, however, Filipinos across the archipelago perceived it as a great affront that their territories continued to be administered by an imperial power. Vice President Elpidio Quirino characterized these growing public sentiments, declaring in the months following independence that "vigor and justice swept through our scattered islands from the northern hills . . . to the southernmost province [which was technically the Turtle Islands] and gathered all the Filipinos into one nation."[45] Elsewhere across Southeast Asia, there was considerable interest in the fate of the islands as an indicator of unfolding decolonization and a case study in colonial-postcolonial territorial rivalry.[46]

Legally, the islands were Philippine territories, but Sabah's maritime traffic operating out of the port of Sandakan had depended on the navigational beacon at Taganak Island since 1923.[47] And since 1930, the United States had pledged to allow Sabah's continued administration over the islands "in perpetuity." Lighthouses tamed dark and obstacle-ridden waters, and colonial economic recovery after the war feasibly hinged on their continued operation. But unbeknownst to Sabah's new colonial government, the lighthouse at Taganak had been destroyed by the Japanese in 1942. So great was the postwar devastation and subsequent loss of colonial maritime activity along Sabah's northern coast that the extent of wartime damage was not fully realized until 1947, following a visit to Taganak by a Philippine investigative committee.[48] Colonial authorities knew little about the region: before the war, chartered company and American officials had "left to each other the task of gathering data" about the islands.[49] Despite these blunders, Sabah's government continued to assert its interest in administering the islands "in perpetuity," with Governor Edward Francis Twining staunchly opposing the transfer.[50] Philippine negotiators steadfastly refused to pay for the repairs and future maintenance of the derelict lighthouse and only reluctantly agreed to undertake antismuggling patrols, further complicating discussions. Despite this deadlock, and the staunch objections of Sabah's colonial government, Britain acquiesced to the

Philippines' terms and agreed to hand the islands over. The transfer of administrative rights quietly took place on October 13, 1947.[51]

Buoyed by its recent transition to independence, however, the Philippine government sought a grand public ceremony to showcase what it saw as an emphatic anticolonial victory. Although it was one of the first Southeast Asian countries to transition to self-governance, the Philippines' early independence years were punctuated by major setbacks. American commercial and strategic involvement persisted, and in March 1947 the Philippine government agreed to a series of ninety-nine-year leases allowing the United States to continue operating its military bases across the country.[52] All of this indicated that de facto American colonial interests remained. Indeed, in a damning assertion, Linton H. Foulds, British ambassador to the Philippines, claimed in late 1946 that despite its transition to independence, the Philippines was "less independent" than any British Crown Colony at the time.[53]

Philippine officials organized a handover ceremony to be held at Taganak Island on June 19, 1948. Britain agreed to participate but sent only two officials of middling seniority from Sabah. In contrast to this small British representation, the Philippine delegation was massive, complete with traditional performances and extensive media coverage. The delegation comprised Sulu royals, local functionaries, and high-ranking politicians from Manila, such as Diosdado Macapagal, who would later become president in December 1961.[54] Perhaps most notable, however, was the announcement that Princess Tarhata Kiram, the niece of Sultan Jamalul Kiram II, would serve as deputy governor of the Turtle Islands.[55]

Princess Kiram's appointment was significant: it placed a direct descendent of the Sulu Sultanate in a position of authority that suggested a newfound strategic union of Sulu and Manila-based power. It also undid some of the feeling of humiliation felt by Sulu locals following the United States' subjugation of the sultanate in 1915. While Princess Kiram's appointment was met with widespread approval across the Philippines, it was also considered a politicized move. The Philippines' Muslim-majority south had long been wary of influence from the Catholic north, and her appointment was interpreted by some as a shallow attempt at promoting unity along fractious religious lines.[56] It nevertheless proved popular among local Turtle Islanders, the older of whom could recall living under the independent Sulu Sultanate prior to 1915. American writer Agnes Newton Keith, who attended the ceremony, recalled how Princess Tarhata Kiram strode across Taganak's white coralline sands, received with adoration by the island's residents. "There on the wet sand, with their feet in the lapping waves, they gathered in a great, gaping and admiring throng, bowing and even weeping" as they welcomed their leader home, wrote Keith.[57]

When news broke that a descendent of the Sulu Sultanate had been appointed deputy governor of the Turtle Islands, there was mass indignation in Sabah's colonial government. Governor Twining was particularly alarmed, arguing that the Philippines, empowered by the Sulu Sultanate's heirs, was entering a new era of expansionism. Twining feared that the loss of administrative rights over the Turtle Islands might spur claims over the entirety of Sabah.[58] Although the Turtle Islands had been demarcated as part of the Philippine Archipelago since 1930, misconceptions that they were British possessions persisted, sparking concerns over Philippine irredentism and diminishing Western influence. One such article published in the *Sunday Times* in Perth, Australia, lamented how as the "islands are changing hands . . . pinpoints of pink on the map are disappearing."[59] Publicly, however, British officials downplayed the event's significance and stressed that it was not a decolonization moment as the British flag had never flown over the Turtle Islands. Nevertheless, there was widespread excitement across the Philippines. In June 1948, news outlets across the Philippines claimed boldly that "the disintegration of the British Empire was being precipitated by the transfer of the Turtle Islands" and that "on the coming auspicious day the Union Jack will be hauled down and the flag of the new Republic will be victoriously raised in its place."[60] The transfer of the islands and the subsequent handover ceremony were formative moments for the Philippines, representing reinvigorated anticolonial ideals and a conflation of Sulu and Filipino interests. For local Sabahans, it served as a reminder of the functional limitations of chartered company governance and of the lasting effects of disorganized colonial boundaries on regional geopolitics.

The Escalation of Private Territorial Claims over Sabah

By the early 1960s, these once complex and muddied maritime boundaries appeared set in their postcolonial contexts. Although newly imposed Philippine rule had symbolically replaced the outgoing colonial presence in the Sulu Sea, there was little material change. Under Philippine administration, the Turtle Islands would once again become a remote backwater, a distant political symbol of the nation's southernmost archipelagic frontier. But issues of piracy and smuggling, considered at the time endemic features of the Sulu Sea, were again making waves.[61]

In Britain, politicians complained that the Royal Navy had been forced to "perform . . . a continuous anti-piracy role off Borneo and the Philippines" since 1961.[62] Members of Parliament blamed the increase in piracy on the lack of action by the Philippine authorities. MP Ian Orr-Ewing, Civil Lord of the Admiralty, argued that due to Philippine inaction, Sabah faced "armed raids by bandits attacking coastal villages," with the territory's merchant shipping also suffering from predation and "lawlessness on the high seas."[63] Speaking in Sabah's new Legislative Council in September 1962, Governor William Goode urged the Philippines "to help put a stop to the piracy plaguing North Borneo's East Coast . . . [by taking] action against the raiders in their home villages to bring them to justice."[64] Administrators such as Goode saw disorder in the seas as a reflection of how the wider region would fare in the absence of colonial rule. According to the colonial government, Philippine administration of the Turtle Islands since 1947 had precipitated a collapse in regional maritime security. As Jennifer L. Gaynor writes, this alludes to the nineteenth-century colonial theory that asserted that piracy was "the result of the decay of native states."[65] It is unsurprising, then, that colonials in the early 1960s similarly considered piracy a product of ineffective postcolonial regimes and anticolonial disorder. Sulu Sea piracy was undeniably a problem, but it also presented British officials with the opportunity to demonstrate the utility of colonial maritime regulation at a time of diminishing imperial influence elsewhere.

Although maritime raiding had been prevalent along Sabah's coasts for centuries, the uptick in piracy in the early 1960s nevertheless caused alarm.[66] From Sandakan in the north to the smaller fishing and trading communities of Lahad Datu, Semporna, and Tawau in the distant southeast, armed raids became increasingly common between 1961 and 1963. But so too did instances of smuggling increase in frequency, an issue precipitated by the near-total collapse of the colonial government's ability to regulate customs and trade. As reported by Nicholas Chung, a customs officer stationed in Lahad Datu between 1959 and 1961, corrupt colonial bureaucrats in what was considered a hardship post in the remote east coast routinely "bypassed or ignored" their duties and failed to inspect incoming ships. Colonial regulators proved so ineffective that Lahad Datu's docks were increasingly utilized to smuggle goods free from normal tariffs and as a place to load contraband onto vessels destined for ports across the Sulu Archipelago.[67] The decay of maritime order was therefore as much a product of ineffective colonial regulation as it was of postcolonial ineptitude or decay.

Many maritime raiders and smugglers hailed from poor and marginalized communities in the southern Philippines. The concept of "piracy" was heavily politicized, and "colonial discourse . . . presented certain acts of maritime violence as self-evidently piratical," even if such activities were necessary for survival.[68] In the early twenty-first century, recent scholarly interventions have shown how such "depredations could be seasonal or temporary survival strategies which had little to do with any overt, political challenge against a particular state." This was true for many communities across the Sulu Archipelago, the coast of Mindanao, and the wider Philippine Muslim south.[69] Systemically excluded from the wealthier Catholic north, many Suluk, "Moro," and Balangingi Samal societies were derided as *bajak lauts* (sea bandits), a term "loaded . . . with all the familiar connotations of 'pirate.'"[70] Crucially, for the Philippine government, these labels afforded clear distinctions between regular (supposedly law-abiding) Filipino citizens and their (allegedly secessionist-prone) "Moro" compatriots in the south. In this sense, Suluk "pirates," *bajak lauts*, and "savage" "Moros" were considered epistemologically incompatible with the notion of being Filipino. Likewise, the Philippine government resolved to not concern itself with issues of maritime security off the coast of Sabah; that was a British problem, and it was easy to deny that the "pirates" were Filipinos. While strategic disassociation from minority regions in the south enabled the Philippine government to turn a blind eye to its maritime security obligations, these same communities were also a boon in the pursuit of national unity across the archipelago. This dichotomy was no isolated phenomenon.

In February and March 2013, international news headlines reported that an "invasion" had taken place in Sabah, in which hundreds of armed insurgents from the Philippines crossed the Sulu Sea and landed ashore on the outskirts of Lahad Datu.[71] Representing Jamalul Kiram III, the "self-proclaimed" Sultan of Sulu, the insurgents sought to lodge "their ancestral claim" to Sabah and began a week-long standoff with Malaysian security forces.[72] Although the assault was unsuccessful, it raised international awareness of the long-standing tensions in the Sulu Sea and the persistence of age-old territorial claims and maritime conflicts. Whereas in 2013 the Philippine government distanced itself from the actions of the Sulu "invaders," subsequent administrations have expressed their eagerness to again invoke formal territorial claims over Sabah, such as in 2016 and more recently in 2021.[73] The relationship between private territorial claims waged by minority groups in the Philippines, and those asserted by the state itself, has a storied past. As in the 2010s, the development of the Philippines' decision to stake an official claim over Sabah in 1962 arose out of a combination of growing public interest in reviving the Sulu Sultanate, ideological desires to strengthen (and feasibly expand) the postcolonial state, and the personal ambitions of political elites eager to leave their mark.

On January 27, 1961, a consortium of eighteen descendants of the recently deceased Mohammad Pulalum sent a letter to Queen Elizabeth II in Britain. Pulalum was one of numerous individuals who had previously staked a claim to the title of Sulu's Sultan following the death of Sultan Jamalul Kiram II in

1936. The letter declared Pulalum's son, Salip Ali, as the new heir to Sulu. Royal to royal, the letter sought to make Sulu's plight known to the British Crown. In the letter, Salip Ali and his seventeen brothers and sisters asserted their "equal and legitimate rights over the possession of British North Borneo" alongside the other vying descendants of Jamalul Kiram II. They decried the injustice of having been denied a chance to exert their sovereignty over Sabah, citing a series of "unwritten laws, customs and traditions" to back up their claim. They argued they too should be entitled to a portion of Sabah's land and the annual cession money outlined in the historical 1878 agreement. They claimed that they had been defrauded by Britain's annexation of Sabah in 1946, and as decolonization loomed in the early 1960s, they were convinced that now was the time to act.[74]

The letter never made it as far as Britain. Early on its unlikely journey to Buckingham Palace it was intercepted and sequestered by British Embassy staff at Manila. The embassy dismissed it as an attempt by "anxious" claimants to avoid being left out, "should there be further pickings as a result of the present manoeuvres of the Kiram descendants."[75] As with many of these burgeoning private claims over Sabah, the colonial government, and the Colonial Office in London, were quick to dismiss them as fraught attempts to increase their political standing back home. Past claims had never materialized and had been easily dismissed by colonial authorities. Indeed, they were no new phenomenon: throughout the early twentieth century, private claims for land and resources in Sabah routinely surfaced and attracted public attention, but they failed to precipitate change.[76] Such claims reveal the intertwined nature of local politics across the Sulu Sea and the increasingly disputed status of British rule in Sabah. Likewise, Britain's swift dismissal of these claims reflected longstanding colonial attitudes toward anticolonial detractors and foreign policy issues facing Sabah, in which external threats and territorial ambiguities were routinely ignored or downplayed.[77]

A few days later, another letter surfaced. In this case, a different set of claimants sent a similar letter to Queen Elizabeth, along with several heads of state and other high-profile recipients across Britain, Spain, the United States, the Philippines, Sabah, Brunei, and even the United Nations. Penned by Datu Mohammad Yachub Attan bin Datu Amilhussin on February 7, 1961, the letter petitioned for himself and fifteen other Sulu dignitaries to also be considered "equal legitimate" heirs to Sulu and thereby claimants to the entirety of Sabah.[78] As with the previous letter, British officials shelved it immediately and did not issue any formal response.

But these burgeoning claims did not go away. The appointment of Nicasio Osmeña, a popular lawyer, by yet another group of Sulu pretenders signaled a further escalation.⁷⁹ Osmeña, who would briefly represent Sheikh Azahari bin Sheikh Mahmud and his Kalimantan Utara movement in 1963, was widely known as a staunch advocate of Sulu and a vocal anticolonial campaigner. Following Britain's formal colonization of Sabah in July 1946, Osmeña had made headlines across the Philippines and Malaya when he declared that Britain "had no right to the 31,000 square miles of oil, mineral and timber domain" in Borneo.⁸⁰ The vast expanse of land and its incalculable bounty of mineral wealth, he argued, ought to be returned to the Philippines, as the successor-in-interest to Sulu.⁸¹

Nicasio Osmeña was also a keen archival researcher. In the early 1960s, he made several trips to investigate colonial records in Spain, where he compiled a large dossier of treaties and land deeds signed in the nineteenth century.⁸² Many of these documents were Spanish-owned copies of records lost by Sultan Jamalul Kiram II, whose deeds, treaties, and even his bejeweled crown were stolen while he was traveling in Singapore in 1898.⁸³ Depending on their translation or interpretation, these records purported to cast doubt on Britain's status in Sabah. The original 1878 transaction signed between Sultan Jamal ul-Azam and Overbeck and Dent was viewed by Britain as an unequivocal cession or purchase. Nicasio Osmeña—and later the Philippine government—contrastingly interpreted it as a temporary arrangement, based on the Malay word *pajakan* (lease) used throughout the text.⁸⁴ Such a lease, Osmeña argued, was akin to a rental agreement that could be terminated at any given point. There is little doubt that Osmeña and the other supporters of Sulu had looked to the Philippine government's 1946 abrogation of Britain's administrative rights over the Turtle Islands for inspiration.

On receiving Osmeña's dossier, the Colonial Office determined immediately to cast it aside, as it had done with Salip Ali's and Datu Mohammad Yachub Attan's correspondence. Many of the documents were written in Spanish, and since the office claimed to lack the "facilities for translation," colonial bureaucrat H. Nield suggested that given "the circumstances we should do nothing further about it." Nield subsequently opined that "if we sent it to Osmeña and asked him to provide a translation he would undoubtedly think that we saw something in his case which we were prepared to investigate. He has no standing in this matter. He is not the accredited representative of the heirs of the Sultan of Sulu and I am sure that we should give him no encouragement whatsoever."⁸⁵

The Colonial Office expressed concern over these proliferating claims but sought to avoid legitimizing them through issuing a response. If metropolitan officials in London were determined to stick their heads in the sand and dismiss the claims, then colonial functionaries in Sabah, too, resolved to ignore the growing interest in acquiring Sabahan territory in the Philippines. Although in 1948 Governor Twining had voiced concerns over Philippine irredentism, his successors in the early 1960s appeared less worried. Governor William Goode, when pressed by journalists about the issue, claimed that "I will be surprised if . . . [the Philippine] government brings a formal claim to North Borneo before an international court." He further added, "I don't think that the people of North Borneo feel that they belong to the Sultan of Sulu."[86]

Although this sequence of private claims over Sabah failed to trigger official backing in the Philippines, the pronouncement of the Anglo-Malayan Malaysia proposal a few months later in May 1961 altered the stakes. Politicians across the Philippines had long observed Sabah with interest but were reluctant or unable to act. Talk of Sabah's inclusion in the proposed Malaysian Federation, however, made everything more urgent. Similarly, by late 1961, Nicasio Osmeña's arguments appeared to be gaining popularity. Filipinos across the archipelago increasingly questioned whether Britain's rights over Sabah could be revoked. Indeed, that Britain continued to pay so-called "shares of the annual cession money" to the heirs and successors of Sulu was perceived as a further indicator of a lease relationship rather than a permanent cession.[87] But there were sticking points. The 1878 treaty was worded in such a way that it granted Overbeck and Dent (and their successors) sovereignty over Sabah "in perpetuity" and "until the end of time."[88] Though these words were firm markers of permanence, the agreement had been configured by "rogue" agents of empire. Additionally, the fact the Spanish and subsequent American colonial administrations had acknowledged the chartered company's Sabah rights in 1885 and 1898, respectively, made it difficult for the Philippines to renege.[89] Even though it was problematic for a postcolonial state to be held accountable for the decisions of its former overlords, there was little that could be done. The legacies of nineteenth-century imperial dealings thus continued to shape questions of postcolonial sovereignty.

These disputes over translation and questions of whether Britain owned or leased its Borneo territory have been the mainstay of many historical debates over the years.[90] In aligning with either the British or the Philippine side, each of these successive orthodox interpretations retains a prominent national bias, supporting either a colonial or a nationalist agenda.[91] In seeking to step beyond these outdated national disputes, however, a more pertinent approach would be not simply to consider the validity of foreign rule in the region by identifying the existence of treaties—for this accords them a sense of legitimacy that fails to account for colonial coercion—but rather to consider them as complex legal machinations conducted by imperial agents. These paper deeds were often acquired by means of deception and obfuscation. Acts of colonization seldom, if ever, had firm legal foundations; it is folly to argue that Britain's hold over Sabah had legitimate origins, but it is equally unavailing to claim that the territory today should become part of the Philippines, for this ignores decades in which societies and cultural identities developed and transformed during the colonial and postcolonial periods. Sabah's pronounced ethnic and cultural diversity meant that while many people maintained transnational links with ethnic groups in neighboring regions (such as in Indonesian Kalimantan, Sulawesi, and the southern Philippines) others fiercely defended their local autonomy, indigeneity, and increasingly their Sabahan identity, too.

The Philippine Claim to Sabah

By late 1961, public opinion in the Philippines had become fixated on the Sabah question. People across Manila and other metropolitan hubs expressed anger and "surprise that their government had not taken the matter up" with Britain directly, as it had done concerning the Turtle Islands in 1946.[92] With the advancement of the Anglo-Malayan plan to form Malaysia, Filipino desires to stake a claim over Sabah gained urgency. Nationalist newspapers capitalized on this interest and fanned the flames of irredentism. The Manila-based *Philippines Free Press*, in particular, spun revanchist commentaries and editorials to an eager public. Considered a "respected and influential" magazine by some, the *Philippines Free Press* "launched an intensive campaign designed to spur governmental action."[93]

Throughout 1961, regional opposition to Projek Malaysia intensified across wider Southeast Asia, with Indonesia labeling it a neocolonial plot and vocal opposition emerging in Brunei. But the Philippines, under President Carlos Garcia, lacked the anticolonial outlook that characterized Sukarno's regime. Though advocating a "Filipino First" policy that attempted to resist American influence, the Garcia administration could not satisfy the popular desire for anticolonial action as advocated by Leon Ma. Guerrero III and Claro M. Recto, among other leading Filipino nationalists.[94] Political organizations across the country, ranging from the Philippine Trade Union Council to fringe communist groups, called for the Philippine government to lodge a claim over Sabah.[95] Despite this interest in Bornean territory and the widespread unease over Sabah's planned merger with Malaysia among the political establishment, the Philippines continued to exercise "very friendly relations" with Britain and Sabah.[96] But following the administration change with the inauguration of President Diosdado Macapagal on December 31, 1961, relations across the Sulu

Sea appeared set to worsen. In contrast to outgoing President Garcia, Macapagal was an outspoken critic of British colonial rule in Sabah. Macapagal's involvement in the Turtle Islands transfer, in which he represented the Department of Foreign Affairs, was formative.[97] Indeed, he was later quoted as saying that "if the Turtle Islands could become part of Philippine territory as a right, why not North Borneo?"[98] As Gerald Sussman suggests, the new president "wished to represent himself as a genuine independent nationalist" and to distance his government from the allegations of CIA interference that had hindered previous administrations.[99]

These factors, combined with ever-increasing political pressure to act, eventually led to President Macapagal's public announcement on June 22, 1962, of his "desire to see the territory [of Sabah] included as part of the national territory of the Republic of the Philippines."[100] The intensity of public—and by June 1962, official—interest in claiming Sabah was heightened by a growing sense of urgency over Sabah's impending decolonization.[101] While claiming the territory from Britain could feasibly be defended as an anticolonial action, once Sabah merged with the already-independent Malaya, such a claim would risk appearing irredentist or expansionist. As one editorial in the *Straits Times* stated in July 1962, "The moment Malaysia becomes a reality the Philippine case ... will be directed not against Britain but against fellow Asians—people with whom the Filipinos feel bonds of friendship, even of kinship."[102]

Malaysia-skeptics across Southeast Asia were gripped with a sense of urgency. Indeed, Kalimantan Utara's and the Philippines' respective claims over Sabah were highly analogous and interlinked, motivated by the same desires to act in this moment of geopolitical fluidity before Malaysia crystallized.[103] Despite seeking similar, largely overlapping, territory—which symbolically mirrored the historical entanglement of the Sulu and Brunei sultanates—the two movements coexisted, shared common objectives, and contributed to the growth of anti-Malaysia sentiments.[104] As discussed in chapter 3, in the aftermath of the failed Brunei Rebellion Sheikh Azahari fled to the Philippines, where he courted Filipino nationalists for support. Although Azahari's Kalimantan Utara plan conflicted with the Philippines' territorial claims, nationalists in the Philippines believed that these differences could be easily resolved. Congressman Godofredo Ramos, for instance, suggested that Kalimantan Utara could secure territory in Sarawak and Brunei while sparing the bulk of Sabah for the Philippines.[105] Likewise, in a secret meeting between Azahari and Princess Tarhata Kiram, brokered by Nicasio Osmeña in January 1963, a pact was formulated to divide the British Borneo territories between Kalimantan Utara and the Philippines.[106]

As with the Brunei Rebellion, colonial officials were caught off guard by the Philippine claim. What had been considered extremely unlikely by Governor Goode in January 1962 had occurred in a highly publicized spectacle just five months later.[107] When pressed by reporters for a response, Goode "declined to comment," while the official British reaction was to reject the claim with "vigour and promptness."[108] Unsurprisingly, public responses in Sabah revealed considerable indignation. Representing the territory's Chinese community, Khoo Siak Chiew said that his supporters rejected the claim "totally and unconditionally." Orang Kaya Kaya Mustapha bin Harun similarly dismissed the claim as "false and without foundation," while Donald Stephens declared that if the Philippines wished to seize Sabah, it would be "over our bodies."[109] Beyond Sabah, however, the claim elevated the Philippines in the eyes of regional anticolonialists. Support was won in Indonesia, where it was welcomed as a boost to the region's anticolonial struggle. Indonesian newspapers, for example *Harian Rakyat*, reported that it symbolized a new "Djakarta/Manila axis" in which "the Bandung Spirit of the Sukarno/Macapagal doctrine will now grow far stronger."[110] Sabah appeared increasingly surrounded.

In the Philippines, politicians worked to advance the claim while navigating considerable diplomatic blowback.[111] Although the United States publicly presented a "hands off" stance, its support for Projek Malaysia was already on the record, and it was unlikely to back anything that might threaten the Malaysia plan.[112] Salvador P. Lopez, the Philippines' acting secretary of foreign affairs, downplayed concerns that the claim would destabilize Southeast Asia, suggesting that the dispute would not cause "undesirable repercussions in Malaya and Borneo." Lopez further stressed to British officials that it would not "lead to territorial claims being put forward by other Southeast Asian countries."[113] While President Macapagal asserted that Sabah was part of the Sulu Sultanate and therefore a sovereign Philippine territory, he also framed the claim as a matter of regional security.[114] Nationalist elites in the Philippines voiced concerns that Sabah would be vulnerable to communist subversion should it become part of the Malaysian Federation. Indeed, in his January 1963 State of the Nation Address, Macapagal claimed that Malaya would not be able to "insure for long the security of North Borneo for the free world . . . [from the] potent communist threat on the Asian mainland."[115] Macapagal wanted to avoid having a "communist territory . . . at the southern frontier of the Philippines," an outcome he described as a "grave and intolerable" scenario.[116] These concerns, however, were little more than repackaged Cold War rhetoric, deployed to downplay allegations of Philippine neocolonial expansionism. As noted by Danny Wong Tze Ken, such fears were overblown because Sabah "was never under communist threat," and much of its population espoused staunchly anticommunist views.[117] Parallels can be drawn between the Philippines' apparent concerns about communism in the 1960s and the emergence of another threat in later years: that of radical Muslim separatist groups in the Philippine south and their putative links to terrorist organizations based in Sabah.[118] That both foreign policy threats perceptibly emerged from the "southern frontier"—a space synonymous with rebellion, secessionism, and extremism—indicates the extent to which Sabah was simultaneously configured in the official psyche as an existential danger and a desirable asset for the Philippines, at once threatening and yet also vital for the nation's future. This mirrors the treatment of minority groups across the Philippine south, which is purportedly beset with *bajak lauts* while also serving as the crux of the nation's myths of archipelagic unity and claims to Melayu legitimacy.

Unlike Kalimantan Utara, which broadcast rampant threats of violence and destruction on its clandestine radio stations, Salvador Lopez assured Britain that any dispute arising from the Philippines' claim could be "settled peacefully and in an atmosphere of goodwill and amity."[119] This outward promise of cordiality suggested a distinction between the methods employed by the Philippines and Kalimantan Utara. Although both sought to acquire territory in Sabah, the former was also preoccupied with maintaining relations with the member states of the Association of Southeast Asia (ASA).[120] The Philippines sought to play both the radical anticolonial savior and the conformist actor. Indeed, some Western analysts at the time voiced support for the Philippine claim, especially when contrasted with Indonesia's subsequent "Ganyang Malaysia" campaign during the Konfrontasi.[121] H. B. Jacobini, for instance, argued in 1964 that the Philippines' approach was "meticulously correct" and that Britain's "disinclination . . . to consider this claim" was indicative of colonialist condescension and constituted the root cause of the dispute.[122]

Other political commentators, in contrast, feared that the claim would lead to outright "conflict," arguing that it "constitute[d] an obstacle to the formation of . . . Malaysia."[123] Many Western observers at the time considered the successful creation of Malaysia key in countering the perceived threat of communism and in safeguarding the Borneo territories from regional advances. Despite Philippine assurances, concern and indignation ran rife throughout Sabah. Indigenous leaders across the territory were particularly "angry and hostile," while the colonial administration continued to hope that the Philippine claim "would not interfere with consideration on Malaysia."[124] Ultimately, while the claim failed to gain momentum beyond the nationalist reportage and public declarations made in the Philippines, it remained a key national objective.

Deadlock and the Road to Maphilindo as an Alternative to Malaysia

Over the following months, opposition to the Malaysia plan continued to intensify across Southeast Asia. By January 1963, the specter of Kalimantan Utara had cast the region into disarray, while rumors of militants and "secret agents" in the jungles of Borneo stoked panic and alarm.[125] Simultaneously, while the Philippine claim continued to elicit concern in Sabah, Filipino officials were not eager to further advance the claim, nor did the British appear willing to directly engage with it.

In the Philippines, nationalist journalists and politicians published a stream of articles catering to the popular demand for information and news concerning the Sabah dispute. Opinion pieces such as C. Ignacio Rivera's "The Philippines' Claim to North Borneo," published in late December 1962, suggested that the dispute had reignited long-standing territorial ambitions central to the Philippines' national psyche. These articles presented Britain's annexation of Sabah in 1946 as a missed opportunity for Sulu and the Philippines to claim the territory from the defunct North Borneo Chartered Company. The lack of Philippine action, at a time when Sabah's postwar administration was particularly vulnerable, was spun to readers as a national catastrophe. Such articles failed to acknowledge, however, that the Sulu Sultanate had been reduced to merely a symbolic institution, with neither domestic sovereignty nor autonomous foreign policy. Similarly, nationalist discourse avoided the fact that in 1946 the Philippines—fresh from the clutches of Japanese occupation, only recently decolonized, and marred by continuing socioeconomic strife—would have been hard pressed to make any moves on Sabah. The stated purpose of articles such as Rivera's was to highlight that the planned decolonization of Sabah in 1963 presented the heirs of Sulu—and thus the Philippines—with a final moment of geopolitical fluidity in which they could "terminat[e] the lease" and "regain" the territory.[126] With each successive moment of power transfer in Sabah following the initial 1878 treaty (most notably its transition in 1946 to Crown Colony status, and finally the plans for merger with Malaysia in 1963), the territory's ties to Sulu were gradually being eroded. And while sections of the Philippine public continued to push for action, President Macapagal's territorial claim had made no progress: Malaysia's planned formation date inched ever closer, and the opportunity to seize Sabah appeared increasingly slim. The claim had become a defining moment for the Macapagal administration's domestic and international reputation. Inaction could prove disastrous.

Malaya, although long portrayed in conventional historiography as a conformist postcolonial state, was widely perceived by rivals and opponents in Southeast Asia as expansionist.[127] The Malayan government made little attempt to hide its interest in Borneo's natural resources, with the Tunku Abdul Rahman declaring that Sabah and Sarawak "would be good financially [because] . . . they have oil" and other primary products.[128] Yet similar neocolonial attitudes were voiced in the Philippines, with the *Manila Times*, for instance, running a special segment titled "The Philippines' Claim to North Borneo Territory" that contained public contributions and letters on the topic. In one such submission, Manila resident Antonio S. Sannoy declared that "North Borneo has sentimental value to us" and that "by law and by tradition . . . [it] rightly belongs to the Philippines." While urging the government to "regain" the "lost paradise," Sannoy also acknowledged that "in so doing, great tact and diplomacy must be employed in dealing with our SEATO ally, Great Britain, and our ASA partner, the Federation of Malaya."[129] Such moderation, however, was rare, with other submissions calling for the use of military force.

Indeed, writing elsewhere, nationalists such as Federico Macaraeg urged direct action through any means necessary. For Macaraeg, although "Malaya is one of our best friends," the time for cordiality had passed. The Philippines "can't just sit idle while we and the generation of Filipinos yet unborn are squeezed out of our patrimony by diplomatic-political maneuvers," wrote Macaraeg. "Regaining" Sabah was not only an issue of rightful national inheritance, he argued, but also a solution to the great many socioeconomic problems that plagued the country. Macaraeg further argued that "the time is not far off due to the tremendous rate of population increase when we could need additional living space for further growth. Right now, we may have already lost by default this region [Sabah] which is one-third of our present total land area, offering untold riches in oil, rubber, and manganese, and the opportunity to the Filipino nation of attaining to greatness in the future." The promise of "living space," "untold riches," and the opportunity to boost the Philippines' image as an archipelagic nation of Melayu stock were major factors in redoubling public support for the Sabah claim.[130] But such objectives served to cast the Philippines' claim in a similar light to the vying Indonesian and Malayan attempts at incorporating Sabah into their visions of expanded archipelagic-national influence.[131]

Contemporaneously in early 1963, however, rising moderate voices in the Philippines cautioned against expansionist policies and warned of damage to the country's international standing should it press ahead with the claim. On January 8, Senator Lorenzo Sumulong publicly lambasted Macapagal's policy as irridentist and colonialist. Sumulong feared a new era of colonial aggression that threatened the core ideals of postcolonial independence. He claimed that "we now appear as seeking to colonize North Borneo instead of speeding up the ending of colonialism in that neighboring and sister country."[132] Unlike other politicians across the Philippines, Malaya, Indonesia, and Britain, who perceived Sabah as a subnational territory and a resource-rich annex, Sumulong considered it a fully fledged country-in-waiting. The senator's comments elicited considerable anger in the Philippines. Macapagal responded by claiming that Sabah was neither a nation nor a stand-alone country, but rather a territory of Sulu and the Philippines. "Colonialism is the act of taking over a territory which is not yours," wrote Macapagal, who argued that the claim was "based on the premise that North Borneo belongs to the Philippines."[133] He contended that it was perfectly compatible to assert such a claim while "recogniz[ing] the cardinal principle of self-determination."[134] Had it received wider international backing, the Philippine claim might have progressed further. But by early 1963, it was sidelined as an empty threat, with detractors condemning it as a populist appeal replete with colonial-style desires for territory and resources.

Importantly, the British government's refusal to directly engage with the Philippines posed a major obstacle for President Macapagal. The Philippines' options were also limited by the lack of US support.[135] Although the Philippine public remained favorable to claiming Sabah, the president appeared to be running out of options. As Nik Anuar Nik Mahmud has suggested, the dispute had become a matter of dignity for Macapagal: he did not want to go down in history as the president who had failed to fight for his Sabah claim. In this sense, the unwillingness of the British government and its colonial counterpart in Sabah to consider the claim caused great consternation.[136] The press in Malaya reported on this humiliation excitedly, with one editorial declaring in late 1962 that "Britain has refused to negotiate . . . because there is nothing to negotiate."[137]

But Malayan and American policymakers sought to push Britain to enter talks with the Philippines in hopes that they could resolve the dispute peacefully in time for Malaysia's proposed formation date. By January 1963, British officials felt that they had no other choice; Projek Malaysia appeared increasingly under threat.[138] At the behest of American advisors, and compelled by rising instability elsewhere in Borneo, Anglo-Philippine talks were hastily scheduled in London for late January. Indeed, as the British ambassador to the Philippines, John A. Pilcher, wrote, "Much credit is given to the Brunei rebels [Kalimantan Utara] and to the US State Department for dragging us to the conference table."[139] Although publicly, Britain joined the discussions with no "intention to raise the Philippine claim," Pilcher privately expressed an eagerness to resolve the issue.[140] The British government's official line was to promote bilateral action on piracy, condemned by metropolitan officials as the "traditional pastime for the inhabitants of Sulu."[141] But Britain also expected to use the talks to "influence the Philippines to drop its plan to take the North Borneo case to the International Court of Justice or the United Nations" and to prevent the Philippines from colluding with Azahari's Kalimantan Utara movement. Similarly, the Philippine delegation, headed by Emmanuel Pelaez, vice president and secretary of foreign affairs, reportedly "came to London with the determination to turn a deaf ear" to the British arguments.[142] Unsurprisingly, the talks ended in deadlock, with only a vague commitment to promote the "future political stability and progress" of the Borneo territories. While the Anglo-Philippine talks failed to bring an end to the Sabah dispute, they contained mentions of President Diosdado Macapagal's emergent proposal for a "Confederation of Malay States," which offered a way out, perhaps.[143]

While maintaining his opposition toward Projek Malaysia, Macapagal nevertheless sought to improve ties with Malaya and Indonesia. Facing the potential for massive public backlash if he dropped the claim, Macapagal faced the problem of how to maintain it—superficially at least—while also preserving amicable relations with neighboring states. The Philippine claim was thus directed toward the British and framed as anticolonial. Indeed, Macapagal's proposed confederation, termed Maphilindo, promoted "friendly cooperation," "goodwill," and economic development, and it was devised to resolve regional disputes while firmly situating the Philippines among the ranks of Malaya and Indonesia as postcolonial nations of Melayu origin. Simultaneously, while endorsing friendlier ties with Malaya, Macapagal also presented his Maphilindo proposal as an alternative to the Malaysia plan.

The Maphilindo Proclamation

Following the Anglo-Philippine talks in London in January 1963, the leaders of Malaya, the Philippines, and Indonesia agreed to convene in Manila in attempt to resolve the contested status of the British Borneo territories. The Manila Summit, scheduled for early June, saw President Macapagal, Prime Minister the Tunku Abdul Rahman, and President Sukarno deliberate in a reportedly "frank manner and in a most cordial atmosphere." Together they described the summit as arising from a "determination . . . to achieve closer cooperation . . . [and] to chart their common future." The Manila Accord, signed at the end of July 1963, espoused a commitment to maintain "the

MAPHILINDO, THE CONFEDERATION THAT NEVER WAS 151

stability and security of the area from subversion . . . and to ensure the peaceful development of their respective countries."[144]

The outwardly earnest and cordial nature of the Manila Accord appeared as a stark contrast to the violence and political disturbances unfolding on the ground in Sabah and wider British Borneo. By July, Indonesian support for rebel groups had led to a series of armed clashes and raids deep in Sabah's interior and along the remote east coast.[145] Likewise, the Philippines remained staunchly committed to its Sabah claim. Yet the Manila Accord proffered a miraculous, if unlikely, solution to Southeast Asia's spiraling geopolitical instability. Maphilindo, a "Confederation of nations of Malay origin," was born amid this intense ideological rivalry, promoting "brotherliness and cordiality."[146] Detailed in map 3 below, the proposed confederation stretched all the way from Aceh in the far west to Papua in the east.

Local and foreign observers alike were stunned. Almost immediately, Maphilindo elicited great publicity as a venture that "could become the most significant Southeast Asian development in recent years."[147] In Singapore, Soh Tiang Keong claimed excitedly that Maphilindo could become "the world's third biggest economic force after the US and Russia." In possessing a vast territory, complete with massive forest, agricultural, and mineral reserves,

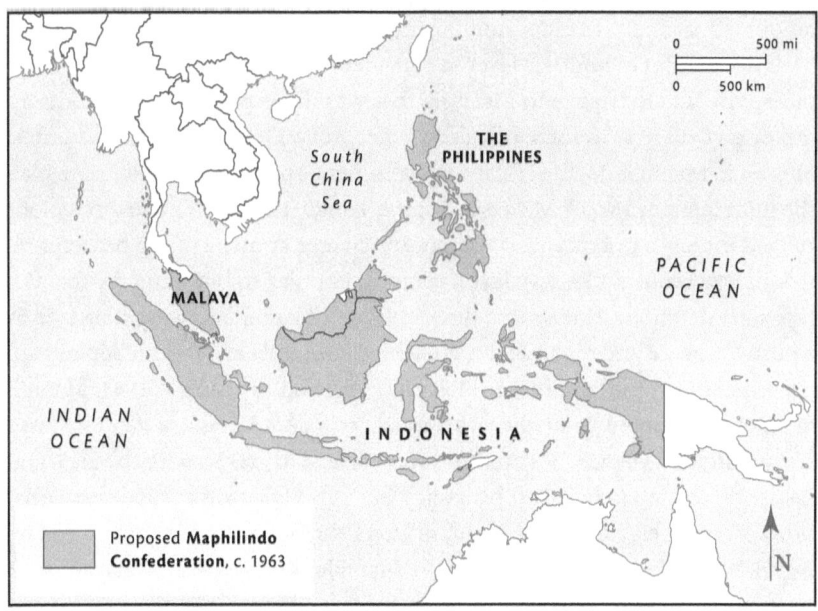

MAP 3. Map detailing the proposed Maphilindo Confederation, circa 1963. Map by Erin Greb Cartography.

Maphilindo would, according to Soh, "control the world's rubber production" and "work one of the biggest deposits of tin, iron and manganese ore."[148] Sabah was to play a central role in this proposed confederation: as a vast territory with untapped resources, it would be of considerable economic value to Malaya, the Philippines, and Indonesia. Simultaneously, the Maphilindo confederation presented a potential solution to the complex and overlapping claims afflicting the territory. Sabah could be split three ways, though at the expense of the Malaysia plan. Through Maphilindo, Sabah would essentially serve as a colonial territory. Although some observers remained cautious about whether Maphilindo would ever be institutionalized to the point of becoming a confederation, it was viewed with considerable optimism and excitement by many in the weeks preceding the formation of Malaysia.[149] Advocates at the time hoped that, even if Maphilindo never materialized, the positivity induced by the proposed confederation would counter the regional hostility surrounding Indonesia's unfolding Konfrontasi, the Philippines' claim, and Projek Malaysia.

This was ultimately wishful thinking, as even in the run-up to the tripartite talks, Kalimantan Utara's subversive efforts continued to serve as a distraction.[150] Indeed, just five days after the Manila Accord and the Maphilindo proclamation, General Abdul Haris Nasution publicly admitted that Indonesia was providing financial and military support for Azahari's movement.[151] Maphilindo therefore represented a colorful diversion. On one level, it amounted to a politicized vision for promoting unity among the peoples of Melayu origin. On another level, it provided both Indonesia and the Philippines with an alternative to Malaysia that was more peaceful than Konfrontasi or any attempt to forcefully acquire territory. Despite widespread public interest in Maphilindo, the Malayan government's primary objective remained the fulfillment of Projek Malaysia. For the Tunku, the Maphilindo discussions offered merely a pragmatic, if temporary, chance at maintaining peaceful relations and reducing anti-Malaysia rhetoric in order to buy time for the Malaysian Federation. At the same time, although Maphilindo was publicized as a push for peace and regional development, Indonesia and the Philippines approached it as a tool to prevent Malaysia's creation. By August 1963, Maphilindo had amounted to neither a regional confederation nor a genuine push toward attaining peace. But Sukarno was particularly taken with the idea, and he continued to anchor it to his policy of "pan-Malayanism" and proclamations of archipelagic unity. Indeed, in late 1963, Sukarno was quoted as saying that "for the sake of greatness, the Maphilindo nations of Malayan stock must unite."[152]

But Sabah's position in these conceptions of Melayu archipelagic unity remained tenuous and disputed. Although the Maphilindo proposal purported to adhere to the ideals of *mushawarah* (consultation) and *mufukat* (consensus of opinion) in its attempts to resolve the Sabah issue, it was ultimately predicated on Sabah's incorporation into a larger confederation, irrespective of local sentiments. Added to this was the fact that many locals in Sabah—in particular, large sections of its Kadazandusun and Chinese populations—did not support the notion of "pan-Malayanism." The same concerns over Malay domination that had undermined the Malaysia plan also shaped people's opinions on Maphilindo.

Despite these uncertainties, however, Maphilindo won considerable support and interest among Western observers and analysts. Maphilindo was praised not only for offering a potential solution to the tensions in Southeast Asia but also for its apparent capacity to become a powerful anticommunist device. In prioritizing fears of communism, Alastair Taylor wrote in 1964 that if Maphilindo transitioned into a more structured political entity, inclusive of Sabah and Sarawak, it would "comprise an overwhelming majority of Malay stock [compared to which] . . . the scattered Chinese enclaves would always remain demographically weak and politically vulnerable." Taylor warned of the growing influence of "Communist China" and asked, "What would serve so well as an institutionalised and armed Maphilindo?"[153]

As an alternative to Malaysia for some, as a temporary opportunity to promote peace for others, and as an anticommunist device for yet more still, the Maphilindo proposal was popularized as an exciting postcolonial project during a period of geopolitical fluidity. But needless to say, Maphilindo did not last long. It swiftly became politicized, with its supporters quick to espouse visions of a united Malay race that left little room for minority participation. It was clear that the promise of Maphilindo was being utilized by the Philippines, Indonesia, and Malaya to meet different ends, whether national aggrandizement, regional expansionism, or obfuscation. Maphilindo was never actualized, but it persisted as a template and a mentality for promoting regional cordiality and consensus-based diplomacy, notions that would live on in subsequent political organizations in Southeast Asia. Despite the downfall of Maphilindo, and the continuing tensions surrounding the Malaysia plan and the subsequent Konfrontasi, the tenets of *mushawarah* and *mufukat*, as enshrined in Macapagal's proposal, would later play a foundational role in the Association of Southeast Asian Nations (ASEAN). It was only in early 1966 that the Tunku Abdul Rahman would finally declare that "Maphilindo is dead" and that it was swiftly "outmoded because it was based on a racialist concept."[154] Maphilindo's purported purpose of creating a powerful union of Malay peoples—often encapsulated in Sukarno's notion of pan-Malayanism—failed to gain traction in Malaya's and Singapore's multiethnic societies. While some

Chinese leaders, such as Tan Siew Sin, president of the Malayan Chinese Association, were initially supportive of Maphilindo—describing it as "enlightened" and to the "benefit of all"—an increasing number of Chinese residents across Malaya and Sabah soon turned cold on the idea, troubled by its anti-Chinese dimensions and uninspired by the calls for pan-Malay unity.[155] For Sabah's wider public, Maphilindo represented the dangers of foreign overlordship and economic domination, with its lure of regional archipelagic aggrandizement offering little reprieve.

From the very outset, Maphilindo and its paradoxical promises of peace and cordiality amid the proliferating Konfrontasi faced an uphill struggle. C. R. Ashwin, of the Australian Department of Foreign Affairs and Trade, argued that it almost immediately "lapsed because of confrontation." He further opined that "it was very much a political creation of the moment aiming at dissolving the Malaysia problem within a wider framework of association."[156] Along these lines, Maphilindo presented yet another path toward decolonization and state creation (and purportedly even further colonization) at a time when foreign powers scrambled for territory and influence over Sabah through the Malaysia plan, the Philippines' claim, and the Kalimantan Utara movement.

Despite the multilateral interest and public excitement surrounding Maphilindo, the proposal failed to progress beyond its initial July 1963 proclamation. Although Maphilindo was consigned to wishful thinking and promises of pan-Melayu unity, the grandiose intentions to create a Southeast Asian economic superpower continued to elicit interest among policymakers, political analysts, and members of the public even after the formation of Malaysia. Beyond this, the events leading up to the Maphilindo proclamation were reflective of the intensity of the regional scrambles for territory over Sabah. As with Kalimantan Utara's attempts to seize control over the British Borneo territories, the Philippines sought to demonstrate its ability to enlarge its archipelagic sphere and strengthen itself economically and strategically while revoking perceived historical aberrations through claiming Sabah. The multiplicity of these contemporaneous claims and dreams of archipelagic expansion centering on Sabah indicates the extent to which regional actors perceived the end of empire as a final moment of geopolitical fluidity before borders and regional alignments were crystallized into their new postcolonial shapes. As journalists in Malaya were quick to point out at the time, geopolitical disputes waged against Western colonial powers were markedly easier to justify and rationalize compared to those lodged against postcolonial neighbors, with whom the "bonds of . . . kinship" would undermine claims and problematize aggression.[157] Indeed, this was one of the major issues that Kalimantan Utara faced when it alienated the very people in Sabah that it set out to impress.

Similarly, although anticolonialism was a common rallying cry at the time—serving as a major motivator in the Philippines' requisition of the Turtle Islands in the late 1940s, and again in its Sabah claim in the early 1960s—postcolonial states adopted a variety of approaches in their attempts at securing territory and reordering political boundaries. That President Macapagal also framed his Sabah claim in terms of countering the perceived threat of communist influences from the south suggests that Southeast Asian political actors were willing to turn to a variety of methods to achieve their ends, including deference to the West's strategic and ideological concerns. As argued throughout this book, Sabah never faced any credible communist threat. But that did not mean that metropolitan advisors in London, American analysts, and even various Malayan and Filipino politicians, were not fearful of perceived communist advances.

Through considering the region's complex maritime entanglements, from the legacies of Tuwan Nahuda Kalayakan and other precolonial folktales to the muddied Sulu Sea boundaries during the end of empire, this chapter has underscored Sabah's status as a territory contested from virtually all directions. Together with chapters 3 and 5, it paints a picture of maritime Southeast Asia as a region beset with vying dreams of archipelagic unity and attempts at securing national certification through territorial expansion. Whether offering demographic and material gains for Malaya, physical territory for the Kalimantan Utara movement, or ideological benefits for the Philippines, Sabah was a cornerstone in the making of postcolonial Southeast Asia.

CHAPTER 5

Creating Malaysia, "A Shotgun Colonial Wedding"

The island of Borneo has been entwined with maritime Southeast Asia's foremost polities for centuries, with its wider socioeconomic connections stretching further across Asia, the Middle East, and Europe. Yet for many foreign observers throughout history the island appeared isolated, situated "at the periphery . . . as if it were a low-lying coral reef barely visible on the distant horizon."[1] In literature, as in contemporary travel writing today, the region is cast as exotic, foreign, and at times even otherworldly.[2] Within Southeast Asia, however, Borneo's centrality was never in doubt. Amid the geopolitical fluidity of emerging postcolonial statehood in the mid-twentieth century, the region gained further significance as a core component in competing visions of archipelagic unity. For postcolonial elites across Malaya, Indonesia, and the Philippines, the Borneo territories were conceptualized as proffering resource wealth, territory, and strategic security, while also enabling politicized claims to legitimacy as one of Southeast Asia's regions of original Melayu stock.

This chapter builds on this book's focus on vying archipelagic dreams by analyzing the Anglo-Malayan attempts to incorporate Sabah into the planned Federation of Malaysia. Projek Malaysia, first publicly announced in May 1961, was devised to achieve both British decolonization goals and Malayan postcolonial state-formation ambitions. Unlike with the instances of decolonization that occurred in other colonial territories across the world, in Southeast Asia

Britain sought to manage its withdrawal in order to preserve its commercial and strategic interests.[3] Malayan policymakers stood to benefit from this arrangement, and they worked closely with their British counterparts to facilitate an orderly colonial departure and to position themselves as future custodians in Borneo. And Malaya, which gained independence in 1957, was increasingly seen in the West as a bulwark against perceived communist advances and thus as critical to strengthen.[4] This view was frequently espoused in Western strategic analyses, with American Embassy officials stationed in Kuala Lumpur noting in April 1962, for instance, that "Malaya is a 'showcase' of democracy in an area which is seriously threatened by communism." The "continued existence of a sound and prosperous Malaya," they argued, would be a "constant refutation of communist propaganda and an example to neighboring countries."[5] Similarly, Western policymakers envisioned the Malaysia concept as a "showcase" of enlightened and progressive decolonization, a model for colonial withdrawal to be applied elsewhere across the British Empire.

Although politicians in Britain and the United States reacted to the perceived threat of communism at the time, it was the territorial claims waged by Indonesia and the Philippines that stoked greater alarm within colonial and local elite circles in Sabah. Yet the received wisdom tends to reflect only the global Cold War paradigm by overinflating Soviet and Chinese geopolitical intentions while also placing too much emphasis on Western responses to these perceived threats.[6] And as with the continuation of colonialist tropes and vagaries in contemporary memoirs and travel writings, the fixation on the lingering specter of communism continues to weigh heavily in accounts of the formation of Malaysia.[7] These historiographical tendencies have clouded explanations of Malaya's colonial-style role in securing Sabah for demographic, territorial, and strategic reasons. Not only did the Malayan political elite consider the British Borneo territories as necessary prerequisites to the inclusion of Singapore in an enlarged federation, but they were also motivated by the contemporaneous rise in interest in Sabahan territory across maritime Southeast Asia. From Malaya's perspective, if it did not subsume Sabah and Sarawak, then surely a competitor would. As discussed in chapters 3 and 4, the emergence of rival territorial claims—both private and official—led to a sharp escalation of tensions over the constitutional future of the Borneo territories. Throughout 1962 and 1963, amid the rise of Kalimantan Utara, Indonesian aggression, the Philippines' claim to Sabah, and the Maphilindo proposal, Projek Malaysia gained urgency and importance for Britain and Malaya. This book therefore paints a picture of contingency that rejects prevailing teleological narratives surrounding the formation of Malaysia. By examining this political potentiality, in which Sabah's role in Malaysia was increasingly uncertain throughout 1962 and

1963, it is possible to cast greater light on the local motivations and dealings that have been otherwise overlooked. Whether concerning the role of key local elites or the wider voice of the public, the effects wrought by local agency cannot be overstated.

This chapter is structured into seven sections. The first section argues for a critical reassessment of Sabah's role in state-making processes, suggesting that its latent political potentiality has been overlooked. Section two examines how Sabah came under increasing foreign interest following the proclamation of the Malaysia plan. Sections three and four look at rising international and local opposition to Projek Malaysia, demonstrating how much of this resistance hinged on disagreements over the inclusion of the Borneo territories. The fifth section lays out the major civil-political developments that took place in the territory following the announcement of the Malaysia plan, most notably the emergence of political parties and the public push for constitutional development. The chapter then turns to the various Anglo-Malayan strategies for advancing the merger, with analysis of performative political enquiries, inducements, and policies of obfuscation. The final section examines the so-called moment of *merdeka* and the creation of Malaysia.

The Political Potentiality of State Making

Scholarship on imperial withdrawal and postcolonial state formation in Southeast Asia tends to view Sabah as a fringe territory that was automatically subsumed into the larger Federation of Malaysia.[8] This approach, however, is inherently teleological, resting on the assumption that Sabah was predestined to serve Anglo-Malayan state-making interests as little more than a passive component. The formation of Malaysia itself is similarly depicted as the inherent, logical outcome of British imperialism in Southeast Asia, an idea that "was not new, having been broached on a number of occasions by the British and various local groups" in Malaya.[9] Any discussion of contingency is typically limited to mentions of regional opposition, but even this, through invoking the ultimately futile Indonesian Konfrontasi, does little to counter the notion advanced by Malayan politicians at the time that Sabah was irrevocably and always part of the broader Melayu archipelagic sphere.

In this sense, Sabah is typically considered only in passing for its role as a constituent piece of the eventual Malaysian state, a token territory enabling Singapore's inclusion in the federation. This results in little agency being afforded to Sabah's public, its local political elite, or even its ruling colonial bureaucracy. Indeed, the colonial bureaucracy is erroneously melted into the broader category of British metropolitan thinking, despite the fact that Sabah's leading colonial administrators were outspoken in their skepticism of, and at times outright opposition to, the idea of decolonizing the territory through Projek Malaysia.[10] The colonial view in Sabah in the late 1950s and early 1960s, which was at variance to that advocated by metropolitan and Malayan policymakers, was that the territory required at least five to ten years of additional colonial guidance before any form of decolonization could be countenanced.[11] And importantly, many local elites and power brokers initially echoed this stance, envisioning that colonial stewardship would persist well into the 1970s to serve as a bulwark against foreign influence, to preserve business interests, and to stem the perceived tyranny of rival ethnic communities. Yet these local perspectives have been all but written out of conventional analyses. Opinions on decolonization and *merdeka* were particularly varied across Sabah, with staunch ideological differences echoing the territory's pronounced ethnic and cultural diversity. These debates were fraught: advocates of merger with Malaysia jostled with supporters of continued colonial rule, while those favoring alignment with Kalimantan Utara or the Philippines railed against those pushing for independent Bornean statehood, and so on.

By reading backwards and consulting correspondence, reportage, and material circulated at the time, it is evident that even on the eve of Malaysia's formation, Sabah's participation was anything but certain. And without Sabah, the creation of Malaysia itself would have been virtually impossible.[12] While the colony's initially nonconformist colonial bureaucrats would be swiftly brought into line to respect the directives from London and Kuala Lumpur—as servants of empire they ultimately had little choice—the same could not be said for all of Sabah's local elites. A softer touch, whether through collaboration, inducements, or coercion, would be required to advance the Malaysia proposal among local power brokers.

Furthermore, through analyzing the dynamic roles played by Sabah's local elites, who despite lacking formal positions of authority in colonial governance were nevertheless politically influential and commanded sizable public support, it is possible to show the extent to which the territory's decolonization experience was a fluid and uncertain process. Countering this historiographical orthodoxy yields two important outcomes: first, it denaturalizes and problematizes the otherwise plain explanations of the formation of Malaysia; and second, it contributes to the uncovering of local agency and public opinion that are otherwise obscured.

Casting new light on these local perspectives in Sabah's late colonial and postcolonial periods is particularly valuable considering the lack of available material concerning grassroots voices. Unlike the vast scale of government records in the colonial archive, there is comparatively little written evidence pertaining to ordinary Sabahans. This is a quandary not unfamiliar to those interested in similar colonial-postcolonial transitions elsewhere across the globe. Widespread illiteracy, failed education programs, poverty, and broader civic dysfunctionality in Sabah had long inhibited the emergence of the types of Western-style party politics observed in many mainstream decolonization cases, rendering the public particularly voiceless. That political parties in Sabah only emerged in the early 1960s is typically viewed as evidence indicating the territory's ostensible lack of maturity.[13] This has led to a failure to recognize the varied local-traditional forms of political agency and civic expression that did exist but that evaded preservation in the official archives owing to a lack of electoral records, written material, and colonial-style bureaucratic addenda. In turn, this has resulted in broad-brush dismissals of Sabah's public as politically immature and passive passengers in Southeast Asian and imperial history.[14] Yet the crystallization of elite voices, explored in chapter 2, reveals strong local efforts to participate in—and at times to dictate the direction of—political discussions. Importantly, this tendency among Sabah's local elite to publicly question colonial authority, condemn administrative neglect, and push for improved prosperity, displays the political potentiality of Sabah's diverse public. These undercurrents of civic participation—always on the verge of exploding into either teeming anticolonial antagonism or vicious ethnocultural conflict, but never quite doing so—served as the engine of Sabah's history. They also wrought major effects on the nature of Britain's eventual withdrawal, the formation of Malaysia, and the reshaping of archipelagic Southeast Asia in a world after empire.

Parallel to this story of local political potentiality in Sabah were the regional crises and contests over its territory, which reached a head between 1961 and 1963. This heady brew of transnational rivalry, expansionism, subversion, and competing dreams of archipelagic unity, explored in chapters 3 and 4, offers invaluable nuance toward better understanding Sabah's decolonization experience. Through this, it is possible to better understand a range of decolonization and state-formation processes in cognate subnational territories across the world.

"Manifest Destiny Syndrome" and the Subjugation of Borneo

Regional contests over Sabah's territory drew interest from the world's foremost powers. In Moscow, the state-owned news agency issued condemnations of Projek Malaysia, categorizing it as an attempt at preserving Western colonial influence.[15] Half a world away, American diplomats in Singapore issued similar criticisms, although instead directed at Malaya's rivals, namely Indonesia and the Philippines because of their competing interest in the British Borneo territories. Indeed, on January 12, 1963, amid rising geopolitical uncertainty in Borneo, Charles F. Baldwin, the US ambassador to Malaya, claimed that Philippine president Diosdado Macapagal and Indonesian president Sukarno were both delusional. In a memorandum to Secretary of State Dean Rusk, Baldwin expressed "serious doubts [concerning their] . . . grasp [on] reality. Both men [are] apparently suffering from manifest destiny syndrome. Each has reached [the] decision that with British withdrawal from Borneo, his country, by geographic proximity, logic of history, and intrinsic worth, is [the] only logical successor."[16]

Charles Baldwin feared that if either the Philippines or Kalimantan Utara (and by virtue of this, Indonesia) took control over Sabah, "an interim period of so-called independence would be followed by an inevitable plea for annexation."[17] Although much of the United States' Southeast Asian strategy revolved around communist containment, there was as early as 1961 growing acknowledgement in American policymaking circles that regional attempts by postcolonial states at expanding into decolonization power vacuums constituted the foremost issue facing maritime Southeast Asia.[18] Robert Donhauser, for instance, claimed in October 1961 that the communist threat was "considerably less . . . acute" than in previous years and that the "communists neither speak for the masses nor represent the 'wave of the future.'"[19] The successful containment of communist forces in Malaya during the Emergency, combined with the perceived lack of civic or political maturity across the seas in Borneo, rendered the threat of foreign annexation by an aggressive neighbor more pressing than subversion of a purely ideological nature. These views also reveal an awareness of the conceptual differences between actual independent self-governance on the one hand and "independence" through merger with, or annexation by, a larger state on the other. In their view, Sabah's independence could not be won through either Kalimantan Utara's or the Philippines' support, as that would result in eventual annexation.

These concerns developed further in response to the publicized interest among Philippine, Indonesian, and Kalimantan Utara elite circles in extending control over Sabah. But how did these territorial designs differ from Projek Malaysia? Were Malaya's claims over Sabah any more justifiable than those of Indonesia, the Philippines, or the Brunei rebels? To an extent, such questions presuppose that the postcolonial future of the Borneo territories was suited only for continued foreign rule. Although there was talk in Sabah of independent statehood, this had failed to draw sufficient public support, and *merdeka* was increasingly framed in terms of merger with, or annexation by, a foreign entity or federation. Independence, merger, and annexation became increasingly intertwined and muddied. Yet few have questioned why independent self-governance was never on the table. Instead, successive colonial-inspired, orthodox, and Malayan nationalist schools of thought have identified supposedly ironclad cultural, ethnic, commercial, and institutional (largely colonial) ties connecting Borneo to the Malayan Peninsula. This act of conceptually shrinking the vast stretch of open sea separating the two distant regions, to connect Borneo and Malaya, suited the colonial agenda in the last days of empire, as it did Malayan politicians eager to incorporate a new territory and its people. Similarly, growing numbers of local Sabahan elites supported alignment with the peninsula as a way of strengthening their newfound political and commercial capital. Through this, the idea of Malaysia was naturalized in Western policymaking as the only logical—and the only strategically secure—product of Britain's imperial withdrawal from Southeast Asia.

But Projek Malaysia was far from a natural, unforced decolonization outcome. It was instead realized through an active process of state creation, coercion, and disenfranchisement, in which elite interests were masked under the guise of local agency. Likewise, this process of federalizing Britain's Southeast Asian empire into an archipelagic bloc was characterized by the forging of artificial links where previously only loose maritime ties had existed.[20] Although the bulk of Sabah's trading was historically oriented north toward Hong Kong, Japan, and Taiwan, rather than laterally facing Malaya in the west, it was the latter, rather than the former, that was chosen as the nexus of the merger.[21] Indeed, commercial records reveal not only that Sabah was a primary exporter of raw materials to Hong Kong but that it was correspondingly dependent on the manufactured goods produced by factories across Cheung Sha Wan, Tai Kok Tsui, and San Po Kong, among other industrial districts throughout the city. This is not to claim that Sabah's peninsular links were commercially irrelevant, but instead that its relationship with Malaya was more akin to rivalry between cognate cultivation and raw material-based economies than the complementary interdependence experienced between Hong Kong and its Bornean partner. Indeed, United Nations economists correlated the unanticipated, short-lived rise in Malayan rubber exports in 1962 to the decrease in production in Sabah, Sarawak, Indonesia, and Vietnam, indicating the extent to which these were competitors each vying for the same diminishing market.[22] Nevertheless, that Sabah was economically entwined with both Malaya and Hong Kong—each separated from it by hundreds of miles of open sea—suggests that it had options.

In cultural and demographic terms, too, the situation proved complex. Although they were protective of their indigenous identity, increasing numbers of coastal Kadazandusuns were by the early 1960s beginning to convert to Islam.[23] By the 1970s, after the formation of Malaysia, they would eventually form a sizable Muslim population, together with the territory's Suluk, Bajau, Brunei, Malay, and other Muslim residents, who would be broadly conceived by peninsular elites as future *bumiputera*. "In embracing the Islamic faith," wrote Herman Luping, increasing numbers of Sabahans began to "separate themselves from their original . . . ethnic identity" and consider themselves as Malays.[24] But this was matched by an increase in ethnic discord among other indigenous communities, with increased opposition to the spread of Islam recorded in *kampongs* across the interior between 1961 and 1963.[25]

Importantly, this was a period of unprecedented demographic change in Sabah. As detailed in table 1 below, between 1951 and 1960 the number of ethnically Chinese residents grew by 41 percent, compared to an increase of only 24 percent among the Kadazandusuns, and 19 percent among the Muruts.[26] Sabah's large Chinse population is frequently mislabeled as a transient immigrant community, despite census records indicating that over 90 percent were born in the colony. These communities were firmly embedded in the socioeconomic fabric of the territory, serving as clerks, technicians, business owners, farmers, traders, laborers, landowners, and administrators, rather than fleeting sojourners. Nevertheless, Sabah's Hakka and Cantonese communities also maintained "long-established connections" with Hong Kong and China.[27] This set them apart from other Sabahan locals, with many of the colony's poor resenting the perceived wealth and influence displayed by their Chinese counterparts. Indeed, as argued by Cameron Cobbold in his report for the Commission of Enquiry to determine public opinion on the Malaysia issue, "The commercial

Table 1 Demographic change in Sabah, 1951–60

ETHNIC GROUP	1951	1960	PERCENTAGE INCREASE
Kadazandusun	117,867	145,650	24
Murut	18,724	22,343	19
Bajau	44,728	61,838	38
Other Indigenous	61,690	80,002	30
Chinese	74,374	104,855	41
European	1,213	1,807	49
Others	15,545	37,833	143
Total	334,141	454,328	36

Source: 1951 and 1960 census data, *Colonial Annual Report: North Borneo 1960* (London: Her Majesty's Stationery Office, 1961), 18.

interests of North Borneo, particularly in the flourishing Chinese business communities of Sandakan and Tawau, lie more with Hong Kong and eastwards than with Singapore."[28]

These economic and demographic links paint a picture of contingency that is valuable in denaturalizing official explanations of the formation of Malaysia. Added to this is the conceptual framework surrounding Sabah's initial colonization in the 1880s, in which early administrators actively modeled the new settlements in Borneo on Hong Kong, the archetype of imperial entrepôt trade. They were even named as such, with the port of Sandakan popularly referred to as "Little Hong Kong." Although late colonial Sabah theoretically held a multitude of options for its postcolonial future, only one was deemed a suitable match by its metropolitan overlords. There was logic to this thinking: postcolonial union between Sabah and Hong Kong would have doubtless provoked uproar and instability. But so too would virtually any proposed merger in a decolonizing world in which independent statehood served as the gold standard. Yet Britain was determined to play a paternalistic role in enforcing a union that it considered demographically, economically, and strategically sound, if also for convenience and to save face. US State Department records indicated widespread concern that the merger would be perceived internationally as coerced. In one such discussion, Projek Malaysia was described to Secretary of State Dean Rusk as a "shotgun colonial wedding," whereby Sabah was being strong-armed into union with Malaya by Britain, the shotgun-wielding parent, to block it from other prying suitors.[29] But since the late 1990s and early 2000s, scholarship has rejected this view, instead asserting that Malaya, not Britain, was the driving force behind merger.[30]

Forced union served imperial as well as Malayan postcolonial interests. The British Borneo territories, having been formally colonized only in 1946, still bore the marks of their anachronistic chartered company and Raj forbears. British and Malayan politicians alike conceived Sabah in particular as a territory too vulnerable (and too valuable) to be independent. Not only did it perceivably lack adequate administrative, infrastructural, and sociopolitical development, but it was also considered defenseless against external security threats. Western security concerns at the time were motivated by the perceived threat of communism, with metropolitan officials warning that Sabah's growing Chinese population would render it increasingly vulnerable. Merger would act as a shield.

Despite the talk of decolonization and equitable merger, however, Borneo continued to be conceived as a colonial territory prized for its commercial and resource wealth. Anglo-Malayan strategies were also informed by the fraught independence wars unfolding elsewhere across the colonial world. As

Anthony Stockwell writes, "The federation of proximate, if disparate, territories was believed to carry administrative, economic and strategic advantages" in times of declining colonial influence. Even in the early 1960s, memories of Britain's wartime collapse in Southeast Asia continued to shape imperial thinking: "It was felt that colonial fragmentation had contributed to the military debacle of 1941–42 and could not be allowed to jeopardize Britain's position" in the future.[31]

While Sabah's colonial government continued to believe it best to delay decolonization until the 1970s, Malayan politicians had long sought to promote cultural and nationalistic links to justify a speedy merger.[32] Foremost among these links was the rise of Malay Bahasa as a national language, which, alongside Islam, served as the one of the two "great vectors of *Melayu* identity" that produced, "at its mad fringes, a powerful ethno-linguistic nationalism."[33] The proposed incorporation of the Borneo territories into a greater Malaysia offered a distinct set of advantages for Malaya. While Britain was primarily concerned with merging Singapore and Malaya for security reasons, many Malayan elites feared that they would lose influence with the inclusion of Singapore's Chinese-majority population.[34] Malaya's prime minister, the Tunku Abdul Rahman, believed that the absorption of Sabah's and Sarawak's non-Chinese inhabitants through Projek Malaysia would "cushion" Malaya from any perceived ethnic imbalance.[35] For the Tunku, it was at first enough to classify Sabah's and Sarawak's residents as non-Chinese, but the ultimate goal remained to consolidate Melayu archipelagic supremacy through recasting them as *bumiputera* and consolidating Melayu identity. Critics were quick to note that despite public promises to maintain diversity and equality, the new federation was never envisaged as a pluralistic "Malaysian Malaysia." As argued by James Ongkili, the "special position" of the ethnic Malays in Malaysia had always been evident. Not only was it widely recognized but it was also "given explicit legal sanction by being written into" the federation's constitution. With British support, Malaya's ruling elite advanced a version of the Malaysia plan that was "inescapab[ly] . . . a *bumiputera*-based undertaking."[36] All of this indicates that the formation of Malaysia was not carried out among equal merger partners but rather was a process geared to aid a peninsular nationalist agenda in the creation of a Melayu-centric archipelagic state.

Key to this process was the inherent flexibility of ideas of indigeneity. In many ways, indigenous identity is a "socially constructed ascription" that numerous groups within a state may claim. Indeed, notions of indigeneity could be invoked (or revoked) to "challenge or support dominant founding myths of nation-states."[37] For the purposes of the Malaysia plan, Sabah's and Sarawak's diverse indigenous populations—who did not ascribe to any unified national identity—were simultaneously considered to be the "definitive" original inhabitants of Borneo and yet also ethnically flexible enough to be morphed into Malayan *bumiputera*.[38] As well as serving the Malayan nationalistic agenda, this also suited the West's preoccupation with countering the perceived communist threat, which so frequently resulted in the arbitrary sidelining of Chinese communities.[39]

International Opposition to the Malaysia Plan

Anglo-Malayan plans to form Malaysia drew international condemnation from the very outset in 1961. As explored in chapters 3 and 4, anti-Malaysia and anticolonial sentiments, which often masked competing designs for territorial expansion, proliferated widely across Brunei, Indonesia, and the Philippines. Although publicized as a pluralistic postcolonial union, the Malaysia plan swiftly gained a reputation internationally for being a neocolonial plot. This was the line adopted by states across the Communist Bloc, too, who turned to the broadcasting of anticolonial material across the airwaves to criticize the West's support for Projek Malaysia.

In an era dominated by Cold War divisions, these critiques of the yet-to-be-formed Malaysian Federation aggravated geopolitical tensions. Although there was no communist presence in Sabah, Western policymakers sought to frame the Malaysia proposal as an attempt at preventing the southward spread of nefarious ideologies. Anglo-Malayan state-making ambitions, according to one channel transmitted by TASS (the Telegraph Agency of the Soviet Union), were but a "new colonial noose" through which Britain would be able to "bind together the remnants of . . . [its] empire in Southeast Asia."[40] Speaking in broadcasts aired by the Korean Central News Agency, North Korean officials decried the plan in February 1963 as a "colonialist plot" designed to enable Britain to "bolster their tottering colonial ruling system . . . and maintain their slave domination over the people there by means of neo-colonialism."[41] Similar views were also expressed by state media outlets in North Vietnam and the People's Republic of China throughout this period. But foreign communist involvement stopped there. While this rhetoric was pervasive, the Communist Bloc was not pulling the strings to undermine Anglo-Malayan interests in Borneo, as Western policymakers argued.

Nevertheless, this stream of anti-Malaysia rhetoric contributed to the creation of a single, common language of condemnation. Identical words and turns of phrase were adopted by distant international actors and regional Southeast Asian neighbors alike in order to convey, in the harshest of terms, what they saw as Malaysia's inherent faults and Britain's continuing misconduct. Foremost within this rhetoric were the allegations of neocolonialism, that the departing colonial power was installing a successor to carry out its bidding through an elaborate state-making scheme. These condemnations were popularized across Southeast Asia by a process of anticolonial mimicry; state-making endeavors, such as Kalimantan Utara, imitated the appearance and function of the world's leading anticolonial movements to advance their own visions of postcolonial statehood. Although many scholars have since dismissed Malaysia's ostensibly neocolonial tendencies, such claims appeared to strike at the very core of postcolonial transitions in Southeast Asia.[42] In many ways a vague term, "neocolonialism" was a charge that could be levied at virtually any state—colonial or postcolonial—attempting to exploit resources, marginalize minority groups, or impose controversial laws. "A term of opprobrium," neocolonialism was utilized by a range of critics "to denote economic subjugation" and political domination after the formal end to colonial rule.[43] Sometimes these international criticisms of Southeast Asian neocolonialism broke rank, with the North Vietnamese government instead issuing a harsh condemnation of the Philippines' vying claim over Sabah in December 1962. One such proclamation aired on North Vietnamese radio described the Philippines as an American satellite that sought to colonize Sabah and spread imperialist influence.[44] Around the same time, a Soviet radio channel attempted to sow seeds of division in the West by claiming that the Maphilindo Confederation was in fact a US-sponsored plot to undermine Projek Malaysia and advance American "colonialist designs." According to Soviet analysts, Borneo was a resource-rich frontier brimming with oil deposits that the Americans were desperate to acquire. They further claimed that the United States was "not averse" to the idea of countering Malaysia because the Anglo-Malayan plan was, they argued, "to a certain degree directed against the [United States'] . . . attempts to strengthen its position in Southeast Asia."[45]

Much of this propaganda can be attributed to the wider backdrop of Cold War hostility. Malcolm MacDonald, British commissioner-general for Southeast Asia, claimed in November 1962 that in spite of the polemical chatter on the radio, Malaysia was "accept[ed] as more or less inevitable." With Britain's—and indeed the West's—strategic hopes pinned on Malaysia, it is small wonder that any prospect of failure would be perceived as an existential threat to its regional influence. Contingency was masked by a commitment to the one plan. By emphasizing Malaysia's inevitability, particularly to its detractors, MacDonald was only further naturalizing the plan as the only acceptable way forward for Sabah and, in so doing, diminishing the validity of all other decolonization routes. International condemnation, of course, would continue, with recurring reports that "Peiping radio ha[d] blasted [the] formation of Malaysia" as neocolonial, further etching these divisions into Asia's geopolitical milieu.[46]

But to what extent was the formation of Malaysia neocolonial? In some regards, Britain struggled to see its own vision of decolonization realized amid its declining influence in Southeast Asia.[47] Furthermore, the act of classifying Malaysia as a British neocolonial project risks obscuring the central role played by Malayan elites in shaping their country's future. Although the Federation of Malaysia derived its constitutional genetics from the long tradition of Britain's attempts to federate the Malayan Peninsula beginning in the late nineteenth century, its defining characteristics lay in its *bumiputera*-centric ethnonational ideals and in its desires to incorporate new overseas territorial possessions, whether in Sumatra or Borneo.[48]

These characteristics were advanced by the Tunku Abdul Rahman and the United Malays National Organisation (UMNO). The ascendency of Malayan nationalist leadership had been evident since the late 1940s and 1950s, when Britain was compelled to acquiesce to pressure exerted by the Malayan Alliance, comprising the UMNO, the Malayan Chinese Association (MCA), and the Malayan Indian Congress (MIC). In so doing, Britain was forced "to proceed faster and further" than intended and abandon various "publicly stated preconditions for independence." The first of these preconditions was Britain's demand that Malaya transition to independence only after the Emergency period had ended. Second, Britain sought to usher in an independence movement that was "genuinely multiracial," but this was soon superseded by the predominance of Malayan ethnonationalism. And third, Britain publicly called for merger between Malaya and Singapore as a precondition for self-governance, a compromise that the Tunku was unwilling to make.[49]

This was the backdrop against which Projek Malaysia was conceived. Malaya had emerged in August 1957 as an independent state grounded in a powerful set of ethnonational ideals. But British policymakers still sought to play their hand in Southeast Asian affairs by seeking to combine Singapore with Malaya, a parting act designed to excise communism from the peninsula by smothering subversive elements in the city-state with *bumiputera* transplants. To achieve this final imperial goal, what better inducement was there to appease skeptical Malayan politicians than offering up the Borneo territories? In this sense, while the allegations that the Malaysia plan was a British neocolonialist scheme may fall short, it is nevertheless evident that colonial-style motivations pervaded elite circles in both Kuala Lumpur and London. Importantly, not only did a "substantial British economic presence survive the transfer of political power" in Malaya in 1957 but the immediate postcolonial years witnessed a "significant revival" of economic interdependence between the two countries.⁵⁰ This lasting economic integration persisted until the 1970s, when the Malaysian government "took on a more proactive role in the economy" and ended its "subservience to big British business."⁵¹ But the continuation of colonial economic interests after decolonization was not necessarily reflective of sustained imperial domination. Although a symbol of lasting foreign interference, colonial business interests were aided by Malayan elites who were eager to avoid "tamper[ing] with established British investment."⁵² Similar concerns over postcolonial economic instability were voiced by local Sabahans who were wary of fiscal and commercial strife after decolonization. Covetous elites often worked to maintain the outgoing colonial system to preserve their own interests while seeking to establish successor systems that were cognate in form and function. But as in Sabah, the precipitous decline in Malaya of once-dependable sources of wealth, such as rubber and tin, signaled economic uncertainty and a need for diversification.⁵³

Merger may have been lambasted as a neocolonial ruse to enable Malaya to tap into Sabah's and Sarawak's resource wealth, but the proposal was widely considered by Malayan policymakers as a major economic risk. For all of Malaya's economic woes, Sabah was faring worse. Its population was poorer, and its economic infrastructure was considerably less developed; if it were incorporated into the planned federation, Malaysia would have to absorb its problems too. In August 1962, Tan Siew Sin, Malaya's finance minister, met with American officials in Kuala Lumpur to discuss prospects for securing financial aid. Although Tan "readily admitted" that at the time Malaya "[did] not appear to be in need of external assistance," he foresaw great political and economic uncertainty after merger. The dilemma facing American policymakers at the time was whether "aid should be extended for the primary purpose of enabling a country to maintain desirable conditions of political and economic freedom."⁵⁴ Since the yet-to-be-formed Malaysian Federation represented a "showcase" for Western interests and since Britain was unable to provide it with sufficient financial aid, the United States concluded that its economic support was ultimately justifiable.

In Singapore, Prime Minister Lee Kuan Yew echoed Tan Siew Sin's concerns. In a discussion with John Kenneth Galbraith, US ambassador to India, in September 1962, Lee stated that while in the "short run prospects for the Federation are favourable," he worried "in the long run . . . about the dependence on tin and rubber." "Substantial industrial alternatives must be found," he claimed.⁵⁵ Among these alternatives was the type of industrial-scale manufacturing observed in Hong Kong, which the new federation's port towns would seek to imitate, combined with the vast resource wealth offered by the Borneo territories. Although Sabah and Malaya faced similar economic issues, the former's timely transition to industrial-scale logging had provided a lifeline for the territory, if one recurringly undermined by a critical lack of labor.[56] Alongside Sabah's tropical hardwoods, deposits of minerals, and extensive fisheries were Sarawak's petrochemical reserves; all these together comprised a vast and largely untapped commercial repertoire.

Although the charge of neocolonialism was most often directed toward Britain and other Western powers, it is nevertheless evident that Malaya (and other postcolonial territories angling to wield influence in Borneo) also exhibited colonial-style motivations and actions. Similarly, the entwined nature of metropolitan and peninsular interests positioned Malaya as a successor state to the outgoing colonial administration in Sabah. By serving as a replacement custodian for the Borneo territories, Kuala Lumpur would receive in exchange vast territorial, resource, and demographic yields.

Local Opposition to the Malaysia Plan

Local responses in Sabah to Projek Malaysia were varied and complex. Despite this, conventional scholarship either reduces the role of Sabah's public to a passive component or glosses over it altogether. Not only is analysis of the local perspective absent in the received wisdom, but the activities of the colonial government are all too frequently folded into the broader category of British metropolitan agendas. This is a critical oversight, considering that it was Sabah's colonial bureaucrats and their local functionaries who were tasked with readying the territory for merger. Moreover, by the time Anglo-Malayan policymakers issued directives in 1961 to hasten the Borneo territories' constitutional advancement toward merger, many in Sabah had already been working steadily toward their own competing visions for self-governance. In order to cast light on local opposition to the Malaysia plan, it is first necessary to disentangle the conflicts between the British colonial and metropolitan agendas. By separating these two distinct groups, it is possible to understand how local objectives in Sabah (whether pertaining to colonial bureaucrats or ordinary residents) differed to those espoused by policymakers in London and national elites in Kuala Lumpur.

One of the more unlikely obstacles to closer union between the British Borneo territories and Malaya ironically emerged from within Sabah's colonial government itself. In 1957, an incipient plan to federalize the Borneo territories was initiated by Sabah's then governor, Roland Evelyn Turnbull, and his counterpart in Sarawak, without instructions from London. Inspired by the federalization of Britain's colonies in Asia, Africa, and the Caribbean in the

1940s and 1950s, Turnbull, together with Anthony Abell, governor of Sarawak, issued simultaneous broadcasts over Radio Sabah and Radio Sarawak urging closer union among the three Borneo territories.[57] Turnbull spoke of the "inevitability of self-determination" and declared that the surest way forward was to "federate with other neighbouring territories."[58] Turnbull also solicited input from other career colonial bureaucrats, such as Robert Scott, governor of Mauritius, who took to Radio Sabah in November 1957 as a guest speaker to discuss the "types of co-operation possible between Sarawak, Brunei, and North Borneo."[59]

Importantly, however, Roland Turnbull's views differed from prevailing metropolitan thinking, which he argued was incorrectly predilected toward Singapore and Malaya. He expressed instead the desirability of "closer association" among Sabah, Sarawak, and Brunei to preserve their character and identity. "We needn't look as far afield as Singapore or Malaya," urged Turnbull. "All we have to do is to look at the history of Borneo. Weren't Sarawak and Sabah once part of the Sultanate of Brunei?"[60] But Turnbull's proposal was hindered by a great many issues, not least by the public's unwillingness to push for political independence at the time, but also by widespread confusion about what his plan meant. Would his proposed federation be merely a loose amalgamation to facilitate streamlined administration? Or would it merge the three into a single postcolonial country? Turnbull attempted to assuage these concerns by emphasizing the flexibility of the proposed federation and assuring the public that each territory's "individuality is worthy of retention." He later clarified that while "federation [and] . . . formal political association" would be in all of their "joint interests," "amalgamation of the three countries into one [would be] impractical even if it were desirable."[61] But people were listening, and Turnbull's proclamations quietly resonated with supporters of an enlarged Brunei Sultanate, as it did with advocates of a larger and more prosperous Bornean federation.

With clear signs of interest from both Sarawak's and Brunei's leadership, Turnbull directed Sabah's Information Office to ascertain the public's reaction to his proposal. Ronald Brooks lamented that while the government "was organized to disseminate information," it had no reliable means for gathering public feedback.[62] This was a recurrent issue in Sabah, which would later cause problems during the Anglo-Malayan Cobbold Commission of Enquiry in 1962.[63] To survey local opinions on questions of future self-government, Sabah's Information Office turned to the tried-and-tested methods of indirect rule: convening with "chiefs" when they sat at Native Court hearings and tasking District Officers to meet with indigenous colleagues across the territory. Brooks also hired a Chinese-speaking district liaison officer to ascertain the opinions of Sabah's Chinese residents.[64] Turnbull's proposal elicited keen interest among certain local elites, with Donald Stephens, a close associate of the governor, advancing a similar vision for an independent Bornean federation also in mid-1957. Popularized as "Stephens' plan for *Merdeka*," it sparked concerns in Britain over rising anticolonial and proindependence sentiments in Borneo.[65] While Stephens's plan was swiftly shot down, Turnbull's idea remained up for debate as a potential, if rather ambiguous, compromise, which advocated closer political ties among the trio of British Borneo territories rather than outright *merdeka*. Having debated Turnbull's plan, the colony's Legislative Council—comprising a mixture of colonial business and local elites—passed a resolution on April 10, 1958, recommending "close constitutional association" among the Borneo territories. One council member, for instance, was supportive of the plan in principle but cautioned the government against prematurely rushing the territory toward constitutional change: "Hurry slowly," they said, "plan by all means but *perlahan perlahan* [slowly slowly]." Others, including Mustapha bin Harun, supported the plan but emphasized the need for greater racial harmony, calling for the "natives" to work together. Donald Stephens, who held close ties to Turnbull, proclaimed the plan "the most momentous discussion ever held" and stated that such "talk of *merdeka* and [of] running their own affairs" boded well for Sabah's future.[66]

Despite eliciting support among Sabah's colonial and local elite circles, Turnbull's plan failed to progress. Colonial attempts at uncovering the opinions of ordinary Sabahans yielded no clear results, while metropolitan officials, who closely monitored the plan's development, turned a blind eye and refused to extend any official endorsement. In London, members of Parliament pressed the secretary of state for the colonies for the latest updates on the Borneo proposal, only to be informed that "no decisions have yet been made."[67] Prevailing assessments at the time that Sabah's and Sarawak's publics were too politically immature to handle independence or complex political choices appeared to gain credence as Turnbull's plan withered and then stalled. "*Perlahan perlahan*" became "stop stop."

With Roland Turnbull's sudden death in December 1960, his proposal would appear to die with him. But its afterlives would persist, proving that communities across Borneo did have the capacity to formulate their own visions for future statehood. Significantly, the nucleus of his proposal—a political union among the three Borneo territories under the auspices of the Sultanate of Brunei—would endure, and it would later gain regional backing and an anticolonial charge with the rise of Sheikh Azahari's Kalimantan Utara movement in 1963.[68] On paper, Turnbull's and Azahari's proposals were strikingly similar. And while these plans would both fall out of favor, Sabah's colonial administration under the leadership of Turnbull's successor, Governor William Goode, would continue to remain out of step with metropolitan agendas, expressing wariness of Projek Malaysia and urging a continuation of colonial rule until the 1970s.

The road to decolonization exposed stark divisions at the very core of Britain's metropolitan-colonial system, in which imperial policymakers in London sought to wrest greater control from overseas administrators over questions of governance and the constitutional future of the colonies. This diminished the sway of career colonial bureaucrats who had for decades ruled overseas territories with relative autonomy. Turnbull's plan was but one attempt at keeping the colonial administration in the driving seat as Sabah hurtled toward decolonization, vying not only against the rising tide of anticolonial forces in Southeast Asia but also against the growing interest in London in dictating the future of its remaining colonies to suit Britain's vestigial imperial interests and diminishing presence on the world stage. This administrative tussle over the nature of decolonization served as a quiet, but nevertheless significant, backdrop to the more public debates over Sabah's future and the formation of the Malaysian Federation.

The announcement of the Malaysia plan in May 1961 elicited widespread concern and upheaval across Sabah. Much of this opposition stemmed from latent ethnic tensions that pervaded the territory's diverse towns and ports. With new arrivals from both interior *kampongs* and overseas, towns such as Sipitang, Jesselton, and Sandakan were growing in size. These rapidly urbanizing populations jostled for standing in both political and commercial spheres, and each sought to play a part in Sabah's constitutional future. Public debates over merger with Malaysia proved immensely divisive, frequently spilling out from restaurants, theaters, and teahouses into the streets. Some incidents even made international news, with reports being made of pro-Malaysia gangs wielding shotguns facing off with anti-Malaysia adversaries.[69] Ideological disagreements in Sabah's urbanizing settlements bred rampant ethnic strife and even xenophobia. Many of Sabah's Kadazandusun communities, for instance, voiced explicitly anti-Chinese, anti-Javanese, and anti-Malayan sentiments, while they were in turn dismissed as politically naïve "natives."

Since the late 1950s, public skepticism toward Malaya had become widespread in Sabah, with influential local leaders such as Donald Stephens publicly condemning the Tunku Abdul Rahman for his alleged "dictator tendencies."[70] Indeed, by the end of the decade, "fear of domination" by Malaya was widespread.[71] With the announcement of the Malaysia plan in 1961, Stephens joined regional Bornean nationalists in Sarawak and Brunei in an attempt to thwart the plan. Together with Sheikh Azahari (who would later establish Kalimantan Utara) and Ong Kee Hui (leader of the Sarawak United People's Party), Stephens founded the United Front Against Malaysia on July 10, 1961. In a public statement, they warned that "any plan in accordance to the pronouncements made by Tengku Abdul Rahman . . . would be totally unacceptable to the people of the three territories."[72]

The majority of Sabah's Chinese communities were also skeptical of Projek Malaysia. Chinese elites in coastal towns were particularly vocal in their opposition to the plan, fearing a loss of influence and access to goods and workers from Hong Kong. Likewise, the proposal was considered unpopular among everyday Chinese residents, who viewed it as "a device to curb or dilute Chinese economic and political influence."[73] But Richard Yap, a Kadazandusun resident, condemned the influence of Sabah's Chinese *towkays* (business owners) and claimed that while the elites were against Malaysia, common Chinese people in Sabah were "all for the concept."[74]

As with other local elites such as Mustapha bin Harun, Donald Stephens was also wary of the growing influence of Chinese communities in the territory. Echoing the colonial preoccupation with communism, many Sabahans were quick to condemn their Chinese counterparts for harboring links to international left-wing movements.[75] Fears of Malayan domination, felt widely among Kadazandusun communities, also bled into opposing fears that they might also be displaced by wealthier Chinese groups. These ethnic tensions contributed in no small part to the swift disintegration of the United Front Against Malaysia later in 1961 and, with it, the plans for an independent Bornean federation that were first proposed by Governor Roland Turnbull in 1958.[76] Although initial grassroots responses to the Malaysia plan revealed a multitude of different perspectives, people's stances gradually came to reflect broader ethnic divides, with little room for individual expression of opinion.

Civil-Political Development at the End of Empire

Writing in mid-1962, Wong Pow Nee, Penang's chief minister, and Ghazali Shafie, permanent secretary to Malaya's Ministry of Foreign Affairs, claimed that the Malaysia plan had elicited "an awakening of political consciousness in the most heartening manner." According to Wong and Shafie, it was the very prospect of Malaysia itself that had roused civic action in Sabah, an ostensibly self-fulfilling process that in turn indicated the territory's readiness for merger.[77] But this ignores the wider patterns of political development in Sabah, with numerous flashpoints, public expressions of discontent, and instances of civic participation occurring throughout the preceding decades. While the Malaysia question may have sparked the creation of political parties, their emergence was but the latest in a series of major sociopolitical transformations in Sabah. Contingency surrounding the territory's role in Projek Malaysia contributed to preexisting rivalries and tensions. Sabah's incipient political parties were thus formed around long-established ethnocultural identities, with the question of Malaysia dictating the ideological direction of party manifestos as either pro- or antimerger.

The largest and most prominent new party was Donald Stephens's United National Kadazan Organization (UNKO). Founded in late 1961 as an ethnically based organization, the UNKO proved extremely popular among grassroots Kadazandusun communities across the west coast and lowland regions. Its promotion of indigenous values resonated deeply with *orang tuas* and their followers across Sabah. Although the party's stance on Malaysia was initially unclear—owing to Stephens's own indecisiveness—it later transformed into one of the most ardent backers of the plan. Similarly pro-Malaysia in outlook was Mustapha's new party, the United Sabah National Organization (USNO), founded in late 1961 as a sister organization to the UMNO in Malaya. Drawing interest among Muslims across Sabah—most notably the Islamized Kadazandusun, Suluk, and Bajau communities—the USNO grew to command a substantial following along Sabah's northern and eastern coasts. In addition to these two major pro-Malaysia parties was the comparatively smaller but still tentatively promerger Sabah Chinese Association (SCA), formed in late 1962 by Khoo Siak Chew and Peter Chin.

Despite the colonial government's attempts to promote the creation of moderate parties, anti-Malaysia views also gained prominence. The Murut- and Kadazandusun-based Pasok Momogun party, established in early 1962 as a breakaway movement from UNKO by brothers Orang Kaya Kaya G. S. Sundang and Orang Kaya Kaya Sedomon Gusanad Kina, emerged as the only sustained voice in Sabah in opposition to Malaysia. Sundang and Sedomon commanded widespread influence and drew support from across the interior and upland regions owing to the legacy of their father, the previous Kadazandusun *huguan siou*, Orang Kaya Kaya Gusanad Kina. Within months, Pasok Momogun gained a substantial following, initially among the Muruts and Kadazandusuns, but later also among Malaysia-skeptic Chinese residents who disagreed with the SCA's pro-Malaysia leaning.

Mustapha bin Harun's and Donald Stephens's respective parties supported the Malaysia plan because they believed that it would "safeguard the interests of natives and Muslims against the educationally and economically superior Chinese." Pasok Momogun's leaders, in marked contrast, "opposed the proposal because [they saw it] . . . as hasty and preferred a gradual transition from British colonial administration to self-governance."[78] They also expressed doubt that indigenous values and customs would be preserved after merger. Ironically, therefore, it was those who opposed the plan who remained largely procolonial, favoring a continuation of the status quo until Sabah could sustain independent statehood.[79] Although many colonial administrators also sought a continuation of the current system, Sundang and Sedomon were dismissed as problematic figures. Colonials voiced concern that they harbored an "emotional dislike for Malays." Sedomon attempted to convey his concerns to the colonial elite. "No matter how sweetly they might talk," Sedomon claimed in conversation with a district officer, they "would later impose the Muslim religion on the native peoples."[80] So great was Sedomon's antipathy toward Malaysia that in a subsequent meeting with Governor William Goode, he declared that "if the British were no longer able to look after the people of North Borneo, then could we not arrange for either the Japanese or the Americans to take over. . . . Even the Japanese would be more acceptable . . . than the Malays. Whatever their misdeeds during the war, they had not interfered with pig keeping or threatened folk with circumcision."[81]

Although these were very real concerns—ordinary Sabahans across the territory were voicing similar fears—the colonial government was wary of rising ethnic discord, particularly anti-Malay sentiments. Dismissed by colonial officials for embracing fickle ethnopolitics, Pasok Momogun's leadership nevertheless presented its followers with a clear roadmap for independence, which, strikingly, was not dissimilar to Governor Roland Turnbull's abortive 1957 plan. Under G. S. Sundang and Sedomon Gusanad Kina's direction, the party pledged to push for union between the three Borneo territories and to install Brunei's Sultan Omar Ali Saifuddin III as *agong* (supreme head or king) after independence.[82] But as Projek Malaysia progressed, few, if any, colonial administrators were willing to extend support to a plan that contravened metropolitan directives.

Although officially people were encouraged to express their views openly, in reality, anti-Malaysia sentiments were condemned and met with reprisals. Orang Kaya Kaya Mohammed Yassin bin Haji Hashim, a local Kadazandusun leader in the Sipitang District on the west coast, for instance, roused concern in the colonial government over his vocal opposition to Malaysia.[83] Colonial officials, eager to maintain leverage over local elites, had long voiced fears that "this kind of native will be drawn into the field of politics."[84] Although Mohammad Yassin had been a celebrated individual—a veteran of administrative service since the 1930s, he was awarded an MBE for his role as a "successful guerilla leader" against the Japanese, and later an OBE for his work in the Executive Council—colonials determined that he was becoming increasingly extremist in outlook and thus presented a threat. Elites such as Mohammed Yassin drew particularly harsh treatment from the colonial government, with officials noting with disdain his propensity to make "ill-considered" anti-British sentiments.[85] But these officials also feared that "relieving them of their duties and their salaries . . . would be to throw them into the arms of political movements" such as Kalimantan Utara. Mohammad Yassin's run-ins with the government began as early as October 1959, when it was alleged that he had been operating a smuggling ring deep in the interior. Informants claimed that he was selling firearms to buyers across the border in Indonesian Kalimantan. This source of ill-gotten wealth, administrators reasoned, would feasibly explain why he was "living well beyond his salary" by spending frivolously "on the entertainment of females" and "drinking even more heavily than usual these days."[86]

Also subject to mounting scrutiny was G. S. Sundang, who was labeled a traitor by pro-Malaysia advocates in late 1962. The Pasok Momogun movement was further discredited when a series of anonymous letters surfaced in the press alleging that key members were communists. To make matters worse, further allegations were made that Sundang was associated with Sheikh Azahari's Kalimantan Utara movement. On December 14, 1962, during the Brunei Rebellion, the government demanded that all political leaders in the Legislative Council "denounce" the uprising and "Azahari's pretensions on behalf of Sabah." While the leaders of the territory's pro-Malaysia parties unanimously condemned the rebellion, Sundang reportedly "remained silent." There was immediate outrage in the council, prompting some UNKO and USNO politicians to claim that Sundang's silence was "tantamount to treason."[87] Bitter infighting, ethnic discord, and disputes over merger would continue to dominate Sabah's budding political scene as it coursed toward the designated date for merger in 1963.

Anglo-Malayan Strategies for Creating Malaysia: Inducements, Obfuscation, and Performative Political Enquiries

Despite a lack of consensus on the Malaysia plan within the colonial government, officials continued to exert pressure on antimerger elements within the territory. But as with Roland Turnbull's failed Borneo federation proposal, administrators lamented the difficulties they faced in recording the public's stance. Added to this were the broader issues of disseminating information across Sabah's remote interior, in which many communities had still not received word of the proposed merger. Although local power brokers and growing numbers of their followers were eagerly voicing their opinions in the colony's main ports and towns, the reality was that many Sabahans throughout rural and forested regions had been left out of the equation. How might they respond to merger? Where did their loyalties lie? Similarly, while there was little that Sabah's public, or even its colonial government, could do to directly counter the plan, short of an all-out uprising, Britain and Malaya needed the territory to appear to enter union willingly. Any sign of popular dissent would threaten to derail the plan. Britain's formal colonization of the Borneo territories in 1946 had prompted localized discontent in Sarawak, while Malaya's ongoing attempts at pushing them toward merger led to embarrassing allegations of neocolonialism. Britain and Malaya were thus "determined that the veneer of legitimacy be attached to the whole process."[88]

Enter the Cobbold Commission of Enquiry.[89] Unlike what happened in Vietnam and Indonesia, for instance, where independence struggles led to the decisive removal of the colonial state and its associated systems, Britain worked with Malaya to advance a prearranged decolonization model for Sabah emphasizing continuity and gradual reform over revolutionary change. Key to this was the implementation of an a priori commission, devised to preempt criticism of Projek Malaysia and absolve Britain and Malaya of any neocolonial charges. The Cobbold Commission of Enquiry into Sabah and Sarawak was announced in late January 1962 under a tight schedule, as Malaysia's proposed formation date of August 31, 1963, loomed ever closer. The enquiry was headed by Cameron Cobbold (ex-governor of the Bank of England), accompanied by two Malayan and two British representatives: Wong Pow Nee (chief minister of Penang) and Ghazali Shafie (permanent secretary to the Ministry of Foreign Affairs in Malaya), and Anthony Abell (former governor of Sarawak) and David Watherston (former chief secretary of Malaya).[90] All of them were vetted as "firm supporters" of Malaysia, although their opinions differed over how, and indeed when, it should be created.[91] The commission's British representatives, including Cobbold, argued that the Borneo territories needed additional "development" and that colonial administrators should remain in charge for an additional five to ten years after merger to ensure a smooth transition.[92] The Malayan representatives, in contrast, rejected this argument and claimed that Sabah and Sarawak were in no way underdeveloped.[93] Notwithstanding these differences, the commission was ultimately devised with clear-cut objectives and led by bureaucrats with the sole task of advancing the Malaysia plan.

The commission drew from historical precedents. Britain and other imperial powers had long utilized preemptive enquiries to configure the creation of new states and the division of territory. The 1919 King-Crane and 1938 Woodhead commissions, for example, served as important touchstones for commission architects in postwar Britain.[94] Indeed, by the time Britain and Malaya opted for a commission in Borneo, enquiries had already developed a long-standing precedent as a tool of governance, obfuscation, and blame avoidance. And while many of these past political enquiries had been undermined by questions surrounding their integrity and neutrality, Anglo-Malayan policymakers nevertheless believed that the Cobbold Commission would counteract the negative publicity and claims of neocolonialism.

But this would be no easy task. Malaya and Britain expected swift results from Cobbold's team, who would tour the two Borneo territories in under two months before publishing their findings in June 1962. Local and regional media outlets were primed to report on the commission's outcomes.[95] The rapid pace of the commission's work, however, surprised many observers at the time who felt that it would surely have to overcome "the formidable task" of making "visits to all residencies and divisions in the territories concerned." Further doubts were raised over the enquiry's candor and meticulousness. As one observer wrote, "No machinery exists at present in Borneo for holding a plebiscite and it would take some months to make preparations for such an operation."[96] In Indonesia, the nationalist newspaper *Merdeka* leveled a scathing condemnation at the commission, claiming that "the proper measurement of whether the people of Northern Borneo wish to join Malaysia or not would be through a referendum that would continue for at least a year."[97]

The effects of Sabah's and Sarawak's vast jungle sprawl on the commission cannot be overstated. "The task was no easy one," wrote Cameron Cobbold, noting the "difficulty of communications," with the "slow means of transport and the distances to be covered."[98] In fact, the commission was so curtailed by Borneo's geography, lack of infrastructure, and sheer size that it could only tour select settlements, mainly larger towns and areas serviced by airfield or jetty. And if it were not for the use of chartered airplanes and the Sarawak governor's own personal "launches and river craft," the enquiry might well have been compromised further. In total, the commission held fifty hearings in thirty-five locations across Sabah and Sarawak while also collecting two thousand affidavits from the public.[99] In his report, Cameron Cobbold conceded that it was ultimately "not possible ... to reach the remoter areas" of Sabah and Sarawak.[100] Those who were illiterate, stranded in the distant uplands, or simply unable to post their submissions, were denied the opportunity to share their views.

Despite the evident political nature of the commission and the manifest problems of data collection, many Western observers were quick to laud it as an accurate "fact-finding survey" of public opinion.[101] That Anglo-Malayan policymakers and international observers were now conceiving the people of Sabah in terms of a "public," rather than a passive and subordinate "colonial population," represented a major conceptual shift. Unsurprisingly, the Malayan and British governments welcomed the recommendations wholesale. But the commission's findings—(1) that a third of respondents favored the Malaysia plan, (2) a third remained indecisive, and (3) a final third were staunchly against it—were vague and left much room for interpretation. The data, including affidavits and actual grassroots commentary, were withheld from public scrutiny and lay dormant in the archive for decades. Considerable uncertainty surrounded the second category of respondents who were undecided. But Cobbold's report assured readers that this indecisive group would be "favourable to the Malaysia project" if certain "conditions and safeguards" regarding "native" rights, representation, and prosperity could be guaranteed. These respondents, the report continued, "would be markedly influenced by a firm expression by [the Sabah and Sarawak] Governments that the detailed arrangements eventually agreed upon are in the best interests of the territories."[102]

Importantly, however, others dismissed public skepticism as a product of poor education and naïveté. A. E. Philipps, a colonial plantation owner, claimed simply that "the native is bewildered."[103] Cameron Cobbold and his team capitalized on widespread public misunderstandings about what Malaysia meant, as well as rife confusion over Sabah's political options. The commission withheld choice: the public was "never offered the alternative of independence, either as separate entities or within a Borneo federation," wrote George Kahin.[104] This meant that supporters of an independent state of Sabah or a postcolonial union comprising the three Borneo territories—of which there were many advocates in the region—had no official way of recording their views. When standing before the commission, respondents could only choose between merger or continued colonial rule. Those who favored independent statehood for Sabah, or who opposed both colonial rule and the Malaysia plan, could not formally lodge their views. Officially, these options were not accepted by the commission. Skeptics were instead assured by Cobbold and his team that Malaysia would ultimately bring *merdeka*, even though this was not a promise that they could realistically make. Resultantly, many were either silenced or placated at the very last moment by false assurances of independence, when in actuality, independence was never on the table.

Some instances of last-ditch persuasion had far-reaching statistical implications, with the voices of a few elites causing disproportionately large swings in the commission's findings. Orang Tua Awang Hashim, a local leader from the west coast, changed his mind at the last minute and summarily declared that he and all 530 inhabitants of Kampong Kawang would now support the proposal because "independence will be gained through Malaysia."[105] It is notable that none of Kampong Kawang's residents had any direct input in Hashim's snap decision when he stood before the commission. But Cobbold, Wong, Shafie, Abell, and Watherston—agents of the Malaysia plan—all did. During the commission's tour there were many such instances of last-minute persuasion, with dramatic effects. This underscored the commission's dual role as both an ostensible fact-finding process and a tool for active political persuasion. While many indigenous leaders and minor elites were swayed by commission members, a rising cohort of power brokers with territory-wide influence stood to make political gains amid the uncertainty and rising polarization in Sabah through actively signaling their new allegiance.

The Cobbold Commission could not have been held at a more fortuitous moment for the territory's foremost power brokers, such as Mustapha bin Harun and Donald Stephens. Mustapha cemented his role as an advocate for Malaysia, which he claimed would counter "bad elements" in the territory.[106] The commission proved similarly beneficial for Stephens, as it granted him the opportunity to publicly reverse his political stance and put his newfound loyalty to Malaysia on the official record. As a newspaper editor and political commentator, Stephens's influence was so pervasive across Sabah that many grassroots leaders and *orang tuas* looked to him for guidance when preparing to stand before the commission. This signaled his utility to Anglo-Malayan policymakers, who were willing to overlook his brief flirtation with the United Front Against Malaysia in 1961. In an affidavit submitted to the commission by one of Stephens's allies, Orang Tua Taib of Kampong Sembulan Tengah wrote that he and his 2,358 subjects would unanimously "accept Malaysia." They would do so without hesitation, he assured the commission, and they would "obey all conditions" that came with it.[107] Similarly, a letter sent on behalf of the 197 "Natives of Bangawan" explained that despite initial misgivings, the Malaysia plan was now attractive because it had been adequately explained.[108] With the commission's arrival, pro-Malaysia solidarity appeared to emerge out of nowhere. In the port towns of Sandakan, Jesselton, and Kudat, locals from all walks of life followed Mustapha's and Stephens's example in throwing their weight behind the plan. It appeared as though no one wanted to be left behind. In Jesselton, a group of Electricity Board workers submitted a pro-Malaysia memorandum that ended with the slogan "We say long live Malaysia."[109] A few blocks down the street, employees of the Jesselton Posts and Telegraph service voiced similar sentiments, declaring "Independence for Sabah; long live Malaysia."[110] A letter submitted by a group of railway mechanics echoed the very same statement: "Long live Malaysia."[111] Radio receivers across Sabah blared this oft-heard song: "Merger and Malaysia Are Sure as the Sun Rises!"[112] There were countless such expressions of public support; pro-Malaysia feeling appeared to spread across the territory in a virulent manner.

But not all voices toed the official line. Amid the sound of pro-Malaysia songs and the clamor for merger, opponents continued to voice their concerns, risking themselves, their families, and their livelihoods amid growing public backlash. Y. K. Wong, a Jesselton local of Hong Kong descent, penned an essay outlining his opposition to Malaysia based on its religious and racial implications. He expressed fears that after merger, religious and ethnic minorities in Sabah would come under threat. Wong also took issue with the idea of a national language, arguing that Malay Bahasa was not suitable for the majority of Sabah's population, who preferred to converse in Cantonese, Mandarin, English, Kadazandusun, or other local languages. He described the Malaysia plan as a "bombshell" that has "done much damage to the hitherto racial harmony which we hold so dear" and stressed the importance of Sabah attaining true independent statehood first. Concluding his essay, Wong declared that "the people of North Borneo will not easily forget how this choice so near within its grasp has been taken away."[113] E. Sadiwah, who worked for a local Kadazandusun cultural association in the town of Inanam, agreed. In an affidavit submitted to the commission, he asked, "Why should we join Malaysia when we have not set up our own [independent] government yet?"[114]

Chang Ah Foo, a gardener from Kudat, argued for a series of "safeguards" to protect Sabah's Chinese, non-Malay, and non-Muslim residents. He stressed the importance of attaining "freedom of speech, freedom of worship and freedom of society" and questioned why Mustapha bin Harun's Islamized indigenous communities should "be placed in the same position as the Malays." If they were to be higher-status citizens, Chang asked, "then what about the Chinese, Indians, Philippines [sic], Eurasians and others?"[115] Malaysia skeptics suffered considerable vitriol in the months leading up to merger, with Sabah's Chinese residents, in particular, bearing the brunt of this growing ethnic discord. In Jesselton, it was not uncommon for advocates of Malaysia to label their opponents as traitors and pariahs, with Talip bin Japar, for instance, claiming that "those who oppose Malaysia are no other than foreigners who have no ties to this country." Talip made no effort to hide the target of his condemnation: "Those foreigners from Hongkong who come here for work . . . should be sent back whenever their contracts expire."[116] Despite this backlash, anti-Malaysia discontent continued to simmer quietly across the territory. But officially, merger was in vogue, and pro-Malaysia advocates were granted a mandate by the state to operate virtually unchecked. This prompted many across Sabah to express fears of reprisal attacks or marginalization. Michael

Wong, a member of Sabah's Legislative Council and the Beaufort District Council, summarized these concerns, stating in his memoranda to the commission that he hoped that his skepticism of Projek Malaysia would not lead others to "simply brand [him] . . . as a communist." Calls for him and his fellow ethnic Chinese residents to go back to Hong Kong and China, he claimed, were "wrong accusations to the good people," most of whom were "born [in Sabah] and have stayed in the country continuously."[117]

If the Cobbold Commission represented an overt attempt at validating Projek Malaysia through gathering public opinion, then Britain and Malaya's policy of ingratiating and appeasing local power brokers represented a more covert method for securing elite support for merger. The Malayan government extended overtures to local elites and administrative officers in Borneo in an attempt to generate pro-Malaysia feeling. This led to the establishment of all-inclusive "study tours" to Kuala Lumpur, in which local officers from Sabah would receive mentorship from their Malayan counterparts on matters of rural development and civil administration while being honored with banquets and entertainment. These tours proved highly popular between 1961 and 1963, with rank-and-file local officers, such as Che Awang Mohammad Thaufeck, K. G. Unnithan, and Miau Shau Kee, for instance, returning to Sabah as staunch advocates of Malaysia.[118] Major political elites, too, were sent on tours designed to influence, ingratiate, and ultimately win over support. As if to make amends for his involvement in the abortive United Front Against Malaysia, Stephens later cofounded the Malaysia Solidarity Committee while on tour in Kuala Lumpur in mid-1962 with Mustapha bin Harun, arguing that Malaysia was now in Sabah's "best long-term interests."[119]

Also considered high-value targets were elites affiliated with Pasok Momogun and other anti-Malaysia elements. Observing the developments in Sabah, Malayan officials described Pasok Momogun as the "only organisation of any consequence" due to its capacity to derail the formation of Malaysia. But Pasok Momogun's leaders could be placated, they reasoned, if their "fear of domination" by Malaya could be "set at rest."[120] G. S. Sundang and Sedomon Gusanad Kina both received invitations to tour Malaya in early 1962, where they would be showered with gifts and inducements and would be encouraged to see value in Projek Malaysia. Sedomon, however, expressed suspicion. In a meeting with Governor William Goode in early February 1962, he claimed that these invitations to Kuala Lumpur were deceptive, as they coincided with the dates of the Cobbold Commission's visit to Sabah. Goode commented that "he [Sedomon] and many other native leaders had received invitations to visit Malaya during the period . . . 14 to 28 [February 1962]. He [said that he] could not possibly accept this as it would mean that he was out of the way when the commission came. I said that I assumed the invitations, of which I had no previous knowledge, had been issued in ignorance of the date of arrival of the commission."[121]

By luring Malaysia-skeptics out of Sabah, Sedomon alleged, the tours would make them unable to share their opinions with the commission. While it was unlikely that Malaya sought to prevent local politicians from standing before the commission, the invitations were doubtless tinged with political overtones. Yet just a few weeks later, in late February, colonial officer M. G. Edge reported that despite Sedomon's initial misgivings, he had in fact accepted the invitation to Malaya. Following his return from Kuala Lumpur, Edge described how Sedomon was "now supposed to be 100% pro-Malaysia and that the reverse of his former stance can be attributed to his comparatively recent visit to . . . Malaya where he was accorded VIP treatment which so over-awed him that the question of Malaysia was 'sold' lock, stock and barrel. . . . Sedomon has intimated that he would like to be invited again."[122]

Although Sedomon did eventually come to support the Malaysia plan, Edge's commentary also reveals the attitudes toward indigenous politicians that pervaded colonial governance at the time, in which contrarian local leaders were depicted as fickle, disloyal, and prone to sudden about-turns in their political views. Colonials attributed this political shift to their "VIP treatment" in Malaya, but local developments in Sabah and observations from across the wider region also informed their views. Speaking to reporters at Kuala Lumpur's Sungai Besi Airport, Sedomon stated that only after his tour of Malaya could he finalize his decision: "After this visit, when I go back to my country, I will be able to tell my people of the progress I have seen in this country [Malaya]. Then only can we tell our people whether we can accept Malaysia or not."[123]

By late 1962, Projek Malaysia appeared to be gaining traction, and its opponents increasingly found themselves at a loss. During this time, Sedomon's brother, G. S. Sundang, witnessed a sharp decline in his political influence, and it became clear that he was losing out to Stephens, Mustapha, and other rival elites who publicly favored merger. In October 1962, in attempt to salvage his withering political career, Sundang agreed to cease his opposition to Malaysia and to partner with Stephens and Mustapha to prepare for merger. When pressed by reporters, Sundang stated that "continued opposition . . . could result in bloodshed among the natives" and, revealingly, that "we don't want to be left out."[124] But it was too late, and Pasok Momogun's decline appeared terminal.

With the ebb of Pasok Momogun's influence, and the continuing growth of the UNKO, the USNO, and the SCA, large portions of Sabah's anti-Malaysia public found themselves lacking a political platform to express their views. Following the territory's first elections in early 1963, Pasok Momogun's decline was etched into the electoral record. Winning in only twelve districts, Pasok Momogun performed poorly compared to the UNKO with thirty-nine, the USNO with fifty-three, and the SCA with twenty-seven seats.[125] Although the party retained influence in its interior strongholds—Murut-majority towns such as Keningau, Beaufort, Kuala Penyut, and Tenom—it drew negligible support in Sabah's larger coastal settlements. After merger, in 1964, what remained of Pasok Momogun would eventually be absorbed by the UNKO to form the United Pasokmomogun Kadazan Organization (UPKO), ostensibly uniting all indigenous communities under a pro-Malaysia banner.

Archipelagic Unity? Merger and the Merdeka Moment

The Federation of Malaysia was created on September 16, 1963, amid proliferating international antagonism and resistance. Despite this hostility and contestation, celebrations proceeded as planned. Banquets, parades, and revelries were held at public and official venues across the newly wedded federation. At the port of Malacca, a series of sports grounds were transformed into outdoor cinemas when at 7:30 p.m. the government projected footage of the "Malaysia Day" celebrations that had unfolded earlier that morning in Sabah and Sarawak. That the film reels could be hurriedly developed, processed, and transported from East to West Malaysia demonstrated the new federation's ostensible close-knit unity. Children gathered to watch the footage from street corners and from inside nearby buildings with windows opened wide. Nearby, in the peninsular city of Johor Bahru, a large public feast began at 8:30 p.m. Later in the evening, in Penang, people gathered in crowds to watch as fireworks thundered in the sky above the Hindu temple. In Seremban, to the south of Kuala Lumpur, a packed itinerary kicked off with a parade through the streets and ended with festivities at the local sports stadium.[126] Under official direction, virtually every city, town, and *kampong* turned out to witness the creation of Malaysia.

The Malaysia Day festivities were no less vibrant in Sabah, where Kota Kinabalu's (formerly Jesselton's) main streets were transformed into sites celebrating state formation, colonial departure, and the official handover. Although many locals continued to lament the failure to obtain true independent statehood, an atmosphere of positivity and excitement for the future prevailed. The celebrations were a highly choreographed affair, having been planned well in advance. On September 15, the day before the creation of Malaysia, Governor Goode departed at 6:00 p.m. after witnessing a "farewell guard of honour." The next day, beginning at 8:00 a.m., a parade was held swearing in Donald Stephens as Sabah's new chief minister, followed by the raising of the new flags and an "announcement made on the birth of Malaysia." Plans were made for festivities to "continue throughout [the] day culminating in [the] evening with . . . fireworks and traditional dancing."[127]

Malaysia emerged in these scenes as a choreographed triumph, a demonstration to supporters and detractors alike that the dream of archipelagic unity had prevailed. Reports detailing the jubilant scenes were disseminated across the globe. But beneath this display lay deep societal divides and unresolved tensions. While many local leaders had been pacified by Malaya—won over by promises of power and influence—many communities continued to fear for their rights and autonomy after merger and amid the imposition of a new national identity. Patterns of resource extraction and exploitation, too, would continue, and the local power brokers who had worked so hard to encourage Sabah's merger would perpetuate colonial-era systems for their new peninsular masters.

Despite the publicity and the official assurances, the formation of the Federation of Malaysia was not an inherent, logical outcome of Britain's imperial withdrawal from Southeast Asia. Rather, as this chapter has demonstrated, it was advanced amid great uncertainty and contingency, in which its advocates had to navigate local, regional, and international opposition to ensure its creation. Anglo-Malayan policymakers and local Bornean power brokers alike had to advance their chosen vision of merger amid regional tumult and vying territorial claims. Even after its creation, during its early years Malaysia was beset with resistance and turmoil both in the peninsula and across Borneo, culminating in the expulsion of Singapore in 1965 and the violent Konfrontasi between 1963 and 1966.

While much of this antagonism can be attributed to the wider backdrop of regional anticolonialism and ethnopolitical tensions, staunch opposition to Anglo-Malayan designs developed in many forms locally, as it did regionally, with the rise of competing state-making ambitions and neocolonial aspirations. The neocolonial attempts to secure territory in Sabah, waged simultaneously by Malaya, the Philippines, Kalimantan Utara, and Indonesia, served as competing visions for expanded statehood and archipelagic unity in postcolonial Southeast Asia.

Locally, too, calls for Bornean unity and Sabahan independence—propagated at first by the colonial administration, and later by an assortment of local power brokers and regional anticolonial nationalists—left indelible marks on the territory's political landscape. Governor Roland Turnbull's proposal, shot down by colleagues in London determined to stake their claim to overseeing Sabah's constitutional future, exposed deep rifts between colonial and metropolitan policymakers. Likewise, the forging of artificial links between Borneo and the Malayan Peninsula to suit both British administrative and Malayan state-making ambitions (based on the common legacies of colonial administration, rather than inherent social and cultural ties) lay the groundwork for what would become Projek Malaysia. As this chapter has discussed, however, Sabah's economic, demographic, and institutional connections to other entrepôts—most notably Hong Kong—drew considerable interest at the time in both public and official circles. This demonstrates that Sabah had options while further serving to denaturalize the Borneo-peninsular links that were being strengthened at the time for administrative convenience and for peninsular interest. Indeed, while Sabah was cast, by Anglo-Malayan design, as a core component in the Federation of Malaysia, its experience of decolonization was paradoxically more akin to that of Hong Kong's handover to China in 1997. Although both territories experienced a transfer of power from one overlord to another, Sabah's decolonization continues to be erroneously framed as an independence or *merdeka* moment.

This chapter ultimately denaturalizes the creation of Malaysia by showing how it was a contingent and proactive process—simultaneously vulnerable to regional antagonism and dependent on the inclusion of Sabah—rather than an inherent one. In so doing, it pushes back against the received wisdom, which teleologically frames the British Borneo territories as predestined for merger. Likewise, this critical reassessment also demonstrates the extent to which Anglo-Malayan designs for state formation were ultimately not dissimilar to the competing attempts to leverage control over Sabah waged by the Philippines, Kalimantan Utara, and Indonesia. Each hinged on the inclusion of the Borneo territories as a set of resource-rich colonies made available by Britain's decision to disengage from its Southeast Asian empire before the territories were able to stand alone as independent states. Furthermore, that Sabah was considered at the time incapable of progressing toward independence is indicative of the lack of agency accorded to its dynamic and heterogenous public. It was a territory robbed of its agency in the moment of decolonization, at a time when merger and state formation ironically hinged on its very inclusion. This echoes the historic instances of annexation and formal colonization between the 1840s and 1940s, which saw the region riven by a sequence of colonizing attempts.

Conclusion
Afterlives

When flying into Kota Kinabalu from the south, the airplane approaches a single tarmac runway that lies parallel to the coast. From the right side of the plane, forests and distant mountains press the city close to the shore. From the left side, the expansive South China Sea extends to the horizon, endlessly blue. As the plane approaches the city, over beaches down below, towns and *kampongs* slide in and out of vision. It flies over Meligan, Papar, and Kinarut, then Putatan and Petagas, now virtually absorbed into Kota Kinabalu's growing urban sprawl.[1] The flight track traces the routes traversed by so many traders, migrants, sojourners, administrators, and fortune seekers in days gone by. Today, Kota Kinabalu is a quintessential Malaysian city, but one that still clings to its Bornean past.

On June 6, 1976, the same route ended in disaster for Donald Stephens: his airplane never made it to Kota Kinabalu International Airport.[2] As the plane approached the city, it came down at 3:41 p.m. in the waters off Kampong Sembulan, a few hundred meters from the runway. Everyone on board perished. Witnesses described how the airplane, a small ten-seater Australian Government Aircraft Factories Nomad, encountered difficulty as it approached for landing. Crowds of onlookers, "hypnotised by the drama unfolding before them," gazed up at the plane as it "stall[ed] then suddenly spiralled downwards into the shallow sea." At the scene of the crash, barely fifteen meters from Sembulan's stilted houses, the sea was reported to have been "dyed crimson," while corpses, luggage, and mechanical parts lay strewn about the wreckage.³ Onlookers remarked how the weather was calm and clear and how the plane seemingly fell from the sky.

The demise of Donald Stephens was felt by many across Sabah. Stephens perished alongside six of his newly inaugurated United Pasokmomogun Kadazan Organization (UPKO) cabinet members, as well as his son Johari Stephens, his bodyguards, and the flight crew.⁴ His government had come to power only months earlier, having succeeded Mustapha bin Harun's United Sabah National Organization (USNO) administration in April 1976.⁵ The incident wiped out virtually the entirety of Sabah's new UPKO government and thrust the state into uncharted waters.

The airplane crash occurred just a couple of miles from Petagas, the town where Donald Stephens's father, Jules Pavitt Stephens, and countless others involved in the Kinabalu Uprising were beheaded by the Japanese in 1944.⁶ And a few miles further to the south lies the *kampong* where his grandfather, Ernest Alfred Pavitt, struck a deal with Orang Tua Limbahau in 1896 to wed Kwai, his grandmother. Pavitt and Kwai's union set in motion a sequence of events that would reshape the boundaries of Sabahan identity, colonial-indigenous relations, and, ultimately, Sabah's transition toward postcolonial statehood and merger with Malaysia.

The occurrence of the disaster so close to one of Sabah's most vital administrative and commercial centers characterizes the precarity that shaped many lives throughout the territory. The safety of even the most politically important lives in Sabah was but a fragile illusion. Almost immediately, allegations of foul play and sabotage circulated. Firsthand accounts of the accident were suppressed by the federal government in Kuala Lumpur, while books covering the events are still banned at the time of writing for their raising of sensitive and unwanted questions.⁷ That the government's official report remains classified elicits further talk of conspiracy. Talk of the "Double Six Tragedy" resurfaces every year as a moment of anguish and intrigue.⁸ The incident brought the Stephenses' story to an abrupt close, but it also cast Sabah further into Malaysia's grasp, and as one international news report described, it "stirred a crisis."⁹ The disaster occurred as the state was beginning to transition toward greater minority inclusion after a period of increased pressure from the peninsula. The preceding decade had been marked by a struggle for influence between marginalized indigenous communities and dominant state-supported ethnic groups. The dwindling fortunes of Sabah's indigenous peoples, who had long lost out to commercial big business, environmental degradation, and metropolitan agenda, were reflected in the outpouring of grief over the tragedy. Many felt that their chances of securing change and representation had perished with the crash. Their *huguan siou* was no more.

The inhabitants of the city of Kota Kinabalu were no strangers to suffering and destruction. Between 1942 and 1945, countless lives were lost, and virtually all of the city's buildings were razed. It was amid this devastation that its inhabitants, a heterogeneous mix of Kadazandusuns, Muruts, Malays, Chinese, Javanese, Eurasians, and a multitude of other ethnic groups, forged a tentative Sabahan identity that was inspired by the anti-Japanese "Kinabalu Guerillas." This civic identity was markedly dissimilar to the nationalist and anticolonialist movements that arose contemporaneously in other colonial territories, however, and after the war's end it soon broke down. It instead resembled a collective push for peace and, in many ways, simply a sense of stability in times of chaos. The crucible of war and the virtually unending specter of geopolitical contestation that characterized everyday life in Sabah since the nineteenth century instilled the public with a popular disdain for radical politics. Colonial rule was often tolerated, if begrudgingly, despite administrative failures and deep inequalities, because it ushered in new economic activity and a sense of political stability, albeit sluggish and profoundly imbalanced. It also prevented any one local ethnic group from gaining the upper hand over the others. This desire to stem the perceived tyranny of rival ethnic communities contributed to popular beliefs in the postwar period that colonial governance should persist until at least the 1970s.[10] When Kalimantan Utara burst onto the scene in early 1963, for instance, it was precisely this aversion to anticolonial radicalism (and the movement's particular brand of violence and brutality) that left Sheikh Azahari bin Sheikh Mahmud's calls for armed rebellion unanswered. Likewise, when the Tunku Abdul Rahman announced Projek Malaysia in 1961, many ordinary Sabahans—Kadazandusuns, Muruts, Chinese, and Suluks, among others—reacted with concern that they would lose out amid the imposition of Melayu values from the peninsula. As the prominent Murut leader Orang Kaya Kaya Sedomon Gusanad Kina claimed in 1962, merger with Malaysia would interfere with the "native" way of life.[11] As Sabah hurtled toward decolonization, many wanted to apply the brakes until a time when the territory could progress toward true *merdeka* as a standalone, autonomous country. All of this, ultimately, demonstrates the extent to which members of the public were actively involved in their own affairs, a far cry from the received wisdom that paints ordinary Sabahans as politically dormant and naïve passengers in the region's history. As this book has demonstrated, popular resistance and (often unconventional) civic participation through the leadership of prominent local power brokers enabled Sabah's public to serve as the engine of its history.

Identifying this collective resistance is not to say that Sabah's public was characterized by unity or a common voice. Although the territory was neither shaped by radical anticolonial groups nor engulfed in violent separatist movements, major divisions and tensions persisted. The ascendency of local power brokers in the early 1960s, each representing distinct ethnic groups, perpetuated these divides and granted some communities disproportionately large influence. After merger with Malaysia, however, many Sabahans turned toward Kuala Lumpur, adopting Melayu values as a sign of fealty to their new metropolitan overlords. Islam, historically confined to Borneo's coastal lowlands and port towns, would subsequently serve as a vector for injecting peninsular Malayan influence into Sabah. Its prevalence increased as key proponents ascended to seats of power after decolonization. Donald Stephens's decision to convert to Islam in 1971, remodeling himself as Tun Muhammad Fuad Stephens, elicited support among Sabah's growing number of Islamized Kadazandusuns. Mustapha bin Harun, in contrast, had long been considered the de facto head of the territory's Muslim communities, and he emerged as a staunch advocate of extending Malayan influence. During his tenure as chief minister from 1967 to 1976, he presided over policies seeking to Islamize and "Malayanize" Sabah's indigenous peoples.[12] This formed a core part of his administration's proclaimed "one language, one culture, one religion" policy, devised to integrate Sabah within Malaysia's Melayu-centric vision of archipelagic unity.[13] In this period, growing numbers of Kadazandusuns—who had previously been animist or Christian—converted to Islam, undermining traditional allegiances to *orang tuas* and local political figures that had long structured indigenous society. The state reclassified these new converts as ethnic Malays and *bumiputera*. Through this reclassification, they were absorbed into Malaysia's dreams of national unity, spanning the Malayan Archipelago from peninsula to Borneo. Under Mustapha bin Harun's tenure as chief minister, the government spearheaded the replacement of local languages with Malay Bahasa, and the Kadazandusun language ceased to be taught in state schools.[14] Lacking effective political representation between 1967 and 1976, many non-Islamized Kadazandusuns were rendered largely voiceless, while Sabah's Chinese communities continued to face marginalization. Other ethnic minorities and indigenous groups fared much worse. Political opponents and advocates of indigenous minority rights were condemned for espousing "anti-Kuala Lumpur" politics.[15]

Meanwhile, the tendrils of foreign commerce and big business burrowed ever deeper into Sabah's rain forests. Despite unprecedented logging and mining, resulting in environmental devastation, these same jungles and distant uplands continue to serve state interests today as places abounding in resource wealth, as they did in the nineteenth century. Indigenous dispossession intensified in the years following merger, with new laws building on colonial-era ordinances that further deprived people of access to their ancestral lands.[16] Although the Kadazandusuns' fortunes had purported to change with Stephens's electoral victory in April 1976, his untimely death, alongside that of many of his UPKO cabinet members in the infamous airplane crash, thrust the new party into turmoil, perpetuating age-old political, ethnic, and cultural divisions. In the postcolonial period, as in the early days of colonial expansion, political authority proved incredibly difficult to implement across the entire territory. Governance was characterized by a constant tussle between factions, and political capital remained anchored to the cosmopolitan port towns at the expense of the interior.

The Federation of Malaysia emerged in September 1963 a widely contested state, with the newly acquired Borneo territories serving as the focal point for regional and international opposition. As this book has demonstrated, Sabah was simultaneously a resource-rich centerpiece for the new federation, a strategically crucial place in British plans for decolonization, and also a focal point for territorial claims waged by the Philippines, Indonesia, and a bevy of smaller state-making projects. Following merger with Malaysia, Sabah and Sarawak would both become violently embroiled in the Konfrontasi, a conflict that was part of Sukarno's "Ganyang Malaysia" campaign. Although the insurgency would end decisively in 1966, the legacies of the conflict endure, particularly in remote border communities.[17] Similarly, Sabah's contested and perennially uncertain status persists even today. The effects of sustained (geo)political strife, inflicted by foreign territorial claims, local resentment toward civic disenfranchisement, land dispossession, and disputes over ethnic and national identities, are profound.[18]

With this in mind, this book has shown how the years leading up to formal decolonization were marked by intense fluidity. Each of the vying attempts at injecting influence, winning over the public, and scrambling for territory and resource access, hinged on the belief that Sabah was malleable and thus attainable. Indeed, in the 1950s and 1960s, Sabah was considered so malleable that Malaya, the Philippines, and Indonesia each sought to use it to crystallize its own dreams of postcolonial statehood, national identity, and archipelagic unity. Despite this sense of contingency in the late colonial period, Sabah's eventual incorporation into the federation set in stone age-old patterns of foreign domination.

Nevertheless, this book denaturalizes the formation of Malaysia by demonstrating that its emergence was not an inherent progression toward independence but rather an outcome made possible only through the complicity of local power brokers, the concerted efforts of Malaya's political elite, and Britain's willingness to expedite the decolonization process. And although underrepresented in the received wisdom, the active participation of Sabah's public wrought major effects by enabling this process of state creation. Despite lacking conventional forms of civic representation and political engagement, ordinary Sabahans rejected Kalimantan Utara's, Indonesia's, and the Philippines' respective advances, calling instead for either continued colonial rule or Projek Malaysia.

For many years, Sabah's cultural, demographic, and economic links to Hong Kong, the southern Philippines, and the rest of Borneo were comparable to—and at times perhaps even stronger than—those of Malaya. What if the United States had cast its weight behind the Philippines' territorial claim over Sabah? What if Maphilindo or Kalimantan Utara had gained greater public support and come to fruition instead? What if—as existing narratives of imperial enfeeblement might entertain—Britain was too weak to defy regional attempts to thwart Projek Malaysia? Or what if Britain had instead decided to push for a Hong Kong–Borneo federation or a fully independent state of Sabah? Official narratives have relied on the idea that Malaysia was the inherent or sole logical outcome of Britain's withdrawal from Sabah. But in so doing, teleological interpretations have naturalized the federation while whitewashing the varied attempts by local and regional actors at leveraging Sabah for their own ends. Perhaps most importantly, the received wisdom has withheld Sabah's agency from view. This book stands as a vital corrective, while also offering an adaptable methodology for reassessing an array of cognate marginal and subnational regions across the world. The comparisons drawn throughout this book between the decolonization experiences of Sabah and Hong Kong represent just one out of many such threads of similarity. The legacies of unfinished decolonization or perpetual colonialism, masked under the guise of postcolonial statehood, continue to shape communities across the Asia Pacific, Africa, the Middle East, and beyond. The pursuit of postcolonial dreams of territorial expansion and national unity comes not without its side effects and its sacrifices.

Chasing Archipelagic Dreams began with a vignette encapsulating the beginnings of the fraught relationship among the colonial state, the environment, and the people caught in between. It drew connections between early colonial functionaries and their descendants, who would in later years shape Sabahan politics and society. Such human stories, viewed alongside the broader administrative and political developments, add depth and perspective. In so doing, the book has investigated key themes, issues, and a familiar cast of

CONCLUSION

characters in the extension of foreign influence in Sabah amid the end of empire.

Foremost among these interrogatives has been to question the received wisdom concerning Britain's withdrawal from empire in Southeast Asia, Sabah's role in the formation of Malaysia, and the series of vying attempts to expand archipelagic spheres of postcolonial influence. Through this questioning, the book reconceptualizes decolonization and postcolonial state formation in Southeast Asia with a view toward offering a portable and adaptable methodology for scholars analyzing cognate subnational territories across the globe, whether in Africa, the Middle East, Europe, Central and South America, or elsewhere in Asia. Likewise, it calls for a reassessment of imperial decline that pays greater attention to the granular, grassroots developments that shaped local society and colonial administrative policy alike. Empire along these peripheries—whether outposts up the Kinabatangan River, lighthouses on contested Sulu Sea islands, or distant interior territories described in paper deeds and tacit agreements made with local leaders—was shaped as much by the broad-brush proclamations and political strategies of metropolitan and colonial governments as it was by the actions of lesser *kampong* leaders, district officers, and the various everyday residents scattered across the territory.

This book has ultimately advanced three main arguments. First, it has contended that international anticolonial projects, state-making attempts, and territorial assertions over Sabah from the late 1940s to the 1960s paradoxically elicited a considerable increase in colonial power and influence on the ground. Second, it has argued that ethnic, social, and political heterogeneity in Sabah led to pronounced local fragmentation and disunity that stymied the development of a cohesive anticolonial movement but nevertheless enabled the emergence of influential local power brokers. Finally, this book asserts that Sabah never fully decolonized. Its merger with Malaysia prompted an extension of colonial-style rule, an intensification of resource extraction, the suppression of local autonomy, and the imposition of an externally configured national identity.

Specifically, as explored in chapter 1, administrative shortfalls amid the imposition of formal colonial rule, combined with wartime devastation, perpetuated suffering into the late 1940s. Even amid the traumas of war ruin, foreign speculators and rogue agents wanted in on Sabah's territory. Chapter 2 built on the focus on economic policy by analyzing the new Crown Colony government's heightened penetration into Sabah's interior. It examined how this affected local communities scattered throughout the territory and how asymmetric economic policies gave rise to a nascent form of anticolonialism. Although they were not in direct pursuit of independent statehood, this cohort of young and increasingly politically engaged individuals sought greater access to the territory's resource wealth. The advent of print media, new ways of vocalizing political thought, and growing criticisms of the colonial government propelled Sabah's public toward an uncertain future.

The third chapter in this book turned to the emergence of Kalimantan Utara and the rapid popularization of radio in the late 1950s, which contributed to major sociopolitical shifts across Southeast Asia. Chapter 4 disentangled Anglo-Philippine geopolitical disputes over a series of island territories off Sabah's northern coast before analyzing the escalation of private and official claims over Bornean territory. It concluded with an investigation of Maphilindo, a proposed transnational confederation of the three postcolonial states and a theoretical route for ousting Britain from Borneo. Chapter 5 examined the emergence and development of the Anglo-Malayan Projek Malaysia, first announced in 1961. It discussed how British and Malayan policymakers worked with local power brokers across Sabah to convince the public to support the Malaysia proposal. By analyzing political commissions of inquiry, regional disputes and attempts to undermine the proposal, and local perspectives, the final chapter demonstrated how Sabah's diverse public served as the engine of the territory's history and how, without Sabah, Malaysia would never have come into being.

NOTES

Prologue

1. Walter H. Medhurst, preface to Frank Hatton, *North Borneo: Explorations and Adventures on the Equator* (London: Sampson Low, Marston, Searle & Rivington, 1886), iii.
2. Joseph Hatton, "Frank Hatton in North Borneo," *The Century Magazine*, vol. 8 (1885): 438–39.
3. Frank Hatton and W. R. Hodgkinson, "Notes on a Natural Oil Obtained from an 'Oil Shale' in North Borneo," August 9, 1881, 1–3, in Colonial Office file (CO) 874/352, the National Archives (TNA), Kew, England.
4. Robert Peckham, for instance, describes how "hunting inculcated those heroic frontier values of resilience and ingenuity, which were seen as most desirable in the male colonial subject." See Peckham, "Game of Empires: Hunting in Treaty-Port China, 1870–1940," in *Eco-Cultural Networks and the British Empire: New Views on Environmental History*, ed. James Beattie, Edward Melillo, and Emily O'Gorman (London: Bloomsbury Academic, 2015), 202.
5. Nicholas J. White, "The Survival, Revival and Decline of British Economic Influence in Malaysia, 1957–1970," *Twentieth Century British History* 14, no. 3 (2003): 223, https://doi.org/10.1093/tcbh/14.3.222.
6. Hatton, "Frank Hatton in North Borneo," 438, 439.
7. Robert Bickers, *Empire Made Me: An Englishman Adrift in Shanghai* (London: Penguin Books, 2004), 15.
8. C. S. Hutchison, *Geology of North-West Borneo: Sarawak, Brunei and Sabah* (Amsterdam: Elsevier, 2005), 1; P. Collenette, *The Geology and Mineral Resources of the Jesselton-Kinabalu Area, North Borneo* (Kuching: Government Printing Office, 1958), 5.
9. P. J. Granville-Edge, *The Sabahan: The Life and Death of Tun Fuad Stephens* (Kuala Lumpur: Writers' Publishing House, 1999), 29.
10. In addition to material exports, Borneo inspired myriad works of fiction in Europe. See, for instance, Joseph Conrad's novels set in Borneo, such as *Almayer's Folly*, and William Somerset Maugham's various short stories, such as "The Outstation" and "Before the Party." Similarly, accounts of explorations to Borneo were read with great interest by colonials at home and abroad. See, for instance, Frederick Boyle, *Adventures Among the Dyaks of Borneo* (1865; repr., Kota Kinabalu: Opus Publications, 2007); Odoardo Beccari, *Wanderings in the Great Forests of Borneo* (1904; repr., Oxford: Oxford University Press, 1989); and Eric Mjöberg, *I Tropikernas Villande Urskogar* [Forest life

and adventures in the Malay Archipelago] (1928; repr., Kota Kinabalu: Natural History Publications [Borneo], 1999).

11. Robert Cribb, Helen Gilbert, and Helen Tiffin, *Wild Man from Borneo: A Cultural History of the Orangutan* (Honolulu: University of Hawaii Press, 2014), 107–8; Jonathan Moran, "Life and Death in a Pitcher," *Natural History* 115, no. 8 (2006): 57.

12. In addition to its environmental and ecological significance, the concept of island "boundedness" is useful in (geo)political and colonial contexts. Sujit Sivasundaram considers how island "boundedness" shaped the course of colonial history in Sri Lanka in *Islanded: Britain, Sri Lanka and the Bounds of an Indian Ocean Colony* (Chicago: University of Chicago Press, 2013), while Lauren Benton discusses the geopolitical role of islands in facilitating colonial expansion in *A Search for Sovereignty: Law and Geography in European Empires, 1400–1900* (Cambridge: Cambridge University Press, 2010).

13. Eric Tagliacozzo, "Onto the Coasts and Into the Forests: Ramifications of the China Trade on the Ecological History of Northwest Borneo, 900–1900 CE," in *Histories of the Borneo Environment: Economic, Political and Social Dimensions of Change and Continuity*, ed. Reed L. Wadley (Leiden: KITLV Press, 2005), 26, https://doi.org/10.1163/9789004454279_004.

14. Granville-Edge, *The Sabahan*, 30.

15. Danny Wong Tze Ken, *Historical Sabah: Community and Society* (Kota Kinabalu: Natural History Publications, 2004), 87–90.

16. Granville-Edge, *The Sabahan*, 30, 32–33.

17. Wong, *Community and Society*, 83–88.

18. Granville-Edge, *The Sabahan*, 35.

19. Wong, *Community and Society*, 89. See also Ooi Keat Gin, *The Japanese Occupation of Borneo, 1941–1945* (London: Routledge, 2011), 98–117.

20. See chapters 2 and 5.

21. "Profile: Donald Stephens," September 11, 1957, 2, in Foreign and Commonwealth Office (FCO) 141/13004, TNA; Granville-Edge, *The Sabahan*, 83.

22. See chapter 2.

23. "Malaysian Air Crash Kills 11," *Sarasota Herald-Tribune*, June 7, 1976, 5; Peter J. Mojuntin, *The Golden Son of the Kadazan* (Seremban: Chang Lithho Press, 1978), 7–11.

24. "Fuad: Sabotage Suspected: Hussein Orders Probe into Plane Crash," *New Nation*, June 7, 1976, 1; Kelimen Sawatan, "Real Cause of Air Crash Never Made Known—Yong," *Borneo Post Online*, December 23, 2011, https://www.theborneopost.com/2011/12/23/real-cause-of-air-crash-never-made-known-yong/.

Introduction

1. Andulon B. Maga to Secretary, Malaysia Commission, February 24, 1962, in CO 947/16, TNA.

2. A. J. Alli Ahmed to Secretary, Malaysia Commission, February 19, 1962, in CO 947/16, TNA.

3. "Big 'Unity' Plan: Tengku on Closer Ties with S'pore, Borneo and Brunei," *Straits Times*, May 28, 1961, 1.

4. "Big 'Unity' Plan," 1.

5. "Note by M. MacDonald of talks with the Sultan of Brunei on 13–14 December," December 18, 1958, Dominions Office (DO) 35/10019, no. 12, E2, in *British Docu-*

ments on the End of Empire: Malaysia, Series B, vol. 8, ed. A. J. Stockwell (London: The Stationery Office, 2004), 14–17. See also Mohammed Noordin Sopiee, "The Advocacy of Malaysia—Before 1961," *Modern Asian Studies* 7, no. 4 (1973): 717–32, https://doi.org/10.1017/S0026749X00013500.

6. Hansard, "Sarawak," 200 Parl. Deb. H.L. (5th ser.) (1956) cols. 328–68.

7. Commissioner-General Malcolm MacDonald to Governor Anthony Abell, May 7, 1954, 1, in FCO 141/12555, TNA.

8. A. J. Stockwell, "Malaysia: The Making of a Neo-Colony?" *Journal of Imperial and Commonwealth History* 26, no. 2 (1998): 141.

9. Stockwell, "Malaysia," 138–56.

10. "The S-E Asian Vacuum," *Singapore Free Press*, August 25, 1961, 1.

11. Danny Wong Tze Ken, *Historical Sabah: Community and Society* (Kota Kinabalu: Natural History Publications, 2004), 125.

12. Wen-Qing Ngoei, *Arc of Containment: Britain, the United States, and Anticommunism in Southeast Asia* (Ithaca, NY: Cornell University Press, 2019), 2.

13. Maya Jasanoff, *The Dawn Watch: Joseph Conrad in a Global World* (London: William Collins, 2017), 125.

14. This is a stark contrast to Brunei's dominant role in maritime Southeast Asia during its heyday in the mid-sixteenth century, when it controlled a vast maritime empire. See, for instance, Barbara Watson Andaya and Leonard Y. Andaya, *A History of Early Modern Southeast Asia, 1400–1830* (Cambridge: Cambridge University Press), 151–66.

15. Eric Tagliacozzo, "Onto the Coasts and Into the Forests: Ramifications of the China Trade on the Ecological History of Northwest Borneo, 900–1900 CE," in *Histories of the Borneo Environment: Economic, Political and Social Dimensions of Change and Continuity*, ed. Reed L. Wadley (Leiden: KITLV Press, 2005), 27, 31–32, https://doi.org/10.1163/9789004454279_004.

16. "North Borneo," 5 Parl. Deb. (4th ser.) (1892) cols. 1808–19.

17. Amarjit Kaur, *Economic Change in East Malaysia: Sabah and Sarawak since 1850* (London: Macmillan, 1998), 3.

18. Steven Press, *Rogue Empires: Contracts and Conmen in Europe's Scramble for Africa* (Cambridge, MA: Harvard University Press, 2017), 11–15.

19. Jasanoff, *Dawn Watch*, 124.

20. David Leake, *Brunei: The Modern Southeast-Asian Islamic Sultanate* (London: McFarland & Company, 1989), 28.

21. In the eighteenth century, the East India Company also sought to utilize Labuan as a port to facilitate trade with southern China. See Leigh R. Wright, "The Anglo-Spanish-German Treaty of 1885: A Step in the Development of British Hegemony in North Borneo," *Australian Journal of Politics and History* 18, no. 1 (1972): 62–75.

22. Press, *Rogue Empires*, 84–86.

23. Press, *Rogue Empires*, 87; Ian Black, "The 'Lastposten': Eastern Kalimantan and the Dutch in the Nineteenth and Early Twentieth Centuries," *Journal of Southeast Asian Studies* 16, no. 2 (1985): 281–91, https://doi.org/10.1017/S0022463400008456.

24. Frank Tatu, "The United States Consul, the Yankee Raja, Ellena and the *Constitution*: A Historical Vignette," *Archipel* 40 (1990): 84, https://www.persee.fr/doc/arch_0044-8613_1990_num_40_1_2667.

25. Kennedy Tregonning, "American Activity in North Borneo, 1865–1881," *Pacific Historical Review* 23, no. 4 (1954): 359–60, 364, https://doi.org/10.2307/3634654.

26. Press, *Rogue Empires*, 133.

27. Press, *Rogue Empires*, 133, and Helmuth Stoecker and Peter Sebald, "Enemies of the Colonial Idea," in *Germans in the Tropics: Essays in German Colonial History*, ed. Arthur J. Knoll and Lewis H. Gann (Westport, CT: Greenwood Press, 1987), 59.

28. Graham Irwin, *Nineteenth-Century Borneo: A Study in Diplomatic Rivalry* (Leiden: Brill, 1955), 196.

29. Press, *Rogue Empires*, 7.

30. Wright, "The Anglo-Spanish-German Treaty of 1885," 71; Martin Meadows, "The Philippine Claim to North Borneo," *Political Science Quarterly* 77, no. 3 (1962): 326.

31. Irwin, *Nineteenth-Century Borneo*, 197.

32. Wright, "Anglo-Spanish-German Treaty," 71, 74.

33. James Francis Warren, *The North Borneo Chartered Company's Administration of the Bajau, 1878–1909: The Pacification of a Maritime, Nomadic People* (Athens: Ohio University, Center for International Studies, 1971), 33.

34. See, for instance, John Gallagher, *The Decline, Revival, and Fall of the British Empire* (Cambridge: Cambridge University Press, 1982); Piero Gleijeses, "Decolonization and the Cold War," in *The Oxford Handbook of the Ends of Empire*, ed. Martin Thomas and Andrew S. Thompson (Oxford: Oxford University Press, 2018), 477–96; and Sarah Stockwell, "Britain and Decolonisation in an Era of Global Change," in Thomas and Thompson, *Oxford Handbook*, 65–84.

35. Wm. Roger Louis, *Ends of British Imperialism: The Scramble for Empire, Suez and Decolonization* (London: I. B. Tauris, 2006), 452.

36. John Darwin, "Imperialism in Decline? Tendencies in British Imperial Policy Between the Wars," *Historical Journal* 23, no. 3 (1980): 659, https://doi.org/10.1017/S0018246X00024936.

37. Darwin, "Imperialism in Decline?," 657.

38. Louis, *Ends of British Imperialism*, 3. There are other examples here too, in which decolonization can be seen to have resulted in the preservation of—or increased—colonial or metropolitan influence after the de jure moment of constitutional independence. Enduring American economic and strategic influences in the Philippines have been explored by Kathleen Nadeau, *The History of the Philippines* (Westport, CT: Greenwood, 2008), 68, and by Kathleen Weekley, "The National or the Social? Problems of Nation-Building in Post–World War II Philippines," special issue, *Third World Quarterly* 27, no. 1: From Nation-Building to State-Building (2006): 97, https://doi.org/10.1080/01436590500369253.

39. Sarah Stockwell notes that it was not uncommon for colonials to claim that India's independence in 1947 was the "fulfilment of an unswerving liberalism" and a completion of the age-old civilizing mission. See Stockwell, "Britain and Decolonisation," 65.

40. Louis, *Ends of British Imperialism*, 452.

41. As John Darwin writes, "The facile notion of successive phases of expansion, stagnation and decline does not stand up to critical scrutiny." See Darwin, *Britain and Decolonisation: The Retreat from Empire in the Post-War World* (London: Macmillan, 1988), 6.

42. Martin Shipway, *Decolonization and Its Impact: A Comparative Approach to the End of the Colonial Empires* (Oxford: Wiley-Blackwell, 2008), 87–113.

43. Indeed, Shipway's book only mentions Malaysia twice in passing. See Shipway, *Decolonization and Its Impact*, 1, 83.

44. Gleijeses, "Decolonization and the Cold War," in Thomas and Thompson, *Oxford Handbook*, 478–87.

45. Hong Kong is often depicted as an anomalous case in British decolonization, although the 1997 Handover is typically seen as the official end of the British Empire. See, for instance, Andrew Higgins, "A Last Hurrah and an Empire Closes Down: China again Master of Hong Kong," *Guardian*, July 1, 1997, https://www.theguardian.com/world/1997/jul/01/china.andrewhiggins; and Edward A. Gargan, "China Resumes Control of Hong Kong, Concluding 156 years of British Rule," *New York Times*, July 1, 1997, https://www.nytimes.com/1997/07/01/world/china-resumes-control-of-hong-kong-concluding-156-years-of-british-rule.html.

46. As explored in chapter 1, many in Australia viewed the British Borneo territories as an important strategic buffer zone to counteract any future Japanese aggression.

47. Vincent Bevins, *The Jakarta Method: Washington's Anticommunist Crusade and the Mass Murder Program that Shaped Our World* (New York: PublicAffairs, 2020), 12.

48. Joseph Chinyong Liow, "Tunku Abdul Rahman and Malaya's Relations with Indonesia, 1957–1960," *Journal of Southeast Asian Studies* 36, no. 1 (2005): 88–89, https://doi.org/10.1017/S0022463405000044.

49. Ngoei, *Arc of Containment*, 115.

50. See, for instance, Francis L. F. Lee et al., "Hong Kong's Summer of Uprising: From Anti-Extradition to Anti-Authoritarian Protests," *China Review* 19, no. 4 (2019): 1–32, https://muse.jhu.edu/pub/250/article/743118; and Joshua Wong, "Hong Kong's International Front Line: Risks and Opportunities," *Journal of International Affairs* 73, no. 2 (2020): 261–68, https://www.jstor.org/stable/26939983.

51. "Group Draws Up Self-Determination Petition for Sarawak and Sabah," *Borneo Post*, August 13, 2014, https://www.theborneopost.com/2014/08/13/group-draws-up-self-determination-petition-for-sarawak-and-sabah/. See also James Chin, "Is Malaysia heading for 'BorneoExit'? Why some in East Malaysia are advocating for secession," *The Conversation*, September 24, 2010, https://theconversation.com/is-malaysia-heading-for-borneoexit-why-some-in-east-malaysia-are-advocating-for-secession-146208; and Johan Arriffin Samad, "The 1963 Malaysia Agreement: Pakatan's Failed Restoration and Perikatan's Fledgling Initiatives," in *Sabah from the Ground: The 2020 Elections and the Politics of Survival*, ed. Bridget Welsh, Vilashini Somiah, and Benjamin Y. H. Loh (Singapore: ISEAS Publishing, 2021), 39–60.

52. Robert Strayer, for instance, has argued for a comparative approach to aid in framing the collapse of the Soviet Union and the decolonization of its constituent states. See Strayer, "Decolonization, Democratization, and Communist Reform: The Soviet Collapse in Comparative Perspective," *Journal of World History*, 12, no. 2 (2001): 375–406, https://doi.org/10.1353/jwh.2001.0042.

53. Muhammad Muslih, "Arab Politics and the Rise of Palestinian Nationalism," *Journal of Palestinian Studies* 16, no. 4 (1987): 77–78, https://doi.org/10.2307/2536721.

54. See, for instance, Yair Wallach, "Creating a Country through Currency and Stamps: State Symbols and Nation-Building in British-Ruled Palestine," *Nations and Nationalism* 17, no. 1 (2010): 1–19, https://doi.org/10.1111/j.1469-8129.2010.00470.x.

55. Yair Wallach, "Trapped in Mirror-Images: The Rhetoric of Maps in Israel/Palestine," *Political Geography* 30, no. 7 (2011): 358, https://doi.org/10.1016/j.polgeo.2011.07.004.

56. Shannon Teoh, "Philippines' Claim over Sabah Becomes Hot Topic in State Polls," *Straits Times*, September 22, 2020, https://www.straitstimes.com/asia/se-asia/philippines-claim-over-sabah-becomes-hot-topic-at-state-polls.

57. *Straits Times*, "Duterte Vows to Pursue Philippine Claim to Sabah," May 27, 2016, https://www.straitstimes.com/asia/se-asia/duterte-vows-to-pursue-philippine-claim-to-sabah; Gregory Poling, Phoebe DePadua, and Jennifer Frentasia, "The Royal Army of Sulu Invades Malaysia," *Centre for Strategic and International Studies: Critical Questions*, March 8, 2013, https://www.csis.org/analysis/royal-army-sulu-invades-malaysia.

58. Michael R. Dove, *The Banana Tree at the Gate: A History of Marginal Peoples and Global Markets in Borneo* (New Haven, CT: Yale University Press, 2011), 247.

59. Jasanoff, *Dawn Watch*, 161.

60. Ann Laura Stoler, *Along the Archival Grain: Epistemic Realities and Colonial Common Sense* (Princeton, NJ: Princeton University Press, 2008), 1.

61. Mary Margaret Steedly, *Rifle Reports: A Story of Indonesian Independence* (Berkeley: University of California Press, 2013), 9.

62. "Extract from R. W. C.'s Diary," June 8, 1962, 93, in FCO 141/13013, TNA.

63. L. C. Hoffman, *Straits Times*, January 19, 1963.

64. "Divorce Off: Aza's Wife Not in Court," *Straits Times*, April 5, 1963, 5; "Azahari's Wife No. 2 to Divorce Him," *Straits Times*, October 28, 1966, 6.

65. Nicholas Tarling, "Kennedy P. G. Tregonning," *Borneo Research Bulletin*, January 1, 2016, https://link.gale.com/apps/doc/A503262432/AONE?u=anon~6beed223&sid=googleScholar&xid=1ee389e3.

66. See, for instance, Wong, *Community and Society*; Kaur, *Economic Change in East Malaysia*; and Ooi Keat Gin, *Post-War Borneo: Nationalism, Empire and State-Building* (London: Routledge, 2013).

67. Kennedy Tregonning, *North Borneo* (London: Her Majesty's Stationery Office, 1960).

68. "Publications, Corona Library Series: North Borneo," October 28, 1958, in CO 1027/299, TNA. R. D. Binford, of the Colonial Office's Publication Division, even remarked that Sabah's Governor Roland Turnbull "was upset" by the criticisms contained in Tregonning's manuscript.

69. Kennedy Tregonning to Jones, memorandum, October 22, 1957, in CO 1027/299, TNA.

70. "Publications, Corona Library Series: North Borneo," October 28, 1958, in CO 1027/299, TNA.

1. From Company State to Crown Colony

1. Hansard, "North Borneo and Sarawak," 461 Parl. Deb. (5th ser.) (1949) cols. 907–20.

2. P. J. Granville-Edge, *The Sabahan: The Life and Death of Tun Fuad Stephens* (Kuala Lumpur: Writers' Publishing House, 1999), 73.

3. Danny Wong Tze Ken, *Historical Sabah: The War* (Kota Kinabalu: Opus Publications, 2010), 149.

4. Ronald J. Brooks, *Under Five Flags: The Story of Sabah, East Malaysia* (Edinburgh: Pentland, 1999), 149.

5. Ueno Itsuyoshi, *An End to a War: A Japanese Soldier's Experience of the 1945 Death Marches of North Borneo*, trans. Mika Reilly (Kota Kinabalu: Opus Publications, 2012), 97.

6. The word "rentice," originating from the Malay *rentas* (traverse), refers to narrow access paths cleared though vegetation to facilitate colonial lines of communication, specifically the laying down and maintenance of telegraph and power lines across North Borneo, Brunei, and Sarawak. See Stella Moo-Tan, ed., *The Diaries of George C. Woolley*, vol. 4 (Kota Kinabalu: Department of Sabah Museum, 2018), 520.

7. Tom Harrisson, "Explorations in Central Borneo," *The Geographical Journal* 114, no. 4 (1949): 147–48, https://doi.org/10.2307/1789578. These activities have been neglected in traditional histories of Sabah's wartime experience, and they reveal how even the most remote indigenous communities became involved in the war effort. Harrisson notes that even though the war officially ended in August 1945, anti-Japanese missions persisted for many years, as isolated groups of Japanese soldiers continued to fight, having not received word of their country's surrender.

8. Harrisson, "Explorations in Central Borneo," 147.

9. "Another Great Trading Company Disappears," *Morning Tribune*, July 15, 1946, 10; "British North Borneo's Goodbye to the Company," *Straits Times*, July 15, 1946, 4.

10. Ueno, *An End to a War*, 94, and Ooi Keat Gin, *Post-War Borneo, 1945–1950: Nationalism, Empire and State-Building* (London: Routledge, 2013), 57–58.

11. Wong, *The War*, 140.

12. Wong, *The War*, 146–48.

13. Hansard, "British North Borneo (Administration)," 414 Parl. Deb. (5th ser.) (1945).

14. Charles. F. C. Macaskie, *End of an Era: The Borneo Reminiscences of C. F. C. Macaskie, C. M. G.* (Kota Kinabalu: Opus Publications, 2011), 8–9. The British Borneo Civil Affairs Unit was abbreviated and often referred to as "BBCAU," which was in turn referred to as "Bikau" by locals.

15. For an in-depth discussion of the Sultanates of Sulu and Brunei and precolonial territorial entanglements, see chapter 3.

16. See, for instance, Gavin Merrick Long, *Australia in the War of 1939–1945*, 1st ser., vol. 7, *The Final Campaigns* (Canberra: Australian War Memorial, 1963); and Graeme Sligo, *Backroom Boys: Alfred Conlon and Army's Directorate of Research and Civil Affairs, 1942–46* (Sydney: Big Sky Publishing, 2016).

17. Ooi Keat Gin, "Prelude to Invasion: Covert Operations before the Re-Occupation of Northwest Borneo, 1944–45," *Journal of the Australian War Memorial*, no. 37 (2002), https://www.awm.gov.au/articles/journal/j37/borneo.

18. Sligo, *Backroom Boys*, 289.

19. Ooi, "Prelude to Invasion."

20. Sligo, *Backroom Boys*, 295, 297.

21. Macaskie, *End of an Era*, 8–9. The Australian Directorate of Research and Civil Affairs, a think tank founded by Alfred Austin Conlon, formed the institutional and intellectual nucleus of the Australian administration in Borneo.

22. Hansard, "Sarawak," 200 Parl. Deb. H.L. (5th ser.) (1956) cols. 329–68.

23. Macaskie, *End of an Era*, 9.

24. Geoffrey Gray, "W. E. H. Stanner: Wasted War Years," in *Scholars at War: Australasian Social Scientists, 1939–1945*, ed. Geoffrey Gray, Doug Munro, and Christine

NOTES TO PAGES 41–45

Winter (Canberra: Australian National University Press, 2012), 97–99, http://press-files.anu.edu.au/downloads/press/p166981/pdf/ch04.pdf.

25. Macaskie, *End of an Era*, 9.

26. Long, *Australia in the War*, 402–3.

27. David Phillips, "Borneo History: Time for a New Look?" *Journal of the Malay Branch of the Royal Asiatic Society* 89, vol. 2 (2016): 56, https://doi.org/10.1353/ras.2016.0024.

28. Macaskie, *End of an Era*, 9.

29. Hansard, "Commonwealth Migration," 166 Parl. Deb. H.L. (5th ser.) (1950) cols. 1228–68.

30. Hansard, "Colonial Affairs," 425 Parl. Deb. (5th ser.) (1946) cols. 238–352

31. Hansard, "Sarawak (Proposed Cession)," 419 Parl. Deb. (5th ser.) (1946) cols. 368–73.

32. Hansard, "Sarawak (Proposed Cession)," 419 Parl. Deb. (5th ser.) (1946) cols. 368–73.

33. Paul Kratostka, ed., introduction to *Southeast Asian Minorities in the Wartime Japanese Empire* (London: RoutledgeCurzon, 2002), 1–2.

34. Hansard, "Sarawak (Proposed Cession)," 419 Parl. Deb. (5th ser.) (1946) cols. 368–73.

35. Hansard, "Sarawak (Act of Cession)," 423 Parl. Deb. (5th ser.) (1946) cols. 337–38.

36. Amarjit Kaur, *Economic Change in East Malaysia: Sabah and Sarawak since 1850* (London: Macmillan, 1998), 118.

37. Hansard, "Sarawak (Act of Cession)," 423 Parl. Deb. (5th ser.) (1946) cols. 337–38.

38. "Stewart's Murder Planned a Year Ago," *Malaya Tribune*, January 10, 1950, 1.

39. Hansard, "Constabulary (Trespass Inquiry)," 430 Parl. Deb. (5th ser.) (1946).

40. Hansard, "British North Borneo," 141 Parl. Deb. H.L. (5th ser.) (1946) cols. 1009–10.

41. "Risings in the North Keppel and Rundum Districts," in CO 874/835, TNA; Andrew Massey, *The Political Economy of Stagnation: British North Borneo Under the Chartered Company, 1881–1946* (Kota Kinabalu: Arkib Negeri Sabah, 2006), 249.

42. Phillips, "Borneo History," 55.

43. "Notes on Local Government and Native Administration," November 13, 1947, 1–2, in FCO 141/17033, TNA.

44. Many members of Parliament were shocked by the voracity at which the Britain's new Labour Government was willing to "transfer for money . . . the sovereign rights of a country." See Hansard, "Colonial Affairs," 425 Parl. Deb. (5th ser.) (1946) cols. 238–352.

45. Hansard, "British Firms, Borneo (Taxation)," 438 Parl. Deb. (5th ser.) (1946) cols. 1752–60.

46. Hansard, "British Firms, Borneo (Taxation)," 438 Parl. Deb. (5th ser.) (1946) cols. 1752–60; and "North Borneo (Financial Position)," 438 Parl. Deb. (5th ser.) (1947) col. 2006.

47. "B.N.B. Co. Turns Down £2,200,000," *Singapore Free Press*, June 19, 1946, 1.

48. "B.N.B. Becomes Colony on July 15," *Straits Times*, June 20, 1946, 3.

49. Hansard, "Colonial Affairs," 425 Parl. Deb. (5th ser.) (1946) cols. 238–352.

50. "B.N.B. Becomes Colony on July 15," *Straits Times*, June 20, 1946, 3.

51. "N. Borneo Settlement Held Up," *Straits Budget*, August 14, 1947, 13.

52. "Award for Br. North Borneo Co.," *Sunday Tribune (Singapore)*, February 27, 1949, 1.

53. "Chartered Company Only Left with $320," *North Borneo News & Sabah Times*, October 18, 1962.

54. Phillips, "Borneo History," 56.

55. See, for instance, Kaur, *Economic Change in East Malaysia*, 118.

56. Ronald J. Brooks, for example, suggests that the postwar period was characterized by a resumption of British rule because many chartered company-era bureaucrats were employed as colonial officers after the war. See Brooks, *Under Five Flags*, 163–64.

57. "Filipinos Say Their Independence Is Real," *Indian Daily Mail*, June 11, 1947, 4.

58. Kathleen Nadeau, *The History of the Philippines* (Westport, CT: Greenwood, 2008), 68; Kathleen Weekley, "The National or the Social? Problems of Nation-Building in Post–World War II Philippines," in "From Nation-Building to State-Building," special issue, *Third World Quarterly* 27, no. 1 (2006): 97, https://doi.org/10.1080/01436590500369253.

59. Max Seitelman, "The Cession of Sarawak," *Far Eastern Survey* 17, no. 3 (1948): 35–37

60. "The Little Empire," *Straits Times*, June 25, 1946, 4.

61. Hansard, "Sarawak," 200 Parl. Deb. H.L. (5th ser.) (1956) cols. 329–68.

62. Hansard, "North Borneo and Sarawak," 461 Parl. Deb. (5th ser.) (1949) cols. 907–20.

63. "North Borneo Joins Empire," *Straits Times*, July 16, 1946, 1.

64. David Phillips, "The 'Migrated Archives' and a Forgotten Corner of Empire: The British Borneo Territories," *Journal of Imperial and Commonwealth History* 44, no. 6 (2016): 1007, https://doi.org/10.1080/03086534.2016.1251557.

65. Phillips, "Borneo History," 56.

66. Hansard, "Sarawak," 200 Parl. Deb. H.L. (5th ser.) (1956) cols. 329–68.

67. Wong, *The War*, 149–50.

68. Peter Lovegrove, "Borneo's Dusuns Rewarded," *Singapore Free Press*, October 29, 1947, 4.

69. "Annual Report of the Department of Immigration and Labour for the Year 1948," 23, in CO 648/23, TNA.

70. Wong, *The War*, 150.

71. Hansard, "British Firms, Borneo (Taxation)," 438 Parl. Deb. (5th ser.) (1947) cols. 1752–60.

72. Arthur G. Tubb, "Report on Accounts and Finances for the Colony of North Borneo," October 31, 1947, 9, in CO 648/23, TNA.

73. "Annual Report on the West Coast Residency for 1921," *State of North Borneo Supplement to the Official Gazette, 1921*, 223, in CO 648/9, TNA.

74. Maureen De Silva, "Javanese Indentured Labourers in British North Borneo, 1914–1932," (PhD diss., School of Oriental and African Studies, University of London, 2009), 61, 193–94, https://eprints.soas.ac.uk/29298/.

75. Michael R. Dove, "Smallholder Rubber and Swidden Agriculture in Borneo: A Sustainable Adaptation to the Ecology and Economy of the Tropical Forest," *Economic Botany* 47, no. 2, (1993): 137, https://doi.org/10.1007/BF02862016.

76. Hansard, "North Borneo and Sarawak," 461 Parl. Deb. (5th ser.) (1949) cols. 907–20.

77. M. C. Cleary, "Plantation Agriculture and the Formulation of Native Land Rights in British North Borneo, c. 1880–1930," *The Geographic Journal* 158, no. 2 (1992): 170–81, https://doi.org/10.2307/3059786.

78. L. W. Jones, "The Decline and Recovery of the Murut Tribe of Sabah," *Population Studies* 21, no. 2 (1967): 133–34, https://doi.org/10.1080/00324728.1967.10405470.

79. David R. Saunders, "'State of Intoxication:' Governing Alcohol and Disease in the Forests of British North Borneo," *eTropic: Electronic Journal of Studies in the Tropics* 20, no. 1 (2021): 15, https://doi.org/10.25120/etropic.20.1.2021.3779.

80. Ranjit D. S. Singh, *The Making of Sabah, 1865–1941: The Dynamics of Indigenous Society* (Kuala Lumpur: University of Malaya Press, 2000), 27.

81. L. W. Jones, *The Population of Borneo: A Study of the Peoples of Sarawak, Sabah, and Brunei* (1966; repr., Kota Kinabalu: Opus Publications, 2007), 18–19.

82. Stephen L. Harp, *A World History of Rubber: Empire, Industry, and the Everyday* (Chichester: Wiley Blackwell, 2016), 17. See also "Refund of Rubber Export Duty," in *Colonial Annual Report: North Borneo 1948* (London: His Majesty's Stationery Office, 1949), 7.

83. Douglas James Jardine, *Administration Report for the Year 1936*, 1937, 30, in CO 648/18, TNA.

84. Hansard, "North Borneo and Sarawak," 461 Parl. Deb. (5th ser.) (1949) cols. 907–20.

85. Mark G. L. Van Nieuwstadt and Douglas Sheil, "Drought, Fire, and Tree Survival in a Borneo Rain Forest, East Kalimantan, Indonesia," *Journal of Ecology* 93, no. 1 (2005): 191–201, https://doi.org/10.1111/j.1365-2745.2004.00954.x.

86. Carolyn Payus et al., "Impact of Extreme Drought Climate on Water Security in North Borneo: Case Study of Sabah," *Water* 12, no. 1135 (2020): 1–19, https://doi.org/10.3390/w12041135.

87. Harrisson, "Explorations in Central Borneo," 148; "Tenom Notes," *British North Borneo Herald*, May 16, 1928, 93, in CO 855/42, TNA.

88. "Annual Report of the Department of Agriculture for the Year 1946," 4, in CO 648/23, TNA.

89. "Production and Labour," in *Colonial Annual Report: North Borneo 1948*, 7.

90. "Annual Report of the Department of Agriculture for the Year 1946," 4–12, in CO 648/23, TNA. Agricultural revenue for July to December 1946 was only 1,785.85 Malayan dollars (£189; $762), while expenditure was 25,976.30 Malayan dollars (£2,840; $11,447).

91. "Annual Report of the Department of Agriculture for the Year 1947," 81, in CO 648/23, TNA.

92. Wm. Roger Louis, *Ends of British Imperialism: The Scramble for Empire, Suez and Decolonization* (London: I. B. Tauris, 2006), 452.

93. "Annual Report of the Department of Agriculture for the Year 1946," 2, in CO 648/23, TNA.

94. Hansard, "British Firms, Borneo (Taxation)," 438 Parl. Deb. (5th ser.) (1947) cols. 1752–60.

95. Harp, *World History of Rubber*, 11.

96. Hansard, "North Borneo and Sarawak," 461 Parl. Deb. (5th ser.) (1949) cols. 907–20.

97. T. G. Cochrane, "Empire Oil: The Progress of Sarawak," *Journal of the Royal Society of Arts* 72, no. 3723 (1924): 308–19.

98. Harp, *World History of Rubber*, 102.

99. "Annual Report for the Department of Immigration and Labour for the Year 1948," 366, in CO 648/23, TNA.

100. Hansard, "Sarawak," 200 Parl. Deb. H.L. (5th ser.) (1956) cols. 329–68.

101. John M. Carroll, *Edge of Empires: Chinese Elites and British Colonials in Hong Kong* (Cambridge, MA: Harvard University Press, 2005), 16.

102. Saw Swee-Hock and Chiu Wing Kin, "Population Growth and Redistribution in Hong Kong, 1841–1975," *Southeast Asian Journal of Social Science* 4, no. 1 (1975): 127, https://doi.org/10.1163/080382476X00101.

103. Lowell Thomas, ed., *Nations of the World: Hong Kong* (Portland, OR: Sawyer's View-Master Series, , n.d.), 5.

104. Ho Yin-Ping, *Trade, Industrial Restructuring and Development in Hong Kong* (Basingstoke, UK: Macmillan, 1992), 4.

105. "Immigrant Labour," in *Colonial Annual Report: North Borneo 1948*, 13.

106. Hansard, "Commonwealth Migration," 166 Parl. Deb. H.L. (5th ser.) (1950) cols. 1228–68.

107. Philip J. Watson, "The History of Rubber Statistics," International Rubber Study Group (1999), 2.

108. Harp, *World History of Rubber*, 102.

109. "U.S. May Cut Natural Rubber Requirements," *Straits Times*, July 20, 1946, 2.

110. Enzo R. Grilli, "Natural Rubber: A Better Future?" *Finance & Development* 18, no. 2 (June 1981): 25, https://doi.org/10.5089/9781616353452.022.

111. "Annual Report of the Department of Immigration and Labour for the Year 1948," 354, in CO 648/23, TNA.

112. Hansard, "Colonial and Middle Eastern Services," 461 Parl. Deb. (5th ser.) (1949) cols. 2043–88.

113. "Possible Use of Italian Labour in North Borneo," 1949, in FO 371/79536, TNA.

114. The idea to populate Borneo with Italian labor was not entirely new. Between 1870 and 1873, the Italian government sought to establish a penal colony at Gaya Bay, on Sabah's west coast. See Graham Irwin, *Nineteenth-Century Borneo: A Study in Diplomatic Rivalry* (Leiden: Brill, 1955), 196.

115. P. Wilkins, memorandum, "Recruitment of Agricultural Labour for North Borneo," August 22, 1947, 1, in CO 167/942/6, TNA. See also Hansard, "Mauritius (Economic Problems)," 506 Parl. Deb. (5th ser.) (1952) cols. 956–64.

116. "Annual Report of the Department of Immigration and Labour for the Year 1948," 358–59, in CO 648/23, TNA.

117. P. Wilkins, memorandum, "Recruitment of Agricultural Labour for North Borneo," 1, August 22, 1947, in CO 167/942/6, TNA.

118. Mr Higham to Mr Sidebotham, memorandum, November 24, 1948, 9–10, in CO 167/942/6, TNA.

119. Mr Higham to Mr Sidebotham, memorandum, November 24, 1948, 9–10, in CO 167/942/6, TNA.

120. David W. John and James C. Jackson, "The Tobacco Industry of North Borneo: A Distinctive Form of Plantation Agriculture," *Journal of Southeast Asian Studies* 4, no. 1, (1974): 93, https://doi.org/10.1017/S002246340001643X.

121. R. C. Wilkinson, "Report on the Project of Emigration from Mauritius to North Borneo," 1949, 3, 10–11, in CO 167/942/6, TNA.

122. "Annual Report of the Department of Immigration and Labour for the Year 1948," 359, in CO 648/23, TNA.

123. Hansard, "Cocos Islands Bill," 536 Parl. Deb. (5th ser.) (1955) cols. 698–734.

124. Hansard, "Christmas Island Bill," 166 Parl. Deb. H.L. (5th ser.) (1958) cols. 996–1005.

125. Hansard, "Commonwealth Migration," 166 Parl. Deb. H.L. (5th ser.) (1950) cols. 1228–68.

126. Hansard, "Malaysia Bill," 252 Parl. Deb. H.L. (5th ser.) (1963) cols. 933–979.

127. John Fisher, "Man on the Spot: Captain George Gracey and British Policy towards the Assyrians, 1917–45," *Middle Eastern Studies* 44 no. 2 (2008): 226, https://doi.org/10.1080/00263200701874875.

2. The (Re-)Emergence of Anticolonial Voices

1. Nordin Ramli, "The History of Offshore Hydrocarbon Exploration in Malaysia," *Energy* 10, no. 3–4 (1985): 457–73, https://doi.org/10.1016/0360-5442(85)90060-X.

2. The term *orang kaya kaya*, literally meaning "rich rich man," denoted societal importance, wealth, and status. It was used to convey respect, akin to a gentleman. While deriving from local traditions, the term was incorporated into the colonial system codified as a formal title. For an explanation of the role of political status in the colonial Dutch East Indies, see Roy Ellen, "On the Contemporary Uses of Colonial History and the Legitimation of Political Status in Archipelagic Southeast Seram," *Journal of Southeast Asian Studies* 28, no. 1 (1997): 78–102, https://doi.org/10.1017/S0022463400015186

3. Michael Dove, *The Banana Tree at the Gate: A History of Marginal Peoples and Global Markets in Borneo* (New Haven, CT: Yale University Press, 2011), 8.

4. Eric Tagliacozzo, "Onto the Coasts and into the Forests: Ramifications of the China Trade on the Ecological History of Northwest Borneo, 900–1900 CE," in *Histories of the Borneo Environment: Economic, Political and Social Dimensions of Change and Continuity*, ed. Reed L. Wadley (Leiden: KITLV Press, 2005), 27, https://doi.org/10.1163/9789004454279_004.

5. Hansard, "Sarawak," 200 Parl. Deb. H.L. (5th ser.) (1956) cols. 329–68.

6. In addition to this, there was also a steady demand for items collected from Borneo's forest, which formed a small but steady source of exports. Such jungle products included rattan, edible birds' nests, animal skins, wild latexes, and sago, among other items.

7. *Colonial Annual Report: North Borneo 1948* (London: His Majesty's Stationery Office, 1949), 29.

8. Government of North Borneo, *Guide to the Timber Industry and Forest Produce Exhibition at the Forest Office* (Sandakan: North Borneo Government Press, 1959), vii, in CO 1069/548, TNA.

9. *Colonial Annual Report: North Borneo 1957* (London: Her Majesty's Stationery Office, 1958), 40–41. For information on Hong Kong's transformation into an industrial manufacturing hub, see Ho Yin-Ping, *Trade, Industrial Restructuring and Development in Hong Kong* (Basingstoke, UK: Macmillan Press, 1992).

10. *Colonial Annual Report: North Borneo 1960* (London: Her Majesty's Stationery Office, 1961), 46–48.

11. Willem Meijer, "Plant Geographic Studies on Dipterocarpaceae in Malesia," *Annals of the Missouri Botanical Garden* 61, no. 3 (1974): 806, https://doi.org/10.2307/2395031.

12. Alexander Shenkin et al., "The World's Tallest Tropical Tree in Three Dimensions," *Frontiers in Forest and Global Change* 2, no. 32 (2019): 3, https://doi.org/10.3389/ffgc.2019.00032; Mary Gagen, "The World's Tallest Known Tropical Tree Has Been Found—and Climbed," *National Geographic*, April 3, 2019, https://www.nationalgeographic.com/environment/article/worlds-tallest-tropical-tree-discovered-climbed-borneo.

13. William W. Bevis, *Borneo Log: The Struggle for Sarawak's Forests* (Seattle: University of Washington Press, 1995), 12.

14. Ooi Jin Bee, *Tropical Deforestation: The Tyranny of Time* (Singapore: National University of Singapore, 1993), 86.

15. See chapter 1. See also Hansard, "North Borneo and Sarawak," 461 Parl. Deb. (5th ser.) (1949) cols. 907–20; and "The Little Empire,'" *Straits Times*, June 25, 1946, 4.

16. See part II (chapters 3, 4, and 5).

17. David Fedman, writing about Japanese-occupied Korea in the early twentieth century, describes a similar process in which Japanese forestry management was predicated on disenfranchising Indigenous communities from accessing forest resources and monopolizing the epistemological parameters of "not just who owned the land but how it could be used." See Fedman, *Seeds of Control: Japan's Empire of Forestry in Colonial Korea* (Seattle: University of Washington Press, 2020), 74.

18. Owen Rutter, *British North Borneo: An Account of its History, Resources and Native Tribes* (London: Constable, 1922), 226.

19. "Risings in the North Keppel and Rundum Districts," in CO 874/835, TNA.

20. See, for instance, David R. Saunders, "'State of Intoxication': Governing Alcohol and Disease in the Forests of British North Borneo," *eTropic: Electronic Journal of Studies in the Tropics* 20, no. 1 (2021): 202–25, https://doi.org/10.25120/etropic.20.1.2021.3779.

21. Stephen L. Harp, *A World History of Rubber: Empire, Industry, and the Everyday* (Chichester: Wiley Blackwell, 2016), 102; Philip J. Watson, "The History of Rubber Statistics," International Rubber Study Group (1999), 2.

22. *Colonial Annual Report: North Borneo 1955* (London: Her Majesty's Stationery Office, 1956), 49–50.

23. Danny Wong Tze Ken, *Historical Sabah: Community and Society* (Kota Kinabalu: Natural History Publications, 2004), 137.

24. Rutter, *British North Borneo*, 226.

25. Harp, *World History of Rubber*, 11.

26. *Colonial Annual Report: North Borneo 1960* (London: Her Majesty's Stationery Office, 1961), 70, 73–74.

27. *Colonial Annual Report: North Borneo 1960*, 72

28. Fenner Brockway, in Hansard, "Malaysia Bill," 681 Parl. Deb. (5th ser.) (1963) cols. 924–1006.

29. Ranjit D. S. Singh, *The Making of Sabah, 1865–1941: The Dynamics of Indigenous Society* (Kuala Lumpur: University of Malaya Press, 2000), 27.

30. "Native Chiefs," 1913–46, in CO 874/815, TNA.

31. E. J. Philipps to A. N. Galsworthy, March 6, 1946, 88, in CO 874/815, TNA, and "Native Chiefs: Classification Scheme," January 14, 1924, in CO 874/815, TNA, 32–4.

32. See, for instance, Iza R. Hussin, *The Politics of Islamic Law: Local Elites, Colonial Authority, and the Making of the Muslim State* (Chicago: University of Chicago Press, 2016); Merima Ali, Odd-Helge Fjelstad, and Abdulaziz B. Shifa, "European Colonization and the Corruption of Local Elites: The Case of Chiefs in Africa," *Journal of Economic Behaviour and Organization* 179 (2020): 80–100, https://doi.org/10.1016/j.jebo.2020.08.043; and Nantang Ben Jua, "Indirect Rule in Colonial and Post-Colonial Cameroon," *Paideuma: Mitteilungen zur Kulturkunde* 41 (1995): 39–47, https://www.jstor.org/stable/40341691. Another relevant example would be to look at the role of elites in colonial Hong Kong and their activities in the period leading up to the 1997 handover, in which old and new elites "scrambled for benefits and jockeyed for position" with both the outgoing British and incoming Chinese colonial overlords. See Ma Ngok, *Political Development in Hong Kong: State Political Society, and Civil Society* (Hong Kong: Hong Kong University Press, 2007), 28.

33. Harry J. Benda, "Political Elites in Colonial Southeast Asia: An Historical Analysis," *Comparative Studies in Society and History* 7, no. 3 (1965): 233–34, https://doi.org/10.1017/S0010417500003662.

34. Rini Kusumawati and Leontine Visser, "Capturing the Elite in Marine Conservation in Northeast Kalimantan," *Human Ecology* 44, no. 3 (2016): 301–10, https://doi.org/10.1007/s10745-016-9830-0.

35. Kusumawati and Visser, "Capturing the Elite," 301–2. Sabah's early colonial period was characterized by a series of violent conflicts between the chartered company and indigenous groups. See, for instance, "Risings in the North Keppel and Rundum Districts," in CO 874/835, TNA; and Andrew Massey, *The Political Economy of Stagnation: British North Borneo Under the Chartered Company, 1881–1946* (Kota Kinabalu: Arkib Negeri Sabah), 249.

36. Harold Nicolson, "The Colonial Problem," *International Affairs* 17, no. 1 (1938): 36, https://doi.org/10.2307/2602169.

37. Ma, *Political Development in Hong Kong*, 28.

38. Tom Phillips and Alex Healey, "'I Should Have Done More': Chris Patten on Leaving Hong Kong without Democracy," *Guardian* (Manchester), June 28, 2017, https://www.theguardian.com/world/2017/jun/28/i-should-have-done-more-chris-patten-leaving-hong-kong-without-democracy-china.

39. Ming K. Chan, "The Legacy of the British Administration of Hong Kong: A View from Hong Kong," *China Quarterly*, 151 (1997): 577, https://doi.org/10.1017/S0305741000046828.

40. Local elections were first held in December 1962. There was little opportunity for public political expression prior to this. See "Candidates for Local Govt. Elections," *North Borneo News & Sabah Times*, December 5, 1962.

41. Ian Black, "Native Administration by the British North Borneo Chartered Company" (PhD diss. Australian National University, 1970), 161.

42. Popular opposition to the poll tax sparked a widespread rebellion in the Rundum District in 1915, and the tax continued to stoke anger and resentment until it was abolished in 1962. "Bill to Abolish Poll Tax in North Borneo Announced," *North Borneo News & Sabah Times*, August 27, 1962. See also "Murut Population: Threat of Extinction and Injustice of Ungraduated Poll Tax," 1935, in CO 531/25/8, TNA; and memorandum, Attorney General to Chief Secretary, February 19, 1960, 38, in FCO 141/13004, TNA.

43. "Annual Report on the West Coast Residency for 1917," 110, in CO 648/8, TNA.

44. Agnes Newton Keith, *White Man Returns* (1951; repr., Kota Kinabalu: Opus Publications, 2008), 101.

45. Alice M. Nah, "(Re)mapping Indigenous 'Race'/Place in Postcolonial Peninsular Malaysia," *Geografiska Annaler*, Series B, *Human Geography* 88, no. 3 (2006): 286–87, https://doi.org/10.1111/j.1468-0459.2006.00222.x.

46. Keith, *White Man Returns*, 101.

47. "The Story of Saudin," *Atlantic*, February 1938; James Sarda, "Saudin—the Murut 'Marco Polo,'" *Daily Express (Sabah)*, November 22, 2009. http://www.dailyexpress.com.my/read/230/saudin-the-murut-marco-polo-/.

48. "The Story of Saudin."

49. James Francis Warren, *The North Borneo Chartered Company's Administration of the Bajau, 1878–1909: The Pacification of a Maritime, Nomadic People* (Athens: Ohio University, Center for International Studies, 1971), 33; Mohammed Jefri Radius, "The Rundum Incident Was More of a War than a Rebellion," *Daily Express (Malaysia)*, April 22, 2012. https://www.dailyexpress.com.my/read.cfm?NewsID=882.

50. Hansard, "Malaysia Bill," 252 Parl. Deb. H.L. (5th ser.) (1963) cols. 933–979.

51. "Fostering of Potential Leaders," July 21, 1961, 5, in FCO 141/13022, TNA.

52. "Fostering of Potential Leaders," 5.

53. "Fostering of Potential Leaders, 1962—Second Half-Year Report," January 8, 1963, 1, in FCO 141/13022, TNA.

54. "Fostering of Potential Leaders, 1962—First Half-Year Report," July 5, 1962, 1–2, in FCO 141/13022, TNA.

55. Yamamoto Hiroyuki, "'Foreigners' Nationalism' in Malaysia: Donald Stephens and K. Bali in Making of Sabah Nationhood," *Jurnal Sejarah* 9, no. 9 (2001): 51.

56. P. J. Granville-Edge, *The Sabahan: The Life and Death of Tun Fuad Stephens* (Kuala Lumpur: Writers' Publishing House, 1999), 52.

57. See the discussion of Stephens's grandfather, Ernest Alfred Pavitt, and his father, Jules Pavitt Stephens, in the prologue of this book.

58. Granville-Edge, *The Sabahan*, 30, 35.

59. "Malaysian Air Crash Kills 11," *Sarasota Herald Tribune*, June 7, 1976, 5; "An Explosion, Then Fuad's Plane Hurtled Down . . . ," *New Nation*, June 8, 1976, 2. The cause of the disaster remains disputed and is the source of continued controversy today. See Kelimen Sawatan, "Real Cause of Air Crash Never Made Known—Yong," *Borneo Post Online*, December 23, 2011, https://www.theborneopost.com/2011/12/23/real-cause-of-air-crash-never-made-known-yong/.

60. Wong, *Community and Society*, 90.

61. Biographical memorandum on Donald Stephens, "The Hon. Donald Stephens," 1957, 10, in FCO 141/13004, TNA.

62. "The Hon. Donald Stephens," 10; and "Note on Existing Policy regarding Native Applicants for Annual Timber Licences," May 23, 1960, 7, in FCO 141/13003, TNA.

63. "The Hon. Donald Stephens," 10.

64. Wong, *Community and Society*, 90.

65. Granville-Edge, *The Sabahan*, 45.

66. "Profile: Donald Stephens," September 11, 1957, 3, in FCO 141/13004, TNA.

67. According to Ooi Keat Gin, there were only six survivors out of 2,400 prisoners of war forced to march from Sandakan to Kuching via Ranau. Ooi Keat Gin, *The Japanese Occupation of Borneo, 1941–1945* (London: Routledge, 2011), 91–98. See also Lynette Ramsay Silver, *Sandakan: A Conspiracy of Silence* (Kota Kinabalu: Opus Publications, 2007).

68. There were frequent reports throughout the nineteenth and early twentieth centuries of outbreaks of "Borneo fever," a catch-all term for dengue fever, malaria, and various unknown ailments. See, for example, *Singapore Free Press and Mercantile Adviser*, August 31, 1899, 8.

69. Luigi Santacroce et al., "*Mycobacterium leprae*: A Historical Study on the Origins of Leprosy and its Social Stigma," *Infez Med* 29, no. 4 (2021): 623–32, https://doi.org/10.53854/liim-2904-18.

70. Granville-Edge, *The Sabahan*, 45–46.

71. "The Hon. Donald Stephens," 1957, 9–10.

72. Granville-Edge, *The Sabahan*, 53.

73. Granville-Edge, *The Sabahan*, 52.

74. For an overview of the Kinabalu Uprising, see Ooi Keat Gin's chapter on anti-Japanese revolts in occupied Borneo in *Japanese Occupation of Borneo*, 98–117.

75. Wong, *Community and Society*, 89.

76. Wong, *Community and Society*, 89.

77. Granville-Edge, *The Sabahan*, 76–77.

78. Herman J. Luping, *Sabah's Dilemma: The Political History of Sabah, 1960–1994* (Kuala Lumpur: Magnus Books, 1994), 21.

79. Fausto Barlocco, "An Inconvenient Birth: The Formation of a Modern Kadazan Culture and its Marginalisation within the Making of the Malaysian Nation (1953–2007)," *Indonesia and the Malay World* 41, no. 119 (2013): 120, https://doi.org/10.1080/13639811.2013.766010.

80. "Profile: Donald Stephens," September 11, 1957, 2, in FCO 141/13004, TNA.

81. Luping, *Sabah's Dilemma*, 21.

82. "The Hon. Donald Stephens," 10.

83. Assistant Commissioner to R. N. Turner, North Borneo Chief Secretary, October 11, 1960, 52, in FCO 141/13004, TNA.

84. Sandakan Resident to R. N. Turner, North Borneo Chief Secretary, October 21, 1960, 54, in FCO 141/13004, TNA.

85. Assistant Commissioner to R. N Turner, October 11, 1960, 52, in FCO 141/13004, TNA.

86. "Profile: Donald Stephens," 2–3.

87. Ronald J. Brooks, *Under Five Flags: The Story of Sabah, East Malaysia* (Edinburgh: Pentland, 1999), 200.

88. Margaret Roff, "The Rise and Demise of Kadazan Nationalism," *Journal of Southeast Asian History* 10, no. 2 (1969): 330, https://doi.org/10.1017/S0217781100004439.
89. Brooks, *Under Five Flags*, 200.
90. Brooks, *Under Five Flags*, 200.
91. Anthony Reid, *Imperial Alchemy: Nationalism and Political Identity in Southeast Asia* (Cambridge: Cambridge University Press, 2009), 192.
92. Fausto Barlocco, *Identity and the State in Malaysia* (London: Routledge, 2014), 46.
93. Reid, *Imperial Alchemy*, 192.
94. Roff, "Kadazan Nationalism," 332.
95. Reid, *Imperial Alchemy*, 192.
96. "Profile: Donald Stephens," 2.
97. Wong, *Community and Society*, 158–59.
98. "Monthly Summary of News for the Period 25 November to 24 December, 1957," 1, in FCO 141/12291, TNA.
99. Roff, "Kadazan Nationalism," 330–31.
100. "North Borneo News and Sabah Times—Monthly Press Review for June 1955," July 2, 1955, 2, in FCO 141/12289, TNA; Granville-Edge, *The Sabahan*, 88.
101. Saunders, "'State of Intoxication,'" 206–8.
102. Reid, *Imperial Alchemy*, 190–91; "North Borneo News and Sabah Times—Monthly Press Review for June 1955," 2, July 2, 1955, in FCO 141/12289, TNA.
103. "North Borneo News and Sabah Times—Monthly Press Review for June 1955," 1.
104. "The Hon. Datu Mustapha bin Datu Harun, O.B.E.," July 13, 1962, 95, in FCO 141/13013, TNA.
105. "Profile: Donald Stephens," 2.
106. Fenner Brockway, in Hansard, "Malaysia Bill," 681 Parl. Deb. (5th ser.) (1963) cols. 924–1006.
107. John Darwin, *Britain and Decolonisation: The Retreat from Empire in the Postwar World* (London: Macmillan, 1988), 283.
108. *Report of the Commission of Enquiry, North Borneo and Sarawak* (London: Her Majesty's Stationery Office, 1962), 65.
109. "Monthly Summary of News," 1.
110. "Monthly Summary of News," 1.
111. Labuan District Officer to Chief Secretary, memorandum, February 25, 1960, 41, in FCO 141/13004, TNA.
112. Papar District Officer to the West Coast Resident, memorandum, October 11, 1957, 6, in FCO 141/13004, TNA.
113. Attorney General to Chief Secretary, memorandum, February 19, 1960, 38, in FCO 141/13004, TNA.
114. Note by R. N. Turner, April 21, 1960, 4–5, in FCO 141/13013, TNA.
115. Note by R. N. Turner, April 21, 1960, 4–5.
116. Conservator of Forests to Chief Secretary, October 21, 1960, in FCO 141/13013, TNA, 74.
117. Conservator of Forests to Chief Secretary, 74.
118. "Application for Licence to Extract Timber: Jambongan Island," June 8, 1960, 298, in FCO 141/13013, TNA.
119. "The Hon. Datu Mustapha bin Datu Harun, O.B.E.," 95.

120. "The Hon. Datu Mustapha bin Datu Harun, O.B.E.," 95.
121. Biographical profile, Datu Mustapha bin Datu Harun, O.B.E., May 23, 1960, 53, in FCO 141/13013, TNA.
122. "Extract from R. W. C.'s Diary," June 8, 1962, 93, in FCO 141/13013, TNA.
123. Biographical profile, Datu Mustapha bin Datu Harun, O.B.E., 53.
124. Note by R. N. Turner, February 27, 1961, 17, in FCO 141/13013, TNA.
125. "The Hon. Datu Mustapha bin Datu Harun, O.B.E.," 95–96.

3. The Rise of the Kalimantan Utara Movement

1. Danny Wong Tze Ken argues that unlike Malaya and Sarawak, Sabah "was never under communist threat." See *Historical Sabah: Community and Society* (Kota Kinabalu: Natural History Publications, 2004), 125.

2. In 1950, Indonesian politician Mohammed Yamin declared that it was imperative for Indonesia to take over the three British Borneo territories in order to counter Western colonialism. See "Bid for British Borneo," *Singapore Free Press*, January 31, 1950, 8.

3. See chapter 4.

4. "Monthly Summary of News for the Period 25 November to 24 December, 1957," 1, in FCO 141/12291, TNA.

5. Ronald J. Brooks, *Under Five Flags: The Story of Sabah, East Malaysia* (Edinburgh: Pentland, 1999), 200.

6. Abdul Rahman, *Political Awakening* (Petaling Jaya: Pelanduk Publications, 1986), 73; Ghazali Shafie, *Ghazali Shafie's Memoir: On the Formation of Malaysia* (Kuala Lumpur: Penerbit Universiti Kebangaan Malaysia, 2004), 26.

7. See, for instance, Matthew Jones, "Creating Malaysia: Singapore Security, the Borneo Territories, and the Contours of British Policy, 1961–63," *Journal of Imperial and Commonwealth History* 28, no. 2 (2000): 85–109,https://doi.org/10.1080/03086530008583091.

8. Internal memorandum on the Malaysia proposal, Canberra, January 7, 1963, in National Archives of Australia (NAA), Canberra, A4359, 221/6/2A; Alex Josey, "Nair Warns: This Can Spark a War in S-E Asia," *Straits Times*, February 12, 1963, 16.

9. "Note by M. MacDonald of Talks with the Sultan of Brunei on 13–14 December," December 18, 1958, DO 35/10019, no. 12, E2, in *British Documents on the End of Empire*, series B, vol. 8, *Malaysia*, ed. A. J. Stockwell (London: The Stationery Office, 2004), 14–17. See also Mohammed Noordin Sopiee, "The Advocacy of Malaysia—Before 1961," *Modern Asian Studies* 7, no. 4 (1973): 717–32, https://doi.org/10.1017/S0026749X00013500.

10. Cameron Cobbold to Harold Macmillan, "Personal and Confidential Letter Addressed to the Prime Minister," June 21, 1962, 3, in FCO 141/13046, TNA; *Report of the Commission of Enquiry, North Borneo and Sarawak* (London: Her Majesty's Stationery Office, 1962), 42.

11. Hansard, "Malaysia Bill," 252 Parl. Deb. H.L. (5th ser.) (1963) cols. 933–979.

12. "Monthly Summary of News," 1.

13. "Even 'Volunteers' Cannot Stop Malaysia–Lee," *Straits Times*, January 1, 1963, 1. See also Wen-Qing Ngoei, *Arc of Containment: Britain, the United States, and Anticommunism in Southeast Asia* (Ithaca, NY: Cornell University Press, 2019), 129.

14. "Letter from Sir R. Scott to Mr Lennox-Boyd," January 29, 1959, DO 35/10019, no. 21, in Stockwell, *British Documents*, 31. See also Herman J. Luping, "The Kadazans

and Sabah Politics" (PhD diss., Victoria University of Wellington, 1985), 1–2; and Fausto Barlocco, *Identity and the State in Malaysia* (London: Routledge, 2014), 54–55.

15. Shafie, *On the Formation of Malaysia*, 27–28.
16. "Bid for British Borneo," *Singapore Free Press*, January 31, 1950, 8.
17. "The Little Empire," *Straits Times*, June 25, 1946, 4.
18. Ngoei, *Arc of Containment*, 121.
19. See, for instance, T. N. Harper, *The End of Empire and the Making of Malaya* (Cambridge: Cambridge University Press, 1999).
20. Joseph Chinyong Liow, "Tunku Abdul Rahman and Malaya's Relations with Indonesia, 1957–1960," *Journal of Southeast Asian Studies* 36, no. 1 (2005): 88–89, https://doi.org/10.1017/S0022463405000044.
21. J. D. Legge, *Sukarno: A Political Biography* (New York: Praeger Publishers, 1972), 6.
22. Importantly, such Cold War interpretations overlook local considerations, especially in places where communism was neither prevalent nor considered a grave threat, such as in Sabah.
23. Hansard, "Malaysia Bill," 252 Parl. Deb. H.L. (5th ser.) (1963) cols. 933–979.
24. Taomo Zhou, "Ambivalent Alliance: Chinese Policy towards Indonesia, 1960–1965," *China Quarterly* 221 (2015): 215, https://doi.org/10.1017/S0305741014001544; Ngoei, *Arc of Containment*, 135.
25. See Liow, "Malaya's Relations with Indonesia."
26. Traditionally, studies of US activities in Southeast Asia have been dominated by a focus on the Vietnam War and sporadic moments of CIA involvement, such as the shooting down of an American spy plane over the Maluku Islands in Indonesia in 1958. Over the past few decades greater attention has been paid to CIA involvement in destabilizing Indonesia. See, for instance, Kenneth Conboy and James Morrison, *Feet to the Fire: CIA Covert Operations in Indonesia, 1957–1958* (Annapolis, MD: US Naval Institute Press, 1999); Audrey R. Kahin and George McT. Kahin, *Subversion as Foreign Policy: The Secret Eisenhower and Dulles Debacle in Indonesia* (New York: The New Press, 1995); and Vincent Bevins, *The Jakarta Method: Washington's Anticommunist Crusade and the Mass Murder Program That Shaped Our World* (New York: PublicAffairs, 2020).
27. As Henk Schulte Nordhult writes, "The early years of the Indonesian nation state were . . . characterised by a permanent sense of crisis, caused by political instability and institutional weakness," while the countryside was "plagued by endemic insecurity and the state's inability to maintain 'law and order.'" See Henk Schulte Nordhult, "Indonesia in the 1950s: Nation, Modernity, and the Post-Colonial State," *Bijdragen tot de Taal-, Land- end Volkenkunde* 167, no. 4 (2011): 394, https://doi.org/10.1163/22134379-90003577.
28. Ngoei, *Arc of Containment*, 120.
29. Liow, "Malaya's Relations with Indonesia," 88.
30. Ngoei, *Arc of Containment*, 120; "Monthly Summary of News," 1.
31. Liow, "Malaya's Relations with Indonesia," 98.
32. "Rebels' Families 'Sent to Safety,'" *Straits Times*, March 7, 1958, 1.
33. Kahin and Kahin, *Subversion as Foreign Policy*, 121.
34. Ngoei, *Arc of Containment*, 120. See also Don Beresford, "'Sumatra State' Plot Chiefs are Now in Malaya," *Straits Times*, December 17, 1958, 12.
35. "Obscurity in Indonesia," *Straits Times*, December 27, 1958, 6; "Tengku on Rebels: 'Embarrassing to Malaya,'" *Straits Times*, December 12, 1958, 1.

36. "Tengku Accused of Having Sumatra Designs," *Straits Times*, January 11, 1959, 5. A previous, if ironic, precedent for cross-strait unity was during the Second World War, when the Japanese occupiers merged southern Malaya with the entirety of Sumatra to form a single administrative unit, with Singapore as the capital. This new federation, named Syonan ("brilliant south"), was based on the ostensible ethnic and cultural affinity between peninsular and Sumatran Malays. See Harper, *End of Empire*, 36.

37. Ngoei, *Arc of Containment*, 119.

38. Liow, "Malaya's Relations with Indonesia," 88.

39. Harper, *End of Empire*, 46.

40. Frederick P. Bunnel, "Guided Democracy Foreign Policy: 1960–1965 President Sukarno Moves from Non-Alignment to Confrontation," *Indonesia*, no. 2 (1966): 42, https://doi.org/10.2307/3350755.

41. *Report of the Commission of Enquiry*.

42. Attorney General to Chief Secretary, memorandum, February 19, 1960, 38, in FCO 141/13004, TNA.

43. Parti Rakyat Brunei was inspired by Parti Rakyat Malaya, led by Ahmad Boestaman, whom Azahari had met in 1955. See "Letter from D. C. White to Sir A. Abell Reporting on His First Six Months as British Resident," January 3, 1959, CO 1030/658, no. E13, in Stockwell, *British Documents*, 25.

44. "Brace of Constitutions," *Economist*, October 5, 1957, 28.

45. "Letter from D. C. White to Sir A. Abell," 25.

46. Shafie, *On the Formation of Malaysia*, 28.

47. "Letter from D. C. White to Sir A. Abell," 25.

48. Eileen Chanin, *Limbang Rebellion: Seven Days in December 1962* (Singapore: Ridge Books, 2013), 164; George McT. Kahin, *Southeast Asia: A Testament* (London: RoutledgeCurzon, 2003), 150–51; Shafie, *On the Formation of Malaysia*, 28.

49. Hansard, "Rising In Brunei," 245 Parl. Deb. H.L. (5th ser.) (1962) cols. 415–18.

50. "Support for Azahari's Bogus Revolution," *Straits Times*, January 26, 1963, 8.

51. Sheikh Azahari bin Sheikh Mahmud, also known as A. M. Azahari, was born in Brunei in 1928. After the Second World War, he joined Indonesian anticolonialists in their struggle against the Dutch, returning in the early 1950s to Brunei where he engaged in various business and later political activities. See Stockwell, *British Documents*, 25.

52. "Tidak Akan Menyerah Sa-lagi Belum Merdeka, Tekad Pemberontak" ["We will not surrender before independence, determination of the rebels"], *Berita Harian*, December 11, 1962, 1. Translated from the following in Malay: "*Tatapi perjuangan akan berjaian terus dan kami tidak akan meletakkan senjata sa-hingga penjajah British yang terakhir di-usir keluar dan sa-hingga sa-buah negara kesautan kalimantan utara yang merdeka lahir.*"

53. "Tidak Akan Menyerah,",1.

54. "PAS Bantah Isteri Azahari Di-tahan" ["PAS protests Azahari's wife being detained"], *Berita Harian*, January 3, 1963, 1. Translated from the following in Malay: "*Tindakan tentera British ini merupakan suatu kezaliman terhadap ra'ayat Brunei*"; "*Pemberontakan itu bertujuan membebaskan negeri mereka dari penjajah.*"

55. "PR [Parti Rakyat] Bantah Polis Rampas Risalah 'Revolusi' Brunai" ["PR protests seizure of Brunei 'revolution' brochures"], *Berita Harian*, January 22, 1963, 3.

56. United States Embassy, London to Secretary of State Dean Rusk, telegram, December 11, 1962, in National Security Files (NSF), series 1, box 11, Borneo (general), John F. Kennedy Presidential Library (JFK Library), Boston, MA; "PR Bantah Polis", 3; "Zaini–Won't Betray Cause, Says Aza," *Straits Times*, January 29, 1963, 1.

57. "PAS Bantah Isteri Azahari Di-tahan," 1.

58. In one such incident, the Singaporean police seized sixty-one copies of a pamphlet that was due to be disseminated among followers. See "PR Bantah Polis," 3.

59. "Zaini–Won't Betray Cause, Says Aza," *Straits Times*, January 29, 1963, 1.

60. Joseph Scalice, "Crisis of Revolutionary Leadership: Martial Law and the Communist Parties of the Philippines, 1959–1974" (PhD diss., University of California, Berkeley, 2017), 159, https://escholarship.org/uc/item/2mc0496x.

61. "Azahari 'To Accept Volunteers,'" *Straits Times*, January 22, 1963, 1.

62. Alex Josey, "I Meet Azahari," *Straits Times*, January 19, 1963, 10.

63. "Support for Azahari's Bogus Revolution," *Straits Times*, January 26, 1963, 8.

64. Josey, "I Meet Azahari," 10. In some records, Zulkipli's name is spelled "Zulkifli."

65. Josey, "I Meet Azahari," 10; "Azahari Speaks," *Straits Times*, January 19, 1963, 10.

66. L. C. Hoffman, *Straits Times*, January 19, 1963.

67. Alex Josey, "Ace up Salim's Sleeve: Indonesia Will Be First to Recognise Aza," *Straits Times*, February 10, 1963, 1.

68. Alex Josey, "It's Touch and Go: Our Men Wait Outside," *Straits Times*, February 7, 1963, 1. It was reported that Abdullah Salim Mohamed spoke with a "strong Indonesian accent," leading the Malayan delegation to question whether he was an Indonesian agent.

69. Josey, "It's Touch and Go," 1.

70. "'Fiasco' Says Jek of Moshi Talks," *Straits Times*, February 11, 1963, 1.

71. Gerard McCann, "Where Was the *Afro* in Afro-Asian Solidarity? Africa's 'Bandung Moment' in 1950s Asia," *Journal of World History* 30, no. 1–2 (2019): 90, https://doi.org/10.1515/9789400604346-006.

72. Josey, "Ace up Salim's Sleeve," 1.

73. R. L., "Amid Disaster, the Good Life," *Straits Times*, January 31, 1963, 6.

74. R. N. Turner, "Note on Interview with Miss Helen Chung at the Secretariat," December 14, 1962, 1, in FCO 141/13003, TNA; *Report of the Commission of Enquiry*, 40–54.

75. "Azahari Speaks, 10.

76. "Press Analysis: Philippine North Borneo Claim and the Revolt in the North Borneo Territories," December 20–26, 1962, in FO 371/169985, TNA. Cipriano Cid, according to Joseph Scalice, "was a known quantity, forever on the fringes of the [Philippine] Communist Party and intimately associated with its leadership." See Scalice, *Crisis of Revolutionary Leadership*, 127, 159.

77. Nik Anuar Nik Mahmud, *Tuntutan Filipina Ke Atas Borneo Utara* [The Philippine claim to North Borneo] (Kuala Lumpur: Penerbit Universiti Kebangsaan Malaysia, 2009), 78.

78. "Voice from the Past," *Economist*, May 19, 1962, 661.

79. Acting Secretary of Foreign Affairs Salvador P. Lopez to British ambassador John A. Pilcher, *Official Gazette*, June 22, 1962.

80. "Salip Ali Sultan Mohammad Pulalum to the Queen of England," January 27, 1961, 1–3, in FO 371/160051, TNA; "Datu Mohammad Yachub Attan bin Datu Amilhussin to the Queen of England," February 7, 1961, 1–2, in FO 371/160051, TNA.

81. "Memorandum for the Colonial Office, Her Majesty's Government, from N. Osmeña," January 29, 1961, 2, in FO 371/160051, TNA.

82. "British Right to Borneo Challenged," *Malaya Tribune*, July 17, 1946, 7.

83. Mahmud, *Tuntutan Filipina*, 78.

84. Hoffman, *Straits Times*, January 19, 1963.

85. The voracious public appetite for gossip and information about Azahari even extended to rumors about his two wives, Raja Shamsiati binte Raja Putra and Saibah Azahari, whom he left behind in Borneo, and the media circulated accusations that he was a "woman-chaser." See, for instance, "Court Hitch: Aza's Wife Must Wait for Divorce," *Straits Times*, March 5, 1963, 18; and "Azahari's Wife: New Snag in Divorce Request," *Straits Times*, March 28, 1963, 11.

86. "The Improbable Azahari," *Straits Times*, February 22, 1963, 1. A British Army representative cast doubt on this, commenting that it was "a very impractical way to descend from a civil airliner and a highly improbable accomplishment."

87. "Kesenyapan Azahari" ["Azahari's silence"], *Berita Harian*, February 20, 1963, 4. Translated from the following in Malay: "*Dunia tentu hairan apa-kah tela terjadi kapada ketua pemberontak Brunei.*"

88. "Kesenyapan Azahari," 4.

89. "Voice of the Kalimantan Utara Freedom Fighters (Clandestine)," October 30, 1963, 1, in CIA-RDP81–00770R000100050017–7, General CIA Records. Between its first broadcast on March 5, 1963, and October 1963, the radio station ran a daily segment between 11:50 GMT and 12:30 GMT.

90. "'Rebel' Broadcasting Stations in Indonesia," 1962–3, in 2012/0012491, *Arkib Negara Malaysia* (National Archives of Malaysia, ANM), Kuala Lumpur, 16.

91. "'Rebel' Broadcasting Stations in Indonesia," 1962–3, 16, in 2012/0012491, ANM. The above formatting, including enjambment, reflects how it was recorded by colonial officials in 1963.

92. Brooks, *Under Five Flags*, 192.

93. Geoffrey Geldard, "Rebel Radio Propaganda Lies Anger People of Sarawak," *Straits Times*, May 1, 1963, 16.

94. Geldard, "Rebel Radio Propaganda Lies," 16.

95. "Azahari 'To Accept Volunteers,'" 1; Josey, "Ace Up Salim's Sleeve," 1.

96. Geldard, "Rebel Radio Propaganda Lies," 16.

97. Geldard, "Rebel Radio Propaganda Lies," 16.

98. "14 Held in Sarawak," *Straits Times*, January 3, 1963, 1; "Another Exclusive," *Straits Times*, January 19, 1963, 1; *Borneo Bulletin*, May 26, 1962, cited in Haji Harun bin Haji Abdul Majid, *Rebellion in Brunei: The 1962 Revolt, Imperialism, Confrontation and Oil* (London: Tauris, 2007), 76.

99. "Another Exclusive," 1.

100. "'Rebel' Broadcasting Stations in Indonesia," 16.

101. David Easter, *Britain and the Confrontation with Indonesia, 1960–66* (London: Tauris Academic Studies, 2012), 42.

102. During the 1930s and 1940s, international radio broadcasting became increasingly propagandized and weaponized. During the Second World War, radio was a cen-

tral tool in disseminating information and propaganda, and by 1945 politicized airwaves "had engulfed every continent." See James Wood, *History of International Broadcasting* (London: Peter Peregrinus, 1994), 49. Additionally, during the Vietnam War, the airwaves became a central battleground between North Vietnamese and American-sponsored radio stations, with counterinsurgency and subversive propaganda being beamed across the entire region in the late 1950s and 1960s. See Gregory M. Tomlin, *Murrow's Cold War: Public Diplomacy for the Kennedy Administration* (Lincoln: University of Nebraska Press, 2016), 234.

103. The United Kadazan National Organisation Executive Committee, "Memorandum on Malaysia for consideration of the Commission of Enquiry on Malaysia," February 22, 1962, "Cobbold Submissions—Associations," 13, in CO 947/17, TNA.

104. Edwin Jurriens, *From Monologue to Dialogue: Radio and Reform in Indonesia* (Leiden, KITLV Press, 2009).

105. Jennifer Lindsay, "Making Waves: Private Radio and Local Identities in Indonesia," special issue on Language and Media, *Indonesia*, no. 64 (1997), 106, 110–11, https://doi.org/10.2307/3351437.

106. Jurriens, *From Monologue to Dialogue*, 10.

107. Uwe Aranas, *The History of Wireless Telegraphy in British North Borneo* (Kota Kinabalu: Department of Sabah Museum, 2018), 31, 230–31.

108. Fausto Barlocco, "Between the Local and the State: Practices and Discourses of Identity among the Kadazan of Sabah (East Malaysia)" (PhD diss. Loughborough University, 2008), 59, https://repository.lboro.ac.uk/articles/thesis/Between_the_local_and_the_state_practices_and_discourses_of_identity_among_the_Kadazan_of_Sabah_East_Malaysia_/9480593/1.

109. Brooks, *Under Five Flags*, 191.

110. British colonial administrators were particularly sensitive to the threat of Communist subversion during the 1950s due to the Malayan Emergency, as well as proliferating Cold War tensions. See, for instance, Alexander N. Shaw, "British Counterinsurgency in Brunei and Sarawak, 1962–1963: Developing Best Practices in the Shadow of Malaya," *Small Wars & Insurgencies* 27, no. 4 (2016): 704–5, https://doi.org/10.1080/09592318.2016.1190052. Danny Wong Tze Ken has also argued that unlike Malaya and Sarawak, Sabah "was never under communist threat." See Wong, *Community and Society*, 125.

111. Brooks, *Under Five Flags*, 192.

112. Brooks, *Under Five Flags*, 192–93.

113. "C-plan Course," *Straits Times*, January 22, 1959, 2; "Dari Borneo ka-London" ["From Borneo to London"], *Berita Harian*, August 28, 1959, 2.

114. "Monthly News Summary for April, 1956," 1–3, in FCO 141/13002, TNA.

115. "Monthly News Summary for March, 1956," 2, in FCO 141/13002, TNA.

116. Aranas, *History of Wireless Telegraphy*, 230–31.

117. "Monthly Summary of News for the Period 25 May to 24 June, 1957," in FCO 141/13002, TNA.

118. "Radio Seeking Information," *Straits Times*, December 15, 1958, 9.

119. Brooks, *Under Five Flags*, 194, and Aranas, *History of Wireless Telegraphy*, 233–34.

120. "One Radio Station Helps Another," *Straits Times*, February 22, 1961, 5. The upgrade cost one hundred thousand Malayan dollars, a significant amount at the time.

121. Benedict Anderson has remarked on the significance of print media in the creation of new national identities, while Michelle Hilmes argues that this effect was even more pronounced with the proliferation of radio. See Benedict Anderson, *Imagined Communities: Reflections on the Origin and Spread of Nationalism* (London: Verso, 1983); 35 and Hilmes, "Radio and the Imagined Community," in *The Sound Studies Reader*, ed. Jonathan Sterne (London: Routledge, 2012), 351.

122. The exception here was Donald Stephens's *Sabah Times*, first published in 1953.

123. "Extracts from broadcasts by Radio Kalimantan Utara, the Voice of the Freedom Fighters of Northern Borneo," May 20, 1963, 39, in 2012/0012491, ANM.

124. Chanin, *Limbang* Rebellion, 167.

125. Quoted from Steven Farram, "*Ganyang!* Indonesian Popular Songs from the Confrontation Era, 1963–1966," *Bijdragen Tot De Taal-, Land- En VolkenKunde* 170, no. 1 (2014): 6–7, https://doi.org/10.1163/22134379-17001002.

126. An important exception to this trend is David Easter's "British Intelligence and Propaganda during the 'Confrontation,' 1963–1966," *Intelligence and National Security* 16, no. 2 (2001): 83–102 https://doi.org/10.1080/714002893.

127. American observations in December 1962 reveal the movement's early attempts to gain recognition through the United Nations, although by June and July 1963 it had become largely discredited. See Bob Donhauser to Dean Rusk, telegram, December 14, 1962, in NSF, series 1, box 11, Borneo (general), JFK Library.

128. "'Rebel' Broadcasting Stations in Indonesia," 18.

129. Easter, "British Intelligence and Propaganda," 90.

130. Anonymous, to Secretary, Malaysia Commission, n.d., 102, in CO 947/16, TNA.

131. Easter, "British Intelligence and Propaganda," 90.

132. "'Rebel' Broadcasting Stations in Indonesia," 18.

133. "Extracts from broadcasts by Radio Kalimantan Utara, the Voice of the Freedom Fighters of Northern Borneo," May 20, 1963, 39, in 2012/0012491, ANM.

134. "'Rebel' Broadcasting Stations in Indonesia," 16.

135. Anonymous, to Secretary, Malaysia Commission, 102.

136. Donhauser to Rusk, telegram, December 28, 1962.

137. "Zulkifli: Loyalty of Borneo Is to Soekarno," *Straits Times*, May 17, 1963, 9.

138. See chapter 5.

139. Matthew Jones, *Conflict and Confrontation in South East Asia, 1961–1965* (Cambridge: Cambridge University Press, 2001), 84.

140. Loo W. K., Andrew Lin, and Tsien Chi Bang to Malaysia Commission of Enquiry, memorandum, "Cobbold Submissions—Individuals,' February 21, 1962, 2, in CO 947/16, TNA.

141. Tom Rice, "Merdeka for Malaya: Imagining Independence across the British Empire," in *The Colonial Documentary Film in South and South-East Asia*, ed. Ian Aitken and Camille Deprez (Edinburgh: Edinburgh University Press, 2017), 46.

142. "Zulkifli: Loyalty of Borneo Is to Soekarno," 9.

143. "'Rebel' Broadcasting Stations in Indonesia," 16.

144. "Monthly Summary of News for the Period 25 November to 24 December, 1957," 1.

145. "'Rebel' Broadcasting Stations in Indonesia," 16.

146. Speech by President Sukarno, *Antara News Agency*, May 15, 1963, 6, in 2012/0012491, ANM.

147. Ngoei, *Arc of Containment*, 120–21.
148. "'Support for Rebellion in Sumatra' Decision," *Straits Times*, September 26, 1963, 20.
149. United Nations Malaysia Mission Report, "Final Conclusions of the Secretary-General," September 14, 1963.
150. "The Facts in Borneo," *Straits Times*, October 7, 1963, 10.

4. Maphilindo, the Confederation That Never Was

1. Research by oceanographers has demonstrated how the Sulu Sea—a body of water enclosed by Palawan, Borneo, Mindanao and the various Sulu islands—is prone to developing massive rogue waves, or solitons, with amplitudes spanning tens of meters. It is considered a dangerous and unpredictable sea. See, for example, David C. Chapman et al., "Evidence of Internal Swash Associated with Sulu Sea Solitary Waves," *Continental Shelf Research* 11, no. 7 (1991): 591–99, https://doi.org/10.1016/0278-4343(91)90014-W; and Anthony K. Liu, John R. Apel, and James R. Holbrook, "Nonlinear Internal Wave Evolution in the Sulu Sea," *Journal of Physical Oceanography* 15, no. 1 (1985): 1613–24, https://doi.org/10.1175/1520-0485(1985)015%3C1613:NIWEIT%3E2.0.CO;2.

2. As Heather Sutherland argues, orthodox histories have tended to compartmentalize the region into colonial and later national bounds, viewing them in isolation from wider transnational and transregional processes. This has the effect of obscuring important connections and interactions. See Sutherland, "Southeast Asian History and the Mediterranean Analogy," *Journal of Southeast Asian Studies* 34, no. 1 (2003): 1–20, https://doi.org/10.1017/S0022463403000018. For a more recent examination of the maritime boundary between Sabah and the Philippines, see David R. Saunders, "Dimming the Seas around Borneo: Contesting Island Sovereignty and Lighthouse Administration amidst the End of Empire, 1946–1948," *TRaNS: Trans-Regional and -National Studies of Southeast Asia* 7, no. 2 (2019): 181–207, https://doi.org/10.1017/trn.2019.5.

3. See, for instance, "Duterte Vows to Pursue Philippine Claim to Sabah," *Straits Times*, May 27, 2016, https://www.straitstimes.com/asia/se-asia/duterte-vows-to-pursue-philippine-claim-to-sabah; and Gregory Poling, Phoebe DePadua, and Jennifer Frentasia, "The Royal Army of Sulu Invades Malaysia," *Centre for Strategic and International Studies: Critical Questions*, March 8, 2013, https://www.csis.org/analysis/royal-army-sulu-invades-malaysia.

4. Eric Tagliacozzo argues that from the 1850s onwards Borneo took on a "truly regional importance" in trades of goods across maritime Southeast Asia. See Tagliacozzo, "Borneo in Fragments: Geology, Biota, and Contraband in Trans-National Circuits," *TRaNS: Trans-Regional and -National Studies of Southeast Asia* 1, no. 1 (2013): 63–85, https://doi.org/10.1017/trn.2012.8.

5. Amarjit Kaur, *Economic Change in East Malaysia: Sabah and Sarawak since 1850* (London: Macmillan, 1998), 31.

6. In addition to the historical political linkages, northern Borneo and the southern Philippines were ethnically and culturally intertwined, with its people stemming from "the same racial stock" and sharing common "customs and traditions." See Paridah Abd. Samad and Darusalam Abu Bakar, "Malaysia-Philippines Relations: The Issue of Sabah," *Asian Survey* 32, no. 6 (1992): 556, https://doi.org/10.2307/2645160.

7. The name Maphilindo was derived from the first few syllables of each of the participant states: "**Ma**[laya]-**Phil**[ippines]-**Indo**[nesia]."

8. "Tuwan Nahuda" is often considered a tragedy, and in recalling death, love, and suffering, it tends to be recited orally in times of mourning, ritual observances, and wakes. See Muham Julasman, "Tuwan Nahuda," in *Voices from Sulu: A Collection of Tausug Oral Traditions*, ed. Gerard Rixhon (Manila: Ateneo de Manila University Press, 2010), 326–38.

9. The Suluk (or Tausūg) people are an ethnic group from the southern Philippines (particularly Mindanao, Jolo, and Palawan) and coastal parts of northern Borneo, including Sabah and Indonesia's North Kalimantan. Together with other indigenous communities in Sabah, they are considered among the original inhabitants of the region. The community's relationship with the Sulu Sea, and the wider maritime region surrounding Borneo, is a fundamental aspect of their identity. As Vilashini Somiah argues, many Suluks in Sabah are committed to the "idea of the sea as their country." Throughout history, the Sulu Sea has served an important role, allowing seafaring communities to navigate an "alternative geography," "interchange[ing] between common 'landmarks' (such as islands and coastlines) and unique 'seamarks' (shallow, tame, and merciless waters) to pinpoint their location." See Somiah, *Irregular Migrants and the Sea at the Borders of Sabah, Malaysia: Pelagic Alliance* (Cham: Palgrave Macmillan, 2021), 156–57.

10. Julasman, "Tuwan Nahuda," 328–30.

11. Julasman, "Tuwan Nahuda," 326.

12. Ranjit D. S. Singh, *The Making of Sabah, 1865–1941: The Dynamics of Indigenous Society* (Kuala Lumpur: University of Malaya Press, 2000), 92–94.

13. See, for instance, Volker Schult, "Sulu and Germany in the Late Nineteenth Century," *Philippine Studies* 48, no. 1 (2000): 81, http://www.philippinestudies.net/ojs/index.php/ps/article/view/439/4567.

14. Mesrob Vartavarian describes how the prosperity of local sultanates in the southern Philippines was historically determined by their "access to overseas commerce." In later years, however, the once-fortunate maritime positioning of these polities, such as the Sultanate of Maguindanao, meant that they were more easily targeted and overrun by Spain, whereas other polities that were either located deep in the hinterland (such as the Sultanate of Buayan) or overseas (such as the Sultanate of Sulu) retained independence. See Vartavarian, "Imperial Ambiguities: The United States and Philippine Muslims," *South East Asia Research* 26, no. 2 (2018): 3, https://doi.org/10.1177/0967828X18769224.

15. James Francis Warren, *The Sulu Zone: The Dynamics of External Trade, Slavery, and Ethnicity in the Transformation of a Southeast Asian Maritime State, 1768–1898* (Singapore: Singapore University Press, 1981), 3.

16. James Francis Warren, "Slave Markets and Exchange in the Malay World: The Sulu Sultanate, 1770–1878," *Journal of Southeast Asian Studies*, 8, no. 2 (1977): 162, https://doi.org/10.1017/S0022463400009322.

17. Singh, *Making of Sabah*, 93–94; Ian Black, *A Gambling Style of Government: The Establishment of the Chartered Company's Rule in Sabah, 1878–1915* (Kuala Lumpur: Oxford University Press, 1983), 3–4.

18. See, for instance, Kenneth R. Hall, "Upstream and Downstream Unification in Southeast Asia's First Islamic Polity: the Changing Sense of Community in the Fif-

teenth Century 'Hikyat Raja-Raja Pasai' Court Chronicle," *Journal of the Economic and Social History of the Orient* 44, no. 2 (2001): 198, https://doi.org/10.1163/1568520017 53731042; and Elizabeth Lambourn, "Tombstones, Texts and Typologies: Seeing Sources for the Early History of Islam in Southeast Asia," *Journal of the Economic and Social History of the Orient* 51, no. 2 (2008): 254, https://doi.org/10.1163/156852008X 307447.

19. Cesar Adib Majul, "Political and Historical Notes on the Old Sulu Sultanate," *Journal of the Malaysian Branch of the Royal Asiatic Society* 38, no. 1 (1965): 25–26, https://www.jstor.org/stable/41491838.

20. H. Otley Beyer, "Brief Memorandum on the Government of the Sultanate of Sulu and the Powers of the Sultan During the 19th Century," *Philippine International Law Journal* 2, no. 1 (1946; repr. 1963): 325–26.

21. Warren, *Sulu Zone*, 6.

22. Eric Tagliacozzo, "Kettle on a Slow Boil: Batavia's Threat Perceptions in the Indies' Outer Islands, 1870–1910," *Journal of Southeast Asian Studies* 31, no. 1 (2000): 71, https://doi.org/10.1017/S0022463400015885.

23. Nicholas Tarling, *Sulu and Sabah: A Study of British Policy towards the Philippines and North Borneo from the Late Eighteenth Century* (Oxford: Oxford University Press, 1978), 1.

24. Martin Meadows, "The Philippine Claim to North Borneo," *Political Science Quarterly* 77, no. 3, (1962): 326, https://doi.org/10.2307/2146308; Nestor Martinez Nisperos, *Philippine Foreign Policy on the North Borneo Question* (Ann Arbor, MI: University Microfilms International, 1981), 73.

25. Steven Press, *Rogue Empires: Contracts and Conmen in Europe's Scramble for Africa* (Cambridge, MA: Harvard University Press, 2017), 8, 11 51. For an earlier account of the American attempts to colonize sections of the Borneo coast in the 1860s, see Kennedy Tregonning, "American Activity in North Borneo, 1865–1881," *Pacific Historical Review* 23, no. 4 (1954): 357–72, https://doi.org/10.2307/3634654.

26. Schult, "Sulu and Germany," 81.

27. Black, *Gambling Style of Government*, 4.

28. Nisperos, *North Borneo Question*, 73.

29. Long after the formation of the North Borneo Chartered Company, sections of Sabah's interior remained beyond the colonial grasp. Termed by D. S. Ranjit Singh as "independent rivers," large tracts of hinterland above the east coast continued to be administered by Sulu *datus* and their subordinates, known as *jajahan*, who functioned as settlers, traders, and local chiefs. See Singh, *Making of Sabah*, 51.

30. "Letter of Francis B. Harrison to Vice President and Secretary of Foreign Affairs Elpidio Quirino," February 27, 1947, in "Selected Documents Relating to the Philippine Claim to North Borneo," *Philippine International Law Journal* 2, no. 1 (1946; repr., 1963): 333; "British Right to Borneo Challenged," *Malaya Tribune*, July 17, 1946, 7.

31. Beyer, "Brief Memorandum," 327–31.

32. Hansard, "Address in Reply to Her Majesty's Most Gracious Speech," 297 Parl. Deb. H.L. (5th ser.) (1968) cols. 268–348.

33. H. B. Jacobini, "Fundamentals of Philippine Policy Towards Malaysia," *Asian Survey* 4, no. 11 (1964): 1145, https://doi.org/10.2307/2642665.

34. See, for instance, Tagliacozzo, "Kettle on a Slow Boil," 71–72; and Warren, *Sulu Zone*, 6.

35. Tarling, *Sulu and Sabah*, 300.
36. "Memorandum: Carpenter Agreement," *Official Gazette*, March 22, 1915.
37. For an in-depth study of this regional geopolitical contest and territorial overlap, see Saunders, "Dimming the Seas Around Borneo," 181–207.
38. "Convention regarding the boundary between the Philippine Archipelago and the State of North Borneo, with exchange of notes," January 2, 1930, Cmd. 3622, in CO 531/22/5, TNA.
39. Saunders, "Dimming the Seas Around Borneo," 183.
40. "New Philippines Republic Has Ambitions," *Indian Daily Mail*, July 19, 1946, 1.
41. Elpidio Quirino to Linton H. Foulds, Minister to the Philippines, memorandum, September 19, 1946, Cmd. 8320, Treaty Series No. 58, p. 2, in FO 93/149/3/0, TNA.
42. "Letter of Francis B. Harrison," 333–34.
43. "Memorandum: Carpenter Agreement."
44. "New Philippines Republic Has Ambitions," 1. See also Norizan Kadir and Suffian Mansor, "Menghidupkan Semula Institusi Kesultanan Sulu Melalui Tetutan ke atas Sabah, 1962–1986" [Reviving the Sultanate of Sulu through its claim over Sabah, 1962–1986], *Akademika* 87, no. 3 (2017): 123, http://ejournal.ukm.my/akademika/issue/view/949.
45. Elpidio Quirino, "Nationhood and Father Burgos," 1947, in *The Making of the Filipino Nation and Republic*, ed. Jose V. Abueva (Manila: University of the Philippines Press, 1998), 172.
46. "Philippine Govt Claiming British N. Borneo Islands," *Malaya Tribune*, July 19, 1946, 3.
47. Saunders, "Dimming the Seas Around Borneo," 196.
48. Quirino to Foulds, telegram, August 13, 1947, 67, in CO 537/2180, TNA.
49. Laurence H. Odell, "Philippines Urged to Survey Outlying Neglected Islands," *Far Eastern Review Survey* 8, no. 10 (1939): 119, https://doi.org/10.2307/3023095.
50. Telegram, Charles Jeffries to A. N. Galsworthy, October 2, 1947, 37–38, in CO 537/2180, TNA.
51. Manuel Roxas, "Providing for the Administration of the Turtle and Mangsee Islands," Philippine Government Executive Order No. 95, *Official Gazette*, October 13, 1947.
52. The 1946 Bell Trade Act, for instance, granted American citizens and businesses unfettered access to resources and lands in the Philippines. Kathleen Nadeau, *The History of the Philippines* (Westport, CT: Greenwood, 2008), 68; and Kathleen Weekley, "The National or the Social? Problems of Nation-Building in Post–World War II Philippines," in "From Nation-Building to State-Building," special issue, *Third World Quarterly* 27, no. 1 (2006): 97, https://doi.org/10.1080/01436590500369253.
53. L. H. Foulds to E. Bevin, memorandum, November 21, 1946, in FO 371/34344, TNA.
54. The attendance of Diosdado Macapagal as a Department of Foreign Affairs official was important, especially considering his subsequent role in the Philippines' 1962 claim over Sabah.
55. "Woman Rules Turtle Isles: American Educated Princess Becomes Deputy Governor," *Reading Eagle*, January 1, 1948, 16.
56. Yvonne Yazbeck Haddad and John L. Esposito, *Islam, Gender, and Social Change* (New York: Oxford University Press, 1998), 214.

57. Agnes Newton Keith, *White Man Returns* (1951; repr., Kota Kinabalu: Opus Publications, 2008), 251.

58. Governor Twining to Foulds, telegram, February 18, 1948, 43–44, in CO 537/4254, TNA.

59. Peter C. Richards, "A New Flag Now Flies over the 'Turtle Island,'" *Sunday Times* (Perth), December 14, 1947, 18.

60. Keith, *White Man Returns*, 245–46.

61. See, for instance, "More Cases of Borneo Piracy Despite R.N. Patrols," *Singapore Free Press*, September 13, 1961, 1; "A Big Increase in Piracy in N. Borneo," *Straits Budget*, December 27, 1961, 16; and "20 Filipino Pirate Suspects Arrested," *Straits Times*, October 4, 1962, 1.

62. Hansard, "Vote A Numbers," 673 Parl. Deb. H.L. (5th ser.) (1963) cols. 964–1137.

63. Hansard, "Borneo (Piracy)," 641 Parl. Deb. (5th ser.) (1961) col. 96.

64. "Britain Asks Manila to Help Stop Piracy," *Straits Times*, September 14, 1962, 5.

65. Jennifer L. Gaynor, "Piracy in the Offing: The Law of the Lands and The Limits of Sovereignty at Sea," *Anthropological Quarterly* 85, no. 3 (2012): 850, https://doi.org/10.1353/anq.2012.0036.

66. Singh, *Making of Sabah*, 72–74.

67. Nicholas Chung, *Under the Borneo Sun: A Tawau Story* (Kota Kinabalu: Natural History Publications, 2005), 77–79.

68. Gaynor, "Piracy in the Offing," 846.

69. Tagliacozzo, "Kettle on a Slow Boil," 71–72.

70. Gaynor, "Piracy in the Offing," 847–88.

71. Poling, DePadua, and Frentasia, "Royal Army of Sulu"; Steve Finch, "Fighting and Fallout in Sabah," *The Diplomat*, March 5, 2013, https://thediplomat.com/2013/03/fighting-and-fallout-in-sabah/; Jeremy Grant, "'Sultan of Sulu' Invasion of Borneo Creates Problems in Malaysia, Philippines," *Washington Post*, March 4, 2013, https://www.washingtonpost.com/world/asia_pacific/sultan-of-sulu-invasion-of-borneo-creates-problems-in-malaysia-philippines/2013/03/04/b33829a8-84f2-11e2-98a3-b3db6b9ac586_story.html.

72. Poling, DePadua, and Frentasia, "Royal Army of Sulu."

73. See, for instance, "Duterte Vows to Pursue Philippine Claim to Sabah," *Straits Times*, May 27, 2016, https://www.straitstimes.com/asia/se-asia/duterte-vows-to-pursue-philippine-claim-to-sabah; and Amy Chew, "Secret Plot to Invade Malaysia's Sabah with Sulu Militia Hatched in Southern Philippines: Security Source," *South China Morning Post*, December 9, 2021, https://www.scmp.com/week-asia/politics/article/3158966/secret-plot-invade-malaysias-sabah-sulu-militia-hatched-southern.

74. "Salip Ali Sultan Mohammad Pulalum to the Queen of England," January 27, 1961, 1–3, in FO 371/160051, TNA.

75. British Embassy, Manila, to South-East Asia Department, Foreign Office, February 18, 1961, in FO 371/160051, TNA, 1.

76. "British Right to Borneo Challenged," *Malaya Tribune*, July 17, 1946, 7.

77. For instances of governmental ineptitude and laxness in the Sulu Sea, see Saunders, "Dimming the Seas Around Borneo," 181–207.

78. "Datu Mohammad Yachub Attan bin Datu Amilhussin to the Queen of England," February 7, 1961, 1–2, in FO 371/160051, TNA.

79. "Memorandum for the Colonial Office, Her Majesty's Government, from N. Osmeña," January 29, 1961, 2, in FO 371/160051, TNA.

80. "British Right to Borneo Challenged," 7.

81. In early 1963, Nicasio Osmeña claimed that Britain had paid the North Borneo Company £29 million for the territory when it formally annexed it in July 1946, and that such a sum was owed to the heirs of Sulu. This claim was firmly rejected by the Foreign Office, which alleged that such a sum was a great exaggeration. A smaller payment of £1.4 million was paid to the company in 1949. See John A. Pilcher to Fred Warner, memorandum, January 9, 1963; and Departmental Distribution, Foreign Office to British Embassy, Manila, January 16, 1963, in FO 371/169985, TNA.

82. Pilcher to Warner; Departmental Distribution, Foreign Office to British Embassy.

83. Tarling, *Sulu and Sabah*, 314. In addition to losing considerable amounts of money and jewelry, the sultan also lost his crown and "a treaty between himself and the Government of Sandakan." See also Federico Macaraeg, "Borneo Claim by PI Pressed," *The Forum*, December 20, 1961.

84. "Memorandum for the Colonial Office, Her Majesty's Government, from N. Osmeña," 2.

85. H. Nield to J. I. McGhie, memorandum, February 8, 1961, 1, in FO 371/160051, TNA.

86. "'N. Borneo: A Formal Claim Unlikely," *Straits Times*, January 17, 1962, 9.

87. "For Foreign Office Concurrence," memorandum, February 1961, 1, in FO 371/160051, TNA.

88. R. N. Turner to H. Nield, January 30, 1961, 1, in FO 371/160051, TNA.

89. Leigh R. Wright, "The Anglo-Spanish-German Treaty of 1885: A Step in the Development of British Hegemony in North Borneo," *Australian Journal of Politics and History* 18, no. 1 (1972): 74.

90. See, for instance, Cesar Adib Majul, "Political and Historical Notes on the Old Sulu Sultanate," *Journal of the Malaysian Branch of the Royal Asiatic Society* 38, no. 1 (1965): 24–42, https://www.jstor.org/stable/41491838; Jacobini, "Fundamentals of Philippine Policy," 1144–51; Orlando M. Hernando, "The Philippine Claim to North Borneo," (MA diss., Kansas State University, 1965), 1–75; Meadows, "Philippine Claim to North Borneo," 321–35; and Samad and Bakar, "Malaysia-Philippines Relations," 554–67, among other studies.

91. Indeed, these conventional debates continue to garner public interest, with considerable back-and-forth over the Philippines' more recent Sabah claims. See, for instance, Lucio Blanco Pitlo III, "Why the Philippines' Sabah Claim against Malaysia Isn't a Land Grab," *South China Morning Post*, September 18, 2020, https://www.scmp.com/week-asia/opinion/article/3101954/why-philippines-sabah-claim-against-malaysia-isnt-land-grab; and, in contrast, Bunn Nagara, "Why the Philippines Has No Justifiable Claim to Sabah and Never Had," *South China Morning Post*, November 1, 2020, https://www.scmp.com/week-asia/opinion/article/3107859/why-philippines-has-no-justifiable-claim-sabah-and-never-had.

92. British Embassy, Manila, to South-East Asia Department, Foreign Office, December 6, 1961, 1, in FO 371/160051, TNA.

93. Meadows, "Philippine Claim to North Borneo," 323.

94. Gerald Sussman, "Macapagal, the Sabah Claim and Maphilindo: The Politics of Penetration," *Journal of Contemporary Asia* 13, no. 2 (1983): 211, https://doi.org/10.1080/00472338380000141.

95. "Press Analysis: Philippine North Borneo Claim and the Revolt in the North Borneo Territories," December 20–26, 1962, in FO 371/169985, TNA.

96. "Formal Claim Unlikely," 9.

97. Diosdado Macapagal, "State-of-the-Nation Message to the Congress of the Philippines," *Official Gazette*, January 28, 1963. See also Sussman, "Macapagal," 211–12.

98. "Macapagal Says: Claim Based on Regional Security, Too," *Straits Times*, January 4, 1963, 18.

99. Sussman, "Macapagal," 211.

100. Acting Secretary of Foreign Affairs Salvador P. Lopez to British Ambassador John A. Pilcher, *Official Gazette*, June 22, 1962. See also "Philippines Claims Sovereignty in British-Ruled North Borneo," *New York Times*, June 23, 1962, 1.

101. "Regional Cooperation in South East Asia," n.d., 1, in NAA, A1838, 3006/9/6 Part 1.

102. "Cobbold and Manila," *Straits Times*, July 1, 1962, 10.

103. See chapter 3.

104. *Harian Rakyat*, February 22, 1964, in "Malaysia/Indonesia Policy," February 25, 1964, in NAA, A1209, 1963/6637 part 5.

105. "Press Analysis: Philippine North Borneo Claim."

106. Nik Anuar Nik Mahmud, *Tuntutan Filipina Ke Atas Borneo Utara* [The Philippine claim to North Borneo] (Kuala Lumpur: Penerbit Universiti Kebangsaan Malaysia, 2009), 78.

107. "Formal Claim Unlikely, 9.

108. "Anger in Borneo," *Straits Times*, June 24, 1962, 1; "Britain Rejects Manila's Borneo Claim," *Straits Times*, February 2, 1963, 1.

109. "Anger in Borneo," 1.

110. *Harian Rakyat*, February 22, 1964, in "Malaysia/Indonesia Policy."

111. "N. Borneo Claim: Future Action," *Straits Times*, December 5, 1962, 15.

112. "Anger in Borneo," 1.

113. Lopez to. Pilcher, June 22, 1962.

114. "Macapagal Says," 18. See also Amando Respicio Boncales, "A Historical Discourse of the Philippine Claim over Sabah" (PhD diss., Northern Illinois University, 2013), 24.

115. Macapagal, "State-of-the-Nation Message."

116. Boncales, "Historical Discourse," 24; Macapagal, "State-of-the-Nation Message."

117. Danny Wong Tze Ken, *Historical Sabah: Community and Society* (Kota Kinabalu: Natural History Publications, 2004), 125.

118. See, for instance, Laura Steckman, "The Abu Sayyaf–ISIS Nexus: Rising Extremism and its Implications for Malaysia," *Counter Terrorist Trends and Analyses* 8, no. 5 (2016): 18, https://www.rsis.edu.sg/wp-content/uploads/2016/05/CTTA-May-2016.pdf.

119. Lopez to Pilcher.

120. British Embassy, Manila, to South-East Asia Department, Foreign Office, December 6, 1961, 1.

121. See, for instance, Sussman, "Macapagal," 210–28.

122. Jacobini, "Fundamentals of Philippine Policy," 1144–45.

123. Meadows, "Philippine Claim to North Borneo," 321.

124. "N. Borneo Leaders Angry and Hostile," *Straits Times*, June 28, 1962, 1.

125. "'Rebel' Broadcasting Stations in Indonesia," 18, in 2012/0012491, ANM.

126. C. Ignacio Rivera, "The Philippines Claim to North Borneo," December 1962, in FO 371/160051, TNA.

127. See, for instance, Wen-Qing Ngoei, *Arc of Containment: Britain, the United States, and Anticommunism in Southeast Asia* (Ithaca, NY: Cornell University Press, 2019), 120.

128. Tan Tai Yong, *Creating "Greater Malaysia": Decolonization and the Politics of Merger* (Singapore: Institute of Southeast Asian Studies, 2008), 53.

129. "The Philippines' Claim to North Borneo Territory," *Manila Times*, December 1962, in FO 371/160051, TNA.

130. Federico Macaraeg, "Borneo Claim by PI Pressed," *The Forum*, December 20, 1961.

131. Yong, *Creating "Greater Malaysia,"* 53; Ngoei, *Arc of Containment*, 120.

132. "Senator: Borneo Claim 'Wrong,'" *Straits Times*, January 8, 1963, 16.

133. "Macapagal Attacks the 'Drop Claim' Senator," *Straits Times*, March 28, 1963, 20.

134. Macapagal, "State-of-the-Nation Message."

135. John A. Pilcher to Foreign Office, memorandum, January 10, 1963, in FO 371/169985, TNA.

136. Mahmud, *Tuntutan Filipina*, 70–71, 79.

137. "The Borneo Claim," *Straits Times*, December 31, 1962, in FO 371/169985, TNA.

138. Mahmud, *Tuntutan Filipina*, 86.

139. John A. Pilcher to Fred A. Warner, memorandum, January 2, 1963, in FO 371/169985, TNA.

140. Outward Telegram from Commonwealth Relations Office to British Embassies in Kuala Lumpur, Canberra and Wellington, December 29, 1962, 1–2, in CO 1030/954, TNA.

141. "Talks with the Philippine Government: Items for the Agenda," January 4, 1963, 14, in CO 1030/954, TNA; "Barter Trade and Smuggling between Sulu, Indonesia and Borneo," 1960–62, in CO 1030/1285, TNA.

142. Mahmud, *Tuntutan Filipina*, 92. Translated from the following in Malay: *"Jangkaan British bahawa persidangan itu akan dapat mempengaruhi Filipina supaya mennggugurkan racangannya untuk membawa kes Borneo Utara ke Mahkamah Antarabangsa atau Pertubuhan Bangsa-bangsa Bersatu."*

143. "Anglo-Philippine Communiqué (London)," *Journal of the American Chamber of Commerce of the Philippines* 39, no. 2 (1963): 74.

144. Manila Accord between the Philippines, the Federation of Malaya and Indonesia, signed at Manila, July 31, 1963, 550 United Nations Treaty Series 8029, at 345, https://treaties.un.org/doc/publication/unts/volume%20550/volume-550-i-8029-english.pdf.

145. "Indonesian Attitude against Borneo, North Kalimantan and Brunei," 3, in 2012/0012392, ANM. Similar incidents occurred in Sarawak, in which, for example, a series of armed insurgents raided a police station in Tebedu near the Indonesian border

in April 1963. See "60 Armed Men Raid Sarawak Police Station and Capture Guns," *Straits Times*, April 13, 1963, 1.

146. "Manila Accord."
147. "Maphilindo and Malaysia," *New York Times*, August 6, 1963, 30.
148. Soh Tiang Keong, "Maphilindo Seen as Third Force," *Straits Times*, August 14, 1963, 12.
149. Alastair M. Taylor, "Malaysia, Indonesia—and Maphilindo," *International Journal* 19, no. 2 (1964): 168, https://doi.org/10.1177/002070206401900202.
150. As late as December 1963, communist groups in Vietnam and China voiced their "strong support" for the "people of Kalimantan Utara." See "Hanoi sokong Azahari" [Hanoi supports Azahari], *Berita Harian*, December 10, 1963, 3.
151. Speech by General Nasution, Antara News Agency, August 6, 1963, 24, in 2012/0012491, ANM.
152. Taylor, "Malaysia, Indonesia—and Maphilindo," 168–69.
153. Taylor, "Malaysia, Indonesia—and Maphilindo," 169–70.
154. Notes on "Prospects for Maphilindo," June 1966, in FO 370/2878, TNA; "Regional Cooperation in South East Asia." .
155. "Maphilindo Is Not against the Chinese in Malaysia, Tan," *Straits Times*, August 7, 1963, 18.
156. "Regional Cooperation in South East Asia."
157. "Cobbold and Manila," 10.

5. Creating Malaysia, "A Shotgun Colonial Wedding"

1. James T. Collins, "Contesting Straits Malayness: The Fact of Borneo," *Journal of Southeast Asian Studies* 32, no. 3 (2001): 385, https://doi.org/10.1017/S0022463401000212.
2. Suhana binti Sarkawi and Datu Sanib bin Said, "Borneo in the Eyes of Joseph Conrad," *Jurnal Kalijaga* 2, no. 1 (2013): 16–19.
3. This followed a similar approach to that deployed by the United States in the Philippines. See, for instance, Kathleen Nadeau, *The History of the Philippines* (Westport, CT: Greenwood, 2008); and Kathleen Weekley, "The National or the Social? Problems of Nation-Building in Post–World War II Philippines," in "From Nation-Building to State-Building," special issue, *Third World Quarterly* 27, no. 1 (2006): 85–100, https://doi.org/10.1080/01436590500369253. On Britain's continued economic presence in Malaysia, see Shakila Yacob and Nicholas J. White, "The 'Unfinished Business' of Malaysia's Decolonisation: The Origins of the Guthrie 'Dawn Raid,'" *Modern Asian Studies* 44, no. 5 (2010): 919–60, https://doi.org/10.1017/S0026749X09990308; and Nicholas J. White, *British Business in Post-Colonial Malaysia, 1957–1970: "Neocolonialism" or "Disengagement"?* (London: RoutledgeCurzon, 2004).
4. See Wen-Qing Ngoei, *Arc of Containment: Britain, the United States, and Anticommunism in Southeast Asia* (Ithaca, NY: Cornell University Press, 2019), in particular chapter 4, 114–48.
5. Ambassador Charles F. Baldwin to Department of State, memorandum, April 1, 1962, in NSF, series 1, box 140, Malaya/Malaysia, JFK Library.
6. Recent literature tends to perpetuate colonial-era assessments of the communist threat, arguing that it was primarily Cold War pressures that instigated the formation

of Malaysia, overlooking other factors. See, for instance, A. J. Stockwell, "Malaysia: The Making of a Neo-Colony?" *Journal of Imperial and Commonwealth History* 26, no. 2 (1998): 138–56, https://doi.org/10.1080/03086539808583029.

7. Interestingly, Cheng Guan Ang has argued (see *Southeast Asia's Cold War: An Interpretive History* [Honolulu: University of Hawaii Press, 2018], 110), that the formation of Malaysia is "seldom viewed through a Cold War lens," due to the receding local "communist threat" in Malaya after the Malayan Emergency. Despite this claim, numerous scholars have sought to situate the formation of Malaysia within a wider framework dominated by the perceived threat of Soviet or Chinese communist influences. Typically, such scholarship takes the form of counterinsurgency or Konfrontasi analyses, such as Alexander N. Shaw's "British Counterinsurgency in Brunei and Sarawak, 1962–1963: Developing Best Practices in the Shadow of Malaya," *Small Wars & Insurgencies* 27, no. 4 (2016): 702–25, https://doi.org/10.1080/09592318.2016.1190052; and John Subritzky's "Britain, *Konfrontasi*, and the End of Empire in Southeast Asia, 1961–65," *Journal of Imperial and Commonwealth History* 28, no. 3 (2000): 209–27, https://doi.org/10.1080/03086530008583106.

8. These publications depict Sabah's and Sarawak's publics as politically underdeveloped, and thus as lacking agency. See, for instance, Barbara Watson Andaya's and Leonard Y. Andaya's section on the formation of Malaysia in *A History of Malaysia* (Basingstoke, UK: Macmillan, 1982), in addition to R. Catley's "Malaysia: The Lost Battle for Merger," *Australian Outlook* 21, no. 1 (1967): 44–60, https://doi.org/10.1080/10357716708444261; and Robert O. Tilman's "Malaysia: The Problems of Federation," *Political Research Quarterly* 16, no. 4 (1963): 897–911, https://doi.org/10.1177/106591296301600409.

9. Andaya and Andaya, *History of Malaysia*, 270.

10. Matthew Jones, *Conflict and Confrontation in South East Asia, 1961–1965* (Cambridge: Cambridge University Press, 2001), 79.

11. Ronald J. Brooks, *Under Five Flags: The Story of Sabah, East Malaysia* (Edinburgh: Pentland, 1999), 200.

12. There are many reasons for this, but chief among these was the Malayan government's unwillingness to countenance merger with Singapore without the simultaneous inclusion of the Borneo territories, owing to perceived demographic and racial imbalances. See Stockwell, "Making of a Neo-Colony?," 149–50.

13. Andaya and Andaya, *History of Malaysia*, 272.

14. See, for instance, early texts such as Y. L. Lee, "The Population of British Borneo," *Population Studies* 15, no. 3 (1962): 226–43, https://doi.org/10.1080/00324728.1962.10406073; and more recently John Darwin, *Britain and Decolonisation: The Retreat from Empire in the Post-War World* (London: Macmillan, 1988), 283; and Mat Zin Bin Mat Kib, "Christianization in Sabah and the Development of Indigenous Communities: A Historical Study," *Journal of the Malaysian Branch of the Royal Asiatic Society* 77, no. 1 (2004): 53–65, https://www.jstor.org/stable/41493514.

15. Moscow TASS (Telegraph Agency of the Soviet Union), "Plan for Malaysia New colonial Noose," July 19, 1962, *Daily Report*, Foreign Broadcast Information Service, Foreign Radio Broadcasts (FBIS-FRB)-62-140.

16. Charles F. Baldwin to Dean Rusk, memorandum, Secretary of State, January 12, 1963, in NSF, series 1, box 140, Malaya/Malaysia, JFK Library.

17. Baldwin to Rusk.

18. This was at variance from the early-1950s obsession over the threat of ideological subversion that was feared to emanate from Indochina. By the late 1950s and early 1960s, Malaya was increasingly perceived in the West as having emerged from "enlightened colonial administration" as an anticommunist bastion. See Ngoei, *Arc of Containment*, 45.

19. Robert Donhauser to Dean Rusk, Secretary of State, October 16, 1962, in NSF, series 1, box 140, Malaya/Malaysia, JFK Library.

20. Hansard, "Sarawak," 200 Parl. Deb. H.L. (5th ser.) (1956) cols. 329–68.

21. Sabah's imports from Hong Kong in 1955 were virtually on par with those of Malaya. But by 1960, its purchases from Hong Kong would outstrip even those of its other commonwealth partners, with a total value of 16,000,000 Malayan dollars ($) compared to the $12,200,000 worth of goods brought in from Malaya. See "Commerce," in *Colonial Annual Report: North Borneo 1955* (London: Her Majesty's Stationery Office, 1956), 30–31; and "Commerce," in *Colonial Annual Report: North Borneo 1960* (London: Her Majesty's Stationery Office, 1961), 50.

22. United Nations, *World Economic Survey*, pt. 2, "Current Economic Developments" (United Nations: New York, 1964), 48.

23. Herman J. Luping, "The Kadazans and Sabah Politics" (PhD diss., Victoria University of Wellington, 1985), 1–2. See also Fausto Barlocco, *Identity and the State in Malaysia* (London: Routledge, 2014), 54–55.

24. Luping, "The Kadazans and Sabah Politics," 1–2.

25. William A. C. Goode, notes from interview with O.K.K. Sedomon Gusanad Kina, February 7, 1962, in FCO 141/13012, TNA.

26. "Population," in *Colonial Annual Report: North Borneo 1960* (London: Her Majesty's Stationery Office, 1961), 18.

27. "Population," in *Colonial Annual Report: North Borneo 1958* (London: Her Majesty's Stationery Office, 1959), 17–18.

28. Cameron Cobbold, "Section A: Enquiry in North Borneo," in *Report of the Commission of Enquiry, North Borneo and Sarawak* (London: Her Majesty's Stationery Office, 1962), 31.

29. Jones to Dean Rusk, Secretary of State, December 27, 1962, in NSF, series 1, box 11, Borneo (general), JFK Library.

30. See Stockwell, "Making of a Neo-Colony?," 138–56.

31. Stockwell, "Making of a Neo-Colony?," 141.

32. Donna J. Amoroso, *Traditionalism and the Ascendency of the Malay Ruling Class in Colonial Malaya* (Petaling Jaya: Strategic Information and Research Development Centre, 2014), 226–27.

33. Rachel Leow, *Taming Babel: Language in the Making of Malaysia* (Cambridge: Cambridge University Press, 2018), 180.

34. See, for instance, George McT. Kahin, *Southeast Asia: A Testament* (London: RoutledgeCurzon, 2003), 150.

35. Stockwell, "Making of a Neo-Colony?," 149–50.

36. James P. Ongkili, "The 'Dacing' in Sabah and Sarawak," *Southeast Asian Affairs* (1975): 113, https://www.jstor.org/stable/27908247.

37. Alice M. Nah, "(Re)mapping Indigenous 'Race'/Place in Postcolonial Peninsular Malaysia," *Geografiska Annaler*, Series B, *Human Geography* 88, no. 3 (2006): 285, https://doi.org/10.1111/j.1468-0459.2006.00222.x. For a study on indigeneity and aboriginality

in colonial Malaya, see Sandra Khor Manickam's *Taming the Wild: Aborigines and Racial Knowledge in Colonial Malaya* (Singapore: National University of Singapore Press, 2015), especially 1–4.

38. Luping, "The Kadazans and Sabah Politics," 1.

39. As Wen-Qing Ngoei writes, the West's hostility toward communist-controlled China was part of an "extant distrust of Southeast Asia's Chinese." Ngoei, *Arc of Containment*, 29.

40. Moscow TASS, "New Colonial Noose.".

41. Pyongyang KCNA (Korean Central News Agency), "Malaysia Federation Is Colonialist Plot," February 12, 1963, *Daily Report*, FBIS-FRB-63-030.

42. See Stockwell, "Making of a Neo-Colony?," 138–56.

43. David Fieldhouse, *Colonialism 1870–1945: An Introduction* (London: Macmillan, 1983), 8.

44. "Brunei People Are Struggling for Freedom," Hanoi, December 21, 1962, *Daily Report*, FBIS-FRB-62-248.

45. Moscow TASS, "U.S. Plan Counters U.K. Malaysian Scheme," December 17, 1962, *Daily Report*, FBIS-FRB-62-246.

46. Notes on interview with Malcom Macdonald, contained in Robert Donhauser to Dean Rusk, Secretary of State, memorandum, November 8, 1962, in NSF, series 1, box 140, Malaya/Malaysia, JFK Library.

47. Stockwell, "Making of a Neo-Colony?," 138.

48. Tracing the genealogy of the federation to the Federated Malay States offers valuable nuance. See, for instance, H. Conway Belfield's *Handbook of the Federated Malay States* (London: Edward Stanford, 1902); and Eunice Thio's "Some Aspects of the Federation of the Malay States," *Journal of the Malaysian Branch of the Royal Asiatic Society* 40, no. 2 (1967): 3–15, https://www.jstor.org/stable/41491921.

49. Stockwell, "Making of a Neo-Colony?," 144–45.

50. Nicholas J. White, "The Survival, Revival and Decline of British Economic Influence in Malaysia, 1957–1970," *Twentieth Century British History* 14, no. 3 (2003): 223, https://doi.org/10.1093/tcbh/14.3.222.

51. White, *British Business in Post-Colonial Malaysia*, 2–3.

52. White, "British Economic Influence in Malaysia," 223.

53. Junid Saham has noted that although Malaya's "economic progress" was "impressive" throughout the 1950s and early 1960s, "the potential for enhancing economic growth lay in diversifying the economy" beyond traditional economic staples. See Saham, *British Industrial Investment in Malaysia, 1963–1971* (Kuala Lumpur: Oxford University Press, 1980), 8.

54. Charles F. Baldwin to Department of State, memorandum, August 1, 1962, in NSF, series 1, box 140, Malaya/Malaysia, JFK Library.

55. John Kenneth Galbraith to Charles F. Baldwin, regarding interview with Lee Kuan Yew, September 24, 1962, in NSF, series 1, box 140, Malaya/Malaysia, JFK Library.

56. Amarjit Kaur, *Economic Change in East Malaysia: Sabah and Sarawak since 1850* (London: Macmillan, 1998), 166.

57. J. R. Angel, "The Proposed Federation of Sarawak, North Borneo and Brunei: the Development and Decline of the British Borneo Concept" (PhD diss., University of Sydney, 1963), 248–53.

58. Roland Turnbull, quoted in Brooks, *Under Five Flags*, 200–201.
59. "Monthly Summary of News for the Period 24 October to 23 November, 1957," 2, in FCO 141/12291, TNA.
60. Roland Turnbull, quoted in Brooks, *Under Five Flags*, 200–201.
61. Roland Turnbull, quoted in J. R. Angel, "Proposed Federation," 253.
62. Brooks, *Under Five Flags*, 201.
63. See David R. Saunders, "Brokering a Postcolonial Malaysia: How Local Elites Shaped the Cobbold Commission, 1961–63," *Critical Military Studies*, Published ahead of print, November 10, 2023, https://doi.org/10.1080/23337486.2023.2268958.
64. Brooks, *Under Five Flags*, 201.
65. See chapter 2.
66. "North Borneo Legislative Council Meeting," Department of Information Services, April 10, 1958, PressR19580410d, National Archives of Singapore (NAS).
67. Hansard, "North Borneo, Brunei and Sarawak (Union)," 587 Parl. Deb. (5th ser.) (1958).
68. See chapter 3.
69. "Supporters of Borneo Parties Row over Flag," *Straits Times*, May 29, 1962.
70. "Monthly Summary of News for the Period 25 November to 24 December, 1957," 1, in FCO 141/12291, TNA.
71. Recommendations made by Wong Pow Nee and Ghazali Shafie, in *Report of the Commission of Enquiry*, 65.
72. "United Front Plan," *Straits Times*, July 10, 1961, 1.
73. Justus van der Kroef, "The Dynamics of Communism in Malaysia," *Communist Affairs* 3, no. 3 (1965): 8, https://doi.org/10.1016/0588-8174(65)90022-7.
74. "Chinese Towkays 'Against Malaysia' in Sabah," *Straits Budget*, June 20, 1962.
75. Mary F. Somers Heidhues, "Peking and the Overseas Chinese: The Malaysian Dispute," *Asian Survey* 6, no. 5 (1966): 276, https://doi.org/10.2307/2642537.
76. Mohamad Yusop, "The Malaysia Plan and the First Brunei Elections, 1962," *Journal of the Malay Branch of the Royal Asiatic Society* 71, no. 1 (1998): 68, https://www.jstor.org/stable/41493352.
77. Wong and Shafie, in *Report of the Commission of Enquiry*, 65. See also Danny Wong Tze Ken, "The Name of Sabah and the Sustaining of a New Identity in a New Nation," *Archipel* 89 (2015): 173, https://journals.openedition.org/archipel/495.
78. Faisal S. Hazis, "Domination, Contestation, and Accommodation: 54 Years of Sabah and Sarawak in Malaysia," *Southeast Asian Studies* 7, no. 3 (2018): 343, https://doi.org/10.20495/seas.7.3_341.
79. "Report by M. G. Edge, Superintendent, Special Branch, on His Visit to the Interior," February 22–27, 1963, 6, in FCO 141/13009, TNA.
80. Notes on O.K.K. Sedomon, February 7, 1962, in FCO 141/13012, TNA.
81. William A. C. Goode, notes from interview with O.K.K. Sedomon Gusanad Kina, February 7, 1962, in FCO 141/13012, TNA.
82. Goode, notes from interview with O.K.K. Sedomon Gusanad Kina, .
83. Macmillan to Brook, June 21, 1962, in Prime Minister's Office (PREM) 11/3867, TNA, quoted in Jones, *Conflict and Confrontation*, 84–85.
84. District Officer for Beaufort to Resident, memorandum, February 13, 1957, in FCO 141/13009, TNA.
85. C. Perkin to C. S., memorandum, October 22, 1959, in FCO 141/13009, TNA.

86. District Officer for Beaufort to Resident, memorandum, February 13, 1957, in FCO 141/13009, TNA; and Mohammed Yassin, Biographical Note, March 1963, 1, in FCO 141/13009, TNA.

87. R. N. Turner, "Note on Interview with Miss Helen Chung at the Secretariat," December 14, 1962, 1, in FCO 141/13003, TNA.

88. Jones, *Conflict and Confrontation*, 79.

89. For analysis on the Cobbold Commission, and on how local Sabahan elites shaped the enquiry and the formation of Malaysia, see Saunders, "Brokering a Postcolonial Malaysia."

90. Notably, Abell had previously gained note for advocating Turnbull's 1958 Borneo federation plan, but by 1962 his loyalties lay with Projek Malaysia.

91. Cameron Cobbold to Harold Macmillan, "Personal and Confidential Letter Addressed to the Prime Minister," June 21, 1962, 3, in FCO 141/13046, TNA.

92. Recommendation by Anthony Abell and David Watherston, in *Report of the Commission of Enquiry*, 54.

93. Wong and Shafie, in *Report of the Commission of Enquiry*, 65.

94. See, for instance, Ussama Makdisi, "Anti-imperialism, Missionary Work, and the King-Crane Commission," in *Empire's Twin: US Anti-imperialism from the Founding Era to the Age of Terrorism*, ed. Ian Tyrrell and Jay Sexton (Ithaca, NY: Cornell University Press, 2015), 118–36; Matthew Kraig Kelly, *The Crime of Nationalism: Britain, Palestine, and Nation-Building on the Fringe of Empire* (Oakland: University of California Press, 2017); and Gregory J. Shibley, "Revisiting Hitti's Thoughts on Palestine and Arab Identity," *Arab Studies Quarterly* 41, no. 2 (2019): 150–71, https://doi.org/10.13169/arabstudquar.41.2.0150.

95. "Cobbold on His Way to Kuching," *Singapore Free Press*, February 19, 1962; "Cobbold Team in Jesselton–Then a Rest," *Straits Times*, February 26, 1962.

96. T. E. Smith, "Proposals for Malaysia," *The World Today* 18, no. 5 (1962): 199, https://www.jstor.org/stable/40393401.

97. Excerpt from *Merdeka*, quoted in "Terserah kpd British, kata akhbar Jakarta" ["It's up to the British, said the Jakarta press"], *Berita Harian*, August 7, 1963, 1.

98. Cobbold, *Report of the Commission of Enquiry*, 19.

99. Hamilton F. Armstrong, "The Troubled Birth of Malaysia," *Foreign Affairs* 41, no. 4 (1963): 683, https://www.foreignaffairs.com/articles/asia/1963-07-01/troubled-birth-malaysia.

100. Cobbold, *Report of the Commission of Enquiry*, 9.

101. L. A. Sheridan, "Constitutional Problems of Malaysia," *International and Comparative Law Quarterly* 13, no. 4 (1964): 1349, https://doi.org/10.1093/iclqaj/13.4.1349; Richard Allen, "Britain's Colonial Aftermath in South East Asia," *Asian Survey* 3, no. 9 (1963): 403–14, https://doi.org/10.2307/3023461.

102. Cobbold, *Report of the Commission of Enquiry*, 44–45.

103. "Some notes on 'Malaysia' presented to the Cobbold Commission by A. E. Philipps, Tuaran Estate, North Borneo," March 6, 1962, in CO 947/16, TNA.

104. George McT. Kahin, "Malaysia and Indonesia," *Pacific Affairs* 37, no. 3 (1964): 256, https://doi.org/10.2307/2754974.

105. Orang Tua Awang Hashim to Secretary, Malaysia Commission, February 24, 1962, in CO 947/16, TNA.

106. "Chinese Towkays 'Against Malaysia.'"

107. Orang Tua Taib to Secretary, Malaysia Commission, February 26, 1962, in CO 947/16, TNA.

108. Residents of Begawan to Cameron Cobbold, February 22, 1962, in CO 947/16, TNA.

109. Thirty-three members of the North Borneo Electricity Board to Secretary, Malaysia Commission, February, 1962, in CO 947/16, TNA.

110. Asmat Abdullah and Abdul Rahman Bidin to Secretary, Malaysia Commission, February 24, 1962, in CO 947/16, TNA.

111. Forty-five workers of the Locomotive Shop to Secretary, Malaysia Commission, February, 1962, in CO 947/16, TNA.

112. Eileen Chanin, *Limbang Rebellion: Seven Days in December 1962* (Singapore: Ridge Books, 2013), 167.

113. Y. K. Wong to Secretary, Malaysia Commission, February 27, 1962, in CO 947/16, TNA.

114. E. Sadiwah to Secretary, Malaysia Commission, February 24, 1962, in CO 947/16, TNA.

115. Chang Ah Foo to Secretary, Malaysia Commission, February 24, 1962, in CO 947/16, TNA.

116. Talip bin Japar to Secretary, Malaysia Commission, n.d., 1962, in CO 947/16, TNA.

117. Michael Wong to Secretary, Malaysia Commission, February 22, 1962, in CO 947/16, TNA.

118. "Study Tour of Malaya," *North Borneo News & Sabah Times*, November 24, 1962.

119. Wong and Shafie, in *Report of the Commission of Enquiry*, 65.

120. Wong and Shafie, *Report of the Commission of Enquiry*, 65.

121. Notes on O.K.K. Sedomon.

122. "Report by M. G. Edge," 7.

123. "Team from N. Borneo Arrives to Decide on Malaysia," *Straits Times*, November 8, 1962, 5.

124. "New Move to Join Sabah Alliance 'To Avoid Bloodshed,'" *Straits Times*, October 30, 1962.

125. Henry Robert Glick, "The Chinese Community in Sabah and the 1963 Election," *Asian Survey* 5, no. 3 (1965): 145, https://doi.org/10.2307/2642404.

126. Ahad, "Seluroh Bandar Sedang Mengator Sambutan" ["Welcoming celebrations across the cities"], *Berita Harian*, September 16, 1963, 3.

127. William A. C. Goode to United Kingdom Commissioner Singapore, High Commissioner Kuala Lumpur, High Commissioner Brunei and Governor of Sarawak, August 1, 1963, in FCO 141/13082, TNA.

Conclusion

1. The *kampong* where Ernest Alfred Pavitt travelled to in 1896 was located just south of Kota Kinabalu, while Petagas was the site of a Japanese internment camp and numerous wartime executions between 1942 and 1945. Many of these towns and *kampongs* have complicated, storied pasts.

2. Donald Stephens was known at this time as Tun Muhammed Fuad Stephens, after having converted to Islam in 1971.

3. Bernard Sta Maria, *Peter J. Mojuntin, the Golden Son of the Kadazan* (Seremban: Chang Lithho Press, 1978), 8–11.

4. The United Pasokmomogun Kadazan Organization (UPKO) was founded in June 1964, resulting from the merger of the United National Kadazan Organisation (UNKO) and Pasok Momogun, which were founded in 1961 and 1962 respectively.

5. Hamdan Aziz, "*Double Six* Tragedy and Implications of Political Development in Sabah, Malaysia," *SOSIOHUMANIKA: Jurnal Pendidikan Sains Sosial dan Kemanusiaan* 6, no. 1 (2013): 89, https://journals.mindamas.com/index.php/sosiohumanika/article/view/483.

6. Danny Wong Tze Ken, *Historical Sabah: Community and Society* (Kota Kinabalu: Natural History Publications, 2004), 89.

7. Bernard Sta Maria's biography *Peter J. Mojuntin, the Golden Son of the Kadazan* has been banned in Malaysia by the federal government since 1978. See, for instance, Joe Fernandez, "Book Casts Shadow on Sabah History," *Free Malaysia Today News*, June 16, 2014; and Eileen Ng, "Ban on Book about Ex-Sabah Leader Stays, Says Zahid," *Malaysian Insider*, May 25, 2015.

8. Aziz, "*Double Six* Tragedy," 89–96.

9. David A. Andelnian, "Plane Crash Stirs a Crisis in Sabah," *New York Times*, June 8, 1976, 7, https://www.nytimes.com/1976/06/08/archives/plane-crash-stirs-a-crisis-in-sabah-death-of-chief-minister-and.html.

10. Ronald J. Brooks, *Under Five Flags: The Story of Sabah, East Malaysia* (Edinburgh: Pentland, 1999), 200.

11. Notes on O.K.K. Sedomon, February 7, 1962, in FCO 141/13012, TNA.

12. Björn Åsgård, "Ethnic Awareness and Development: A Study of the Kadazan Dusun, Sabah, Malaysia" (Honours diss., University of Gothenburg, 2002), 12.

13. Fausto Barlocco, *Identity and the State in Malaysia* (London: Routledge, 2014), 54–55.

14. Åsgård, "Ethnic Awareness and Development," 12.

15. Maria, *Peter J. Mojuntin*, 20; James P. Ongkili, *Nation-Building in Malaysia: 1946–1974* (Singapore: Oxford University Press, 1985), 187.

16. David R. Saunders, "The Friction of Distance in Borneo: Migration, Economic Change and Geographic Space in Sabah," *World History Connected* 17, no. 3 (2020), https://worldhistoryconnected.press.uillinois.edu/17.3/Sabha.html.

17. See, for instance, Laurens Bakker and Jay Crain, "Trade, Transnationalism and Ethnic Infighting: Borders of Authority in Northeastern Borneo," in *Transnational Flows and Permissive Polities: Ethnographies of Human Mobilities in Asia*, ed. Barak Kalir and Malini Sur (Amsterdam: Amsterdam University Press, 2012), 109–26.

18. See "Duterte Vows to Pursue Philippine Claim to Sabah," *Straits Times*, May 27, 2016, https://www.straitstimes.com/asia/se-asia/duterte-vows-to-pursue-philippine-claim-to-sabah; and Amy Chew, "Secret Plot to Invade Malaysia's Sabah with Sulu Militia Hatched in Southern Philippines: Security Source," *South China Morning Post*, December 9, 2021, https://www.scmp.com/week-asia/politics/article/3158966/secret-plot-invade-malaysias-sabah-sulu-militia-hatched-southern.

Bibliography

Archival Sources

United Kingdom

The British Library
The National Archives of the United Kingdom (TNA)
    Colonial Office (CO) Records
    Dominions Office (DO) Records
    Foreign and Commonwealth Office (FCO) Records
    Foreign Office (FO) Records
    Prime Minister's Office (PREM) Records

United States

    Central Intelligence Agency (CIA) Records
    Foreign Broadcast Information Service (FBIS)
    John F. Kennedy Presidential Library

Malaysia

    Arkib Negara Malaysia (National Archives of Malaysia) (ANM)

Australia

    National Archives of Australia (NAA)

Published Sources

Unauthored News Articles

"14 Held in Sarawak." *Straits Times*, January 3, 1963.
"20 Filipino Pirate Suspects Arrested." *Straits Times*, October 4, 1962.
"60 Armed Men Raid Sarawak Police Station and Capture Guns." *Straits Times*, April 13, 1963.
"Anger in Borneo." *Straits Times*, June 24, 1962.
"Another Exclusive." *Straits Times*, January 19, 1963.
"Another Great Trading Company Disappears." *Morning Tribune*, July 15, 1946.
"Award for Br. North Borneo Co." *Sunday Tribune* (Singapore), February 27, 1949.
"Azahari Speaks." *Straits Times*, January 19, 1963.

"Azahari 'To Accept Volunteers.'" *Straits Times*, January 22, 1963.
"Azahari's Wife: New Snag in Divorce Request." *Straits Times*, March 28, 1963.
"Azahari's Wife No. 2 to Divorce Him." *Straits Times*, October 28, 1966.
"B.N.B. Becomes Colony on July 15." *Straits Times*, June 20, 1946.
"B.N.B. Co. Turns Down £2,200,000." *Singapore Free Press*, June 19, 1946.
"Bid for British Borneo." *Singapore Free Press*, January 31, 1950.
"A Big Increase in Piracy in N. Borneo." *Straits Budget*, December 27, 1961.
"Big 'Unity' Plan: Tengku on Closer Ties with S'pore, Borneo and Brunei." *Straits Times*, May 28, 1961.
"Bill to Abolish Poll Tax in North Borneo Announced." *North Borneo News & Sabah Times*, August 27, 1962.
"Brace of Constitutions." *Economist*, October 5, 1957.
"Britain Asks Manila to Help Stop Piracy." *Straits Times*, September 14, 1962.
"Britain Rejects Manila's Borneo Claim." *Straits Times*, February 2, 1963.
"British North Borneo's Goodbye to the Company." *Straits Times*, July 15, 1946.
"British Right to Borneo Challenged." *Malaya Tribune*, July 17, 1946.
"Candidates for Local Govt. Elections." *North Borneo News & Sabah Times*, December 5, 1962.
"Chartered Company Only Left with $320." *North Borneo News & Sabah Times*, October 18, 1962.
"Chinese Towkays 'Against Malaysia' in Sabah." *Straits Budget*, June 20, 1962.
"Cobbold and Manila." *Straits Times*, July 1, 1962.
"Cobbold on His Way to Kuching." *Singapore Free Press*, February 19, 1962.
"Cobbold Team in Jesselton–Then a Rest." *Straits Times*, February 26, 1962.
"Court Hitch: Aza's Wife Must Wait for Divorce." *Straits Times*, March 5, 1963.
"C-Plan Course." *Straits Times*, January 22, 1959.
"Dari Borneo ka-London." *Berita Harian* [Daily News], August 28, 1959.
"Divorce Off: Aza's Wife Not in Court." *Straits Times*, April 5, 1963.
"Duterte Vows to Pursue Philippine Claim to Sabah." *Straits Times*, May 27, 2016, https://www.straitstimes.com/asia/se-asia/duterte-vows-to-pursue-philippine-claim-to-sabah
"Even 'Volunteers' Cannot Stop Malaysia–Lee." *Straits Times*, January 1, 1963.
"An Explosion, Then Fuad's Plane Hurtled Down . . ." *New Nation*, June 8, 1976.
"The Facts in Borneo." *Straits Times*, October 7, 1963.
"'Fiasco' Says Jek of Moshi Talks." *Straits Times*, February 11, 1963, 1.
"Filipinos Say Their Independence Is Real." *Indian Daily Mail*, June 11, 1947.
"Fuad: Sabotage Suspected: Hussein Orders Probe into Plane Crash." *New Nation*, June 7, 1976.
"Group Draws Up Self-Determination Petition for Sarawak and Sabah." *Borneo Post*, August 13, 2014. https://www.theborneopost.com/2014/08/13/group-draws-up-self-determination-petition-for-sarawak-and-sabah/.
"Hanoi Sokong Azahari." *Berita Harian*, December 10, 1963.
"The Improbable Azahari." *Straits Times*, February 22, 1963.
"Kesenyapan Azahari." *Berita Harian*, February 20, 1963.
"The Little Empire.'" *Straits Times*, June 25, 1946.
"Macapagal Attacks the 'Drop Claim' Senator." *Straits Times*, March 28, 1963.

"Macapagal Says: Claim Based on Regional Security, Too." *Straits Times*, January 4, 1963.
"Malaysian Air Crash Kills 11." *Sarasota Herald-Tribune*, June 7, 1976.
"Maphilindo and Malaysia." *New York Times*, August 6, 1963.
"Maphilindo Is Not against the Chinese in Malaysia, Tan." *Straits Times*, August 7, 1963.
"Memorandum: Carpenter Agreement." *Official Gazette*, March 22, 1915.
"More Cases of Borneo Piracy Despite R.N. Patrols." *Singapore Free Press*, September 13, 1961.
"N. Borneo Claim: Future Action." *Straits Times*, December 5, 1962.
"N. Borneo Leaders Angry and Hostile." *Straits Times*, June 28, 1962.
"N. Borneo Settlement Held Up." *Straits Budget*, August 14, 1947.
"N. Borneo: A Formal Claim Unlikely." *Straits Times*, January 17, 1962.
"New Move to Join Sabah Alliance 'To Avoid Bloodshed.'" *Straits Times*, October 30, 1962.
"New Philippines Republic Has Ambitions." *Indian Daily Mail*, July 19, 1946.
"North Borneo Joins Empire." *Straits Times*, July 16, 1946.
"Obscurity in Indonesia." *Straits Times*, December 27, 1958.
"One Radio Station Helps Another." *Straits Times*, February 22, 1961.
"PAS Bantah Isteri Azahari Di-tahan," *Berita Harian*, January 3, 1963.
"Philippine Govt Claiming British N. Borneo Islands." *Malaya Tribune*, July 19, 1946.
"Philippines Claims Sovereignty in British-Ruled North Borneo." *New York Times*, June 23, 1962.
"PR [Parti Rakyat] Bantah Polis Rampas Risalah 'Revolusi' Brunai." *Berita Harian*, January 22, 1963.
"PR Bantah Polis Rampas Risalah 'Revolusi' Brunai." *Berita Harian*, January 22, 1963.
"Radio Seeking Information." *Straits Times*, December 15, 1958.
"Rebels' Families 'Sent to Safety.'" *Straits Times*, March 7, 1958, 1.
"The S-E Asian Vacuum." *Singapore Free Press*, August 25, 1961.
"Senator: Borneo Claim 'Wrong.'" *Straits Times*, January 8, 1963.
"Stewart's Murder Planned a Year Ago." *Malaya Tribune*, January 10, 1950.
"The Story of Saudin." *Atlantic*, February 1938.
"Study Tour of Malaya." *North Borneo News & Sabah Times*, November 24, 1962.
"Support for Azahari's Bogus Revolution." *Straits Times*, January 26, 1963.
"'Support for Rebellion in Sumatra' Decision." *Straits Times*, September 26, 1963, 20.
"Supporters of Borneo Parties Row over Flag." *Straits Times*, May 29, 1962.
"Team from N. Borneo Arrives to Decide on Malaysia." *Straits Times*, November 8, 1962.
"Tengku Accused of Having Sumatra Designs." *Straits Times*, January 11, 1959.
"Tengku on Rebels: 'Embarrassing to Malaya.'" *Straits Times*, December 12, 1958.
"Terserah kpd British, kata akhbar Jakarta." *Berita Harian*, August 7, 1963.
"Tidak Akan Menyerah Sa-lagi Belum Merdeka, Tekad Pemberontak." *Berita Harian*, December 11, 1962.
"United Front Plan." *Straits Times*, July 10, 1961.
"U.S. May Cut Natural Rubber Requirements." *Straits Times*, July 20, 1946.
"Voice from the Past." *Economist*, May 19, 1962.

"Woman Rules Turtle Isles: American Educated Princess Becomes Deputy Governor." *Reading Eagle*, January 1, 1948.
"Zaini–Won't Betray Cause, Says Aza." *Straits Times*, January 29, 1963.
"Zulkifli: Loyalty of Borneo Is to Soekarno." *Straits Times*, May 17, 1963.

Authored Sources

Abdul Majid, Haji Harun bin Haji. "The Brunei Rebellion: December 1962, the Popular Uprising." MPhil diss., King's College, London, 2006.
Ahad. "Seluroh Bandar Sedang Mengator Sambutan." *Berita Harian*, September 16, 1963.
Ali, Merima, Odd-Helge Fjelstad, and Abdulaziz B. Shifa. "European Colonization and the Corruption of Local Elites: The Case of Chiefs in Africa." *Journal of Economic Behaviour and Organization* 179 (2020). 80–100. https://doi.org/10.1016/j.jebo.2020.08.043.
Allen, Richard. "Britain's Colonial Aftermath in South East Asia." *Asian Survey* 3, no. 9 (1963): 403–14. https://doi.org/10.2307/3023461.
Amoroso, Donna J. *Traditionalism and the Ascendency of the Malay Ruling Class in Colonial Malaya*. Petaling Jaya: Strategic Information and Research Development Centre, 2014.
Andaya, Barbara Watson, and Leonard Y. Andaya. *A History of Early Modern Southeast Asia, 1400–1830*. Cambridge: Cambridge University Press, 2015.
Andaya, Barbara Watson, and Leonard Y. Andaya. *A History of Malaysia*. Basingstoke, UK: Macmillan, 1982.
Andelnian, David A. "Plane Crash Stirs a Crisis in Sabah." *New York Times*, June 8, 1976. https://www.nytimes.com/1976/06/08/archives/plane-crash-stirs-a-crisis-in-sabah-death-of-chief-minister-and.html.
Anderson, Benedict. *Imagined Communities: Reflections on the Origin and Spread of Nationalism*. London: Verso, 1983.
Ang, Cheng Guan. *Southeast Asia's Cold War: An Interpretive History*. Honolulu: University of Hawaii Press, 2018.
Angel, J. R. "The Proposed Federation of Sarawak, North Borneo and Brunei: the Development and Decline of the British Borneo Concept." PhD diss., University of Sydney, 1963.
"Anglo-Philippine Communiqué (London)." *Journal of the American Chamber of Commerce of the Philippines* 39, no. 2 (1963).
Aranas, Uwe. *The History of Wireless Telegraphy in British North Borneo*. Kota Kinabalu: Department of Sabah Museum, 2018.
Armstrong, Hamilton F. "The Troubled Birth of Malaysia." *Foreign Affairs*, 41, no. 4 (1963). https://www.foreignaffairs.com/articles/asia/1963-07-01/troubled-birth-malaysia.
Åsgård, Björn. "Ethnic Awareness and Development: A Study of the Kadazan Dusun, Sabah, Malaysia," Honours diss., University of Gothenburg, 2002.
Aziz, Hamdan. "*Double Six* Tragedy and Implications of Political Development in Sabah, Malaysia." *SOSIOHUMANIKA: Jurnal Pendidikan Sains Sosial dan Kemanusiaan* 6, no. 1 (2013): 89–96. https://journals.mindamas.com/index.php/sosiohumanika/article/view/483.

Bakker, Laurens, and Jay Crain. "Trade, Transnationalism and Ethnic Infighting: Borders of Authority in Northeastern Borneo." In *Transnational Flows and Permissive Polities: Ethnographies of Human Mobilities in Asia*, edited by Barak Kalir and Malini Sur, 109–26. Amsterdam: Amsterdam University Press, 2012.

Barlocco, Fausto. "An Inconvenient Birth: The Formation of a Modern Kadazan Culture and Its Marginalisation within the Making of the Malaysian Nation (1953–2007)." *Indonesia and the Malay World* 41, no. 119 (2013): 116–41. https://doi.org/10.1080/13639811.2013.766010.

Barlocco, Fausto. "Between the Local and the State: Practices and Discourses of Identity among the Kadazan of Sabah (East Malaysia)." PhD diss., Loughborough University, 2008. https://repository.lboro.ac.uk/articles/thesis/Between_the_local_and_the_state_practices_and_discourses_of_identity_among_the_Kadazan_of_Sabah_East_Malaysia_/9480593/1.

Barlocco, Fausto. *Identity and the State in Malaysia*. London: Routledge, 2014.

Beccari, Odoardo. *Wanderings in the Great Forests of Borneo* Oxford: Oxford University Press, 1989. First published 1904.

Belfield, H. Conway. *Handbook of the Federated Malay States*. London: Edward Stanford, 1902.

Benda, Harry J. "Political Elites in Colonial Southeast Asia: An Historical Analysis." *Comparative Studies in Society and History*. 7, no. 3 (1965): 233–51. https://doi.org/10.1017/S0010417500003662.

Benton, Lauren, *Search for Sovereignty: Law and Geography in European Empires, 1400–1900*. Cambridge: Cambridge University Press, 2010.

Beresford, Don. "'Sumatra State' Plot Chiefs are now in Malaya." *Straits Times*, December 17, 1958.

Bevins, Vincent. *The Jakarta Method: Washington's Anticommunist Crusade and the Mass Murder Program that Shaped Our World*. New York: PublicAffairs, 2020.

Bevis, William W. *Borneo Log: The Struggle for Sarawak's Forests*. Seattle: University of Washington Press, 1995.

Beyer, H. Otley. "Brief Memorandum on the Government of the Sultanate of Sulu and the Powers of the Sultan During the 19th Century." *Philippine International Law Journal* 2, no. 1 (1963): 325–26. First published 1946.

Bickers, Robert. *Empire Made Me: An Englishman Adrift in Shanghai*. London: Penguin Books, 2004.

Black, Ian. *A Gambling Style of Government: The Establishment of the Chartered Company's Rule in Sabah, 1878–1915*. Kuala Lumpur: Oxford University Press, 1983.

Black, Ian. "The 'Lastposten': Eastern Kalimantan and the Dutch in the Nineteenth and Early Twentieth Centuries." *Journal of Southeast Asian Studies* 16, no. 2 (1985): 281–91. https://doi.org/10.1017/S0022463400008456.

Black, Ian. "Native Administration by the British North Borneo Chartered Company." PhD diss., Australian National University, 1970.

Boncales, Amando Respicio. "A Historical Discourse of the Philippine Claim over Sabah." PhD diss., Northern Illinois University, 2013.

Boyle, Frederick. *Adventures Among the Dyaks of Borneo*. Kota Kinabalu: Opus Publications, 2007. First published 1865.

Brooks, Ronald J. *Under Five Flags: The Story of Sabah, East Malaysia*. Edinburgh: Pentland, 1999.

Bunnel, Frederick P. "Guided Democracy Foreign Policy: 1960–1965 President Sukarno Moves from Non-Alignment to Confrontation." *Indonesia* 2 (1966): 37–76. https://doi.org/10.2307/3350755.

Carroll, John M. *Edge of Empires: Chinese Elites and British Colonials in Hong Kong*. Cambridge, MA: Harvard University Press, 2005.

Catley, R. "Malaysia: The Lost Battle for Merger." *Australian Outlook* 21, no. 1 (1967): 44–60. https://doi.org/10.1080/10357716708444261.

Chan, Ming K. "The Legacy of the British Administration of Hong Kong: A View from Hong Kong." *China Quarterly* 151 (1997): 567–82. https://doi.org/10.1017/S0305741000046828.

Chanin, Eileen. *Limbang Rebellion: Seven Days in December 1962*. Singapore: Ridge Books, 2013.

Chapman, David C., Graham S. Giese, Margaret Goud Collins, Rolu Encarnacion, and Gil Jacinto. "Evidence of Internal Swash Associated with Sulu Sea Solitary Waves?" *Continental Shelf Research* 11, no. 7 (1991): 591–99. https://doi.org/10.1016/0278-4343(91)90014-W.

Chew, Amy. "Secret Plot to Invade Malaysia's Sabah with Sulu Militia Hatched in Southern Philippines: Security Source." *South China Morning Post*, December 9, 2021. https://www.scmp.com/week-asia/politics/article/3158966/secret-plot-invade-malaysias-sabah-sulu-militia-hatched-southern.

Chin, James. "Is Malaysia Heading for 'BorneoExit'? Why Some in East Malaysia Are Advocating for Secession." *The Conversation*, September 24, 2010. https://theconversation.com/is-malaysia-heading-for-borneoexit-why-some-in-east-malaysia-are-advocating-for-secession-146208.

Chung, Nicholas. *Under the Borneo Sun: A Tawau Story*. Kota Kinabalu: Natural History Publications, 2005.

Cleary, M. C. "Plantation Agriculture and the Formulation of Native Land Rights in British North Borneo, c. 1880–1930" *The Geographic Journal* 158, no. 2 (1992): 170–81. https://doi.org/10.2307/3059786.

Cochrane, T. G. "Empire Oil: The Progress of Sarawak." *Journal of the Royal Society of Arts* 72, no. 3723 (1924): 308–19.

Collenette, P. *The Geology and Mineral Resources of the Jesselton-Kinabalu Area, North Borneo*. Kuching: Government Printing Office, 1958.

Collins, James T. "Contesting Straits-Malayness: The Fact of Borneo." *Journal of Southeast Asian Studies* 32, no. 3 (2001): 385–95. https://doi.org/10.1017/S0022463401000212.

Colonial Annual Report: North Borneo 1948. London: His Majesty's Stationery Office, 1949.

Colonial Annual Report: North Borneo 1955. London: Her Majesty's Stationery Office, 1956.

Colonial Annual Report: North Borneo 1958. London: Her Majesty's Stationery Office, 1959.

Colonial Annual Report: North Borneo 1960. London: Her Majesty's Stationery Office, 1961.

Conboy, Kenneth, and James Morrison. *Feet to the Fire: CIA Covert Operations in Indonesia, 1957–1958*. Annapolis, MD: US Naval Institute Press, 1999.

Cribb, Robert, Helen Gilbert, and Helen Tiffin. *Wild Man from Borneo: A Cultural History of the Orangutan*. Honolulu: University of Hawaii Press, 2014.

Darwin, John, *Britain and Decolonisation: The Retreat from Empire in the Post-War World*. London: Macmillan, 1988.

Darwin, John. "Imperialism in Decline? Tendencies in British Imperial Policy Between the Wars." *The Historical Journal* 23, no. 3 (1980): 657–79. https://doi.org/10.1017/S0018246X00024936.

De Silva, Maureen. "Javanese Indentured Labourers in British North Borneo, 1914–1932." PhD diss., School of Oriental and African Studies, University of London, 2009. https://eprints.soas.ac.uk/29298/.

Dove, Michael R. *The Banana Tree at the Gate: A History of Marginal Peoples and Global Markets in Borneo*. New Haven, CT: Yale University Press, 2011.

Dove, Michael R. "Smallholder Rubber and Swidden Agriculture in Borneo: A Sustainable Adaptation to the Ecology and Economy of the Tropical Forest." *Economic Botany* 47, no. 2 (1993): 136–47. https://doi.org/10.1007/BF02862016.

Easter, David. *Britain and the Confrontation with Indonesia, 1960–66*. London: Tauris Academic Studies, 2012.

Easter, David. "British Intelligence and Propaganda during the 'Confrontation,' 1963–1966." *Intelligence and National Security* 16, no. 2 (2001): 83–102. https://doi.org/10.1080/714002893.

Ellen, Roy "On the Contemporary Uses of Colonial History and the Legitimation of Political Status in Archipelagic Southeast Seram" *Journal of Southeast Asian Studies* 28, no. 1 (1997): 78–102. https://doi.org/10.1017/S0022463400015186.

Farram, Steven. "*Ganyang!* Indonesian Popular Songs from the Confrontation Era, 1963 1966." *Bijdragen Tot De Taal-, Land- En VolkenKunde* 170 (2014). 1–24. https://doi.org/10.1163/22134379-17001002.

Fedman, David. *Seeds of Control: Japan's Empire of Forestry in Colonial Korea*. Seattle: University of Washington Press, 2020.

Fernandez, Joe. "Book Casts Shadow on Sabah History." *Free Malaysia Today News*, June 16, 2014.

Fieldhouse, David. *Colonialism 1870–1945: An Introduction*. London: Macmillan, 1983.

Finch, Steve. "Fighting and Fallout in Sabah." *The Diplomat*, March 5, 2013. https://thediplomat.com/2013/03/fighting-and-fallout-in-sabah/.

Fisher, John. "Man on the Spot: Captain George Gracey and British Policy towards the Assyrians, 1917–45." *Middle Eastern Studies* 44, no. 2 (2008): 215–35. https://doi.org/10.1080/00263200701874875.

Gagen, Mary. "The World's Tallest Known Tropical Tree Has Been Found—and Climbed." *National Geographic*, April 3, 2019. https://www.nationalgeographic.com/environment/article/worlds-tallest-tropical-tree-discovered-climbed-borneo.

Gallagher, John. *The Decline, Revival, and Fall of the British Empire*. Cambridge, Cambridge University Press, 1982.

Gargan, Edward A. "China Resumes Control of Hong Kong, Concluding 156 Years of British Rule." *New York Times*, July 1, 1997. https://www.nytimes.com/1997/07/01/world/china-resumes-control-of-hong-kong-concluding-156-years-of-british-rule.html.

Gaynor, Jennifer L. "Piracy in the Offing: The Law of the Lands and The Limits of Sovereignty at Sea" *Anthropological Quarterly* 85, no. 3 (2012): 817–57. https://doi.org/10.1353/anq.2012.0036.
Geldard, Geoffrey. "Rebel Radio Propaganda Lies Anger People of Sarawak." *Straits Times*, May 1, 1963.
Gleijeses, Piero. "Decolonization and the Cold War." In *The Oxford Handbook of the Ends of Empire*. edited by Martin Thomas and Andrew S. Thompson, 477–96. Oxford: Oxford University Press, 2018.
Glick, Henry Robert, "The Chinese Community in Sabah and the 1963 Election," *Asian Survey*, 5, no. 3 (1965): 144–51. https://doi.org/10.2307/2642404.
Grant, Jeremy. "'Sultan of Sulu' Invasion of Borneo Creates Problems in Malaysia, Philippines." *Washington Post*, March 4, 2013. https://www.washingtonpost.com/world/asia_pacific/sultan-of-sulu-invasion-of-borneo-creates-problems-in-malaysia-philippines/2013/03/04/b33829a8-84f2-11e2-98a3-b3db6b9ac586_story.html.
Granville-Edge, P. J. *The Sabahan: The Life and Death of Tun Fuad Stephens*. Kuala Lumpur: Writers' Publishing House, 1999.
Gray, Geoffrey. "W. E. H. Stanner: Wasted War Years." In *Scholars at War: Australasian Social Scientists, 1939–1945*, edited by Geoffrey Gray, Doug Munro, and Christine Winter, 95–116. Canberra: Australian National University Press, 2012. http://press-files.anu.edu.au/downloads/press/p166981/pdf/ch04.pdf.
Grilli, Enzo R. "Natural Rubber: A Better Future?" *Finance & Development* 18, no. 2 (June 1981): 1–29. https://doi.org/10.5089/9781616353452.022.
Haddad, Yvonne Yazbeck, and John L. Esposito. *Islam, Gender, and Social Change*. New York: Oxford University Press, 1998.
Hall, Kenneth R. "Upstream and Downstream Unification in Southeast Asia's First Islamic Polity: The Changing Sense of Community in the Fifteenth Century 'Hikyat Raja-Raja Pasai' Court Chronicle." *Journal of the Economic and Social History of the Orient* 44, no. 2 (2001): 198–229. https://doi.org/10.1163/156852001753731042.
Handbook of British North Borneo. London: William Cowie & Sons, 1890.
Harp, Stephen L. *A World History of Rubber: Empire, Industry, and the Everyday*. Chichester: Wiley Blackwell, 2016.
Harper, T. N., *The End of Empire and the Making of Malaya* (Cambridge: Cambridge University Press, 1999).
Harrisson, Tom. "Explorations in Central Borneo." *The Geographic Journal* 114, no. 4 (1949): 129–49. https://doi.org/10.2307/1789578.
Hatton, Joseph. "Frank Hatton in North Borneo." *The Century Magazine* 8 (1885): 437–46.
Hazis, Faisal S. "Domination, Contestation, and Accommodation: 54 Years of Sabah and Sarawak in Malaysia." *Southeast Asian Studies* 7, no. 3 (2018): 341–61. https://doi.org/10.20495/seas.7.3_341.
Heidhues, Mary F. Somers. "Peking and the Overseas Chinese: The Malaysian Dispute." *Asian Survey* 6, no. 5 (1966): 276–87. https://doi.org/10.2307/2642537.
Hernando, Orlando M. "The Philippine Claim to North Borneo." MA diss., Kansas State University, 1965.

Higgins, Andrew. "A Last Hurrah and an Empire Closes Down: China Again Master of Hong Kong." *Guardian* (Manchester), July 1, 1997. https://www.theguardian.com/world/1997/jul/01/china.andrewhiggins.

Hilmes, Michelle. "Radio and the Imagined Community." In *The Sound Studies Reader*, edited by Jonathan Sterne, 351–62.

Ho, Yin-Ping. *Trade, Industrial Restructuring and Development in Hong Kong.*, Basingstoke, UK: Macmillan, 1992.

Hoffman, L. C. *Straits Times*, January 19, 1963.

Hussin, Iza R. *The Politics of Islamic Law: Local Elites, Colonial Authority, and the Making of the Muslim State.* Chicago: University of Chicago Press, 2016.

Hutchison, C. S. *Geology of North-West Borneo: Sarawak, Brunei and Sabah.* Amsterdam: Elsevier, 2005.

Irwin, Graham. *Nineteenth-Century Borneo: A Study in Diplomatic Rivalry.* Leiden: Brill, 1955.

Jacobini, H. B. "Fundamentals of Philippine Policy Towards Malaysia." *Asian Survey* 4, no. 11 (1964): 1144–51. https://doi.org/10.2307/2642665.

Jasanoff, Maya. *The Dawn Watch: Joseph Conrad in a Global World.* London: William Collins, 2017.

John, David W., and James C. Jackson. "The Tobacco Industry of North Borneo: A Distinctive Form of Plantation Agriculture." *Journal of Southeast Asian Studies* 4, no. 1 (1974): 88–106. https://doi.org/10.1017/S002246340001643X.

Jones, L. W. "The Decline and Recovery of the Murut Tribe of Sabah." *Population Studies* 21, no. 2 (1967): 133–57. https://doi.org/10.1080/00324728.1967.10405470.

Jones, L. W. *The Population of Borneo: A Study of the Peoples of Sarawak, Sabah, and Brunei.* Kota Kinabalu: Opus Publications, 2007. First published 1966.

Jones, Matthew. *Conflict and Confrontation in South East Asia, 1961–1965.* Cambridge: Cambridge University Press, 2001.

Jones, Matthew. "Creating Malaysia: Singapore Security, the Borneo Territories, and the Contours of British Policy, 1961–63." *Journal of Imperial and Commonwealth History* 28, no. 2 (2000): 85–109. https://doi.org/10.1080/03086530008583091.

Josey, Alex. "Ace up Salim's Sleeve: Indonesia Will Be First to Recognise Aza." *Straits Times*, February 10, 1963.

Josey, Alex. "I Meet Azahari," *Straits Times*, January 19, 1963.

Josey, Alex. "It's Touch and Go: Our Men Wait Outside." *Straits Times*, February 7, 1963.

Josey, Alex. "Nair Warns: This Can Spark a War in S-E Asia." *Straits Times*, February 12, 1963.

Jua, Nantang Ben. "Indirect Rule in Colonial and Post-Colonial Cameroon." *Paideuma: Mitteilungen zur Kulturkunde* 41 (1995): 39–47. https://www.jstor.org/stable/40341691.

Julasman, Muham. "Tuwan Nahuda." In *Voices from Sulu: A Collection of Tausug Oral Traditions*, edited by Gerard Rixhon. Manila: Ateneo de Manila University Press, 2010.

Jurriens, Edwin. *From Monologue to Dialogue: Radio and Reform in Indonesia.* Leiden: KITLV Press, 2009.

Kadir, Norizan, and Suffian Mansor. "Menghidupkan Semula Institusi Kesultanan Sulu Melalui Tetutan ke atas Sabah, 1962–1986" [Reviving the Sultanate of Sulu through its claim over Sabah, 1962–1986]. *Akademika* 87, no. 3 (2017): 123–36. http://ejournal.ukm.my/akademika/issue/view/949.

Kahin, Audrey R., and George McT. Kahin. *Subversion as Foreign Policy: The Secret Eisenhower and Dulles Debacle in Indonesia.* New York: New Press, 1995.

Kahin, George McT. "Malaysia and Indonesia." *Pacific Affairs* 37, no. 3 (1964): 253–70. https://doi.org/10.2307/2754974.

Kahin, George McT. *Southeast Asia: A Testament* London: RoutledgeCurzon, 2003.

Kaur, Amarjit. *Economic Change in East Malaysia: Sabah and Sarawak since 1850.* London: Macmillan, 1998.

Keith, Agnes Newton, *White Man Returns.* Kota Kinabalu: Opus Publications, 2008. First published 1951.

Kelly, Matthew Kraig. *The Crime of Nationalism: Britain, Palestine, and Nation-Building on the Fringe of Empire.* Oakland: University of California Press, 2017.

Kib, Mat Zin Bin Mat. "Christianization in Sabah and the Development of Indigenous Communities: A Historical Study." *Journal of the Malaysian Branch of the Royal Asiatic Society* 77, no. 1 (2004): 53–65. https://www.jstor.org/stable/41493514.

Kratostka, Paul, ed. Prologue in *Southeast Asian Minorities in the Wartime Japanese Empire.* London: RoutledgeCurzon, 2002.

Kusumawati, Rini, and Leontine Visser. "Capturing the Elite in Marine Conservation in Northeast Kalimantan." *Human Ecology* 44, no. 3 (2016): 301–10. https://doi.org/10.1007/s10745-016-9830-0.

Lambourn, Elizabeth. "Tombstones, Texts and Typologies: Seeing Sources for the Early History of Islam in Southeast Asia." *Journal of the Economic and Social History of the Orient* 51, no. 2 (2008): 252–86. https://doi.org/10.1163/156852008X307447.

Leake, David. *Brunei: The Modern Southeast-Asian Islamic Sultanate.* London: McFarland, 1989.

Lee, Francis L. F., et al. "Hong Kong's Summer of Uprising: From Anti-Extradition to Anti-Authoritarian Protests." *China Review* 19, no. 4 (2019): 1–32. https://muse.jhu.edu/pub/250/article/743118.

Lee, Y. L. "The Population of British Borneo" *Population Studies* 15, no. 3 (1962): 226–43. https://doi.org/10.1080/00324728.1962.10406073.

Legge, J. D. *Sukarno: A Political Biography.* New York: Praeger Publishers, 1972.

Leow, Rachel. *Taming Babel: Language in the Making of Malaysia.* Cambridge: Cambridge University Press, 2018.

Lindsay, Jennifer. "Making Waves: Private Radio and Local Identities in Indonesia." In special issue on Language and Media, *Indonesia*, no. 64 (1997), 105–23. https://doi.org/10.2307/3351437.

Liow, Joseph Chinyong. "Tunku Abdul Rahman and Malaya's Relations with Indonesia, 1957–1960." *Journal of Southeast Asian Studies* 36, no. 1 (2005): 87–109. https://doi.org/10.1017/S0022463405000044.

Liu, Anthony K., John R. Apel, and James R. Holbrook. "Nonlinear Internal Wave Evolution in the Sulu Sea." *Journal of Physical Oceanography* 15, no. 1 (1985): 1613–24. https://doi.org/10.1175/1520-0485(1985)015%3C1613:NIWEIT%3E2.0.CO;2.

Long, Gavin Merrick. *Australia in the War of 1939–1945*, 1st ser., vol. 7., *The Final Campaigns*. Canberra: Australian War Memorial, 1963.

Louis, Wm. Roger. *Ends of British Imperialism: The Scramble for Empire, Suez and Decolonization*. London: I. B. Tauris, 2006.

Lovegrove, Peter. "Borneo's Dusuns Rewarded." *Singapore Free Press*, October 29, 1947.

Luping, Herman J. "The Kadazans and Sabah Politics." PhD diss., Victoria University of Wellington, 1985.

Luping, Herman J. *Sabah's Dilemma: The Political History of Sabah, 1960–1994*. Kuala Lumpur: Magnus Books, 1994.

Ma, Ngok. *Political Development in Hong Kong: State Political Society, and Civil Society*. Hong Kong: Hong Kong University Press, 2007.

Macapagal, Diosdado. "State-of-the-Nation Message to the Congress of the Philippines." *Official Gazette*, January 28, 1963.

Macaraeg, Federico. "Borneo Claim by PI Pressed." *The Forum*, December 20, 1961.

Macaskie, Charles. F. C. *End of an Era: The Borneo Reminiscences of C. F. C. Macaskie, C. M. G.* Kota Kinabalu: Opus Publications, 2011.

Mahmud, Nik Anuar Nik. *Tuntutan Filipina Ke Atas Borneo Utara* [The Philippine claim to North Borneo]. Kuala Lumpur: Penerbit Universiti Kebangsaan Malaysia, 2009.

Majul, Cesar Adib. "Political and Historical Notes on the Old Sulu Sultanate." *Journal of the Malaysian Branch of the Royal Asiatic Society* 38, no. 1 (1965): 23–42. https://www.jstor.org/stable/41491838.

Makdisi, Ussama. "Anti-imperialism, Missionary Work, and the King-Crane Commission." In *Empire's Twin: US Anti-imperialism from the Founding Era to the Age of Terrorism*, edited by Ian Tyrrell and Jay Sexton, 118–36. Ithaca, NY: Cornell University Press, 2015.

"Malaysian Air Crash Kills 11." *Sarasota Herald Tribune*, June 7, 1976.

Manickam, Sandra Khor. *Taming the Wild: Aborigines and Racial Knowledge in Colonial Malaya*. Singapore: National University of Singapore Press, 2015.

Manila Accord between the Philippines, the Federation of Malaya and Indonesia, signed at Manila, July 31, 1963. 550 United Nations Treaty Series 8029. https://treaties.un.org/doc/publication/unts/volume%20550/volume-550-i-8029-english.pdf.

Maria, Bernard Sta. *Peter J. Mojuntin, the Golden Son of the Kadazan*. Seremban: Chang Lithho Press, 1978.

Massey, Andrew. *The Political Economy of Stagnation: British North Borneo Under the Chartered Company, 1881–1946*. Kota Kinabalu: Arkib Negeri Sabah, 2006.

McCann, Gerard. "Where was the *Afro* in Afro-Asian Solidarity? Africa's 'Bandung Moment' in 1950s Asia." *Journal of World History* 30, no. 1–2 (2019): 93–120. https://doi.org/10.1515/9789400604346-006.

Meadows, Martin. "The Philippine Claim to North Borneo." *Political Science Quarterly* 77, no. 3 (1962): 321–35. https://doi.org/10.2307/2146308.

Medhurst, Walter H. "Preface." In *North Borneo: Explorations and Adventures on the Equator*, by Frank Hatton. London: Sampson Low, Marston, Searle & Rivington, 1886.

Meijer, Willem. "Plant Geographic Studies on Dipterocarpaceae in Malesia." *Annals of the Missouri Botanical Garden* 61, no. 3 (1974): 806. https://doi.org/10.2307/2395031.
Mjöberg, Eric. *I Tropikernas Villande Urskogar* [Forest life and adventures in the Malay Archipelago]. Kota Kinabalu: Natural History Publications (Borneo), 1999. First published 1928.
Mojuntin, Peter J. *The Golden Son of the Kadazan*. Seremban: Chang Lithho Press, 1978.
Moo-Tan, Stella, ed. *The Diaries of George C. Woolley*, vol. 4. Kota Kinabalu: Department of Sabah Museum, 2018.
Moran, Jonathan "Life and Death in a Pitcher." *Natural History* 115, no. 8 (2006): 56–62.
Muslih, Muhammad. "Arab Politics and the Rise of Palestinian Nationalism." *Journal of Palestinian Studies* 16, no. 4 (1987): 77–94. https://doi.org/10.2307/2536721.
Nadeau, Kathleen. *The History of the Philippines*. Westport, CT: Greenwood, 2008.
Nagara, Bunn. "Why the Philippines Has No Justifiable Claim to Sabah and Never Had." *South China Morning Post*, November 1, 2020. https://www.scmp.com/week-asia/opinion/article/3107859/why-philippines-has-no-justifiable-claim-sabah-and-never-had.
Nah, Alice M. "(Re)mapping Indigenous 'Race'/Place in Postcolonial Peninsular Malaysia." *Geografiska Annaler. Series B, Human Geography* 88, no. 3 (2006): 285–97. https://doi.org/10.1111/j.1468-0459.2006.00222.x.
Ng, Eileen. "Ban on Book about ex-Sabah Leader Stays, Says Zahid." *Malaysian Insider*, May 25, 2015.
Ngoei, Wen-Qing. *Arc of Containment: Britain, the United States, and Anticommunism in Southeast Asia*. Ithaca, NY: Cornell University Press, 2019.
Nicolson, Harold. "The Colonial Problem." *International Affairs* 17, no. 1 (1938): 32–50. https://doi.org/10.2307/2602169.
Nisperos, Nestor Martinez. *Philippine Foreign Policy on the North Borneo Question*. Ann Arbor, MI: University Microfilms International, 1981.
Nordhult, Henk Schulte. "Indonesia in the 1950s: Nation, Modernity, and the Post-Colonial State." *Bijdragen tot de Taal-, Land- end Volkenkunde*. 167, no. 4 (2011): 386–404. https://doi.org/10.1163/22134379-90003577.
Odell, Laurence H. "Philippines Urged to Survey Outlying Neglected Islands." *Far Eastern Review Survey* 8, no. 10 (1939): 119–20. https://doi.org/10.2307/3023095.
Ongkili, James P. "The 'Dacing' in Sabah and Sarawak." *Southeast Asian Affairs* (1975): 109–14. https://www.jstor.org/stable/27908247.
Ongkili, James P. *Nation-Building in Malaysia: 1946–1974*. Singapore: Oxford University Press, 1985.
Ooi, Jin Bee. *Tropical Deforestation: The Tyranny of Time*. Singapore: National University of Singapore, 1993.
Ooi, Keat Gin. *The Japanese Occupation of Borneo, 1941–1945*. London: Routledge, 2011.
Ooi, Keat Gin. *Post-War Borneo: Nationalism, Empire and State-Building*. London: Routledge, 2013.
Ooi, Keat Gin, "Prelude to Invasion: Covert Operations before the Re-occupation of Northwest Borneo, 1944–45." *Journal of the Australian War Memorial*, no. 37 (2002). https://www.awm.gov.au/articles/journal/j37/borneo.

Payus, Carolyn et al. "Impact of Extreme Drought Climate on Water Security in North Borneo: Case Study of Sabah" *Water* 12, no. 1135 (2020): 1–19. https://doi.org/10.3390/w12041135.

Peckham, Robert. "Game of Empires: Hunting in Treaty-Port China, 1870–1940." In *Eco-Cultural Networks and the British Empire: New Views on Environmental History*, edited by James Beattie, Edward Melillo, and Emily O'Gorman, 202–232. London: Bloomsbury Academic, 2015.

Phillips, David. "Borneo History: Time for a New Look?" *Journal of the Malay Branch of the Royal Asiatic Society* 89, vol. 2 (2016): 45–65. https://doi.org/10.1353/ras.2016.0024.

Phillips, David. "The 'Migrated Archives' and a Forgotten Corner of Empire: The British Borneo Territories." *Journal of Imperial and Commonwealth History* 44, no. 6 (2016): 1007. https://doi.org/10.1080/03086534.2016.1251557.

Phillips, Tom, and Alex Healey. "'I Should Have Done More': Chris Patten on Leaving Hong Kong without Democracy." *Guardian* (Manchester), June 28, 2017. https://www.theguardian.com/world/2017/jun/28/i-should-have-done-more-chris-patten-leaving-hong-kong-without-democracy-china.

Pitlo III, Lucio Blanco. "Why the Philippines' Sabah Claim against Malaysia Isn't a Land Grab." *South China Morning Post*, September 18, 2020. https://www.scmp.com/week-asia/opinion/article/3101954/why-philippines-sabah-claim-against-malaysia-isnt-land-grab.

Poling, Gregory, Phoebe DePadua, and Jennifer Frentasia. "The Royal Army of Sulu Invades Malaysia." *Centre for Strategic and International Studies: Critical Questions*, March 8, 2013. https://www.csis.org/analysis/royal-army-sulu-invades-malaysia.

Press, Steven. *Rogue Empires: Contracts and Conmen in Europe's Scramble for Africa*. Cambridge, MA: Harvard University Press, 2017.

Quirino, Elpidio. "Nationhood and Father Burgos." In *The Making of the Filipino Nation and Republic*, edited by Jose V. Abueva, 172. Manila: University of the Philippines Press, 1998. First published 1947.

R. L. "Amid Disaster, the Good Life." *Straits Times*, January 31, 1963.

Radius, Mohammed Jefri. "The Rundum Incident Was More of a War than a Rebellion." *Daily Express* (Malaysia), April 22, 2012. https://www.dailyexpress.com.my/read.cfm?NewsID=882.

Rahman, Abdul. *Political Awakening*. Petaling Jaya: Pelanduk Publications, 1986.

Ramli, Nordin. "The History of Offshore Hydrocarbon Exploration in Malaysia." *Energy* 10, no. 3–4 (1985): 457–73. https://doi.org/10.1016/0360-5442(85)90060-X.

Reid, Anthony. *Imperial Alchemy: Nationalism and Political Identity in Southeast Asia*. Cambridge: Cambridge University Press, 2009.

Report of the Commission of Enquiry, North Borneo and Sarawak. London: Her Majesty's Stationery Office, 1962.

Rice, Tom. "Merdeka for Malaya: Imagining Independence across the British Empire." In *The Colonial Documentary Film in South and South-East Asia*, edited by Ian Aitken and Camille Deprez, 45–62. Edinburgh: Edinburgh University Press, 2017).

Richards, Peter C. "A New Flag Now Flies over the 'Turtle Island.'" *Sunday Times* (Perth), December 14, 1947.

Roff, Margaret. "The Rise and Demise of Kadazan Nationalism." *Journal of Southeast Asian History* 10, no. 2 (1969): 326–43. https://doi.org/10.1017/S0217781100004439.

Roxas, Manuel. "Providing for the Administration of the Turtle and Mangsee Islands." Philippine Government Executive Order No. 95, *Official Gazette*, October 13, 1947.

Rutter, Owen. *British North Borneo: An Account of its History, Resources and Native Tribes*. London: Constable, 1922.

Saham, Junid. *British Industrial Investment in Malaysia, 1963–1971*. Kuala Lumpur: Oxford University Press, 1980.

Samad, Johan Arriffin. "The 1963 Malaysia Agreement: Pakatan's Failed Restoration and Perikatan's Fledgling Initiatives." In *Sabah from the Ground: The 2020 Elections and the Politics of Survival*, edited by Bridget Welsh, Vilashini Somiah, and Benjamin Y. H. Loh, 39–60. Singapore: ISEAS Publishing, 2021.

Samad, Paridah Abd., and Darusalam Abu Bakar. "Malaysia-Philippines Relations: The Issue of Sabah." *Asian Survey* 32, no. 6 (1992): 554–67. https://doi.org/10.2307/2645160.

Santacroce, Luigi, Raffaele Del Prete, Ioannis Alexandros Charitos, and Lucrezia Bottalico. "*Mycobacterium leprae*: A Historical Study on the Origins of Leprosy and Its Social Stigma." *Infez Med* 29, no. 4 (2021): 623–32. https://doi.org/10.53854/liim-2904-18.

Sarda, James. "Saudin—the Murut 'Marco Polo.'" *Daily Express* (Sabah), November 22, 2009. http://www.dailyexpress.com.my/read/230/saudin-the-murut-marco-polo-/.

Sarkawi, Suhana binti, and Datu Sanib bin Said. "Borneo in the Eyes of Joseph Conrad." *Jurnal Kalijaga* 2, no. 1 (2013): 10–20.

Saunders, David R. "Brokering a Postcolonial Malaysia: How Local Elites Shaped the Cobbold Commission, 1961–63." *Critical Military Studies*. Published ahead of print, November 10, 2023. https://doi.org/10.1080/23337486.2023.2268958.

Saunders, David R. "Dimming the Seas around Borneo: Contesting Island Sovereignty and Lighthouse Administration amidst the End of Empire, 1946–1948." *TRaNS: Trans-Regional and -National Studies of Southeast Asia* 7, no. 2 (2019): 181–207. https://doi.org/10.1017/trn.2019.5.

Saunders, David R. "The Friction of Distance in Borneo: Migration, Economic Change and Geographic Space in Sabah." *World History Connected* 17, no. 3 (2020). https://worldhistoryconnected.press.uillinois.edu/17.3/Sabha.html.

Saunders, David R. "'State of Intoxication:' Governing Alcohol and Disease in the Forests of British North Borneo." *eTropic: Electronic Journal of Studies in the Tropics* 20, no. 1 (2021): 202–225. https://doi.org/10.25120/etropic.20.1.2021.3779.

Saw, Swee-Hock and Chiu Wing Kin. "Population Growth and Redistribution in Hong Kong, 1841–1975." *Southeast Asian Journal of Social Science* 4, no. 1 (1975): 123–30. https://doi.org/10.1163/080382476X00101.

Sawatan, Kelimen. "Real Cause of Air Crash Never Made Known—Yong." *Borneo Post Online*, December 23, 2011. https://www.theborneopost.com/2011/12/23/real-cause-of-air-crash-never-made-known-yong/.

Scalice, Joseph. "Crisis of Revolutionary Leadership: Martial Law and the Communist Parties of the Philippines, 1959–1974." PhD diss., University of California, Berkeley, 2017.
Schult, Volker. "Sulu and Germany in the Late Nineteenth Century." *Philippine Studies* 48, no. 1 (2000): 80–108. http://www.philippinestudies.net/ojs/index.php/ps/article/view/439/4567.
Seitelman, Max. "The Cession of Sarawak." *Far Eastern Survey* 17, no. 3 (1948): 35–37.
Shafie, Ghazali. *Ghazali Shafie's Memoir: On the Formation of Malaysia*. Kuala Lumpur: Penerbit Universiti Kebangaan Malaysia, 2004.
Shaw, Alexander N. "British Counterinsurgency in Brunei and Sarawak, 1962–1963: Developing Best Practices in the Shadow of Malaya." *Small Wars & Insurgencies* 27, no. 4 (2016): 702–25. https://doi.org/10.1080/09592318.2016.1190052.
Shenkin, Alexander, Chris J. Chandler, Doreen S. Boyd, Toby Jackson, Mathias Disney, Noreen Majalap, Reuben Nilus et al. "The World's Tallest Tropical Tree in Three Dimensions." *Frontiers in Forest and Global Change* 2, no. 32 (2019): 3. https://doi.org/10.3389/ffgc.2019.00032.
Sheridan, L. A. "Constitutional Problems of Malaysia." *International and Comparative Law Quarterly* 13, no. 4 (1964): 1349–67. https://doi.org/10.1093/iclqaj/13.4.1349.
Shibley, Gregory J. "Revisiting Hitti's Thoughts on Palestine and Arab Identity." *Arab Studies Quarterly* 41, no. 2 (2019): 150–71. https://doi.org/10.13169/arabstudquar.41.2.0150.
Shipway, Martin. *Decolonization and its Impact: A Comparative Approach to the End of the Colonial Empires*. Oxford: Wiley-Blackwell, 2008.
Silver, Lynette Ramsay. *Sandakan: A Conspiracy of Silence*. Kota Kinabalu: Opus Publications, 2007)
The Singapore Free Press and Mercantile Adviser, August 31, 1899.
Singh, Ranjit D. S. *The Making of Sabah, 1865–1941: The Dynamics of Indigenous Society*. Kuala Lumpur: University of Malaya Press, 2000.
Sivasundaram, Sujit. *Islanded: Britain, Sri Lanka and the Bounds of an Indian Ocean Colony*. Chicago: University of Chicago Press, 2013.
Sligo, Graeme. *Backroom Boys: Alfred Conlon and Army's Directorate of Research and Civil Affairs, 1942–46*. Sydney: Big Sky Publishing, 2016.
Smith, T. E. "Proposals for Malaysia." *The World Today* 18, no. 5 (1962): 192–200. https://www.jstor.org/stable/40393401.
Soh, Tiang Keong. "Maphilindo Seen as Third Force." *Straits Times*, August 14, 1963.
Somiah, Vilashini. *Irregular Migrants and the Sea at the Borders of Sabah, Malaysia: Pelagic Alliance*. Cham: Palgrave Macmillan, 2021.
Sopiee, Mohammed Noordin. "The Advocacy of Malaysia—Before 1961." *Modern Asian Studies* 7, no. 4 (1973): 717–32. https://doi.org/10.1017/S0026749X00013500.
Steckman, Laura. "The Abu Sayyaf–ISIS Nexus: Rising Extremism and its Implications for Malaysia." *Counter Terrorist Trends and Analyses* 8, no. 5 (2016): 16–21. https://www.rsis.edu.sg/wp-content/uploads/2016/05/CTTA-May-2016.pdf.
Steedly, Mary Margaret. *Rifle Reports: A Story of Indonesian Independence*. Berkeley: University of California Press, 2013.

Stockwell, A. J. "Malaysia: The Making of a Neo-Colony?" *Journal of Imperial and Commonwealth History* 26, no. 2 (1998): 138–56. https://doi.org/10.1080/03086539808583029.

Stockwell, A. J., ed. *British Documents on the End of Empire*, series B, vol. 8, *Malaysia*. London: The Stationary Office, 2004.

Stockwell, Sarah. "Britain and Decolonisation in an Era of Global Change." In *The Oxford Handbook of the Ends of Empire*, edited by Martin Thomas and Andrew S. Thompson, 65–84. Oxford: Oxford University Press, 2018.

Stoecker, Helmuth, and Peter Sebald. "Enemies of the Colonial Idea." In *Germans in the Tropics: Essays in German Colonial History*, edited by Arthur J. Knoll and Lewis H. Gann (Westport, CT: Greenwood Press, 1987).

Stoler, Ann Laura. *Along the Archival Grain: Epistemic Realities and Colonial Common Sense*. Princeton, NJ: Princeton University Press, 2008.

Strayer, Robert. "Decolonization, Democratization, and Communist Reform: The Soviet Collapse in Comparative Perspective." *Journal of World History* 12, no. 2 (2001): 375–406. https://doi.org/10.1353/jwh.2001.0042.

Subritzky, John. "Britain, Konfrontasi, and the End of Empire in Southeast Asia, 1961–65." *Journal of Imperial and Commonwealth History* 28, no. 3 (2000): 209–27. https://doi.org/10.1080/03086530008583106.

Sussman, Gerald. "Macapagal, the Sabah Claim and Maphilindo: The Politics of Penetration" *Journal of Contemporary Asia* 13, no. 2, (1983): 210–28. https://doi.org/10.1080/00472338380000141.

Sutherland, Heather. "Southeast Asian History and the Mediterranean Analogy." *Journal of Southeast Asian Studies* 34, no. 1 (2003): 1–20. https://doi.org/10.1017/S0022463403000018.

Tagliacozzo, Eric. "Borneo in Fragments: Geology, Biota, and Contraband in Trans-national Circuits." *TRaNS: Trans-Regional and -National Studies of Southeast Asia* 1, no. 1, (2013): 63–85. https://doi.org/10.1017/trn.2012.8.

Tagliacozzo, Eric. "Kettle on a Slow Boil: Batavia's Threat Perceptions in the Indies' Outer Islands, 1870–1910." *Journal of Southeast Asian Studies* 31, no. 1 (2000): 70–100. https://doi.org/10.1017/S0022463400015885.

Tagliacozzo, Eric. "Onto the Coasts and Into the Forests: Ramifications of the China Trade on the Ecological History of Northwest Borneo, 900–1900 CE." In *Histories of the Borneo Environment: Economic, Political and Social Dimensions of Change and Continuity*, edited by Reed L. Wadley, 25–59. Leiden: KITLV Press, 2005. https://doi.org/10.1163/9789004454279_004.

Tan, Tai Yong,. *Creating "Greater Malaysia": Decolonization and the Politics of Merger*. Singapore: Institute of Southeast Asian Studies, 2008.

Tarling, Nicholas. "Kennedy P. G. Tregonning." *Borneo Research Bulletin*, January 1, 2016. https://link.gale.com/apps/doc/A503262432/AONE?u=anon~6beed223&sid=googleScholar&xid=1ee389e3.

Tarling, Nicholas. *Sulu and Sabah: A Study of British Policy towards the Philippines and North Borneo from the Late Eighteenth Century*. Oxford: Oxford University Press, 1978.

Tatu, Frank. "The United States Consul, the Yankee Raja, Ellena and the *Constitution*: A Historical Vignette." *Archipel* 40 (1990): 79–90. https://www.persee.fr/doc/arch_0044-8613_1990_num_40_1_2667.

Taylor, Alastair M. "Malaysia, Indonesia—and Maphilindo." *International Journal* 19, no. 2 (1964): 155–71. https://doi.org/10.1177/002070206401900202.
Teoh, Shannon. "Philippines' Claim over Sabah Becomes Hot Topic in State Polls." *Straits Times*, September 22, 2020. https://www.straitstimes.com/asia/se-asia/philippines-claim-over-sabah-becomes-hot-topic-at-state-polls.
Thio, Eunice. "Some Aspects of the Federation of the Malay States." *Journal of the Malaysian Branch of the Royal Asiatic Society* 40, no. 2 (1967): 3–15. https://www.jstor.org/stable/41491921.
Thomas, Lowell, ed. *Nations of the World: Hong Kong*. Portland, OR: Sawyer's View-Master Series, n.d.).
Tilman, Robert O. "Malaysia: The Problems of Federation." *Political Research Quarterly* 16, no. 4 (1963): 897–911. https://doi.org/10.1177/106591296301600409.
Tomlin, Gregory M. *Murrow's Cold War: Public Diplomacy for the Kennedy Administration*. Lincoln: University of Nebraska Press, 2016.
Tregonning, Kennedy. "American Activity in North Borneo, 1865–1881." *Pacific Historical Review* 23, no. 4 (1954): 357–72. https://doi.org/10.2307/3634654.
Tregonning, Kennedy. *North Borneo*. London: Her Majesty's Stationery Office, 1960.
Ueno, Itsuyoshi. *An End to a War: A Japanese Soldier's Experience of the 1945 Death Marches of North Borneo*. Translated by Mika Reilly. Kota Kinabalu: Opus Publications, 2012.
United Nations. *World Economic Survey*. Pt. 2, "Current Economic Developments." United Nations: New York, 1964.
Van der Kroef, Justus. "The Dynamics of Communism in Malaysia." *Communist Affairs* 3, no. 3 (1965): 4–10. https://doi.org/10.1016/0588-8174(65)90022-7.
Van Nieuwstadt, Mark G. L., and Douglas Sheil. "Drought, Fire, and Tree Survival in a Borneo Rain Forest, East Kalimantan, Indonesia." *Journal of Ecology* 93, no. 1 (2005): 191–201. https://doi.org/10.1111/j.1365-2745.2004.00954.x.
Vartavarian, Mesrob. "Imperial Ambiguities: The United States and Philippine Muslims." *South East Asia Research* 26, no. 2 (2018): 132–46. https://doi.org/10.1177/0967828X18769224.
Wallach, Yair. "Creating a Country through Currency and Stamps: State Symbols and Nation-Building in British-Ruled Palestine." *Nations and Nationalism* 17, no. 1 (2010): 1–19. https://doi.org/10.1111/j.1469-8129.2010.00470.x.
Wallach, Yair. "Trapped in Mirror-Images: The Rhetoric of Maps in Israel/Palestine" *Political Geography* 30, no. 7 (September 2011): 358–69. https://doi.org/10.1016/j.polgeo.2011.07.004.
Warren, James Francis. *The North Borneo Chartered Company's Administration of the Bajau, 1878–1909: The Pacification of a Maritime, Nomadic People*. Athens: Ohio University, Center for International Studies, 1971.
Warren, James Francis. "Slave Markets and Exchange in the Malay World: The Sulu Sultanate, 1770–1878." *Journal of Southeast Asian Studies* 8, no. 2 (1977): 162–75. https://doi.org/10.1017/S0022463400009322.
Warren, James Francis. *The Sulu Zone: The Dynamics of External Trade, Slavery, and Ethnicity in the Transformation of a Southeast Asian Maritime State, 1768–1898*. Singapore: Singapore University Press, 1981.
Watson, Philip J. "The History of Rubber Statistics." International Rubber Study Group, 1999.

Weekley, Kathleen. "The National or the Social? Problems of Nation-Building in Post–World War II Philippines." In "From Nation-Building to State-Building," special issue, *Third World Quarterly* 27, no. 1 (2006): 85–100. https://doi.org/10.1080/01436590500369253.

White, Nicholas J. *British Business in Post-Colonial Malaysia, 1957–1970: "Neocolonialism" or "Disengagement"?* London: RoutledgeCurzon, 2004.

White, Nicholas J. "The Survival, Revival and Decline of British Economic Influence in Malaysia, 1957–1970." *Twentieth Century British History* 14, no. 3 (2003): 222–42. https://doi.org/10.1093/tcbh/14.3.222.

Wong, Danny Tze Ken. *Historical Sabah: Community and Society.* Kota Kinabalu: Natural History Publications, 2004.

Wong, Danny Tze Ken. *Historical Sabah: The War.* Kota Kinabalu: Opus Publications, 2010.

Wong, Danny Tze Ken. "The Name of Sabah and the Sustaining of a New Identity in a New Nation" *Archipel* 89 (2015): 161–78. https://journals.openedition.org/archipel/495.

Wong, Joshua. "Hong Kong's International Front Line: Risks and Opportunities." *Journal of International Affairs* 73, no. 2 (2020): 261–68. https://www.jstor.org/stable/26939983.

Wood, James. *History of International Broadcasting.* London: Peter Peregrinus, 1994.

Wright, Leigh R. "The Anglo-Spanish-German Treaty of 1885: A Step in the Development of British Hegemony in North Borneo." *Australian Journal of Politics and History* 18, no. 1 (1972): 62–75.

Yacob, Shakila and Nicholas J. White. "The 'Unfinished Business' of Malaysia's Decolonisation: The Origins of the Guthrie 'Dawn Raid.'" *Modern Asian Studies* 44, no. 5 (2010): 919–60. https://doi.org/10.1017/S0026749X09990308.

Yamamoto, Hiroyuki. "'Foreigners' Nationalism' in Malaysia: Donald Stephens and K. Bali in Making of Sabah Nationhood." *Jurnal Sejarah* 9, no. 9 (2001): 49–70.

Yusop, Mohamad. "The Malaysia Plan and the First Brunei Elections, 1962." *Journal of the Malay Branch of the Royal Asiatic Society* 71, no. 1 (1998): 55–73. https://www.jstor.org/stable/41493352.

Zhou, Taomo. "Ambivalent Alliance: Chinese Policy towards Indonesia, 1960–1965." *China Quarterly* 221 (2015): 208–28. https://doi.org/10.1017/S0305741014001544.

Index

Note: locators with *n* denote footnotes. *Page numbers in italics refer to figures.*

Abang Ahmend Zulkipli, 109, 121
Abell, Anthony, 171, 178, 181
Afro-Asian Conference (Moshi, Tanganyika), 110–111, 115, 126
agriculture, colonial government policies, 37, 51–56. *See also* cash crops
Ahmed, A. J. Alli, 10
Alam bin Datu Jinurain, 79
Anak Sabah (Sons of Sabah), 79
Anak Siti Khatijah, *20*
Antanum, Ontoros, 54
anticolonialism: asserting postwar control over Sabah and, 41–42; in Brunei, 107–108; economic issues and, 64, 71, 72; ethnic divisions and, 194–195; Philippine claim to Sabah and, 145; increase in colonial power in Sabah and, 30; Indonesia and, 121–122; local elites and, 10–11, 65, 77–78, 96–97; of Mustapha, 96–97; postwar suffering and emergence of, 97–98; Radio Kalimantan Utara and, 116
anticolonial opposition, 93–98
Anti-Japanese Martyrs' Affairs Office, 49
anti-Malaysia politicians on Sabah, lobbied to support Malaysia plan, 183–185
anti-Malaysia sentiment in Sabah, 14, 166–167, 173–174, 182–183, 190–191; political parties and, 175–177
archipelagic unity in Southeast Asia, Britain and, 48
Arusap bin Sokongan, 76–77
Ashwin, C. R., 154
Association of Southeast Asia (ASA), 146
Association of Southeast Asian Nations (ASEAN), 153
Australian administration of Sabah, 35–36, 40–41
Awang Abdul Hapidz bin Laksamana, 109
Awang Hashim, 180–181

Azahari, Saibah, 29
Azahari bin Sheikh Mahmud, 216n51; Brunei Rebellion and, 102, 108–109; calls for rebellion, 190; in Indonesia, 113, 115; Kalimantan Utara movement and, 103, 109–113; *merdeka* and, 122–123; Osmena and, 141; in Philippines, 144; Radio Kalimantan Utara and, 114–116; United Front Against Malaysia and, 174; wives of, 29, 218n85. *See also* Kalimantan Utara movement

Bajaus, 17, 51–52, 83, 90, 129, 163, 175
Balangingi Samal communities, 139
Baldwin, Charles F., on manifest destiny syndrome of Southeast Asian leaders, 161
Barlocco, Fausto, 87
Barlow, John, 45
Batavia Radio Association, 117
Benda, Harry, 73
Berhala Island, 4, 49, 82, 130
Berita Harian (newspaper), 113, 115
Bevins, Vincent, 26
Bevis, William, 66
Beyer, Henry Otley, 132
Bickers, Robert, 3
Black, Ian, 132
Blamey, Thomas, 40
Boestaman, Ahmad, 216n43
Bombay Burmah Trading Corporation, 71
Borneo: colonial fascination with, 5; colonialism and natural resources of, 2, 4, 11, 17, 48–49; connections to Malaya, 162; desire for territory in, 127–128; failed attempts to form independent federation, 15; lure of natural resources of, 65, 152, 164–165; regional importance of, 221n4; relation to Philippines, 127–129, 130–131, 221n6

255

Borneo fever, 212n68
Borneo Mail (newspaper), 88
Borneo Planning Unit, 39, 40
boundedness, island, 198n12
Brassey, Thomas, 17–18
Britain: desire to combine Singapore and Malaya, 168; importance and advantages of Projek Malaysia for, 104–105, 156–158, 164; interest in Borneo, 19; Kalimantan Utara and, 111–112; Malaya, support for the Sumatran rebels, and, 106–107; Malayan independence and, 168–169; piracy in Sulu Sea and, 137–138, 150; plan to retain control of Sabah postwar, 39–42; postwar annexation/colonization of Sabah, 10, 37, 39, 44–48, 226n81; postwar annexation of Sarawak, 42–44; question of whether Borneo territory owned or leased, 142–143; strategies for creating Malaysia, 177–185; takeover of North Borneo Chartered Company, 44–46, 226n81; talks about Philippines' claim to Sabah, 149–150; transfer of Turtle Islands to Philippines, 135–136
British Borneo Civil Affairs Unit, 39–41
British Borneo Timber Company, 71
British Empire, study of decolonization, 24
British metropolitan policymakers: Brunei Rebellion and, 108; fear of spread of communism and, 118, 155, 164; Philippine territorial claims in Sabah and, 141–142, 150; indirect rule and, 74; labor shortages in Sabah and, 57–58, 61; logging industry and, 68–69; Projek Malaysia and, 10–11, 13–14, 25–26, 38, 97–98, 101, 159, 164, 170–171, 173, 176, 187, 194; radio propaganda and, 118, 119; rubber industry and, 55, 56
British metropolitans, Projek Malaysia and, 170, 171–173
Brooke, James, Sarawak territory and, 18, 131–132
Brooke, Vyner, 42, 43
Brooks, Ronald J., 36, 86–87, 118, 171–172
Brunei: colonization and, 18–19; Kalimantan Utara and, 15; North Borneo Chartered Company and, 19–20; Projek Malaysia and, 12, 103, 107–113; Turnbull plan and, 122, 170–171
Brunei Rebellion, 102, 103, 108–109, 125, 145, 177
Brunei Sultanate, 17, 18, 39, 130, 131–132
Bulungan Sultanate, 17, 39, 130

Cantonese community, 15, 118, 163, 182
cash crops: colonial government's emphasis on, 53, 54–55, 58–59; reinvigoration of, 56–62
Chang Ah Foo, 182
Chan Wing Cheong, 79
Che Awang Mohammad Thaufeck, 183
Chin, Peter, 175
China: connections to Borneo, 15, 17, 65; market for Borneo hardwoods in, 66; migration to Borneo from, 53, 95, 118
Chinese communities on Sabah, 72; conflict with Mustapha, 95–96; education system and, 87–88; growth of, 163; Maphilindo and, 154; marginalization of after federation, 191; Projek Malaysia and, 13, 174, 183; Sabah independence and, 123–124; wariness of among local elites, 174
Chinese War Victims Relief Association, 49
Chung, Nicholas, 138
Cid, Cipriano, 112
civil-political development in Sabah, 174–177
climate, Borneo, 53–54
Cobbold, Cameron, 163–164, 178, 179, 180
Cobbold Commission of Enquiry, 10, 112, 171, 178–182, 184
Cobbold Commission Report, 163–164
Cocos Islands, relocation of population to Sabah and Singapore, 60
Cold War, formation of Malaysia and, 105, 166–168, 230n7. *See also* communism
colonial competition over Borneo, 131–132
colonial documents, as research sources, 28, 29–30
colonial government. *See* Crown Colony government
colonialism: post–World War II, 62; rethinking postwar, 41–42; as route to postwar rehabilitation and development, 47
colonial patronage, systems of, 93–98
colonial rule: ethnic rivalry and, 190; expansion of in postwar Sabah, 48–50, 194; Sabah's merger with Malaysia and extension of type of, 191–192, 194. *See also* Crown Colony government; North Borneo Chartered Company
colonials, relationship to indigenous peoples, 3–4
colonization in South China Sea, 17–18
communism: claims to Sabah and threats of, 145–146; fear of Communist subversion, 219n110; Maphilindo as answer to fears

of, 153; Projek Malaysia and fear of, 13, 14–15, 105, 164; Projek Malaysia proposed as bulwark against, 157; as purported reason for territorial claims, 155; as threat to Sabah, 101; US and containment of in Southeast Asia, 161
Communist Bloc, Projek Malaysia and, 166
Conlon, Alfred Austin, 40–41, 62
Cope, Edith, 7, 80
Cope, Henry William, 7, 80, 83
Cowie, William Clark, 20, 133
Crown Colony government, 22–23, 37; agricultural policy, 51–62; annexation of Sabah from North Borneo Chartered Company, 10, 37, 39, 44–48, 226n81; assumption would remain in power into the 1970s, 102, 165; attitude toward indigenous politicians, 184; concern over claims of Sulu Sultanate, 141–143; elite management and control over resources, 93–95; expanded colonial rule in Sabah and, 37, 48–50; finances of, 50; focus on industry and resource extraction, 63; independence movement in Sabah and, 91; keeping tabs on Stephens and his newspaper, 88; labor policy, 56–62; Philippines' claim to Sabah and, 145; piracy and Philippine control of Turtle Islands, 138; political parties and rising ethnic discord and, 176; Projek Malaysia and, 170–173; Radio Kalimantan Utara and, 114–115, 116; Radio Sabah and, 118–119; regulation and expansion of logging by, 69–72; relations with local and indigenous elites, 73, 77, 85, 86

Daily Express (newspaper), 88
decolonization: colonial influence persisting after, 200n38; grassroots resistance movements, 27; historiography of, 23–26; of Hong Kong, 201n45; political elites and, 10–11; popular opinion on, 9–10; Sabah and, 15–16; Stephens' role in, 7–8
Dent, Arthur, private colonization on Borneo and, 19, 131, 132, 141, 142
Dingle, John, 94
discrimination against local population by colonials, 76–77
Donhauser, Robert "Bob," 121–122, 161
"Double Six Tragedy," 188–189
Douglas-Hamilton, George, 122
Dove, Michael, 28, 65
Drahman (guide), 1–2, 3

dual mandates, 74
Dutch East Indies, radio in, 117
Dyce, R. K., 49

Easter, David, 121
East India Company, Labuan and, 199n21
East Malaysia, role in Projek Malaysia and, 14–15
ecological effects of logging on Sabah, 71
economic disenfranchisement, public interest in issues of, 93–94
Edge, M. G., 184
elite capture, 74
Elizabeth II, 139, 140
entrepôt trade, colonial settlement of Borneo and, 164
ethnic communities: elites and competing, 73; fear of Malay dominance, 190; struggle for influence between indigenous communities and, 189–190
ethnic divisions, 72; anticolonialism and, 194–195; colonial rule and, 190; in Legislative Council, 95–96; Malaysia Federation and, 98; *merdeka* and, 90–92, 122; political parties and, 176; Sabah's reaction to Projek Malaysia and, 173
ethnic imbalance, Projek Malaysia to offset, 128, 165
Eurasians: social position of, 6–7, 80–81; Stephens' social position as, 86. *See also* mixed-race

Fa Hsien, 17
Farram, Steven, 120
Federation of Malaysia: creation/emergence of, 185–187, 192–193. *See also* Projek Malaysia
food shortages on Sabah, 38, 50, 51, 54, 60
foreign labor, import of to Sabah, 53, 56, 57–61
Foulds, Linton H., 136

Galbraith, John Kenneth, 169
Ganyang Malaysia campaign, 15, 125, 126, 146, 192
Garcia, Carlos, 143
Gaynor, Jennifr L., 138
Gleijeses, Piero, 25
Goode, William: Philippine claim to Sabah and, 142, 145; on invitations to visit Malaya, 183–184; Malaysia Day and, 186; on piracy, 138; Sedomon and, 176; wariness of Projek Malaysia, 173

Granville-Edge, P. J., 82
Guerrero III, Leon Ma., 143
Gusanad Kina, 75–76, 78, 84, 85, 175

Haji Abdul bin Rahim, 95
Hakka community, 163
Hall, George, 43
Hare, William, 48, 60–61
Harian Rakyat (newspaper), 145
Harrison, Francis B., 134
Hashim Jalilul Alam Aqamaddin, *20*
Hatton, Frank, 1–2, 3, 5
Hatton, Joseph, 1–2
Hewitt, P. M., 92
Hoffman, L. C., 110
Hong Kong: colonization of, 17; decolonization of, 201n45; demand for Borneo timber, 66, 68; Dent and, 19; elite collaboration with colonial state in, 74; Sabah's links to, 13, 15, 26, 162, 163–164, 174, 187, 193, 231n21; socioeconomic transformation in, 56–57
Ho Yin-Ping, 57
huguan siou, Stephens as, 84–87
Hunter, Douglas, 85–86

independence movement on Sabah. *See merdeka*
indigeneity, flexibility of ideas of, 165–166
indigenous communities: colonial government logging policies and, 70–71; lack of postwar aid for, 49–50; migration from interior to coastal areas, 59–60; role in World War II, 36–37, 38; struggle for influence between ethnic groups on Sabah and, 189–190; supposed loyalty to colonials, 3–4
indigenous economy, effect of large-scale logging on, 59–60, 64, 93–94
indigenous elites: colonial treatment of, 84, 85; logging licenses and influence over, 93–94; *merdeka* and, 90–92; political rise of Stephens, 84–87
indigenous labor, opposition to use of, 59–60
indigenous people: policies to Islamize and Malayanize, 191; uprisings against North Borneo Chartered Company rule, 21
indigenous politicians, attitude of colonial government towards, 184. *See also* Mustapha bin Harun; Stephens, Donald
indirect rule of Sabah's colonial government, 73–75

Indonesia: ambition to incorporate British Borneo into, 102; anticolonial struggle in, 42–43; Azahari in, 113, 115; depictions of postcolonial, 26–27; early years of nation state, 215n27; Philippine claim to Sabah and, 145; Kalimantan Utara and, 15, 102, 103, 121–125, 151, 152; Konfrontasi, 15, 27, 125, 146, 152, 153–154, 158, 192; radio in, 116–117; Radio Kalimantan Utara and, 115–116; reaction to Projek Malaysia in, 13–14, 105–107, 143; Sabah's postcolonial transition and, 11
intelligentsia, Japanese execution of Sabah's, 77, 104
interior, Sabah's, 223n29; gauging reaction to Projek Malaysia in, 177–182; increase in logging and government control over, 69–70; influence of indigenous elites in, 75–76; resource extraction in following merger with Malaya, 191–192, 194
international opinion: on Britain's colonization of Sabah, 47; on Kalimantan Utara, 111–112; on Projek Malaysia, 166–170
Islam: Kadazandusuns converting to, 163; Melayu identity and, 165; Sulu Sultanate and, 131; as vector for Malayan influence in Sabah, 191. *See also* Mustapha bin Harun
Italy: interest in establishing penal colony in Borneo, 21; interest in importing labor from, 207n114
Itsuyoshi, Ueno, 36

Jackson, H., 49
Jacobini, H. B., 146
Jamal ul-Azam, 19, 132–133
Jamalul Kiram II, 133–135, 139–140, 141
Japan: Borneo timber and, 66, 68, 209n17; execution of Sabah's intelligentsia, 77, 104; indigenous communities fighting occupation, 36–37, 38, 83; occupation of Sabah during World War II, 10, 22, 35–36, 203n7
Jasanoff, Maya, 16, 28
Jesselton, 6, 9, *12*, 173; Japanese invasion of, 41; postwar conditions in, 36, 45, 48; support for Projek Malaysia in, 181–182. *See also* Kota Kinabalu
Jesselton Revolt, 77
Johnson, G. R., 85–86
Johnson, Martin and Osa, 76
Josey, Alex, 109–110
jungle economy, 64, 93
jungle productions, 208n6

INDEX 259

Kadazandusun language, Stephen's newspaper and, 88, 89–90

Kadazandusuns, 72; conflict between Muslims and, 96; conversion to Islam among, 163, 191; fear of domination by Malays, 91–92, 174; fighting Japanese, 37; formal education for, 87–88; growth of population, 163; Kinabalu Uprising and, 83; North Borneo Chartered Company and, 44; Pasok Momogun party and, 175, 185; relocation to coast, 38; Stephens as leader of, 7–8, 78, 84, 89–90; United National Kadazan Organization and, 175; view of Malaya, 102

Kahin, George, 180

Kalimantan Utara movement: aversion to anticolonial radicalism and, 190; Azahari and, 108–113; Britain using talks to prevent Philippine collusion with, 150; claim to Sabah, 144; emergence of, 15, 195; links with Indonesia, 102–103, 121–125, 151, 152; map of proposed state, *110*; Pasok Momogun movement and, 177; Radio Kalimantan Utara, 102, 103, 114–116; Sabah's rejection of, 121, 123–125, 126, 155; subversive efforts in Sabah, 151, 152; Turnbull proposal and, 172–173

Kampong Pau, Arusap and, 76

Kaur, Amarjit, 29

Keith, Agnes Newton, 76, 136

Keith, Harry G., 70, 76

Ken, Danny Wong Tze, 29, 81, 145

Kennedy Bay Timber Company, 71

Khoo Siak Chiew, 95, 96, 145, 175

Kimanis Bay, 18–19

"Kinabalu Guerillas," 190

Kinabalu Uprising, 7, 83, 189

Kinabatangan River, exploring, 1, 2, 5

Kinghorn, Ernest, 55, 56

Konfrontasi, 15, 27, 125, 146, 152, 153–154, 158, 192

Korean Central News Agency, 166

Kota Kinabalu, 186, 188–189, 190

Kusumawati, Rini, 73–74

Kwan Yui Ming, 95

Kwok, Albert, 83

labor shortages: agricultural, 53; imported from Hong Kong, 57; interest in importing Italian laborers and, 207n114; plan to import labor from Mauritius, 58–60; on Sabah, 37, 38

Labuan, 18, 19, 21, 92

Lacsina, Ignacio, 112

Langford-Holt, John, 42

Lee Kuan Yew, 169

Legislative Council: Brunei Rebellion and, 177; composition of, 75; ethnic conflict within, 95–96; ethnic divisions and, 95; Goode on piracy, 138; Mustapha and, 95, 96–97, 98; Stephens and, 86–87, 91, 98; Turnbull's plan and, 172; Wong and, 183

Leopold (Belgium), 18

leprosy, Stephens and, 82

Limbahau, 6, 189

Liow, Joseph Chinyong, 106

literacy rates on Sabah, 87; radio's effectiveness and, 119–120

literature set in Borneo, 197n10

"Little Empire," 48, 62, 69

"Little Hong Kong," Sandakan referred to as, 164

local elites: acceptance of British postwar annexation, 46; classification of elites, 73; collaboration with state, 73–75; colonial state control over formation of, 78–79; decolonization and, 10–11; ethnicity and, 191; formation of, 72–75; indigenous political authority and, 75–79; indirect rule and, 73–75; logging policies and, 71–72; Projek Malaysia and, 64, 159–160, 162, 183–185

logging: expansion of in Sabah, 64, 65–72, 76; government use of logging licenses to influence local power, 93–95

Long, Gavin Merrick, 41

Lopez, Salvador P., 145, 146

Louis, Wm. Roger, 24, 54

Lovegrove, Peter, 49

Luping, Herman, 84, 163

Macapagal, Diosdado: Philippine claims to Sabah and, 112, 129, 143–145, 147, 149, 150, 155, 161; improving ties with Malaya and Indonesia, 150; Manila Accord and, 150–151; Taganak Island handover and, 136

Macaraeg, Federico, 148

MacArthur, Douglas, 39–40

Macaskie, Charles F. C., 40, 44

MacDonald, Malcolm, 167–168

Maga, Andulon B., 9–10

Malaya: designs on Borneo, 103–107, 162; economic progress of, 232n53; expansionist plans of, 26–27, 102, 105–107, 148; importance of Projek Malaysia for, 156–158; independence from Britain, 168–169; partnership with Britain, 104–105; perceived as anticommunist bastion, 231n18;

260 INDEX

Malaya (continued)
  relations with Sabah, 162; rubber exports, 55; Sabah annexation as risk for, 169–170; Sabah's postcolonial transition and, 11; Sabah's incorporation to offset ethnic imbalances, 128, 165; skepticism toward in Sabah, 173–174; strategies for creating Malaysia, 177–185; Sumatra and, 106–107. *See also* Projek Malaysia
Malayan Alliance, 168
Malayan Chinese Association (MCA), 168
Malayan elites, Projek Malaysia and, 11, 14, 168
Malayan Emergency, 12–13, 14, 104–105, 119, 219n110
Malayan ethnonationalism, 11, 14, 168
Malayan Indian Congress (MIC), 168
Malayan newspapers on Kalimantan Utara, 113
Malayan People's Action Party, 124
Malay Bahasa language, 165, 182, 191
Malays (Melayu): adoption of Melayu values after merger with Malaysia, 163, 191; Borneo and, 156; community on Sabah, 72; fear of domination by, 91–92
Malaysia: ethnocultural divisions and, 98; reclassification of Islamic converts, 191; rivalry with Kalimantan Utara, 110. *See also* Projek Malaysia
Malaysia Day festivities, 185–186
Malaysia Solidarity Committee, 183
Malcolm, Neill, 45
Ma Ngok, 74
manifest destiny syndrome, 160–166
Manila, Azahari in, 109
Manila Accord, 150–151
Manila Summit, 150
Manila Times (newspaper), 148
Maphilindo, 195, 222n7; failure of, 154–155; map of proposed confederation, *151*; proposal for, 31, 128–129, 147–155; USSR on, 167
maritime Southeast Asia, Sabah and, 16–17, 127, 128, 129–133
Mat Salleh, 77
Mauritius, 58–60, 171
Melayu identity, Malay Bahasa, Islam, and Projek Malaysia, 165–166. *See also* Malays
Meligan, 9–10, 11, 188
Mengkabong, *20*
merdeka (independence): Azahari and, 122–123; lack of public support for, 90–93, 162; local calls for, 186–187; Radio Kalimantan Utara and, 114–116; Sabah and Sarawak and, 121, 122; Stephens' role in, 7–8, 90–93, 172
Miau Shau Kee, 183
mixed-race population on Sabah, 6–7, 80–81
Mohamed, Abdullah Salim, 110–111
Mohammad Yachub Attan bin Datu Amilhussin, 140
Mohammed Yassin bin Haji Hashim, 176–177
Moro communities, 139
Mountbatten, Louis, 39
Mount Kinabalu, 119
Muruts, 76; agriculture and, 51, 53, 59; anticolonialism and, 54, 124–125; effect of war on, 38, 50; elite of, 75.78; fighting Japanese, 37; growth of population, 163; interior and, 53, 59, 72; Kinabalu Uprising, 83; North Borneo Chartered Company and, 44; Pasok Momogun party and, 175, 185; population decline in *kampongs*, 53; racism against, 76; view of Malaya, 102, 190; wild rubber and, 56
Muslih, Muhammad, 27
Muslim community on Sabah: after formation of Malaysia, 163; Mustapha bin Harun as leader of, 78, 94, 95–97, 191
Mustapha bin Harun, 85, 189; as anticolonial power broker, 64; as chief minister, 191; Cobbold Commission and, 181; colonial state's effort to disparage, 29; Philippine claim to Sabah and, 145; influence of, 78; as leader of Sabah Muslims, 78, 94, 95–97, 191; local politics and, 95–97; logging license and, 94–95; Sabah's postcolonial transition and, 23; support for Projek Malaysia, 183; Turnbull plan and, 172; United Sabah National Organization and, 175; wariness of growing Chinese community influence, 174

Nasution, Abdul Haris, 152
national identity, print media, radio, and creation of, 220n121
nationalism on Sabah, 22, 25, 27, 72, 89
natural resources: extracted from North Borneo, 2–3; Projek Malaysia and desire for Borneo's, 164–165. *See also* logging; rubber industry
Negara Kesatuan Kalimantan Utara (Unitary State of Northern Borneo): Azahari and, 109–113; failure of, 125–126. *See also* Kalimantan Utara movement

INDEX 261

neocolonialism: attempts to gain Sabah and, 186; Cobbold Commission and, 179; Projek Malaysia and allegations of, 13–14, 105–106, 167–170
Nicolson, Harold, 74
Nield, H., 141
Nik Anuar Nik Mahmud, 149
Non-Aligned Movement, Kalimantan Utara and, 110–110
North Borneo Chartered Company, 5; administration of Turtle Islands and, 134; British government annexation of territory from, 10, 37, 39, 44–46, 226n81; classification of local elites and, 73; colonial expeditions to Sabah's interior, 1–2; 1878 treaty and, 142; end of, 35; establishment of, 6, 19–20, 21; expunged from Sabah by Japanese, 22; Hatton and, 1–2, 3; purchase of Borneo titles, 131, 132; radio network and, 117
North Borneo Herald (newspaper), 83
North Borneo News & Sabah Times (newspaper): letters to regarding Radio Sabah, 119; Stephens and, 83, 85, 87–90, 92
North Borneo Timbers, 71
North Borneo War Victims Fund Ordinance, 50
North Korea, on Projek Malaysia, 166
North Vietnam, on Philippines' claim over Sabah, 167
Nusantara, 114, 116, 125

Omar Ali, 20
Omar Ali Saifuddin III, 176
"one language, one culture, one religion" policy, 191
Ong Kee Hui, 174
Ongkili, James, 165
Ontoros Antanum, 77
Oodeen (guide), 1–2, 3
Ooi Keat Gin, 29
orang kaya kaya, 73, 208n2
Orr-Ewing, Ian, 138
Osmeña, Nicasio: Azahari and, 141; on British payment to North Borneo Company, 226n81; Philippine claims over Sabah and, 112–113, 140–141, 142; pact to divide British Borneo territories between Kalimantan Utara and Philippines, 144
Overbeck, Gustavus von, 19, 131, 132, 141, 142

padi (rice) farming, 51, 52, 54, 56, 58
Palestinian nationalism, 27

pan-Malayanism, Sabah and, 151, 152, 153
Parashorea malaanonan/*Parashorea tomentella*, 66, 67
Parti Rakyat Brunei (Brunei People's Party), 107–109, 216n43
Parti Rakyat Malaya, 216n43
Pasok Momogun party, 175–177, 183–184, 185, 236n4
Pavitt, Ernest Alfred, 5–6, 80, 189, 235n1
Pavitt, Jules Stephen, 6. See also Stephens, Jules Pavitt
Pavitt, Kwai, 6, 80, 189
petrochemical industry in Sarawak, 55–56, 63–64
Petty-Fitzmaurice, George, 105
Philippines: criticism of territorial claim to Sabah, 148–149; Kalimantan Utara and, 112–113; opposition to British colonization of Sabah and Sarawak, 47; Projek Malaysia and, 14, 15; public support for claims to Sabah, 147, 148; raiders and smugglers from southern, 138–139; Sabah's links to southern, 127–129, 130–131, 193, 221n6; Sabah's postcolonial transition and, 11; Spanish colonial control over, 130; sultanates in, 222n14; Sulu Sea islands and, 129; territorial claims to Sabah, 102, 112–113, 134–135, 139–149, 151; Turtle Islands and, 134–136; US colonization of, 133. *See also* Maphilindo
"Philippines' Claim to North Borneo, The" (Rivera), 147
Philippines Free Press (newspaper), 143
Philippine Trade Union Council, 112, 143
Philipps, A. E., 180
Phillips, David, 41, 49
Pilcher, John A., 149–150
piracy in Sulu Sea, 137–139, 150
political authority: indigenous, 75–79; in postcolonial period, 190–192
political development in Sabah, 174–177
political parties on Sabah: emergence of, 160, 175; Projek Malaysia and, 175–176
poll tax, 211n42
postcolonial state formation, Sabah and, 101–102
Press, Steven, 21, 131
print media: creation of national identity and, 220n121; emergence of local, 65, 83, 87–90. *See also individual newspapers*
private charities, to kickstart postwar recovery, 49

private colonization on Borneo, 131–132. *See also* North Borneo Chartered Company
private logging concerns, government favor for, 70–71
Projek Malaysia: aggression against Sukarno and, 124; allegations of neocolonialism and, 13–14, 105–106, 167–170; Anglo-Malayan strategies for, 177–185; appeasing local elites for support, 183–185, 195; Borneo conceived as colonial territory for resource wealth, 164–165; Cobbold Commission of Enquiry and, 10, 37, 39, 44–48, 112, 226n81; Cold War and, 105, 166–168, 230n7; colonial administrators' skepticism about, 159; creators of, 98; ethnic imbalance issue and, 128, 165; fear of foreign rule and, 121–122; geopolitical instability and concerns triggered by, 11–16; geopolitical strife on Sabah and, 102; idea of indigeneity and, 165–166; importance of for Britain and Malaya, 156–158; inclusion of Singapore and, 12, 13, 103, 157, 165, 168, 169–170; initial reaction to in Sabah, 173–174; international opinion on, 160–161, 166–170; Kalimantan Utara movement's opposition to, 102; local opposition in Sabah to, 121–122, 170–174; Malayan Emergency and, 104–105; Maphilindo proposed as alternative to, 147–150, 152; Philippine claims to Sabah and, 142, 143–144; popular opinion in Saban about, 9–10; public opinion in Sabah about, 9–10, 107, 121–122, 159–160, 170–174; radio propaganda for, 120; reaction to in Brunei, 107–113; regional opposition to, 143–144, 146, 147; revealed by Rahman, 103–104; Sabah political parties and, 175–176; state making and, 162–166; traditional Sabah elites and, 64; USSR condemnation of, 160–161
public concerns, lack of forum to express on Sabah, 75
public opinion: in Sabah about Projek Malaysia, 9–10, 107, 121–122, 159–160, 170–174; in Sabah on British postwar annexation of, 44–45, 46–47; in Sarawak on British annexation, 43–44, 46
Pulalum, Mohammad, 139–140
Pulalum, Salip Ali, 140, 141

Quirino, Elpidio, 134, 135

racial superiority, colonial claims of, 49–50, 76–77
racism towards mixed-race population, 80–81
radio: creation of national identity and, 220n121; influence on Southeast Asia, 195; use as political tool, 116–118, 218–219n102
Radio Kalimantan Utara, 102, 103, 114–116, 119; anti-Malaysian propaganda on, 120–123; end of, 126; public rejection of message on, 121, 123–124
Radio Republik Indonesia, 117
Radio Sabah, 103, 118–120, 123, 171
Radio Sarawak, 171
Rahman, Abdul: anticommunism and, 105; expansionism and, 27; interest in Borneo's natural resources, 148; Malayan nationalism and, 168; Manila Accord and, 150; on Maphilindo, 153; Projek Malaysia and, 11–13, 165, 190; Radio Kalimantan Utara on, 120; speech revealing Projek Malaysia, 103–104; Stephens' condemnation of, 173; suspected neocolonial designs of, 104; Western perception of, 105, 106
Rajaratnam, S., 14
Ramos, Godofredo, 112, 113, 144
Recto, Claro M., 143
regional security, Philippine claim to Sabah and, 145–146
Reid, Anthony, 87
"rentice," 203n6
research sources, 28–30
resistance movements, postcolonial, 27–28. *See also* Kalimantan Utara movement
Revolutionary Government of the Republic of Indonesia (PRRI), 106–107
rice farming, 51, *52*, 54, 56, 58
Rivera, D. Ignacio, 147
Roff, Margaret, 87, 89
rubber industry, 51–*52*, 54–56, 63; importing labor for, 57–58
Rundum rebellion, 54
Rusk, Dean, 161, 164
Rutter, Owen, 69

Sabah: alarm over Sulu princess named to administer Turtle Islands, 137; anticolonialism in, 64, 77–78; Australian administration of at end of war, 35–36, 40–41; British postwar colonization of, 44–48; as center of maritime Southeast Asia, 127, 128, 129–133; civil-political development in, 174–177; Cobbold Commission and, 177–182; colonial claims to, 16–22; decolonization of, 9–10, 15–16, 23–26; demographic change on, 163–164; disputed claims over title of Sultan of Sulu and, 139–142; disputed status of British rule in, 140; early 1960s debate over control of, 10–11; emergence of political parties in, 160, 175; escalation of private territorial claims over, 137–143; evaluating territorial claims for, 161–162; expansion of logging in, 64, 65–72; experience of mixed-race minorities in, 6–7, 80–81; fear of external domination on, 101–102; Philippine territorial claims to, 102, 112–113, 134–135, 139–149, 151; foreign incursion into, 16–17, 22, 139; import of foreign labor to, 57–61; involvement in Konfrontasi, 192; Japanese occupation of, 10, 22, 35–36; labor shortages in, 37, 53, 57–61; lack of complete decolonization in, 30; lack of public support for independence on, 162; links to Hong Kong, 13, 15, 26, 162, 163–164, 174, 187, 193, 231n21; links to southern Philippines, 127–129, 130–131, 193, 221n6; local fragmentation in, 30; Malaya and risk of acquiring, 169–170; Malaysia Day festivities on, 185–186; Maphilindo proposal and, 152–154; map of, 12; merger with Malaysia and extension of colonial-style rule, 191–192, 194; Muslim population of, 78, 94, 95–97, 163, 191; neocolonial attempts to gain, 186; perception of common Melayu heritage in, 128; postwar rehabilitation of, 48–49; public reaction to Radio Kalimantan Utara in, 115–116; radio in, 117–120; relations with Malaya, 162; role in state-making, 158–160; shift in public political awareness in, 126; situating in history, 22–28; slavery in, 7; as source of natural resources, 2–3, 4, 11, 17, 48–49, 65, 152, 164–165; state of after World War II, 35–39; strategic location of, 16–17; Turnbull plan and, 122, 170–173; violence and political disturbances in, 151. *See also* Crown Colony government; interior; local elites; North Borneo Chartered Company; Projek Malaysia

Sabahan identity, 143; Kota Kinabalu and, 190

Sabah Chinese Association (SCA), 175, 184–185

Sabah Sarawak Keluar Malaysia, 27
Sadiwah, E., 182
sago production, 51, 53
Sandakan, 1, 2, 5, 130, 134, 164, 173, 182; views of, 80, 81
Sandakan Harbor, 4
Sandakan Recreation Club, Stephens' incident at, 85–86
Sandison, J. R., 119
Sanin bin Pandin, 79
Sannoy, Antonio S., 148
Sarawak: British annexation of after war, 42–44; Cobbold Commission of Enquiry and, 178–182; colonial government and post-colonial plan for, 170–172; involvement in Konfrontasi, 192; logging in, 66; petrochemical industry in, 55–56, 63–64; postwar, 49; private colonization of, 131–132; Projek Malaysia and, 12, 14, 103, 107; sale to Brooke, 18, 131–132; as source of natural resources, 2–3; Turnbull plan and, 122
Sarawak United People's Party, 174
Saudin bin Labutau, 76–77
Scott, Robert, 171
Sedomon Gusanad Kina, 175–176, 183–184, 190
Seitelman, Max, 47
Semananjung Melayu, 115, 125
Sembulan Tengah, 181
Shafie, Ghazali, 174, 178, 181
Shamsiati (Azahari's wife), 109
Shamsiati binte Raja Putra, 29
Shipway, Martin, 24–25
Shorea faguetiana, 66
Siasi, 130
Singapore: colonization of, 17; Projek Malaysia and, 12, 13, 103, 157, 165, 168, 169–170; race riots in, 121; Stephens' in, 82–83; support for Maphilindo in, 151–152
slavery in Sabah, 7
Sligo, Graeme, 39–40
smuggling, in Sulu Sea, 137–139
Soh Tiang Keong, 151–152
South China Sea, colonization throughout, 17–18
Southeast Asia: Borneo and postcolonial states of, 128–129; colonization of Sarawak and Sabah and British role in, 47–48; emergence of radio in, 116–120; fear of expansionism in, 105; perception of expansionist Malaya, 148; Projek Malaysia and, 11; Projek Malaysia and tensions created in,

Southeast Asia (*continued*) 103–104; Sabah and Sarawak as contested territory in, 125; Sabah's increasing timber trade with, 66, 68–69; US activities in, 215n26
Southeast Asian Treaty Organization (SEATO), 105
Spain: claims in Borneo, 21; colonial treaty records and land deeds from, 141; Philippine sultanates and, 222n14
state-making, political potentiality of, 158–160
Steedly, Mary Margaret, 28
Stephens, Donald (Tun Fuad Stephens), 7–8; anti-Malaysian sentiment, 173–174; childhood, 80; Cobbold Commission and, 181; conversion to Islam, 191, 235n2; as critic of colonial rule, 64, 65; death of, 8, 188–189, 192; discrimination against, 81–82; on Philippine claim to Sabah, 145; grant to study journalism in United Kingdom, 88; influence of over Kadazandusuns, 78; *merdeka* and, 7–8, 90–93, 172; name change after conversion to Islam, 235n2; as newspaper editor, 83, 87–90; questions regarding death of, 189–190; rise of, 79–87; Sabah's postcolonial transition and, 23; in Singapore, 82–83; support for Projek Malaysia, 181, 183; swearing in as chief minister of Sabah, 186; Turnbull and, 86–87; United National Kadazan Organization and, 175
Stephens, Jules Pavitt, 7–8, 80, 82, 83, 189
Stewart, Duncan, 44
Stockwell, Anthony, 165
Stoler, Ann Laura, 28
Straits Times (newspaper), 47–48, 109–110, 115, 144
Sukarno, 143, 161; Ganyang Malaysia campaign, 15, 125, 126, 192; Kalimantan Utara and, 123, 124; Manila Accord and, 150; Maphilindo and, 152; popular depiction of, 105
Sulari, 130
sultanates: Philippine, 222n14. *See also* Brunei Sultanate; Bulungan Sultanate; Sulu Sultanate
Suluks, 90, 139; Islam and, 96, 163, 175; Kinabalu Uprising and, 83; Mustapha and, 96; Projek Malaysia and, 190; "Tuwan Nahuda," 129–130, 133–134, 222n8
Sulu Sea, 127; contested territory in and around, 133–137; dangers of, 221n1; maritime boundaries in, 129–133; piracy and smuggling in, 137–139; Suluks and, 222n9

Sulu Sea islands, Philippines and, 129
Sulu Sultanate, 17, 130–131; claims to title of Sultan, 139–142; demise of following cession, 131, 132–133; Kalimantan Utara and descendants of, 112; territorial claims and, 14, 15, 21, 27–28, 39, 102 134–135; treaty records and land deeds, 141, 142
Sumatra, Malaya and, 106–107
Sumatran rebellion, 116, 124
Sumulong, Lorenzo, 148–149
Sundang, G. S., 175–176, 177, 183, 184
Sunday Times (newspaper), 137
Sussman, Gerald, 144
Syonan, 216n36

Taganak Island, 130; lighthouse on, 134, 135
Tagliacozzo, Eric, 5, 17
Tahau, 130
Talip bin Japar, 182
Tanah Ayer, indigenous attempts to stake claim to, 90–93
Tan Siew Sin, 154, 169
Tapul, 130
Tarhata Kiram, 112, 136–137, 144
Tarling, Nicholas, 131
TASS, 166
Taylor, Alastair, 153
Tentara Nasional Kalimantan Utara (National Army of Northern Borneo), 108, 109
Tho Yeo Ping, 79
timber production in Sabah, 62, 66. *See also* logging industry
Timor-Leste, population migration to Sabah, 61
tobacco estates, 51–52, 59
Torrey, Joseph William, 18–19
treaty records and land deeds, Sulu Sultanate, 141, 142
Tregonning, Kennedy, 29–30
trusteeships, 74
Tubb, Arthur G., 50
Tumonggon, 18–19
Tun Fuad Stephens. *See* Stephens, Donald (Tun Fuad Stephens)
Turnbull, Roland Evelyn: plan for union of Sabah, Sarawak, and Brunei, 122, 170–173, 174, 176, 187; Stephens and, 83, 86–87
Turner, R. N., 30, 85, 94–95, 96
Turtle Islands, 133; as contested territory, 134–136; Philippine takeover of, 155; Princess Tarhata Kiram as deputy director of, 136–137

"Tuwan Nahuda" (folktale), 129–130, 133–134, 222n8
Tuwan Nahuda Kalayakan, 129–130, 155
Twining, Edward Francis: agricultural policy, 54, 60; appeal for charitable donations for Sabah, 50; on Japanese killing of Sabah's intelligentsia, 77; Philippine irredentism and, 142; transfer of Turtle Islands to Philippines and, 135, 137

Ukraine, 27
Union of Filipino Workers, 112
United Front Against Malaysia, 174, 181, 183
United Malays National Organisation (UMKO), 168
United National Kadazan Organisation (UNKO), 175, 184–185, 236n4
United Pasokmomogun Kadazan Organisation (UPKO), 185, 236n4; death of cabinet members with Stephens, 189
United Sabah National Organisation (USNO), 175, 184–185, 189
United States: activities in Southeast Asia, 215n26; colonization of Brunei and, 18–19; control of Turtle Islands, 134–135; Philippine claim to Sabah and, 145, 149; interest in postwar Borneo, 39–40; involvement in Indonesia, 26; Malaya, support for the Sumatran rebels, and, 106–107; military bases in Philippines, 136; Projek Malaysia and, 157, 161; sovereignty over Philippines, 134–135; Sulu Sultanate and, 133
Unnithan, K. G., 183

USSR: condemnation of Projek Malaysia, 160–161; on Maphilindo Confederation, 167

Visser, Leontine, 73–74

Wallach, Yair, 27
Warren, James Francis, 21
Watherston, David, 178, 181
Wen-Qing Ngoei, 27, 106, 124
"West Coast Boys," 79–80, 82
West Indies, proposal for mass emigration to Borneo, 60–61
White, Dennis, 108
"White Rajahs," 39, 42, 131
"wild rubber," 55, 56, 60
Wilkinson, R. C., 59
women, role in Sabah's history, 28–29
Wong, Michael, 182–183
Wong, Y. K., 182
Wong Pow Nee, 174, 178, 181
Wong Tze Ken, Danny, 145–146
Woolley, George Cathcart, 51
World War II: Australian postwar administration of Sabah, 35–36, 40–41; effect of war on Muruts, 38, 50; Japanese occupation of Sabah during, 10, 22, 35–36, 203n7; war damage on Sabah, 35–39

Yamin, Mohammed, 214n2
Yap, Richard, 174

Zaini Haji Ahmed, 109

www.ingramcontent.com/pod-product-compliance
Lightning Source LLC
Chambersburg PA
CBHW030822230426

43667CB00008B/1330